Homemade

how to make hundreds of everyday products fast, fresh, and more naturally

Homemade

how to make hundreds
of everyday products fast,
fresh, and more naturally

Reader's Digest

The Reader's Digest Association, Inc.
Pleasantville, New York • Montreal

Project Staff

EDITOR Don Earnest
DESIGNER Michele Laseau
COVER DESIGN George McKeon
RECIPE EDITOR Nancy Shuker

CONSULTANT-WRITERS

FOOD RECIPES Kim Gayton Elliott
BEAUTY PRODUCTS Jay Ansell, Beth Kalet
HOME REMEDIES Debra Gordon
CLEANING PRODUCTS Steven Schwartz
HOUSE, GARDEN, AND PET PRODUCTS
Delilah Smittle
ILLUSTRATOR Masi + Monkey, Inc.
LAYOUT Edwin Kuo, Rachel Maloney
COPY EDITOR Jeanette Gingold
INDEXER Nan Badgett

Reader's Digest Books

EDITOR IN CHIEF Neil Wertheimer
MANAGING EDITOR Suzanne G. Beason
CREATIVE DIRECTOR Michele Laseau
PRODUCTION TECHNOLOGY MANAGER
Douglas A. Croll
MANUFACTURING MANAGER John L. Cassidy
MARKETING DIRECTOR Dawn Nelson
PRESIDENT AND PUBLISHER, TRADE PUBLISHING
Harold Clarke
PRESIDENT, U.S. BOOKS & HOME ENTERTAINMENT
Dawn Zier

The Reader's Digest Association, Inc.

PRESIDENT AND CHIEF EXECUTIVE OFFICER
Eric Schrier

First printing in paperback 2008

Copyright ©2007 by The Reader's Digest Association, Inc.

Library of Congress Cataloging-in-Publication Data
Homemade : a surprisingly easy guide to making hundreds of
everyday products you would otherwise buy. -- 1st ed.
    p. cm.
Includes index.
ISBN 0-7621-0753-7 (hardcover)
ISBN 978-0-7621-0904-3 (paperback)
1. Home economics. 2. Recipes. I. Earnest, Don, 1938- II.
Reader's Digest Association.
  TX158.H625 2006 640--dc22
                    2006026506

We are committed to both the quality of our products and the service we provide to our customers. We value your comments, so please feel free to contact us.

The Reader's Digest Association, Inc.
Editor-in-Chief
Reader's Digest Books
Reader's Digest Road
Pleasantville, NY 10570-7000

For more Reader's Digest products and information, visit our website:
www.rd.com

Printed in the United States of America

1 3 5 7 9 10 8 6 4 2 (hardcover)
5 7 9 10 8 6   (paperback)

Note to Readers
The information in this book has been carefully researched, and all efforts have been made to ensure its accuracy and safety. The Reader's Digest Association, Inc., and the individual contributing consultant-writers do not assume any responsibility for any injuries suffered or damages or losses incurred as a result of following the instructions in this book. Before taking any action based on information in this book, study the information carefully and make sure that you understand it fully. Observe all warnings. Test any new or unusual repair or cleaning method before applying it broadly, or on a highly visible area or a valuable item. The mention of any brand or product in this book does not imply an endorsement. All prices and product names mentioned are subject to change and should be considered general examples rather than specific recommendations.

The Magic of Homemade

Many of us have a similar shopping ritual. Once a week we go to the grocery store, grab a cart, and load up with a box of this, a bottle of that, and a carton of those and these. Add to that a visit to Wal-Mart, Kmart, or Target for extra supplies, or to the warehouse club for bulk items. It's a whole lot of shopping—and spending—week after week after week.

What do we get with all these packaged products? Sure, good things like reliability and convenience. But there's more. Many everyday items are filled with incomprehensible chemicals and preservatives. You get an overflow of wasteful packaging, too (funny how our garbage cans are so much fuller these days). You also get to see your name-brand products on TV—your dollars pay for all those commercials. And, you get lots of choices—supermarket aisles are packed with mind-boggling variations of the same product.

All of this is modern life, you say. Maybe. But when it gets to the point that a window cleaner has to offer citrus orange or mountain berry flavors to get our attention, consumerism seems a bit out of control.

Our proposed solution: Make things yourself. The little-known truth is that you can replace almost everything you buy at the grocery store with a homemade version that will be cheaper, healthier, yet equally effective. That is exactly what *Homemade* is all about. On these pages, you'll find more than 700 replacement recipes for the most common items bought in stores. Not just food, mind you. Cosmetics, pet supplies, toiletries, cleaners, even everyday medicines can be made at home, easily, quickly, and effectively.

I say this with wholehearted conviction. In our home, my young sons make the barbecue and spaghetti sauces we eat all the time. My wife whips up all-natural mayonnaise, salad dressings, jams, and salsas that make us hum with delight. I whip up cleaners, bread mixes, ice cream, soup stocks, and other pantry items, sometimes just to relax. We save a lot of money. We also have great fun and get a real sense of pride.

You should do the same. These recipes are easy, clever, and unlike those you'll see in other books. You'll love the quality, you'll love the savings, and most of all, you'll love the feeling of accomplishment.

Neil Wertheimer
EDITOR IN CHIEF,
READER'S DIGEST BOOKS

contents

Part Two

health and beauty care for you and yours

*

contents

The Joy of
Homemade Living

Homemade shampoo? Homemade ketchup? Yes, we know it sounds strange, even weird, to make your own shampoo or your own ketchup. After all, most of us are not such dedicated environmentalists or back-to-basics fundamentalists that we feel we must make every product we use from scratch like our homesteading pioneer forebears did a century and a half ago. And picking up a bottle of shampoo or ketchup at the supermarket or drugstore is not that much trouble—and in the grand scheme of things neither seems particularly expensive. And if you are buying a name brand, or even a discount house brand, you can feel relatively confident that you are getting products of reliably consistent quality that will do the job that you want them to do—a shampoo that cleans your hair with lots of bubbly lather or a condiment that will add a tangy sweetness and a bit of extra juiciness to the often dry, bland taste of your burger and fries. The giant multinational food and home products corporations are very adept at putting out innocuous uniform products with a long shelf life and eye-pleasing packaging.

So why bother to make them yourself? There are a great number of reasons that we'll explore on the following pages. For the record, these are not "replication" recipes. We don't claim to have the formula for Formula 409 or the secret of making Coca-Cola. Our versions of everyday products won't smell or look like many of the name-brand products they are replacing. But rest assured that they work—and work terrifically well.

The Rewards of Making It Yourself

As we said earlier, there are a lot of good reasons to make many common household products yourself. The first and most important reason is the real, tangible difference between your homemade product and the manufactured product it replaces. In most cases, you'll find that the quality of the homemade item is outstandingly superior to the store-bought item. Once you have made shampoo or ketchup for yourself, you will immediately know that your homemade version offers rewards that can't be duplicated by the average factory-made product—whether it be the relaxed, more natural feel of your hair after using your homemade shampoo or the richer, more exotic taste of your homemade ketchup.

The same is true of hundreds of other everyday food, beauty, health, cleaning, household, gardening, and even pet products that you routinely pick up at the supermarket, drugstore, or big-box outlet. These include salad dressings, pancake mixes, fresh pasta, pickles, cookies, breads, skin toners, lip balm, aftershave, gargles, toothpaste, pet bird treats, furniture polish, fabric softener, and pest repellents for both the house and garden. All told, you'll find recipes for more than 700 such products in this book.

Another significant reason for making these products yourself is that you'll save money—a lot of money, actually. It may not seem like much for each individual item as you buy it. Just a few dollars here and a few dollars there. But those dollars add up quickly as you buy more and more items. And with savings that range up to more than 90 percent for the homemade replacement versus a name-brand item, cumulative savings can mount rapidly.

But getting better quality and saving money are not the only rewards to be gained by creating your own homemade products. When you make something yourself, you know exactly what goes into it. So you have the enormous satisfaction of knowing that the product you made consists of ingredients that are all natural and healthful—or at least not harmful. And you know for sure that it contains no questionable extenders, stabilizers, or other artificial ingredients. Another reward of making things yourself is that you can adjust the recipe to meet your own needs or taste—making your shampoo less likely to dry out your hair or your ketchup sharper tasting.

When you make something yourself, you also create a lot less waste. And ultimately, when you create an item yourself rather than buying it, you gain a reward that can't be duplicated by anything you buy—a great feeling of self-satisfaction, the self-reliant joy brought on by the realization that you actually made the product yourself.

Here is a more detailed look at these rewards of homemade living.

Saving Money

Although it may seem like a trifling sum at times, you should not overlook the savings when you make something for yourself, because the amount you save really grows the more items you make. And there are very good reasons for this. Every time you buy a bottle of ketchup for the table, shampoo for your hair, salve for an itch, or even liver snaps for your dog, only a very small percentage of the money that you pay goes to cover the costs of making the product. Indeed, if you leave out the actual cost of manufacturing, the ingredients in most products account for only pennies of the purchaser's dollar. What happens to the rest of the money that you plop down at the cashier? It goes to cover the costs of advertising, packaging, shipping, the retailer's rent and light bills, and of course the cashier's salary and her boss's bottom line. Paying a healthy chunk of your shopping dollar for advertising is especially irksome, considering advertising's well-known penchant for grossly inflating the image of a product to entice buyers. If it weren't for the happy faces, cheery jingles, and promises of better living in ads, why else would so many of us, who are otherwise rational, thrifty people, pay good money for cola drinks? After all, they are little more than fizzy water doctored up with sugar, caffeine, artificial flavoring, and brown dye. Actual lab analysis shows that colas are 99.5 percent sugar water; only 0.5 percent is flavoring and color. You can make any number of healthier, more satisfying, better-tasting thirst quenchers in your own kitchen for just a few cents each.

Similarly, a lot of the money you pay for a product goes for packaging—in many cases, the cost of the packaging surpasses the cost of the product itself. So saving your hard-earned cash for better uses is certainly a major reason for making products yourself whenever you can. The chart on page 12 gives some typical examples of how much you can save on a wide variety of products by making them yourself. Try it and watch the savings pile up.

Healthier and More Natural

Saving money, however, is not the only reason for producing your own homemade products. Even more disturbing are the compromises that have to be made to a commercial item's integrity to ensure that it will survive the weeks or months from the time it is manufactured, then shipped and stored, left on the retailer's shelf, and finally picked up and used by you. Depending on the type of product, it is pumped full of stabilizers, plasticizers, extenders, fillers, and other man-made chemicals.

Not all of those additives are there to extend shelf life. Some are added to facilitate the manufacturing process, making the product move faster, release from a mold easier, or create less interference to the smooth flow of production. Other artificial ingredients are added to help the item withstand heat and cold and to be less likely to clump, precipitate, or adhere to packaging.

Still other questionable chemicals are used to cut the cost of using natural ingredients. The best-known villain here is artificial flavoring. Why use expensive, perishable, and difficult-to-handle real strawberries when you can just add a few pinches of a chemical compound that simulates the smell and

real-life examples of savings

Before we started working on this book, we undertook a survey to see what kind of savings you could expect if you created your own homemade replacements for a wide range of brand-name items. Here are the results, and they speak for themselves. The savings are based on typical prices in early 2006 for brand-name items at mainstream suburban outlets near a major Northeastern city versus the comparable cost of ingredients to produce similar quantities of the homemade replacements.

Food	Store Price	Homemade Replacement	Savings
Chi Chi's salsa (16 ounces)	$2.79	$1.38	50%
Smucker's peanut butter (26 ounces)	$4.29	$1.24	71%
Starbucks Frappuccino (38 ounces)	$5.99	$.82	86%
Hershey's cocoa mix (7 ounces)	$3.49	$2.68	23%
Manischewitz chicken noodle soup (15 ounces)	$2.49	$1.15	53%
Aunt Jemima frozen waffles (16 waffles)	$2.99	$1.41	52%
Stubb's barbecue sauce (18 ounces)	$3.89	$1.92	50%
Pepperidge Farm croutons (16 ounces)	$1.79	$.53	70%
Hellmann's mayonnaise (32 ounces)	$3.39	$1.57	53%
Ore-Ida steak fries (28 ounces)	$3.39	$2.20	35%
Häagen-Dazs raspberry sorbet (1 pint)	$3.69	$1.18	68%
Edy's Whole Fruit Bar pops (16 ounces)	$2.75	$1.69	38%

Health, Beauty, and Pet Supplies

Oil of Olay all-day moisturizer (6 ounces)	$9.29	$1.68	82%
Curél moisture therapy lotion (13 ounces)	$7.99	$4.62	42%
Aqua Velva aftershave (3.5 ounces)	$3.69	$.35	90%
Secret Platinum deodorant (2.7 ounces)	$3.69	$.50	86%
Robitussin cough syrup (4 ounces)	$4.69	$2.30	51%
Hall's Plus cherry lozenges (25 lozenges)	$1.99	$.33	83%
Sudafed decongestant (36 pills)	$8.99	$.65	92%
Milk-Bone dog biscuits (19 ounces)	$2.89	$1.91	33%
Whisker Lickins tuna cat treats (4.6 ounces)	$2.08	$.55	73%
Hartz parakeet food (28 ounces)	$3.99	$.87	78%

Household Compounds

Lysol bathroom cleaner (29.3 ounces)	$3.19	$.15	95%
Cascade dishwasher soap (75.2 ounces)	$4.89	$2.96	39%
Pledge lemon furniture spray (12.5 ounces)	$3.79	$2.08	45%
Windex window cleaner (26 ounces)	$3.39	$.15	95%
Elmer's school glue (7.6 ounces)	$1.69	$.19	88%

taste of the berries? Chemical laboratories that support the food, cosmetic, and other industries actually have "sniffing" rooms lined with bottles, each containing a carefully concocted compound and labeled with the name of the fruit, flower, or other natural odors that it emulates. You didn't really believe that "lemon fresh" cleaner contains lemons, did you? No, no more than that "strawberry flavored" ice cream or candy contains real strawberries. They think that you can't taste the difference. But try the real thing side by side with the imitation and there's no question about which is the winner.

In short, anything that you make yourself is likely to be much more natural and more healthful for you than the great majority of manufactured products you buy—whether it's a food, a cosmetic, or a cleaning compound. And in the case of food, it's going to taste a lot fresher.

Suit Your Own Needs

Another great advantage of making products yourself is that you can customize them so that they are just the way you want them. If you like your moisturizer to be fresh smelling and restorative without being greasy and overwhelmingly perfumy, no problem. If you like your chocolate chip cookies to be moist and really chocolaty, no problem. If you want your spaghetti sauce tangier, your gumbo thicker, your ketchup smoother flowing, your mustard spicier, your frozen yogurt tarter, or if the doctor told you to cut back on the salt or sugar, no problem. Even if you are worried that Fido is not getting the right nutrients, no problem. Nearly all of the recipes in this book are flexible and can be readily adjusted to fit your wants or needs. Indeed, we invite you to experiment until you get a product just the way you like it. (Bread and cakes being notable exceptions; always follow the recipe for such baked goods exactly.)

Make Less Waste

In the process of making your own staples, you are going to greatly reduce the amount of useless, environment-damaging waste and garbage you produce. A lot of this is the result of all the packaging you won't be throwing away and all the spray bottles, jars, and such that you will be recycling. But you will also be cutting waste by making your products in batches small enough so that you can easily use them up without having to toss out the last part when it goes bad. For cleaning, laundering, and polishing, you will also be using compounds that are much gentler and less damaging to surfaces and fabrics—and to drains and sewage and septic systems. So when you make it yourself, you do your bit to save the world!

Get Personal Satisfaction

Last but not least among the rewards of making a product yourself is the great sense of personal satisfaction and accomplishment it brings. It's very gratifying to know not only that you can make a staple yourself, but also that you are not dependent on giant corporations and their vulnerable supply chains to satisfy your everyday needs. Being able to fashion our own food, cleaning, and other staples links us with traditions that helped shape us as a people and a nation—traditions of resourcefulness, ingenuity, independence, and self-reliance that stood our ancestors well as they struggled to fashion homes in a strange new land, tame frontiers, and endure the constraints of wartimes and depressions.

Expect to be pleasantly surprised by how really simple and easy it is to make many of the products that you are accustomed to buying ready-made—whether they be peanut butter or pancake mix at your local supermarket, chicken nuggets at a fast-food outlet, lip balm at the cosmetics counter, foot powder at the drugstore, liver snaps at the pet store, furniture polish and bug spray at the home and garden center, or gumdrops at the newsstand. Recipes for these products and more than 700 others are in the chapters that follow. None of the recipes are difficult to make and none call for a lot of ingredients. But first here are some tips that will make your homemade efforts easier and more successful.

Creating Your Own Food Products

The recipes in Part 1 of this book cover some 400 commonly purchased food products that you can make in your own kitchen. There are recipes for making items to stock your pantry, refrigerator, and freezer—or for creating fast on-the-spot replacements for such items. And there are recipes that let you make many foods that you would normally buy already prepared—and spend a great deal of money in the process. All told, they cover condiments, seasonings, sauces, pickled and preserved foods, baked goods, snack food, drinks, convenience dishes, candy, ice cream, and other sweets.

You don't need a large kitchen or a whole battery of equipment to be a good cook, but there are certain well-designed tools that will make your work in the kitchen go faster and more smoothly. Shop for new equipment at a reputable kitchen supply store. Good, sturdy kitchen tools will serve you well for a long, long time and are well worth the initial investment. A Well-Equipped Kitchen (page 16) shows a listing of the pots, pans, and other gear for food preparation and cooking that make life in the kitchen easier.

Before You Start ...

Take stock of your pots and pans. You want your pots and pans to conduct heat evenly (hot spots cause burning and uneven cooking), and you want at least one skillet and one pan with a nonstick interior coating for low-fat cooking. Here are your choices:

- Cast-iron cookware heats slowly and evenly, but needs special care to prevent rust. It is porous and absorbs flavors and reacts badly to some foods, especially acidic ones.

- Enameled cast iron has all the advantages of cast iron, plus it is nonreactive, but it is heavy to lift and you must take care not to chip the enamel.
- Aluminum conducts heat well, but reacts badly with acidic food, and lightweight aluminum pans tend to dent and warp easily.
- Anodized aluminum is a better choice because it is heavier and less prone to warping. Its surface finish makes it less reactive than plain aluminum.
- Clad metal pots are made of several metals fused together to take advantage of each one's properties—copper for even heat and stainless steel for easy cleaning, for example.
- Tin-lined copper pots are beautiful to look at and cook as well as or better than other pans; they are also very expensive and their maintenance is labor-intensive. Not only must they be polished frequently on the outside, but they also must be regularly re-tinned on the inside.

Check out your large appliances. Use an oven thermometer to check that your oven actually registers the heat it is set for. If it is only 5 to 10 degrees off, you can compensate by setting it higher or lower than the recipe requires. If the settings are more than 10 degrees off, call in a repairperson to recalibrate the stove.

Also check the temperatures of your freezer and refrigerator with a refrigerator/freezer thermometer. The freezer should read 0°F and the refrigerator 40°F. If either of them is above those standards, use a colder setting. Also check the door gasket for wear and consider putting in a new gasket to make the door seal tighter. You don't want to risk freezing lots of foods in a freezer that isn't as cold as it should be or risk the deterioration of refrigerated foods that are stored above 40°F.

Evaluate your freezer space. Making your own food is most efficient when you do it in batches large enough to last for a while. When you make a large pot of stock, for example, it will be most useful if you freeze some of it in ice cube trays and the rest in 1-cup or 2-cup containers. If you put the frozen stock cubes in a freezer bag, you will find it easy to add a little stock to a sauce or gravy to make it more flavorful. Save the larger 1- or 2-cup containers for making soups and stews that call for homemade stock.

You also need space for containers of Savory Meat Mix (page 166), which gives you a head start on many fast dinners. Use plastic containers (square ones use freezer space more efficiently than round ones) or heavy-duty plastic zipper bags, which take up even less space. Extra pancakes or waffles or muffins can also be frozen in freezer bags to make speedy but delicious breakfasts. Freezing the best summer and fall offerings of your local farmers' market will require more room too. Once you start stocking up on a regular basis, you may want to consider an auxiliary freezer. But be sure not to locate it in a place where it will be exposed to below-freezing temperatures—like a porch, carport, or unheated garage; freezers, surprisingly, don't work properly when ambient temperatures drop below freezing.

a well-equipped kitchen

When making the food recipes in this book, you don't need any specialized equipment beyond what you would ordinarily use for preparing meals. Here is a list of items that any well-outfitted kitchen should have.

Pots and Pans

10-inch skillet with a tight-fitting lid
7-inch skillet
3-quart saucepan with a tight-fitting lid
1-quart saucepan with a tight-fitting lid
4- to 5-quart Dutch oven or heavy kettle
4-gallon stock pot/pasta pot
Roasting pan, 13 x 9 x 2 inches with rack
Broiler pan with rack

Baking Equipment

2 baking sheets
1 jelly-roll pan
Loaf pan, 9 x 5 x 3 inches
1-quart microwave-safe casserole
2-quart microwave-safe casserole
3 nesting mixing bowls
2 six-cup muffin pans
8-inch or 9-inch cake pans
8-inch or 9-inch pie pans
2 wire cooling racks

Knives

8- to 10-inch chef's knife
2- to 4-inch paring knife
9- to 10-inch serrated bread knife
6-inch utility knife

Small Appliances

Blender or food processor
Coffee maker
Ice-cream maker
Microwave oven
Slow cooker
Waffle iron

Accessories

Candy thermometer
Can opener
Citrus juicer
Colander
Corkscrew
Cutting board
Expandable steamer
Flour sifter
Funnels
Grater
Knife sharpener
Ladle
Long-handled spoon
Measuring cups (dry and liquid)
Measuring spoons
Pancake turner
Pastry blender
Pepper mill
Rolling pin
Rubber spatulas
Salad spinner
Sieves
Slotted spoon
Tongs
Vegetable parer
Whisks
Whistling teakettle
Wooden spoons

As a Precaution ...

- When you preserve any foods by canning them, be especially careful to use only jars intended for canning. Be sure to sterilize the jars and treat the preserves in a hot-water bath (page 72) and to use only fresh seals on the jars. Canning is very safe as long as you observe these simple precautions. This applies to condiments and pickles as well as jams and jellies.
- Keep your knives sharpened. Most kitchen cutting accidents are the result of dull knives. Store knives in a wooden block or on a magnetic rack. Knives in drawers get nicked and lose their sharp cutting edges.
- Take special precautions with raw eggs; salmonella is still a problem; you need to cook the eggs at 160°F for a minute or two to be safe.
- Identify and date everything that you freeze or can. Try to put new packages below the older packages in the freezer and behind the newer jams or pickles on the cupboard shelf.
- If anything you have frozen or canned has an "off" color or odor when you open the package, discard it immediately.

Store leftover foods in covered containers or plastic bags and put them in the refrigerator right away. Never leave cooked meat, poultry, or fish at room temperature for more than two hours, including mealtime. This rule applies to the Thanksgiving turkey too. Foods in a slow cooker are kept at 165°F, just hot enough to kill harmful bacteria.

Creating Health and Beauty Products

Part 2 of this book covers more than 225 homemade beauty and health products and similar products you can make for your pets. You may at first be skeptical about making your own cosmetics or home remedies. It's only natural. Commercial over-the-counter medications and beauty products are both so expensive (and well advertised) and promise so much that you may feel reluctant to compete—or to compromise your skin, hair or health, or that of your pet.

But you should have no such trepidations. Both home remedies and home-made beauty products have a long and honored tradition. And truth be told, many commercial products are little more than dressed-up versions of classic home preparations—whether it be a cough syrup or a spa skin treatment. In the case of homemade cosmetics, it's best to start slowly—with a single mois-turizer, for example, and see how it feels and smells on your skin. Try treating your hair after a shampoo with a vinegar hair rinse. Then try one of the facial masks and a toner. Little by little, you will be won over to these fresh, natural products and want to make more and more of them on a regular basis.

Being able to instantly create your own home remedies is reassuring. You don't have to run to the drugstore or call the doctor every time you or another family member feels a little off. In this book, you'll find more than 100 remedies for the most common ailments that can slow you and your family down—remedies that make life a little more pleasant by making everyday ailments less irritating and long-lived. Hopefully, they'll keep you out of the doctor's office or the emergency room. But remember, home remedies do not take the place of conventional medicine; they complement it. If you don't respond to a home remedy, see a doctor. Let the doctor know how you have treated yourself. Talk to your doctor about the home remedies that have helped you and your family. Doctors will often offer you a few of their own to add to your repertory.

Making your own pet supplies gives you control over the quality of the food and care that your animals receive. Making nontoxic flea dips and ear oils, for example, will keep your dogs and cats healthier and make them less dangerous to the people who pet them. Commercial flea collars and at-the-shoulder dabs are poisonous to people too.

Before You Start ...

Follow the recipe closely. Read the recipes carefully and don't be tempted to use more of any ingredient than what is called for. Make sure you know the difference between regular oils and essential oils. Regular, or "fixed," oils, such as olive oil or canola oil, are the same nonvolatile mostly seed-derived oils that we use for cooking, while essential oils, such as geranium, lavender, or lemon oils, are highly concentrated volatile distillations of leaves and flowers much like perfume (see page 240). They are called essential because they capture the essence of the plant. Most essential oils must be diluted in a regular fixed oil before they are applied to the skin. In this case the regular oil is known as a carrier oil. Essential oils are expensive—it takes many, many pounds of leaves or petals to make even a few ounces of these concentrated oils. You need very little essential oil in each recipe; to conserve your supply, keep it in a cool, dark place. Many people keep them in the refrigerator, but this is not recommended if there is any chance that someone may mistake these oils, which are toxic, for a food and ingest them.

Find your ingredients. You can buy the ingredients for most home remedies and beauty products in health food stores, the supermarket, drugstores—or these days on the Internet. Even specialized ingredients are no longer as difficult to find as they once were. But because herbs and essential oils are not regulated by the government, make your purchases at a reputable store to ensure quality. You can buy many dried herbs at the supermarket, but ideally you will eventually grow and dry your own. You can buy seeds or seedlings for many fresh herbs at garden centers and nurseries; plant them in a sunny patch of soil or in pots on a sunny windowsill. If local gardening outlets don't have an herb you want, you can find many mail-order sources on the Internet.

The ingredients for pet foods and care products are found in groceries, pet shops, natural food stores, garden centers, and for a couple of recipes, liquor stores. None of the ingredients are particularly exotic or difficult to locate.

Take care with equipment. Although you use ordinary cookware to make home remedies or beauty products, it is best to keep this equipment separate from your regular kitchenware—to avoid contaminating foodstuffs. A list of the items you may need is given in Home Remedies and Cosmetics Gear (opposite). You can probably pick up whatever you need at garage sales or stores that sell odd lots of equipment for reduced prices. Making pet products doesn't involve any special equipment other than what you probably already have in your kitchen.

Select safe storage jars and dispensers. While shopping, look for small opaque jars with wide mouths and tight-fitting lids for storing your beauty creams or skin ointments. Because they have no preservatives, they need to be kept away from light and air. Any tinted or colored glass—amber, white, or blue—protects creams from light. Keeping a cream in a small container that it fills almost completely protects it from air. In fact, when you use up half a jar of cream, decant the remaining cream into a smaller jar to protect it further. Tight-fitting lids are important to keep out air and prevent evaporation. Cork lids are too porous to be safe.

Also be on the lookout for spray bottles and pint-size bottles with tight lids for mouthwashes and such. Many of the jars that you need you can probably recycle from your regular kitchen and bathroom supplies. It is smart to sterilize any storage jars before you use them (page 72). Wash plastic spray bottles thoroughly in soap and hot water, rinse thoroughly, and let them air-dry.

As a Precaution ...

- If you are taking a prescription drug, talk to your doctor about possible interactions between it and any herbs or essential oils suggested here.
- If you have allergic reactions to any foods or medications, consult your doctor before taking any home remedy that might contain the allergen.
- If you are pregnant, don't take any herbal medications without consulting your doctor.
- Although side effects from using natural cosmetics are uncommon, allergic reactions can occur in susceptible people. If you have a reaction, immediately stop using the product.
- If you are planning to use an herb that is new to you, patch-test it first. Rub the herb against the tender skin on the underside of your arm right above the elbow or in the crease of the elbow. Wait overnight. If redness or another irritation occurs, don't use it.
- Essential oils should not be used on young children or pregnant women. Check with a doctor before using products with essential oils if you have a chronic or acute disorder such as heart disease, epilepsy, asthma, diabetes, or kidney disease.
- Do not swallow or even taste essential oils. Keep bottles and jars sealed and out of the reach of children. Don't keep them in the refrigerator if you have children.
- If an essential oil is accidentally swallowed, do not induce vomiting. Call a poison hotline or get the person to an emergency room immediately.

home remedies and cosmetics gear

You will need nonreactive equipment to protect your health or beauty products from chemical changes in color and odor. That means avoiding uncoated aluminum, iron, or copper cookware.

To make either beauty or health products, you need:
- Glass, stainless steel, or enameled double boiler
- Set of nonreactive mixing bowls
- Stainless steel or ceramic funnel
- Stainless steel measuring and stirring spoons
- Wooden stirring and mashing spoons
- Stainless steel or ceramic lemon squeezer
- Teakettle
- Ceramic tea bowls and cups
- Tea strainer
- Candy thermometer (for cough drops)

Be sure to label each new jar or bottle of a beauty product as you fill it. The label should give the product's name and the date on which it was prepared. If you are planning to give a homemade beauty product as a gift, list its ingredients as well (you don't want to inadvertently cause an allergic reaction). Labeling is important because many of these preparations look alike in the bottle and many have a limited shelf life.

Store natural products in a cool, dark place (page 255), preferably a dry one, and check them often. Heat, moisture, light, and contact with air can all cause deterioration. Particularly in the summer, the refrigerator is probably the safest place to store homemade cosmetics (again, though, not if you have young children). Even in the refrigerator, you should inspect them regularly to be sure they have not lost their potency. If a product is discolored or has a funny smell, chances are it is past its prime. Discard it and make a new batch.

Most of the home remedy recipes are for products that are intended to be used immediately or within a few days, so if you store a remedy at all, the safest place is in the refrigerator. You can keep some ointments and other remedies for longer; each recipe will advise you. If you do keep remedies longer, label and date them.

Making Products for the House and Garden

Part 3 of this book covers more than 115 useful household and gardening products that you can make—including cleaning and polishing compounds, glue and craft supplies, indoor and outdoor pest repellents, weed killers, fertilizers and soil conditioners, even houseplant food and whitewash. Having simple, nontoxic aids and remedies for house and garden undertakings and problems makes maintenance chores much more pleasant—and much, much cheaper. And none of these recipes are difficult to produce.

Cleaning and polishing your home or getting rid of weeds and pests in the garden may produce very gratifying results, but the processes involved can hardly be described as fun. So, it is no wonder that most of us are tempted by heavily promoted new products that promise to make cleaning and polishing, doing the laundry, or weeding and pest control easier and longer lasting. To avoid the drudgery and tedium of cleaning or weeding, such promises seem worth every penny, no matter what the price. But whether you are dealing with a cleanser, a polish, a bleach, a weed spray, or an insecticide, the problem with many of those commercial products is that they contain harsh and toxic chemicals that may be hard on grime, tarnish, stains, bugs, and other undesirable things, but they are also hard on furniture, floors, clothes, and shrubs—and hard on your skin, eyes, and lungs as well.

The good news is that there are many inexpensive, time-proven products that will make help your garden flourish and your house sparkle, smell good, and gleam invitingly without such toxic effects. You probably already have most of the ingredients for these homemade products on hand. Try making up one of the cleaning recipes and using it. It won't take long, cost much money, or require excessive elbow grease. Expect to be happily surprised.

Once you accept that there are easy, inexpensive ways to foil the pests that have plagued your woolens in the past, you won't find putting away winter clothes so onerous. Keeping ants and roaches out of the cupboards is no problem either when you get out the borax. And as you discover inexpensive, nontoxic ways to keep pests out of a summer garden, you may finally be able to raise the herbs and vegetables you have dreamed about with enrichment from your own compost heap. Or you may finally put together the container garden that you have pictured in your sunroom.

Before You Start ...

Find your ingredients. None of the ingredients required for the cleaning, polishing, crafts, gardening, and other household recipes are particularly exotic. If you don't already have them, you can buy most of them at your local supermarket or hardware store. Just keep these tips in mind:

- Get the largest, cheapest sizes of baking soda, cider vinegar, and white vinegar. House brands are fine. You don't need giant sizes of chlorine bleach or ammonia, however, because the recipes that do use them call for very little of either.
- You'll find borax and washing soda among the detergents in a supermarket.
- Look for castile soap, glycerin, and essential oils at health food stores and on many Internet sites.
- Rubbing alcohol is also called isopropyl alcohol, and you can find an inexpensive house brand at any drugstore.
- Boiled linseed oil and materials needed for paints and finishes are available at paint, art supply, or hardware stores. You can find equipment and tallow for candle making at craft stores.
- One traditional cleaning-compound ingredient that you won't be able to find easily or inexpensively is, surprisingly, soap flakes. The last major national brand of soap flakes (Ivory Snow) was converted to a mild detergent more than 30 years ago. But it is very simple to make your own soap flakes by simply lightly grating a bar of pure soap (such as Ivory) on a coarse grater.

Make garden puttering easier. You will need some large containers for mixing soil and making compost tea. You can use plastic garbage cans or find large buckets at janitorial supply stores—or even better, yard sales. If you have unusually clayey, sandy, or other problematic soil, it's best to have the soil tested before adjusting it with homemade nutrients. To get your soil tested, contact your local Cooperative Extension Service—usually affiliated with a state university's agriculture school or listed on the government pages under the U. S. Department of Agriculture.

For potting and taking care of container plants, it's a good idea to devise a potting table, where you can work on your plants and keep extra pots, homemade fertilizers and pesticides, potting soil, and other planting supplies. Like a kitchen counter, the table should be waist high and have shelves above for storage of fertilizers and pesticides out of the reach of children and shelves below for large containers of compost, vermiculite, or sand. You can make such a gardening workstation in the garage or on a covered porch.

As a Precaution …

- Never combine chlorine bleach and ammonia. While either of these powerful cleaning ingredients is perfectly safe to use alone, they can form a deadly noxious gas if they are mixed together.
- Label any cleaning compounds, pesticides, compost teas, and other fertilizers that you make and keep the containers out of the reach of children.
- Wear vinyl gloves to protect your hands when you are mixing and using household and gardening products.
- It is unlikely that anyone might ingest the essential oils used in homemade air fresheners in Chapter 10, but if an essential oil is accidentally swallowed, observe the same precautions noted earlier: Don't induce vomiting; call a poison center or rush the patient to an emergency room.

When You Are Done …

Most of the cleaning and polishing compounds, craft supplies, pest repellents, and other household and gardening compounds in this book are best prepared just before you use them so that you get the maximum potency and best results out of them. Most are so simple to make, anyway, that you can whip them up in only a couple of minutes. But as the recipes advise, you can store some products, such as scouring powders and some cleaning and bug-control compounds, for periods ranging from a few days up to a couple of weeks. When you do, be sure to put them in tightly closed labeled and dated jars or spray bottles.

recycle rags and spray bottles

There are many ways to keep down the cost of household supplies besides using the recipes in the following chapters. One is to recycle worn or outgrown family clothing as rags for cleaning, polishing, and crafts. Cloth diapers make famously good rags. Old cotton T-shirts and underpants are also very good candidates. Well-worn terrycloth towels absorb water better than anything. And best of all, these rags can be tossed in the washer and used over and over again. Also, finish cleaning windows with newspaper. So, you may never buy paper towels again (at least for cleaning) or expensive disposable rags.

Wash out old empty spray bottles and reuse them for your homemade household or gardening products. (If you do need to buy some, try a garden center or a janitorial supply store; they are listed in the yellow pages.)

Part One

in the kitchen

*

chapter 1

Replacements for Pantry Staples

Nowhere do the benefits of making your own pay off more generously than in the kitchen, especially in making replacements for the cereals, condiments,

salad dressings, seasonings, sauces, and mixes that line your pantry shelves. To give them an almost indefinite shelf life, these manufactured staples are more likely than any other food products to be packed with fillers, preservatives, stabilizers, and other unnatural taste-degrading ingredients. In this chapter, you will not only learn how easy it is to make your own all-natural versions of these staples but also discover how much better a homemade creation tastes. Homemade stock has real flavor. And there is nothing like freshly ground peanut butter that melts in your mouth or fresh pasta so delectably light that it makes any sauce seem tastier.

None of the staple substitutes here have the extraordinary shelf life of manufactured products. But you will find healthy nutty breakfast cereals that will keep their fresh taste for weeks, as well as everyday condiments, ranging from ketchup and mustard that will last for months to fresh salsas that are best eaten in a day or two. Most salad dressings and both savory and sweet sauces are also best if used right away—they only take a minute to whip up anyway—but several will keep in the fridge for a couple of days, and there are salad dressing mixes you can prepare ahead. Most herbs and seasonings and dry mixes will keep for weeks or months, as will fresh pasta and stocks if frozen.

breakfast cereals

Toasted Muesli
This is a favorite Swiss-German morning cereal based on oats and fruit. Packaged versions are quite pricey and not nearly as good.

2 cups old-fashioned oats

1/4 cup sunflower kernels

1/4 cup sliced almonds

1/3 cup finely chopped dates

2 tablespoons oat bran

1 cup bran flakes

1/4 cup toasted wheat germ

1/4 cup raisins

1 tablespoon sugar

1. Preheat the oven to 350°F. In a 15 x 10-inch baking pan, combine the oats, sunflower kernels, and almonds. Bake for 10 to 15 minutes or until the almonds are almost golden.

2. In a large bowl, combine the dates and oat bran, and stir to coat the fruit with the bran. Add the toasted oat mixture, bran flakes, wheat germ, raisins, and sugar. Stir to gently combine all the ingredients.

3. Place the muesli in an airtight container or a self-sealing plastic bag. Label and date, and store in a cool, dry place.

Makes 3 1/2 cups (about 7 servings)

Helpful Hint

Why Make Your Own Breakfast Cereals?

Cereals are a frequent drain on the family budget. The homemade alternatives that are shown here have less sugar and salt and more fiber, making them a much healthier choice for you and your family. They are also generally cheaper, if you look for good prices on grains, nuts, seeds, and dried fruits in the bulk aisles of discount health food supermarkets.

Fruit and Nut Cereal
Packed with protein and high in complex carbohydrates, this tasty mix will keep you going well into lunchtime.

2 cups 1-minute oatmeal

1 cup crumbled shredded wheat

1 cup bran or bran cereal

1 cup wheat germ

1 cup unsalted walnuts, almonds, pecans, or cashews

1/2 cup chopped pitted dates

1 cup chopped dried prunes, apricots, pears, apples, or bananas

1 cup light or dark raisins

1 cup instant nonfat dry milk

1. In a large bowl, combine the oatmeal, wheat flakes, bran, wheat germ, and nuts. Add the dates and dried fruit, and toss to combine the ingredients and coat the fruit with the oatmeal mixture. Add the raisins and dry milk, and stir gently to combine the ingredients thoroughly.

2. Place the cereal in an airtight container or self-sealing plastic bag. Label and date, and store for up to 2 months in the refrigerator.

Makes about 9 1/2 cups

Granola

Packed with nutrition and good taste, granola is the ultimate win-win combination. Eat it with milk for breakfast; sprinkle it on fruit, yogurt, or ice cream; incorporate it into crumble toppings for cobblers; crush it to make crusts for pies or cheesecakes—or just grab a handful for a healthy, energy-boosting snack. To cut the cost of homemade granola, check out the bulk sales aisles of health food supermarkets, such as Whole Foods, Sunflower, or Wild Oats.

4 cups old-fashioned rolled oats

1 cup natural wheat and barley cereal

1 cup sliced unblanched almonds

1/2 cup firmly packed light brown sugar

1 teaspoon salt

1 teaspoon ground cinnamon

1/4 cup frozen apple juice concentrate, thawed

1/4 cup water

2 tablespoons butter, melted

2 tablespoons vegetable oil

2 tablespoons honey

1 teaspoon vanilla

Grated zest of 1 orange

1 cup dried pitted cherries

1 cup light seedless raisins

1. Preheat the oven to 300°F. Lightly coat a 15 x 10-inch jelly-roll pan with nonstick cooking spray and set aside.

2. In a large bowl, combine the rolled oats, cereal, almonds, brown sugar, salt, and cinnamon; set aside. In a small bowl, whisk together the apple juice concentrate, water, butter, oil, honey, vanilla, and orange zest. Pour the juice mixture over the oat mixture and toss until all the ingredients are well combined. Spread the mixture evenly in the prepared pan.

3. Bake, stirring every 15 minutes, until golden and slightly crunchy, about 1 hour.

4. Remove the pan to a rack to cool completely, about 1 hour. When cooled, stir in the cherries and raisins. Store in an airtight container.

Makes 7 cups

Oatmeal Mix

Ready-to-eat oatmeal mixes are a godsend on busy mornings when you need a healthy breakfast in a hurry. The prepackaged mixes are pricey. So whip up your own—and vary it depending on your family's tastes.

6 cups quick-cooking oats

1 1/3 cups dry milk

1 cup dried diced or small apples, apricots, banana slices, prunes, raisins, or mixed dried berries

1/4 cup sugar

1/4 cup brown sugar

1 tablespoon ground cinnamon

1 teaspoon salt

1/4 teaspoon ground cloves

1. In a large bowl, combine all the ingredients and toss to mix well.

2. Store the oatmeal mix in an airtight container or self-sealing plastic bag. Label, date, and store in a cool, dry place for up to 6 months.

To use: Shake the mix well before using. In a saucepan, bring 1/2 cup water to a boil. Slowly stir in 1/2 cup of oatmeal mix. Reduce the heat and cook, stirring, for 1 minute. Remove the pan from the heat, cover, and let stand for 1 minute more or until the oatmeal is the desired consistency.

Makes 8 cups

condiments and spreads

Ketchup

Forget about buying this American staple—homemade is so much better and an inspired way to use up those extra tomatoes at the end of summer.

4 quarts (about 24) ripe tomatoes, peeled, cored, and chopped

1 large yellow onion, chopped

1 large red bell pepper, cored, seeded, and chopped

1 1/2 teaspoons celery seed

1 teaspoon mustard seed

1 teaspoon whole allspice

1 stick cinnamon

1 cup firmly packed brown sugar

1 tablespoon salt

1 1/2 cups cider vinegar

1 tablespoon paprika

1. In a large, nonreactive saucepan or Dutch oven over moderate heat, combine the tomatoes, onion, and red bell pepper, and cook until the vegetables are soft. Using a food mill or a sieve, press the vegetables through to make a puree. Return the vegetable puree to the saucepan.

2. Over high heat, cook the vegetable puree rapidly until it is thick and the volume is reduced by about half, about 1 hour.

3. Cut a 4-inch square of cheesecloth. Place the celery seed, mustard seed, allspice, and cinnamon stick in the center, gather up the corners to form a bag, and secure with kitchen string. Add the spice bag, brown sugar, and salt to the tomato mixture. Over low heat, cook the mixture gently for 25 minutes, stirring frequently.

4. Stir in the cider vinegar and paprika. Continue to cook, stirring frequently, until the mixture is thick.

5. Spoon the ketchup into 3 hot, sterilized pint jars, leaving a 1/8-inch space between the top of the ketchup and the rim of the jar. Wipe the rims, cover, and process for 10 minutes in boiling water (see Safe Canning with a Hot-Water Bath, page 72). Cool and test for airtight seals. Label, date, and store in a cool, dark place for up to one year; the ketchup will be ready to eat in 1 week. Once a jar has been opened, store the ketchup in the refrigerator.

Makes 3 pints

Cocktail Sauce

The zesty side to shrimp and other seafood. To dial up the heat, add more horseradish or hot red pepper sauce. This is not only cheaper than bottled cocktail sauce, but you can mix ingredients to suit your taste.

1 cup Ketchup (above) or bottled chili sauce

1 tablespoon prepared horseradish

1 tablespoon lemon juice

1/2 teaspoon Worcestershire sauce

1/8 teaspoon hot red pepper sauce

1. In a small, nonreactive bowl, combine all the ingredients and stir until well blended. Cover the bowl and refrigerate for at least 1 hour before serving.

2. Store in an airtight container in the refrigerator for up to 1 month.

Makes about 1 cup

Mustard

Named for the plant that produces the seeds from which the powder is made, this versatile condiment is easily made and adjusted to suit a particular taste or use. The basic mix includes 2 to 3 tablespoons of a liquid (vinegar, wine, water, flat beer) to about 1/4 cup dry mustard. Other additions can include turmeric (which gives a bright yellow tint), garlic, tarragon, sugar or honey, salt, and more. Use it to spice up hot dogs, hamburgers, or sandwiches, or brush over meats before grilling or roasting.

1/3 cup mustard seed

3 tablespoons dry mustard

1/2 cup cider vinegar

1/2 cup dark beer

2 garlic cloves, minced

1/4 cup firmly packed light brown sugar

3/4 teaspoon salt

1/2 teaspoon ground ginger

1/4 teaspoon ground allspice

1. In a small bowl, combine the mustard seed, dry mustard, and cider vinegar. Cover the bowl with plastic wrap and let the mustard mixture stand at room temperature for 3 hours.

2. In a small saucepan, combine the dark beer, garlic, brown sugar, salt, ginger, and allspice. Stir in the mustard mixture. Over moderate heat, bring the mixture to a boil; reduce the heat to low and simmer for 5 minutes, stirring occasionally.

3. Spoon the mustard into a hot, clean canning jar and seal tightly. Let the mustard cool to room temperature. Store in a cool, dark place and in the refrigerator after opening.

Makes about 2 cups

Mayonnaise

Homemade mayonnaise tastes so good that it improves all the salads and sandwiches it gets used in. Our version is boiled, eliminating any fear of salmonella contamination from raw eggs. You can experiment with lemon juice for the vinegar and different oil. You also might try cayenne for the white pepper.

4 egg yolks

2 tablespoons water

1 tablespoon white wine vinegar

1 1/2 cups vegetable oil (or a combination of vegetable and olive oils)

Pinch ground white pepper

1. In the bowl of a food processor or blender, combine the egg yolks, water, and vinegar, and whirl just until the ingredients are combined. With the motor running, drizzle in the oil *very slowly*; if the oil is added too quickly, it will become a liquid dressing.

2. Transfer the egg mixture to the top of a double boiler and cook until a thermometer placed in the sauce registers 160°F. Stir in the white pepper. Store in the refrigerator for up to 5 days.

Makes 2 1/3 cups

Aioli (Garlic Mayonnaise)

Traditionally served with poached fish, aioli (pronounced eye-oh-lee) can also be used as a dip for fresh vegetables or seafood, or as a salad dressing. Homemade is delicious and much less pricey.

4 egg yolks

2 tablespoons water

1 tablespoon white wine vinegar

1 garlic clove, minced

1/2 cup fresh white bread crumbs

1 1/2 cups extra-virgin olive oil

Pinch ground cayenne pepper

1. In the bowl of a food processor or blender, combine the egg yolks, water, vinegar, garlic, and bread crumbs, and whirl just until the ingredients are combined. With the motor running, drizzle in the oil *very slowly*; if the oil is added too quickly, it will become a liquid dressing.

2. Transfer the egg mixture to the top of a double boiler and cook until a thermometer placed in the sauce registers 160°F. Stir in the cayenne pepper. Store in the refrigerator for up to 5 days.

Makes 3 cups

Tartar Sauce

When you have tasted a homemade version of this classic fish accompaniment, you won't waste your money on prepared tartar sauces.

1/2 cup Mayonnaise (page 29)

1/2 cup reduced-fat sour cream

6 scallions, minced

1/4 cup chopped Bread-and-Butter Pickles (page 67)

2 tablespoons lemon juice

1 tablespoon capers, drained

1 tablespoon minced parsley

1 tablespoon Dijon mustard

1. In a medium bowl, combine all the ingredients and stir until well blended.

2. Cover the bowl and refrigerate for 2 hours or overnight before using. Store in the refrigerator for up to 5 days.

Makes 1 1/4 cups

Spicy Tomato Salsa

Once relegated to Mexican and Southwestern cuisine, salsa has moved permanently into the mainstream. The spiciness can vary from very mild to tongue-burning hot, depending on the variety of chiles used and how many are included. Experiment until you get it just right for your taste. The zesty mix of tomatoes, scallions, and jalapeño peppers in this basic recipe is not just for tortilla dipping; dollop it on grilled chicken breasts, firm fish, in skirt or flank steak fajitas, or omelets.

3 medium ripe tomatoes, cored, seeded, and chopped

3 small scallions, trimmed and coarsely chopped

1 medium jalapeño pepper, cored, seeded, and finely chopped (wear gloves when handling; they burn)

1 garlic clove, minced

3/4 teaspoon salt

1/3 cup coarsely chopped fresh cilantro

1. In a large, nonreactive bowl, combine the tomatoes, scallions, jalapeño pepper, garlic, and salt. Toss to combine all the ingredients well. Let the salsa stand for 1 hour to let the flavors mellow.

2. Just before serving, toss in the chopped cilantro. Serve immediately or store in the refrigerator for up to 2 days.

Makes 3 1/2 cups

Tomato Basil Salsa

An Italian variation on the old favorite, this salsa may tickle your tastes too.

1 pound ripe tomatoes, peeled and chopped

1 small red onion, peeled and chopped

1 garlic clove, crushed

1 tablespoon extra-virgin olive oil

1/4 cup chopped fresh basil

Salt and freshly ground pepper, to taste

1. In a large, nonreactive bowl, combine the tomatoes, onion, garlic, olive oil, and basil; toss to combine all the ingredients. Add salt and pepper.

2. Cover the bowl and refrigerate for 2 to 4 hours to allow the flavors to develop. The salsa is best eaten on the day it is made but will keep, covered, in the refrigerator for 2 to 3 days.

Makes 2 to 3 cups

Salsa Verde

This green homemade salsa is a mixture of fresh herbs, garlic, capers, and salty anchovies that is sensational with seafood.

2/3 cup flat-leaf parsley

2/3 cup fresh basil leaves

1 garlic clove, halved

1/4 cup capers, drained

2 tablespoons chopped anchovies

3 tablespoons red wine vinegar

1/3 cup extra-virgin olive oil

1/2 teaspoon Dijon mustard

Freshly ground black pepper, to taste

1. Combine the parsley, basil, garlic, capers, and anchovies in the container of a food processor or blender. Whirl until the mixture is very smooth.

2. Stir in the vinegar, olive oil, and mustard. Add pepper. Serve immediately or store in the refrigerator for up to 2 days.

Makes about 1 cup

the story behind peanut butter

This will come as no surprise to nutritionists, but peanut butter was originally sold as a health food—which indeed it is, being an excellent source of protein, fiber, and B vitamins. Unlike today, when peanut butter is a staple of most average households, in its early years, it was mostly eaten by wealthy folks who frequented health spas.

Using ground peanuts as a food spread can be traced back to early Native American and African peoples, but for the modern face of marketed peanut butter, you find a name usually associated with another product: cereal. John Harvey Kellogg of Battle Creek, Michigan, was granted the first U.S. patent in 1895 to process peanuts.

Peanut Butter

This American staple can really eat up your budget. Surprisingly, peanut butter is not only cheaper to make at home, but healthier too.

4 cups shelled, salted dry-roasted peanuts

1 tablespoon plus 1 teaspoon safflower or other mild-flavored vegetable oil

For creamy style: Using a food processor or blender, and working in batches, process the peanuts and the oil until the desired consistency is reached. Stop and scrape down the processor container sides as needed.

For chunky style: Using a food processor or blender, coarse chop about 1/3 of the peanuts; set aside. Working in batches, process the remaining peanuts with the oil until the desired consistency is reached. Scrape down the processor container sides as needed. Stir in the chopped peanuts.

To store: Scrape the peanut butter into a clean container with an airtight lid. Store in the refrigerator for up to 1 month.

Makes 1 cup

Apple Butter

Try spreading this on raisin bread or bran muffins—yum! Some apples to use for this butter: Cortland, McIntosh, or Northern Spy. You can buy it, but homemade is much, much better.

3/4 cup unsweetened apple cider or juice

1/3 cup firmly packed light brown sugar

1 teaspoon ground cinnamon

1/2 teaspoon ground cloves

1/2 teaspoon ground allspice

3 pounds (6 medium) apples, peeled, quartered, and cored

1. In the bowl of a food processor or blender, combine the apple cider, brown sugar, cinnamon, cloves, and allspice. Whirl until all the ingredients are well blended. Add the apple quarters, 2 or 3 at a time, and whirl until the apples are pureed.

2. Pour the apple mixture into a large, nonreactive saucepan. Over moderately high heat, bring the mixture to a boil; reduce the heat to low, cover the saucepan, and cook for 1 hour, stirring occasionally. Uncover the saucepan and cook until the apple mixture is thickened, about 1 to 1 1/2 hours longer.

3. Spoon the apple butter into 2 widemouthed, warm, sterilized half-pint jars, leaving a 1/2-inch space between the top of the jam and the rim of the jar (see Safe Canning with a Hot-Water Bath, page 72). Wipe the rims, cover, label, and date. Store the jam in the refrigerator for up to 3 weeks or in the freezer for up to 1 year.

Makes 2 half-pint jars

salad dressings

Classic Vinaigrette

The classic salad dressing that can be (and should be) whipped up just before serving, then used sparingly over the freshest mixed greens. Since all the ingredients used in vinaigrette are pantry staples, this is a gourmet touch that is quick and easy to make and not costly at all.

1/4 cup extra-virgin or virgin olive oil

4 teaspoons vinegar (white wine, red wine, tarragon, etc.) or fresh lemon juice

1/2 teaspoon salt

Freshly ground pepper, to taste

In a small, nonreactive bowl, whisk together all the ingredients until well blended. Use immediately.

Makes 1/4 cup

Herb Vinaigrette

Fresh herbs give a heightened taste to this vinaigrette that you will never get from a bottled version.

1/4 cup extra-virgin or virgin olive oil

4 teaspoons vinegar (white wine, red wine, tarragon, etc.) or fresh lemon juice

1 tablespoon minced fresh herb, such as tarragon, basil, chives, or parsley

1/2 teaspoon salt

Freshly ground pepper, to taste

In a small, nonreactive bowl, whisk together all the ingredients until well blended. Use immediately.

Makes 1/4 cup

Mustard Vinaigrette

This is a classic dressing often served in good French restaurants.

1/4 cup extra-virgin or virgin olive oil

4 teaspoons vinegar (white wine, red wine, tarragon, etc.) or fresh lemon juice

1 teaspoon Dijon mustard

1/2 teaspoon salt

Freshly ground pepper, to taste

In a small, nonreactive bowl, whisk together all the ingredients until well blended. Use immediately.

Makes 1/4 cup

Garlic Vinaigrette *Experiment with different vinegars and/or lemon juice when you make this dressing.*

1/4 cup extra-virgin or virgin olive oil

4 teaspoons vinegar (white wine, red wine, tarragon, etc.) or fresh lemon juice

1 clove blanched and chopped garlic or 1 clove pressed garlic

1/2 teaspoon salt

Freshly ground pepper, to taste

In a small, nonreactive bowl, whisk together all the ingredients until well blended. Use immediately.

Makes 1/4 cup

flavored oil

Surprisingly easy to make and packing a powerful flavor punch in salads, flavored oils make fabulous gifts too. Make these oils in small quantities, because they are perishable. Lower-moisture herbs such as rosemary, thyme, or summer savory, or spices such as coriander seed or chiles are the best choices.

To make a flavored oil, all you need are several sprigs of fresh herbs or whole spices and olive oil (enough to fill bottles).

1. Spread the herbs or spices on a clean work surface. Using a rolling pin, gently press down on the herbs or spices just to lightly bruise them.

2. In a small saucepan over low heat, warm the olive oil. Add the herbs or spices, and let steep for several minutes. Using a slotted spoon, transfer the herbs or spices to sterilized bottles, distributing them equally. Pour the warm oil on top of the herbs or spices, leaving a 1/4-inch space between the top of the oil and the rim of the bottle. Wipe the rims, cover tightly, and refrigerate for at least 2 days to allow the herbs or spices to infuse the oil.

3. Strain the oil into a new set of sterilized bottles, adding a fresh herb sprig or whole spice to each bottle. Wipe the rims, cover, label, and date. Store in the refrigerator for up to 1 month. Keep refrigerated after the oil is opened.

Balsamic Vinaigrette *Use the best balsamic vinegar and olive oil that you can afford for this dressing.*

1/4 cup extra-virgin or virgin olive oil

4 teaspoons balsamic vinegar

1 tablespoon minced fresh basil

1/2 teaspoon salt

Freshly ground pepper, to taste

In a small, nonreactive bowl, whisk together all the ingredients until well blended. Use immediately.

Makes 1/4 cup

Orange and Almond Oil Dressing
A delicate variation on a classic vinaigrette base, this dressing uses orange juice in place of vinegar.

3 tablespoons orange juice

4 tablespoons almond oil

2 tablespoons canola, sunflower, or extra-virgin olive oil

Salt and freshly ground pepper, to taste

1. In a small, nonreactive bowl, combine the orange juice, almond oil, and vegetable or olive oil. Whisk together until the ingredients are well blended. Add salt and pepper. Whisk vigorously again just before using.

2. Store in an airtight container for up to 1 week in the refrigerator; bring to room temperature and whisk well before using.

Makes about 1/2 cup

Raspberry Vinaigrette
Sweet, tart, tangy—this will quickly become a family favorite. Homemade is better and half the price of the bottled version.

2 jars (12 ounces each) seedless raspberry preserves

1 1/4 cups sugar

1/4 cup water

1/3 cup chopped sweet onion

1/4 cup balsamic vinegar

1 tablespoon dried tarragon

1 tablespoon curry powder

1 teaspoon ground white pepper

1 teaspoon ground black pepper

1 cup extra-virgin or virgin olive oil

1. In a large, nonreactive saucepan over high heat, combine the raspberry preserves and 3/4 cup of the sugar to a boil. Remove the saucepan from the heat and let cool slightly. Pour the raspberry mixture into the bowl of a food processor or blender. Add the water, onion, vinegar, tarragon, curry powder, white pepper, black pepper, and the remaining sugar.

2. Cover and whirl, adding the olive oil in a slow, steady stream, until the ingredients are well blended and the dressing has a smooth consistency. Use immediately or store in an airtight container in the refrigerator for up to 1 week. Bring to room temperature and whisk vigorously before using.

Makes about 4 cups

Buttermilk Dressing Mix
This mix is easy to make and keep on hand for whenever you need a creamy dressing for salad or dip for crudités. It is cheap and convenient and wonderful.

4 1/2 cups buttermilk powder

1 1/2 cups freeze-dried chives

1/2 cup dried dill, crumbled

1/2 cup sugar

1/4 cup dry mustard

1. Whisk together all the ingredients until well blended.

2. Store the mix in an airtight, 2-quart jar in the refrigerator for up to 1 month.

Makes about 7 cups

Buttermilk Dressing

This is a delicious dressing for any tossed green or Caesar-style salad as well as for bean or pasta salads.

10 tablespoons Buttermilk Dressing Mix (opposite)

1 cup warm water

1/4 cup cider vinegar

2 tablespoons sour cream or plain yogurt

1. Whisk together all the ingredients until well blended.
2. Let the mixture stand at room temperature for 1 hour, then stir until all the ingredients are well blended and the dressing is a smooth, creamy consistency.

Makes about 2 cups

flavored vinegar

It's easy to make your own herb-flavored vinegars, which add a great subtle taste to salads, especially ones dressed with just oil and vinegar. But remember, the finished results depend on using a high-quality vinegar as the base.

To make flavored vinegar, you only need:

Several sprigs fresh herbs as desired

High-quality vinegar (enough to fill the desired number of bottles)

Here's how to proceed:

1. Spread the herbs on a clean work surface. Using a rolling pin, gently press down on the herbs just to lightly bruise them enough to release their flavor. Place 1 sprig in each sterilized bottle.

2. In a large, nonreactive saucepan over high heat, bring the vinegar to a boil. Pour the hot vinegar over the herb sprigs in each bottle. Cover the bottles and place them in a sunny windowsill for at least 2 weeks to allow the herbs to infuse the vinegar. Turn each bottle daily.

3. Place a fresh herb sprig into each of a new set of sterilized bottles. Strain the vinegar, discarding the old herbs. Pour the flavored vinegar into the new set of bottles, over the fresh herb sprigs. Cover, label, and date. Store the flavored vinegar in a cool, dark place for up to a year; the vinegar will be ready for use in 2 weeks. Store the flavored vinegar in the refrigerator after opening.

Herb Dressing Mix

All the taste—none of the preservatives! That's what makes this mixture such a delicious bargain.

1/2 cup dried parsley, crumbled

1/4 cup dried oregano, crumbled

1/4 cup dried basil, crumbled

1/4 cup dried marjoram, crumbled

1/4 cup sugar

2 tablespoons fennel seed, crushed

2 tablespoons dry mustard

1 tablespoon ground black pepper

1. In a large, 1-quart jar, combine all the ingredients. Cover the jar and shake until all the herbs are well mixed.
2. Store the Herb Dressing Mix in a cool, dry, dark place for up to 6 weeks.

Makes 2 cups

Herb Dressing

You can adjust the strength of this eye-opening dressing by increasing or decreasing the amount of Herb Dressing Mix you add.

2 tablespoons Herb Dressing Mix (page 37)

1 1/2 cups warm water

2 tablespoons olive oil

5 tablespoons white or tarragon vinegar

2 garlic cloves, crushed

1. In a small, nonreactive bowl, whisk together all the ingredients until well blended. Let the dressing stand at room temperature for 30 minutes; whisk vigorously again and use.

2. Store the dressing in an airtight jar or bottle in the refrigerator for up to 1 week.

Makes 2 cups

Ranch Dressing Mix

Classic, creamy, dreamy—this mix makes it easy to whip up some ranch dressing on demand, for tossing with salads, dipping with crudités, or soothing the fires of Buffalo wings.

2 tablespoons plus 2 teaspoons dried minced onion

1 tablespoon dried parsley, crumbled

2 1/2 teaspoons paprika

2 teaspoons sugar

2 teaspoons salt

2 teaspoons pepper

1 1/2 teaspoons garlic powder

1. In a small, airtight container, combine all the ingredients. Cover and shake vigorously to blend.

2. Store in a cool, dry, dark place for up to 1 year.

Makes about 6 tablespoons

Helpful Hint

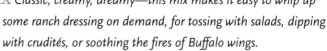

Make Your Own Cost-Effective Croutons

A wonderful way to use up stale bread, croutons are so easy to prepare it makes no sense to spend extra money to buy them. Cut bread slices into 1/2-inch cubes. In a large skillet over moderate heat, heat extra-virgin olive oil. Add the bread cubes and sauté, stirring constantly, until the cubes are well coated, golden in color, and crisp. Transfer the cubes to paper towels and let drain. Add to salads or float on soups. Store in airtight containers.

To add more flavor to your croutons, sauté garlic slices or sprigs of herbs or even chile peppers in the olive oil. Remove and discard the flavorings before adding the bread cubes to the flavored oil.

Ranch Dressing
To make a lower-fat version of this dressing, substitute fat-free mayonnaise for the regular mayonnaise. Buttermilk is made from skim milk, so it is already low in fat and calories. If you don't use buttermilk often, buy a box of dry buttermilk powder and simply make as much as you need when you need it. If you'd like a thicker consistency for dipping, stir the Ranch Dressing Mix into 1 cup sour cream or plain yogurt.

1 container Ranch Dressing Mix (opposite)
1 cup mayonnaise
1 cup buttermilk

In a small, nonreactive bowl, whisk together all the ingredients until the dressing has a smooth, creamy consistency.

Makes about 2 cups

Blue Cheese Dressing
You can make this tangy treat or any of the other prepared salad dressings that follow from scratch and keep them on hand in the refrigerator. They are all easy to make and cost very little compared to commercial brands.

1 1/2 cups mayonnaise
1/2 cup sour cream
1/4 cup cider vinegar
4 teaspoons sugar
1/2 teaspoon dry mustard
1 teaspoon minced fresh garlic
2 teaspoons minced onion
1 cup (4 ounces) crumbled blue cheese

In a small, nonreactive bowl, combine all the ingredients except the blue cheese. Whisk to blend until the dressing has a smooth, creamy consistency. Gently stir in the blue cheese. Cover the bowl and refrigerate for at least 2 hours before serving. Store, covered, in the refrigerator.

Makes 2 cups

Light Blue Cheese Dressing
Rich and creamy and loaded with flavor—you won't guess this is a lower-fat cousin. And it is much better than lower-calorie commercial dressings.

1/2 cup fat-free mayonnaise
2 tablespoons 1% milk
1 tablespoon lemon juice
1/2 teaspoon sugar
1 teaspoon minced fresh garlic
1/4 teaspoon dry mustard
1/2 cup (2 ounces) crumbled blue cheese

In a small, nonreactive bowl, combine all the ingredients except the blue cheese. Whisk to blend until the dressing has a smooth, creamy consistency. Gently stir in the blue cheese. Cover the bowl and refrigerate for at least 2 hours before serving. Store, covered, in the refrigerator.

Makes about 1 cup

French Dressing

You probably have all the ingredients for this creamy favorite in your pantry. It takes just a few minutes to prepare and is much more delicious than the pricey bottled variety.

1 cup ketchup
1/2 cup reduced-fat mayonnaise
3 tablespoons cider vinegar
3 tablespoons honey
2 tablespoons water
1 tablespoon olive oil
1 teaspoon lemon juice
1/2 teaspoon dry mustard
1/4 teaspoon salt

In the bowl of a food processor or blender, combine all the ingredients. Whirl until all the ingredients are well blended and the dressing has a smooth, creamy consistency. Store in an airtight container in the refrigerator.

Makes 2 1/2 cups

Italian Dressing

Nothing tastes better—or is more pleasing to the pocketbook—than homemade Italian dressing.

1/4 cup extra-virgin or virgin olive oil
1/4 cup red wine vinegar
1 garlic clove, minced
1 teaspoon finely chopped onion
1/2 teaspoon dry mustard
1/2 teaspoon celery seed
1/2 teaspoon paprika
1/4 teaspoon Italian Herb Blend (page 42)
2-4 tablespoons sugar or sugar substitute equivalent

In a small, airtight container, combine all the ingredients. Cover and shake vigorously to blend all the ingredients well. Use immediately or store in the refrigerator overnight.

Makes 2/3 cup

Thousand Island Dressing

For a lighter version of this dressing, substitute low- or nonfat mayonnaise or nonfat yogurt for the regular mayonnaise. If you use homemade mayonnaise, it will please both your palate and your budget. In many parts of the country, this is called Russian dressing.

2 cups mayonnaise
1/4 cup chili sauce
1/4 cup pickle relish

1. In a small, nonreactive bowl, stir together all the ingredients until well blended and the dressing has a smooth, creamy consistency.
2. Store in an airtight container in the refrigerator.

Makes 2 1/2 cups

seasonings

Bouquet Garni

This famous combination uses either fresh herb sprigs or dried leaves. It can be added to soups, stews, and any moist-heat cooked meat and poultry dishes.

1/2 bay leaf
2 sprigs parsley
1 sprig thyme

1. Cut a piece of cheesecloth about 4-inches square. Lay the herbs in the center of the cheesecloth, then bring the corners of the cloth together to form a bundle around the herbs. Tie the top of the bundle with kitchen string.

2. Add herb bundle to soup or stew. Once the cooking is finished, the bundle can easily be removed and discarded.

Fines Herbes

This classic blend of four herbs enhances the flavor of fish, poultry, egg dishes, or cooked vegetables.

4 tablespoons dried parsley, crumbled

4 teaspoons dried tarragon, crumbled

4 teaspoons dried chervil, crumbled

4 teaspoons dried chives, finely chopped

1. In a self-sealing plastic bag or container with a tight-fitting lid, combine all the herbs.

2. Label and date, and store at room temperature. Use within 3 months.

how to dry herbs

With a little attention, herbs will grow for almost anyone and in almost any climate. And drying fresh herbs that you have grown yourself will really save you money at the grocery store. For best flavor, try to use dried herbs within 4 to 6 months after preserving them.

Air-drying: Pick fresh herbs. Gather the herbs in bunches and tie each bunch of stems with string, leaving a long end. Using the long end, hang the herb bunches upside down in a cool, dry place until they are completely dried.

Drying in an electric oven: Preheat oven to 100°F. Spread the herbs in a single layer over a baking sheet with a rim. Set the baking sheet in the oven until the herbs are completely dried, about 50 minutes.

Drying in a gas oven: Preheat oven to 200°F, then turn off the oven. Place the baking sheet with the herbs in the warm oven, close the door, and let the herbs sit until completely dried, about 50 minutes.

Herbes de Provence

This popular French mixture can be sprinkled over meats, fish, or poultry before grilling; stirred into rice, couscous, or other grain mixtures; added to omelets or scrambled eggs; or whisked with oil and vinegar for a lovely salad dressing.

6 teaspoons dried oregano, crumbled

3 teaspoons dried basil, crumbled

3 teaspoons dried sweet marjoram, crumbled

3 teaspoons dried thyme, crumbled

1 1/2 teaspoons dried mint, crumbled

1 1/2 teaspoons dried rosemary, crumbled

1 1/2 teaspoons dried sage leaves, crumbled

1 teaspoon fennel seed, crumbled

1. In a mortar, blender, or food processor, combine all the herbs. Crush or pulse-chop them to the consistency desired.
2. Place the herb mixture in a self-sealing plastic bag or airtight container, label, and date. Keep in a dry place at room temperature. Use within 3 months.

Italian Herb Blend

This well-loved herb mix is almost essential in pasta dishes and sprinkled on pizza. It is also delicious with chicken or firm fish.

6 tablespoons dried basil, crumbled

3 tablespoons dried oregano, crumbled

2 tablespoons dried parsley, crumbled

2 tablespoons dried thyme, crumbled

1 teaspoon dried garlic

1. In a self-sealing plastic bag or airtight container, combine all the ingredients.
2. Label and date, and store in a dry place at room temperature. Use within 3 months.

freezing herbs

Freezing herbs protects their flavor even more than drying them, in the opinion of many knowledgeable cooks. How you freeze an herb depends on whether you want to freeze it as a whole sprig or as chopped leaves frozen in an ice cube.

Whole sprigs: Wash and spin-dry sprigs of bushy herbs using a salad spinner. Pack in self-sealing freezer bags, label, date, and freeze. Remove leaves as needed, returning the sprigs to the bags, resealing, and refreezing.

Chopped leaves in ice cubes: Chop leaves of herbs such as chive or parsley. Place 1 tablespoon of the chopped herb into each container in an ice-cube tray. Pour just enough water into each container to cover the herbs and freeze. Pop out the frozen herb cube, place in self-sealing freezer bags, label, date, and freeze. When using in a recipe, just add the cube and let it melt.

Chili Powder

You don't have to pay fancy prices for fancy spice mixes. Make your own and then slowly start adding a little more of one ingredient or a little less of another until you have your own favorite variation. You can adapt this recipe to your own taste, making it spicier by adding more cayenne pepper or milder by adding less, and adding more or less of each spice.

- 3 tablespoons ground chile peppers or paprika
- 1 tablespoon ground cumin
- 1 teaspoon ground turmeric
- 1 teaspoon dried oregano, finely crumbled
- 1 teaspoon garlic powder
- 1/8-1 teaspoon ground cayenne pepper
- 1/4 teaspoon salt
- 1/4 teaspoon ground black pepper

1. Combine all the ingredients in an airtight container. Shake until all the spices are well blended.

2. Store in a cool, dark place for up to 6 months.

Makes about 1/4 cup

Creole Seasoning Mix

This is a spice sensation to sprinkle over popcorn or freshly baked pretzels, French fries, chicken pieces, or to use in Creole or Cajun dishes.

- 2/3 cup ground cayenne pepper
- 1/2 cup plus 2 teaspoons salt
- 1/4 cup garlic powder
- 1/4 cup onion powder
- 1/4 cup chili powder
- 2 tablespoons plus 2 teaspoons ground black pepper

1. Combine all the ingredients in an airtight container. Shake until all the spices are well blended.

2. Store in a cool, dark place for up to 6 months.

Makes 2 cups

Southwest Seasoning Mix

Sprinkle this taste of the Southwest over meats or seafood before grilling, over veggies, or over freshly popped popcorn. Stirring 1 tablespoon of this seasoning mix into 1 cup sour cream, then chilling, makes a fabulous dip.

1/4 cup chili powder

1/4 cup onion powder

2 tablespoons ground cumin

2 tablespoons ground coriander

2 tablespoons dried oregano, crumbled

2 tablespoons dried basil, crumbled

1 tablespoon dried thyme, crumbled

1 tablespoon garlic powder

1. Combine all the ingredients in a container with a tight-fitting lid. Shake until all the spices are well blended.

2. Store in a cool, dark place for up to 6 months.

Makes 1 cup

Make It a Gift

Give a Useful Jar of Herbs

Jars of herb mixtures are always welcome in a cook's home, especially if you have grown the herbs yourself. You can even make herb or spice bags with cheesecloth and kitchen twine, then place the bags in a mason jar—all the cook needs to do is pull out a bag and pop it into whatever's cooking to add fabulous flavor.

Seasoned Coating Mix

This is a fabulous addition to fried or baked chicken and pork recipes.

2 cups sifted all-purpose flour

1 tablespoon paprika

2 teaspoons dried marjoram, crumbled

2 teaspoons dried thyme, crumbled

2 teaspoons onion powder

2 teaspoons garlic powder

1 teaspoon dried rosemary, crumbled

1/2 teaspoon salt

1/4 teaspoon ground black pepper

1. In a self-sealing plastic bag, combine all the ingredients. Seal the bag and shake it to mix the ingredients thoroughly.

2. Label and date the bag, and store in a cool, dry place for up to six months.

Makes enough to coat 20 pork chops or four chickens

Caribbean Spicy Meat Rub

A pungent sweet and spicy blend to rub onto just about any kind of meat before grilling, this meat rub can also be added to sauces and stews. Or stir 4 tablespoons of the rub into 2 tablespoons vegetable oil and heat just until the aromas are released, then add to any marinade for tougher cuts of meat.

3 tablespoons brown sugar

2 tablespoons paprika

2 teaspoons dry mustard

2 teaspoons garlic salt

1 1/2 teaspoons dried basil, crumbled

1 teaspoon ground coriander

1 teaspoon dried savory, crumbled

1 teaspoon dried thyme, crumbled

1 teaspoon black pepper

1 teaspoon ground cumin

1 crushed bay leaf

1. Combine all the ingredients in an airtight container. Shake until all the spices are well blended.

2. Store in a cool, dark place for up to 6 months.

Makes about 1/2 cup

Green Curry Paste

This recipe and the one that follows are two staples of Thai cooking. You'll be surprised how often you'll find yourself reaching for these pastes to add a little exotic, exuberant flavor to your meals. You can find many of the ingredients in Asian cooking specialty stores. Stir this paste into poultry or vegetable dishes, or add to more delicately flavored meat dishes. To really release the flavors, sauté the paste in a little vegetable oil before using it.

4 shallots, chopped

1 teaspoon shrimp or anchovy paste

3 garlic cloves, quartered

2 dried kaffir lime leaves, crushed, or 1 teaspoon lime zest

1 piece (4 inches long) fresh lemongrass, inner stalk chopped

1 tablespoon coriander seeds

1 tablespoon sliced fresh ginger

1 teaspoon freshly grated nutmeg

1 teaspoon cumin seeds

1 teaspoon white peppercorns

6 green chiles, seeded and quartered

3-4 tablespoons coconut cream

1. In the container of a food processor or blender, combine all the ingredients. Whirl until all the ingredients are well blended and the mixture is smooth.

2. Use the paste at once or place in an airtight container, cover with vegetable oil, and store in the refrigerator for up to 4 days. Or pack the paste into an ice-cube tray, freeze, pop out the paste cubes, and store in a self-sealing, freezer-safe plastic bag in the freezer, and use the cubes as needed in recipes.

Makes about 3/4 cup

Red Curry Paste

Keep the milk handy when you dine on this spicy Thai delight—though you can adjust the heat by adding or subtracting the fresh red chiles. (Milk puts out chile fires better than water.) As with the Green Curry Paste (page 45), sautéing the paste in a little oil before using it allows the flavors to be fully released.

3-6 fresh red chiles, stemmed but not seeded

4 shallots, quartered

1 red onion, cut into eighths

4 garlic cloves, quartered

1 piece lemongrass, 4 inches long, inner stalk chopped

1/4 cup fresh cilantro leaves

2 kaffir lime leaves, minced

Zest of 2 limes

1 tablespoon toasted coriander seeds

1 teaspoon grated nutmeg

1 teaspoon cumin seeds

1 teaspoon white peppercorns

2 teaspoons shrimp or anchovy paste

1. In the container of a food processor or blender, combine the red chiles, shallots, red onion, garlic, lemongrass, cilantro, lime leaves and zest, coriander seeds, nutmeg, cumin seeds, and white peppercorns. Whirl until all the ingredients are well blended and the mixture is smooth.

2. In a skillet over medium-low heat, dry-roast the shrimp or anchovy paste for 2 to 3 minutes, stirring constantly. Add to the chile mixture and process to blend all the ingredients until smooth. Use the paste at once or place in a container with a tight-fitting lid, cover with vegetable oil, and store in the refrigerator for up to two weeks.

Makes about 1 cup

Curry Powder

Just about every family in India has a curry recipe. Try making the basic recipe below, then adding or subtracting one of the following until you make your own personal curry powder: cumin seeds, turmeric, mace, black peppercorns, fennel seeds, crushed red pepper flakes, coriander, cinnamon, nutmeg, cloves, tamarind, or cardamom seeds.

1/4 cup ground coriander

2 tablespoons ground turmeric

2 teaspoons ground cumin

2 teaspoons ground ginger

2 teaspoons ground allspice

1 teaspoon ground cinnamon

1 teaspoon ground celery seed

1 teaspoon ground black pepper

1/4 teaspoon ground cayenne pepper

1. Combine all the ingredients in an airtight container. Shake until all the spices are well blended.

2. Store in a cool, dark place for up to 6 months.

Makes about 1/2 cup

marinades

Red Wine Marinade

1/4 cup dry red wine

2 scallions, chopped

2 tablespoons balsamic vinegar

1/2 teaspoon dried rosemary

2 tablespoons olive oil

2 garlic cloves, minced

1/2 teaspoon salt

1/2 teaspoon black pepper

The purpose of any marinade is twofold: An acid (lemon juice, vinegar) breaks down the fibers in tough pieces of meat, and the seasonings infuse the meat with piquant flavor. Try marinating chunks of beef or lamb in this rich-tasting mixture before grilling them on skewers for kabobs. You don't need to buy an expensive packaged marinade.

In a small, nonreactive bowl, combine all the ingredients. Stir to blend all the ingredients well. Pour the marinade into a large, self-sealing bag and add the lamb or beef to be marinated. Place the bag in the refrigerator for at least 4 hours or overnight.

Mustard Marinade

1/3 cup lemon juice

2 scallions, chopped

2 tablespoons soy sauce

2 tablespoons Dijon mustard

2 tablespoons olive oil

1/4 teaspoon hot
red pepper sauce

Use this tasty mixture to marinate boneless chicken breasts, either for straight grilling or cut into cubes for kabobs. You don't need packaged marinades.

1. In a small bowl, combine all the ingredients. Stir to blend well. Pour the marinade into a large, self-sealing bag and add the poultry to be marinated.

2. Place the bag in the refrigerator for at least 4 hours or overnight.

make your own meat tenderizer

Yes, you can buy powdered meat tenderizer, and it won't break your budget, but why buy it when you probably already have several things on hand that will do just as good a job, are healthier, and will add flavor along with the tenderizing action? Almost any acid-based liquid will work.

Beer: Surprise! Place the meat in a nonmetallic dish (glass or enameled), pour a can of beer over it, place it in the refrigerator, and let it sit for 1 hour. For even more tenderizing action, leave the meat sitting in the beer overnight, turning once or twice. If you're slow-cooking the meat (the best cooking method for tough cuts), use beer as part of the cooking liquid.

Buttermilk: This acidy milk makes another great meat tenderizer when used as a marinade.

Lemon juice: If you grow your own lemons, you have a terrific tenderizer for nothing! Lemon juice breaks down tough fibers quickly and easily—and adds a bright citrus taste as well.

Vinegar: Is there anything that vinegar can't do? Soak a tough piece of meat in 1 or 2 cups of vinegar overnight in the refrigerator to tenderize it. Any vinegar will do the job—try different vinegars with different meats to find out which combinations you like the best.

Lemon Herb Marinade
Lovely with lamb chops, this is also great with chicken. It is easy, inexpensive, and delicious.

3 tablespoons vegetable oil

1 teaspoon grated lemon zest

3 tablespoons lemon juice

2 garlic cloves, minced

1 teaspoon dried rosemary, crumbled

1/2 teaspoon dried thyme, crumbled

1/2 teaspoon salt

1/4 teaspoon black pepper

1. In a small, nonreactive bowl, combine all the ingredients. Stir to blend all the ingredients well. Pour the marinade into a large, self-sealing bag and add the lamb, meat, or poultry to be marinated.

2. Place the bag in the refrigerator for at least 4 hours.

Orange Ginger Marinade
Lovely for marinating scallops or lending a sweet, tangy flavor to shrimp or fish, this easy-to-make mixture rivals any prepared marinade.

1/4 cup soy sauce

2 scallions, chopped

1/3 cup orange juice

2 teaspoons grated fresh ginger

2 tablespoons olive oil

2 tablespoons grated orange zest

1 garlic clove, minced

1. In a small, nonreactive bowl, combine all the ingredients. Stir to blend all the ingredients well. Pour the marinade into a large, self-sealing bag and add the seafood to be marinated.

2. Place the bag in the refrigerator for 30 minutes to 1 hour.

Asian Marinade
Sensational with shrimp, this marinade is also good with chicken or flank steak. Compare your own version with bottled ones and you'll be glad you saved the money. If salt is an issue, use low-sodium soy sauce.

1/4 cup lemon juice

1/2 teaspoon salt

2 tablespoons dark sesame oil

1 large garlic clove, minced

1 tablespoon soy sauce

1. In a small, nonreactive bowl, combine all the ingredients. Stir to blend all the ingredients well. Pour the marinade into a self-sealing bag and add the seafood, meat, or poultry to be marinated.

2. Place the bag in the refrigerator for at least 1 hour.

cooking stocks

Beef Stock

At the heart of every great soup, there is a great stock. Although canned broth is convenient, it is really not as flavorful as your own stock. Plus, when you make your own, you have the satisfaction of knowing exactly what goes into it—and what doesn't. When you buy the beef for this rich-tasting stock, ask the butcher to break up the bones into pieces small enough to fit into your stockpot or Dutch oven. This will be cheaper, tastier, and far less salty than most canned broths.

4 pounds meaty beef bones, including marrow and shinbones, or knucklebones

2 yellow onions, thickly sliced

2 carrots, thickly sliced

2 stalks celery with leaves, sliced

6 sprigs fresh parsley

2 small bay leaves

1 sprig fresh thyme or 1/2 teaspoon dried thyme, crumbled

10 black peppercorns

1 tablespoons salt

1. Preheat the oven to 400°F. Place the beef bones, onions, and carrots in a roasting pan and roast until the bones turn a rich brown, for 30 to 45 minutes.

2. Transfer the mixture to a large stockpot or Dutch oven. Add the celery, parsley, bay leaves, thyme, peppercorns, and salt. Add enough water to cover the bone mixture (about 5 quarts).

3. Add a little water to the roasting pan and stir to scrape up the browned bits. Pour the liquid and bits into the stockpot.

4. Place the stockpot over moderately high heat, and slowly bring the mixture to a boil, using a slotted spoon to skim off and discard any fat or scum that rises to the surface. Reduce the heat, partly cover the stockpot, and simmer gently for 3 to 4 hours.

5. Line a fine sieve with cheesecloth and set it over a large bowl. Slowly pour the stock through the sieve; discard the solids. Let the stock cool to room temperature. Pour the stock into serving-size, airtight containers; cover, label, and date. Store the stock in the refrigerator for a week or the freeze for up to 6 months. If fat congeals on top of the stock while refrigerated or frozen, remove and discard before using the stock.

Makes 3 quarts

Helpful Hint

Make Your Own Bouillon Cubes

No one can deny the convenience of bouillon cubes, but you don't have to spend your hard-earned money to have them on hand. When cooking a pot of stock, occasionally cook the liquid down to 2 cups—it will be thick and intense in both flavor and color. Let the reduced stock cool completely, then pour it into ice-cube trays and place the trays in the freezer. When the stock cubes are solid, remove them from the ice-cube trays, wrap each in foil, and store the cubes in a labeled and dated self-sealing freezer bag. Each cube will make 1 cup of soup.

Chicken Stock
You can use the same technique to make turkey stock with your leftover holiday bird.

5 1/2-pound stewing hen or 2 pounds chicken wing tips, necks, and backs

3 stalks celery, sliced

1 large carrot, sliced

1 large onion, quartered

1 leek, sliced

6 sprigs fresh parsley

1/2 teaspoon dried thyme

1 bay leaf

1 teaspoon salt

1/2 teaspoon black peppercorns

1. In a large saucepan or Dutch oven, combine all the ingredients. Add enough water to cover the chicken mixture (about 10 to 12 cups). Over moderately low heat, bring the mixture slowly to a boil, using a slotted spoon to skim off and discard any fat or scum that rises to the surface.

2. Reduce the heat, partly cover the saucepan, and simmer gently until the stock is well flavored, about 3 hours. The longer you simmer the stock, the richer the flavor.

3. Line a fine sieve with cheesecloth and set it over a large bowl. Slowly pour the stock through the sieve; discard the solids. Let the stock cool to room temperature. Pour the stock into serving-size, airtight containers; cover, label, and date. Store the stock in the refrigerator for a week or freeze for up to 6 months. If fat congeals on top of the stock while refrigerated or frozen, remove and discard before using the stock.

Makes 2 quarts

Fish Stock
An elegant base for seafood soups and stews, this delicately flavored stock can also be used as a poaching liquid for whole fish. Be careful not to overcook fish stock; too much cooking can destroy the complex flavor. After making the stock, use the cooked fish in salads or spreads.

1 1/2 pounds whole white-fleshed fish, such as cod, snapper, or scrod, cleaned and scaled

1-2 stalks celery, sliced

1 small onion, sliced

1 cup white wine or juice of 1 lemon

6-8 cups cold water

3 sprigs fresh parsley

1 sprig fresh thyme or 1/2 teaspoon dried thyme, crumbled

1 small bay leaf

1/2 teaspoon salt

1/2 teaspoon black peppercorns

1. Cut off the fish head, slit open the fish, and remove the bones. In a large saucepan, combine the fish fillets, head, and bones. Add the celery, onion, wine or lemon juice, water, parsley, thyme, bay leaf, salt, and peppercorns. Over moderately high heat, bring the mixture to a boil, using a slotted spoon to skim off and discard any fat or scum that rises to the surface.

2. Reduce the heat to very low and barely simmer the stock, uncovered, until the fish fillets are just cooked, about 5 minutes. Using a slotted spoon, lift out the fish fillets and set them aside to drain.

3. Continue to simmer the broth for 15 minutes longer.

4. Line a fine sieve with cheesecloth and set it over a large bowl. Slowly pour the stock through the sieve; discard the solids. Let the stock cool to room temperature. Pour the stock into serving-size, airtight containers; cover, label, and date. Store in the refrigerator for a week or the freezer for up to six months.

Makes 1 1/2 quarts

clarifying stock

To have stock that is beautifully clear and tantalizing, you must clarify it after cooking. There are two methods for clarifying stock: The first will yield fairly clear results; the second method will be very clear.

Straining: Line a fine sieve with cheesecloth and pour the stock through; this will remove any small solids in the stock.

Egg-white method: Separate 2 eggs and whisk together the whites; crush the eggshells. Add the whites and shells to the stock and slowly bring to a simmer, uncovered. When the whites begin to set, pour the stock through a cheesecloth-lined sieve or colander; any particles will be trapped in the egg whites. Discard whites and shells.

Vegetable Stock

A creative way to use vegetable peelings, leftover vegetables, or the parts full of nutrition but not generally served with the vegetables, such as mushroom stems, broccoli and cauliflower stalks, and celery tops. That makes homemade vegetable stock very economical and much better than vegetable cubes.

1/4 cup (1/2 stick) unsalted butter

5 onions, peeled and chopped

2 leeks, halved lengthwise, cleaned, and sliced

2 whole garlic cloves

4 carrots, chopped

4 stalks celery with leaves, chopped

6-8 dried mushrooms

1 small bunch fresh parsley

1 sprig fresh thyme or 1/2 teaspoon dried thyme, crumbled

1 tablespoon salt

1/2 teaspoon ground allspice

Pinch nutmeg or mace

4 quarts cold water

1 tablespoon red wine vinegar *(optional)*

1 fresh red chile, halved and seeded *(optional)*; wear gloves when handling; they burn

1. In a large saucepan or Dutch oven over moderate heat, melt the butter. Add the onions, leeks, and garlic, and cook, stirring, until the onions are golden, 5 to 8 minutes. Add the carrots, celery, mushrooms, parsley, thyme, salt, allspice, nutmeg or mace, and cold water.

2. Bring the mixture slowly to a boil, using a slotted spoon to skim off and discard any fat or scum that rises to the surface. Reduce the heat, partly cover the saucepan, and simmer gently for 2 hours, adding more water as needed to maintain the level at about 3 quarts. If using, add the red wine vinegar and red chile, and simmer for 30 minutes longer.

3. Line a fine sieve with cheesecloth and set it over a large bowl. Slowly pour the stock through the sieve, gently pressing with a wooden spoon to squeeze all the liquid from the solids; discard the solids and the red chile. If desired, clarify the stock (see Clarifying Stock, above). If a thicker stock is desired, do not discard the solids when straining; puree about 1/2 cup of the cooked vegetables and stir the puree back into the stock. Let the stock cool to room temperature. Pour the stock into serving-size, airtight containers; cover, label, and date. Store the stock in the refrigerator for a week or the freezer for up to 6 months.

Makes about 3 quarts

sauces

Barbecue Sauce

Great with beef, chicken, or pork, this homemade sauce is not only cheaper than bottled ones, but you can customize it to your own family's tastes.

1 medium onion, chopped

1/4 cup vegetable oil

1 cup ketchup

3/4 cup water

2 tablespoons Worcestershire sauce

2 tablespoons sugar

1/4 cup cider vinegar

2 tablespoons mustard

1 teaspoon salt

1/2 teaspoon ground black pepper

1. In a medium, nonreactive saucepan over low heat, combine all the ingredients. Simmer, uncovered, for 20 minutes; remove the saucepan from the heat and let the sauce cool.

2. Store in an airtight container in the refrigerator for up to 1 week, or frozen for up to 6 months.

Makes about 2 1/2 cups

Pan Gravy

This is the finishing touch for any roast. Real pan gravy is made using the drippings from roasted meat or poultry, but you can also used homemade stock or canned broth (the flavor will be less intense, but it will work). Authentic gravy doesn't come in a can or a packet.

1/4 cup pan drippings from roast meat or poultry

Melted butter, as needed

2 cups Beef Stock (page 49) or Chicken Stock (page 50), or canned beef or chicken broth

1/4 cup all-purpose flour

Salt and freshly ground pepper, to taste

1. In a 1-cup measure, pour the pan drippings to equal 1/4 cup. If needed, add melted butter to reach the desired amount. Pour the drippings into a large skillet and set aside.

2. Place the roasting pan with the remaining drippings over moderate heat. Stir in the stock or broth and simmer, stirring to loosen any browned bits on the pan, about 1 minute.

3. Place the skillet over moderate heat and heat the drippings for 1 minute. Blend in the flour and cook, whisking, until the flour is a nutty brown, for 1 to 2 minutes. Gradually add the stock, whisking constantly, and cook until the mixture boils and thickens.

4. Reduce the heat to moderately low and simmer, stirring occasionally, for 2 to 3 minutes longer. Add salt and pepper. If the gravy is lumpier than desired, strain through a sieve. Transfer the gravy to a heated gravy boat and serve immediately.

Makes 2 cups

Demiglaze Sauce

This is a beautiful homemade sauce for meats like lean pork that don't produce enough drippings of their own to make gravy. Far better than canned or packaged gravy mixes, it's cheaper too.

1/4 cup unsalted butter

2 ounces Black Forest or Virginia ham, chopped

1 medium onion, chopped

1 carrot, thinly sliced

1/4 cup all-purpose flour

4 cups Beef Stock (page 49) or canned beef broth

1 1/2 cups Chicken Stock (page 50) or canned broth

2 tablespoons tomato paste

1/2 teaspoon salt

1/4 teaspoon dried thyme

1/4 teaspoon ground black pepper

1/2 cup dry red wine

1. In a large, heavy saucepan over moderate heat, melt the butter or margarine. Add the ham and cook, stirring frequently, until lightly golden, abut 8 minutes. Add the onion and cook, stirring frequently, until it is soft, about 5 minutes. Add the carrot and cook until it is tender, about 5 minutes.

2. Sprinkle the flour over the vegetable mixture and stir until it is blended. Gradually add 3 cups of the beef stock, the chicken stock, tomato paste, salt, thyme, and pepper, stirring constantly. Cook, stirring frequently and skimming off any scum that rises to the surface, until the sauce thickens and thickly coats the back of a spoon, about 30 minutes. Strain the sauce through a sieve and discard the solids.

3. Stir in the remaining cup of beef stock and the red wine and cook, uncovered, until the sauce reduces to 3 1/2 cups.

Makes 3 1/2 cups

Espagnole Sauce

Simple, yet rich, this is another brown sauce for lean meats that don't produce drippings. Homemade is tastier, less salty, and cheaper than canned or packaged brown gravy

1/4 cup unsalted butter

2 ounces Black Forest or Virginia ham, chopped

1 medium onion, chopped

1 carrot, thinly sliced

1/4 cup all-purpose flour

3 cups Beef Stock (page 49) or canned beef broth

1 1/2 cups Chicken Stock (page 50) or canned broth

2 tablespoons tomato paste

1/2 teaspoon salt

1/4 teaspoon dried thyme

1/4 teaspoon black pepper

1. In a large, heavy saucepan over moderate heat, melt the butter or margarine. Add the ham and cook, stirring frequently, until lightly golden, abut 8 minutes. Add the onion and cook, stirring frequently, until it is soft, about 5 minutes. Add the carrot and cook until it is tender, about 5 minutes.

2. Sprinkle the flour over the vegetable mixture and stir until it is blended. Gradually add the beef and chicken stocks, tomato paste, salt, thyme, and pepper, stirring constantly. Cook, stirring frequently and skimming off any scum that rises to the surface, until the sauce thickens and thickly coats the back of a spoon, about 30 minutes. Strain the sauce through a sieve and discard the solids.

Makes 3 cups

Mushroom Wine Sauce

Many a steak lover considers this sauce ambrosia, but it is equally good with veal or chicken. Store-bought mushroom gravies just don't come close in taste or economy.

1/4 cup (1/2 stick) unsalted butter or margarine

2 ounces Black Forest or Virginia ham, chopped

1 medium onion, chopped

1 carrot, thinly sliced

1/4 cup all-purpose flour

3 cups Beef Stock (page 49) or canned beef broth

1 1/2 cups Chicken Stock (page 50) or canned chicken broth

2 tablespoons tomato paste

1/2 teaspoon salt

1/4 teaspoon dried thyme, crumbled

1/4 teaspoon black pepper

3 tablespoons butter

2 shallots, minced

8 ounces button, shiitake, or portobello mushrooms, thinly sliced

2/3 cup dry red wine

1. In a large, heavy saucepan over moderate heat, melt the butter or margarine. Add the ham and cook, stirring frequently, until lightly golden, abut 8 minutes. Add the onion and cook, stirring frequently, until it is soft, about 5 minutes. Add the carrot and cook until it is tender, about 5 minutes.

2. Sprinkle the flour over the vegetable mixture and stir until it is blended. Gradually add the beef and chicken stocks, tomato paste, salt, thyme, and pepper, stirring constantly. Cook, stirring frequently and skimming off any scum that rises to the surface, until the sauce thickens and thickly coats the back of a spoon, about 30 minutes. Strain the sauce through a sieve and discard the solids.

3. In a large skillet over moderate heat, melt the butter. Add the shallots and cook until soft. Add the mushrooms and cook until tender. Add the red wine, increase the heat, and boil, uncovered, until the mixture is reduced by half.

4. Add the mushroom mixture to the sauce, stirring until the ingredients are well blended.

Makes 3 1/2 cups

how to clarify butter

Clarified butter is essential to making certain sauces, such as hollandaise, and for dipping artichoke leaves or steamed lobster. By clarifying butter, you are removing the milk solids, leaving a clear, golden, rich oil.

In a small saucepan over very low heat, melt a stick (1/2 cup) of butter. When the butter has completely liquefied but not yet begun to cook, remove the saucepan from the heat and let the butter stand until the white milk solids sink to the bottom. Place a piece of cheesecloth over a small glass bowl. Carefully pour the golden-yellow liquid butter into the bowl through the cheesecloth; be careful to stop pouring when the white solids begin to move. Remove the cheesecloth and store the clarified butter, covered, in the refrigerator until ready to use.

Béarnaise Sauce

Adding immediate elegance to almost any meal, egg sauces, notably this Béarnaise sauce and the Hollandaise Sauce that follows, are among the most refined. Once made with either raw eggs or eggs only lightly cooked in a double boiler, these recipes cook the eggs enough to remove any fear of salmonella contamination. Slow and steady is the rule when cooking egg sauces—or you may scramble your culinary plans. Béarnaise is a sauce served with filet mignon in the finest restaurants for the finest prices. Jars sold in specialty food stores just don't measure up.

1/3 cup chopped fresh tarragon

2 tablespoons white wine vinegar

1 tablespoon minced shallot

2 egg yolks

2 tablespoons water

1/4 teaspoon salt

6 tablespoons clarified unsalted butter (see How to Clarify Butter, opposite), liquid but not hot

1/8 teaspoon white pepper

1. In a small saucepan over moderately high heat, combine the tarragon, white wine vinegar, and shallot, and cook for 1 to 2 minutes. Remove the saucepan from the heat and let cool.

2. In a 1-quart saucepan over moderately high heat, combine the egg yolks, water, salt, and tarragon mixture, and bring to a boil, whisking constantly.

3. Remove the saucepan from the heat. The mixture will begin to curdle, but continue whisking until the mixture becomes smooth. Stir in the clarified butter, 1 tablespoon at a time. Add the pepper and stir until the mixture is smooth and well blended.

Makes 1 cup

Hollandaise Sauce

Try hollandaise drizzled over fresh, steamed asparagus, broccoli, or cauliflower, or over delicate poached fish. It is a must for eggs Benedict or Florentine. Homemade simply tastes best; it also costs less.

2 egg yolks

2 tablespoons water

1/4 teaspoon salt

1 tablespoon lemon juice

6 tablespoons clarified unsalted butter (see How to Clarify Butter, opposite), liquid but not hot

1/8 teaspoon white pepper

1. In a 1-quart saucepan over moderately high heat, combine the egg yolks, water, salt, and lemon juice, and bring to a boil, whisking constantly.

2. Remove the saucepan from the heat. The mixture will begin to curdle, but continue whisking until the mixture becomes smooth. Stir in the clarified butter, 1 tablespoon at a time. Add the pepper and stir until the mixture is smooth and well blended.

Makes 1 cup

Basic White Sauce

Thin, medium, or thick, white sauce is the most versatile of all sauces and can be adapted to suit many a dish. Thin white sauce serves as a base for creamy soups or stews; medium white sauce is added to casseroles and creamed vegetable mixtures, or used as a base for other sauces; thick white sauce works as a binder or a base for dishes like soufflés or croquettes. Making your own white sauce, starting with this basic white sauce, allows you to make all kinds of other recipes, such as the three that follow.

1 tablespoon butter or margarine

1 tablespoon all-purpose flour

1 cup hot milk

1/4 teaspoon salt

1/8 teaspoon white or black ground pepper

1. In a small heavy saucepan over low heat, melt the butter. Add the flour and cook, whisking constantly, until the mixture is smooth, 2 to 3 minutes; do not let the flour brown. Gradually stir in the milk.

2. Increase the heat to moderate and cook, stirring constantly, until the sauce is thickened and smooth, and no raw flour taste remains, about 3 to 5 minutes. Remove the saucepan from the heat and stir in the salt and pepper.

3. To store, lay plastic wrap directly on the surface of the sauce to prevent a skin from forming. Let the sauce cool to room temperature, then refrigerate until needed. Reheat the sauce in the top of a double boiler.

Makes 1 cup

Cheese Sauce

Remember that you can choose the kind of cheese to use for this homemade sauce. Cheddar is classic, but there are many other possibilities. Pour over potatoes or steamed vegetables for a starter.

1 tablespoon butter or margarine

1 tablespoon all-purpose flour

1/2 teaspoon dry mustard

1 cup hot milk

1/2-3/4 cup shredded sharp cheddar cheese

1/4 teaspoon salt

1/8 teaspoon white or black ground pepper

1. In a small heavy saucepan over low heat, melt the butter. Add the flour and dry mustard, and cook, whisking constantly, until the mixture is smooth, 2 to 3 minutes; do not let the flour brown. Gradually stir in the milk.

2. Increase the heat to moderate and cook, stirring constantly, until the sauce is thickened and smooth, and no raw flour taste remains, about 3 to 5 minutes. Remove the saucepan from the heat and stir in the cheese, salt, and pepper.

3. To store, lay plastic wrap directly on the surface of the sauce to prevent a skin from forming. Let the sauce cool to room temperature, then refrigerate until needed. Reheat the sauce in the top of a double boiler.

Makes 1 1/4 cups

Dijon Mustard Sauce *This is wonderful with ham or poached or grilled fish.*

1 tablespoon butter or margarine

1 tablespoon all-purpose flour

1 cup hot milk

2 tablespoons Dijon mustard

1 teaspoon white wine vinegar

1/4 teaspoon salt

1/8 teaspoon white or black ground pepper

1. In a small heavy saucepan over low heat, melt the butter. Add the flour and cook, whisking constantly, until the mixture is smooth, 2 to 3 minutes; do not let the flour brown. Gradually stir in the milk.

2. Increase the heat to moderate and cook, stirring constantly, until the sauce is thickened and smooth, and no raw flour taste remains, about 3 to 5 minutes. Remove the saucepan from the heat and stir in the mustard, vinegar, salt, and pepper.

3. To store, lay plastic wrap directly on the surface of the sauce to prevent a skin from forming. Let the sauce cool to room temperature, then refrigerate until needed. Reheat the sauce in the top of a double boiler.

Makes 1 cup

Mushroom Sauce *Serve this creamy mushroom sauce with roast meat or poultry, or use in casseroles. It is a far cry from canned mushroom soup or sauces.*

3 tablespoons butter or margarine

1 tablespoon all-purpose flour

1 cup hot milk or Beef Stock (page 49)

1/2 cup chopped mushrooms

1/4 teaspoon salt

1/8 teaspoon white or black ground pepper

1. In a small heavy saucepan over low heat, melt 1 tablespoon of the butter. Add the flour and cook, whisking constantly, until the mixture is smooth, 2 to 3 minutes; do not let the flour brown. Gradually stir in the milk or, if a darker sauce is desired, the beef stock.

2. In a small skillet over moderate heat, melt the remaining 2 tablespoons of butter. Add the mushrooms and cook, stirring, for 3 minutes.

3. Increase the heat to moderate and cook, stirring constantly, until the sauce is thickened and smooth, and no raw flour taste remains, about 3 to 5 minutes. Remove the saucepan from the heat and stir in the mushrooms, salt, and pepper.

4. To store, lay plastic wrap directly on the surface of the sauce to prevent a skin from forming. Let the sauce cool to room temperature, then refrigerate until needed. Reheat the sauce in the top of a double boiler.

Makes 1 cup

dessert sauces

Blueberry Syrup
This fresh homemade syrup is mouthwatering over bread pudding, pound cake, ice cream, or pancakes.

4 cups blueberries,
  fresh or frozen

2 thin strips (1 x 3 inches)
  lemon zest

3 cups water

3 cups sugar

1 tablespoon lemon juice

1. In a large saucepan, using a wooden spoon, crush the berries. Add the lemon zest and 1 cup of the water and, over moderate heat, bring the mixture to a simmer. Reduce the heat to low and cook, uncovered, for 5 minutes without simmering.

2. Line a colander or large sieve with cheesecloth and set it over a large bowl. Pour the berry mixture through the colander, squeezing the cheesecloth to extract all of the juice; there should be about 2 cups of blueberry juice. Discard the solids.

3. In a saucepan over moderately high heat, combine 2 cups of water and the sugar, and bring to a boil, stirring until the sugar is dissolved. Continue boiling, without stirring, until a candy thermometer reads 260°F.

4. Add the blueberry mixture. Boil, uncovered, for 1 minute. Remove from heat and let cool. Stir in lemon juice. Store in an airtight container in the refrigerator for up to 1 month.

Makes 3 1/2 cups

Raspberry Sauce
Simple and sensational, this quick, inexpensive sauce will quickly become a kitchen staple to serve over other fruits, sherbets, or ice cream.

1/2 cup sugar

1/2 cup water

2 tablespoons Grand Marnier
  or other orange-flavored
  liqueur

2 cups fresh raspberries or
  dry-pack frozen raspberries

1. In a small saucepan over high heat, bring the sugar and water to a boil. Remove the pan and let the syrup cool.

2. Add the Grand Marnier and raspberries, and stir gently; let stand for 2 minutes. Pour through a sieve into a bowl, pressing to remove the seeds; discard solids.

Makes about 3/4 cup

Mango and Passion Fruit Sauce
This sauce uses fresh fruit and can't be matched by a prepared sauce in a can or a freezer package.

1 large mango, peeled and
  cut up

1/2 cup (6-8 fruits) passion
  fruit pulp

1. In a food processor or blender, combine the mango and passion fruit pulp. Whirl until the mixture is a smooth puree.

2. Place in the refrigerator to chill before serving.

Makes 1 cup

Custard Sauce
No packaged vanilla pudding or custard mix can create this classic, creamy, vanilla-tinged sauce also known as crème anglaise.

1 1/2 cups milk
1/4 cup sugar
1/8 teaspoon salt
3 egg yolks, lightly beaten
3/4 teaspoon vanilla

1. In a medium saucepan over low heat, combine the milk, sugar, and salt, and heat just until small bubbles appear on the surface. In a medium bowl, whisk 1/4 cup of the milk mixture into the egg yolks, then stir back into the pan. Cook over low heat, whisking constantly, until the mixture coats the back of a spoon, about 10 minutes.

2. Remove the saucepan from the heat and strain the mixture through a sieve into a medium bowl. Stir in the vanilla. Let the sauce cool to room temperature and refrigerate, covered, until ready to serve.

Makes about 1 1/2 cups

Fruit Coulis
Here is a versatile sauce that can take advantage of berries in season—or less costly frozen ones the rest of the year. You can use raspberries, blueberries, blackberries, and of course, strawberries. You can also use fresh peaches or apricots—just lightly poach them before pureeing.

1/2 pint fresh berries or
  1 package (8 ounces)
  frozen berries
Sugar, to taste

1. Rinse and drain the berries thoroughly (frozen berries do not require rinsing). In the bowl of a food processor or blender, whirl the berries until they form a smooth puree. If desired, add a little sugar while pureeing.

2. Press the mixture through a sieve and discard any solids or seeds. Taste and add additional sugar, if desired.

3. Place the sauce in the refrigerator to chill before serving. Store in an airtight container in the refrigerator for up to 2 days.

Makes about 1 cup

Butterscotch Sauce
Of course, you can buy butterscotch sauce. Try this versatile version warm over ice cream in summer or over hot gingerbread in the fall and you'll always make it yourself.

3/4 cup (1 1/2 sticks)
  unsalted butter
1 1/2 cups firmly packed
  brown sugar
1/8 teaspoon salt
1 cup heavy cream
1 teaspoon vanilla extract

1. In a small saucepan over low heat, melt the butter. Add the sugar, salt, and cream, and stir until the sugar has dissolved. Simmer for 8 to 10 minutes over low heat, stirring continuously so that the sugar doesn't crystallize. Remove the saucepan from the heat and stir in the vanilla.

2. Serve warm or cold. Can be refrigerated in a covered container for up to a week.

Makes about 2 1/2 cups

Replacements for Pantry Staples   **59**

Chocolate Sauce

Swiss dark and semisweet chocolate, and Dutch cocoa, combine in a rich triple-chocolate knockout that can't be matched at any price.

2 tablespoons Dutch processed cocoa

3 tablespoons cold water

1/2 cup (1 stick) unsalted butter

6 ounces Swiss dark chocolate

4 ounces semisweet chocolate

1 cup boiling water

1 cup firmly packed light brown sugar

3/4 cup granulated sugar

1/2 cup light corn syrup

1/4 teaspoon salt

1 teaspoon vanilla

1. In a glass measuring cup, combine the processed cocoa and water, and stir until completely dissolved. In the top of a double boiler over low heat, melt the butter. Add the cocoa, and the dark and semisweet chocolate, then stir in the boiling water, brown and granulated sugars, corn syrup, and salt.

2. Set the top of the double boiler over moderate heat, and bring the mixture to a boil; boil, uncovered, for 5 minutes (7 minutes for a thicker sauce that will harden when it comes into contact with ice cream). Remove the saucepan from the heat and let the sauce cool to room temperature, then stir in the vanilla.

Makes about 2 1/2 cups

Hot Chocolate Sauce

This irresistible sauce should be made at the last minute and served piping hot over ice cream or frozen yogurt.

1/3 cup milk

1/2 cup heavy cream

1/4 cup sugar

7 ounces bittersweet chocolate, broken up

1. In a small saucepan over low heat, stir together the milk, cream, and sugar.

2. Add the chocolate, stirring until it is melted and a smooth consistency. Serve at once or keep chilled. Reheat slowly before serving.

Chocolate Toffee Sauce

This sauce is like a liquid Heath Bar poured over your ice cream—divine! But also as good as it gets. You can't buy an indulgence like this.

3 ounces semisweet chocolate

1/2 cup heavy cream

1/2 cup toffee candy

In a microwave-safe bowl, microwave the chocolate following the manufacturer's directions until it is melted. Or place the chocolate in a bowl set over simmering water and stir until melted. Stir in the heavy cream and the toffee candy until melted and well blended. Serve warm.

Makes 1 cup

dry mixes

Biscuit and Pancake Mix

This mix will quickly make many favorite breakfast treats—not only biscuits and pancakes but also scones and waffles (pages 141, 142).

6 cups all-purpose flour (or 3 cups all-purpose flour and 3 cups whole wheat flour)

3 1/2 tablespoons baking powder

1 cup instant nonfat dry milk

1 tablespoon salt

1 cup vegetable shortening

1. In a large bowl, combine the flour, baking powder, powdered milk, and salt, and stir until well mixed. Using a pastry blender or 2 knives, cut in the shortening until the biscuit mix resembles coarse meal.

2. Put the mix into a self-sealing bag, label, date, and refrigerate for up to 6 weeks.

Makes about 8 cups

Basic Cake Mix

Don't purchase cake mix—make your own. This basic mix can be stored for 10 to 12 weeks and makes about 16 cups. To test this mix, we suggest that you use it to create the delectable Chocolate Cake (page 117) and Spice Cake (page 116) recipes. It's so flexible that you'll quickly develop your own recipes to fill your family's needs.

8 cups all-purpose flour

6 cups sugar

1/4 cup baking powder

1 1/2 teaspoons salt

2 1/4 cups (1-pound can) vegetable shortening

1. In a large bowl, sift together the flour, sugar, baking powder, and salt. Stir until all the ingredients are well blended.

2. Add the vegetable shortening and, using a pastry blender or two knives, cut the shortening into the flour mixture until it resembles very coarse crumbs.

3. Place the mix in a large, airtight container or a self-sealing plastic bag. Label and date, and store the mix in a cool, dry place or in the refrigerator for 10 to 12 weeks.

Makes about 16 cups

Helpful Hint

Make Your Own Real Vanilla Extract

Every kitchen needs a bottle of vanilla extract—one of the most used flavorings—but as you know, it is not an inexpensive purchase. While imitation vanilla is less expensive, you pay a big price in the loss of that real vanilla flavor. What to do? Make your own.

Place a vanilla bean in a small, clean jar. Pour 3 tablespoons of plain vodka over the vanilla bean. Close the lid tightly and let the mixture stand for four weeks. Remove and discard the vanilla bean before using the extract.

pasta

Egg Pasta #1

Fresh pasta is actually quite easy to make, cooks more quickly than dried pasta, and tastes amazingly light and delicious. There are three steps to making pasta: (1) mixing together a dough, (2) rolling it out and cutting it, and (3) cooking it. You can mix the dough by hand or in a food processor. This is the simplest recipe: The eggs give enough moisture to form a dough.

3 eggs
2 cups all-purpose flour

1. In a large bowl, beat the eggs. Sift in the flour, stirring constantly, until a soft dough forms.

2. On a lightly floured surface, knead the dough until it is smooth and elastic.

3. Roll out and cut the dough by hand or with a pasta machine (see Rolling and Cutting Fresh Pasta, opposite).

4. To cook, bring a large pot of lightly salted water to a boil. Add the pasta. Fresh pasta cooks *very* quickly—thin strands may be cooked by the time they float to the surface of the water; other varieties will cook in about 1 to 2 minutes, ravioli in 6 minutes.

Makes 4 to 6 servings of spaghetti or linguini or enough for a large lasagna

Egg Pasta #2

A little easier to handle, this dough adds olive oil, water, and salt.

2 cups all-purpose flour
2 large eggs
2 teaspoons olive oil
2 tablespoons water
1/2 teaspoon salt

1. On a lightly floured surface, pour the flour in a mound. Using your hands, make a well in the center of the flour mound.

2. In a small bowl, stir together the eggs, olive oil, and water. Slowly pour the egg mixture into the flour well; sprinkle with the salt.

3. Carefully push the flour from around the edges into the well, stirring with your fingers to form a batter. Continue adding flour to the well until the mixture forms a soft dough.

4. Knead the dough for at least 5 minutes or until it is smooth and elastic. Cover the dough with an inverted bowl or plastic wrap, and let it rest for 1 hour before rolling.

5. Roll out and cut the dough by hand or with a pasta machine (see Rolling and Cutting Fresh Pasta, opposite).

6. To cook, bring a large pot of lightly salted water to a boil. Add the pasta. Fresh pasta cooks *very* quickly—thin strands may be cooked by the time they float to the surface of the water; other varieties will cook in about 1 to 2 minutes, ravioli in 6 minutes.

Makes 4 to 6 servings of spaghetti or linguini or enough for a large lasagna

rolling and cutting fresh pasta

By hand: On a lightly floured surface using a long, thin rolling pin, roll out one piece of dough into a thin (1/16 inch thick) 20 x 14-inch rectangle. Lightly flour the top of the dough to prevent sticking. Fold the rectangle of dough in half lengthwise, then fold it again; you should have a 5 x 14-inch rec-tangle—do not press the dough together. Using a very sharp knife or pastry wheel and a ruler or straightedge if needed, cut the sheet of dough into strips, making them as narrow or as wide as you like. Carefully unfold the strips and either hang them gently on a drying rack or lay them flat on dish towels. Let dry for 1 to 2 hours. Fresh pasta must air-dry before cooking or it becomes gluey when boiled.

Using a pasta machine: Following the manufacturer's directions, pass the dough several times through the machine's rollers to knead it and make it elastic. Adjust the rollers closer and closer together as you roll the dough until it is thin enough to cut. Set the machine to cut the desired shapes, and cut. Let the pasta dry on a drying rack or flat on dish towels for 1 to 2 hours.

Processor Dough Pasta

You can make quick work of mixing the dough if you use your food processor instead of your fingers.

2 1/4 cups all-purpose flour
2 eggs
1/4 cup water
1 tablespoon olive oil
1 teaspoon salt

1. Fit a food processor with a plastic dough blade or a metal chopping blade. Combine all the ingredients in the food processor container. Process until the dough rides up in the center, about 20 to 30 seconds.

2. On a lightly floured surface, knead the dough for about 5 minutes or until it is smooth and elastic. Cover the dough with plastic wrap and let it sit for 30 minutes before rolling.

3. Roll out and cut the dough by hand or with a pasta machine (see Rolling and Cutting Fresh Pasta above).

4. To cook, bring a large pot of lightly salted water to a boil. Add the pasta. Fresh pasta cooks *very* quickly—thin strands may be cooked by the time they float to the surface of the water; other varieties will cook in about 1 to 2 minutes, ravioli in 6 minutes.

Makes 4 to 6 servings of spaghetti or linguini or enough for a large lasagna

storing fresh pasta

Let the pasta dry for several hours or until it is dry but not brittle. For long strands of pasta (fettuccine or linguine, for example), when the dough has dried slightly but is still pliable, gently wrap a loose bunch around your fingers to form a "nest." Set the nest to dry completely. For large lasagna rectangles, allow each to dry completely. Then stack the pieces between sheets of wax paper. Store cut pasta in self-sealing plastic bags or airtight containers in the refrigerator for up to 1 week or in the freezer for up to 1 month.

chapter 2

Pickled, Preserved and Frozen Foods

Fewer and fewer of us grow our own fruits and vegetables anymore, but the waning days of summer still present us with an embarrassment of riches as

an avalanche of tomatoes, peppers, cukes, corn, peaches, and other fresh produce flood fruit stands, roadside stalls, and even supermarket shelves. The flavor of this sun-ripened produce is at its peak, and following the simple law of supply and demand, the price is at its lowest. Indeed, you can often get a bushel of tomatoes or peaches for what you would pay for a handful at a less bounteous time of year. The same lower-price, better-taste principle applies to those fruits and vegetables that have different peak seasons—such as strawberries and asparagus in late spring and pumpkins and hard squash in late fall.

The purpose of the recipes in this chapter is to help you take advantage of nature's largess. If you buy fresh vegetables and fruits at their peak and when their prices are most reasonable, you can freeze them and have your "five a day" out of the freezer all winter long—at summer prices and with that unmatchable summer taste. All the instructions you need are in this chapter. Freezing is incredibly simple. With only a bit more effort, you can make your own unbelievably tasty pickles, relishes, and chutneys. And if you also make your own jellies and jams, you will not only save money but also have ready-made presents for hostesses and new neighbors as well.

pickles and relishes

Dill Pickles—Fermentation Method

Dills are the wonderful pickles for which delis are famous. You can easily make your own for lots less. Buy unwaxed cucumbers and try both the fermentation method in this recipe and the fresh-pack method in the next recipe to see which is easier for you and which tastes better to you.

1 gallon water

2/3 cup salt

1 cup white vinegar

4 pounds small to medium (4-5 inches long) pickling cucumbers, unpeeled and scrubbed

15 sprigs fresh dill

30 peppercorns

15 garlic cloves *(optional)*

1. Prepare the brine: In a large, nonreactive bowl, combine 1/2 gallon of the water, 1/3 cup of the salt, and 1/2 cup of the vinegar.

2. Sprinkle half the dill, 15 of the peppercorns, and if using, half the garlic cloves over the bottom of a clean, 1-gallon stone crock. Place the cucumbers on top of the dill-spice mixture, then layer the remaining dill and spices over the cucumbers. Pour the brine over the cucumber mixture to cover. Place a heavy plate on top of the cucumbers and weight it down to keep it below the level of the brine.

3. Set the crock in a moderate (68°F to 72°F), dark place and let the pickles ferment for 1 to 3 weeks. Skim off and discard any scum that forms on top of the brine daily. The pickles are ready when the scum stops forming, the mixture no longer bubbles, and the pickles are olive-green in color with no white spots.

4. Prepare fresh brine: In a large, nonreactive saucepan, combine the remaining 1/2 gallon of water, 1/3 cup of salt, 1/2 cup of vinegar. Drain the pickles; remove and discard the garlic cloves, if used. Divide and ladle the pickles into sterilized 1-quart canning jars. Pour the fresh brine over the pickles in the jars, dividing it equally. Wipe the rims, cover, and process for 15 minutes in boiling water (see Safe Canning with a Hot-Water Bath, page 72). Cool and test for airtight seals. Label, date, and store in a cool, dark place for 4 to 6 weeks. Once a jar has been opened, store the pickles in the refrigerator.

Makes 4 to 6 quarts

Dill Pickles—Fresh-Pack Method

1/3 cup salt

1/2 gallon hot water

4 pounds small to medium (4-5 inches long) pickling cucumbers, unpeeled and scrubbed

4 garlic cloves

8 sprigs fresh dill

4 teaspoons mustard seed

3 tablespoons salt

1 tablespoon sugar

1 1/2 cups vinegar

3 cups water

1. Prepare the brine: In a large, nonreactive bowl, combine 1/3 cup salt and 1/2 gallon hot water. Stir until the salt has completely dissolved. Add the cucumbers to the brine; let stand overnight to pickle.

2. Drain the pickles and discard the soaking brine. Place the pickles, divided equally, into 2 sterilized 1-quart canning jars, packing the pickles so that they are standing on end. Place 2 garlic cloves, 4 dill sprigs, and 2 teaspoons of mustard seed in each jar.

3. In a large, nonreactive saucepan, combine 3 tablespoons salt, 1 tablespoon sugar, 1 1/2 cups vinegar, and 3 cups water. Bring the mixture to a boil. Pour the hot brine over the pickles in the jars, dividing it equally. Wipe the rims, cover, and process for 20 minutes in boiling water (see Safe Canning with a Hot-Water Bath, page 72). Cool and test for airtight seals. Label, date, and store in a cool, dark place for 4 to 6 weeks. Once a jar has been opened, store the pickles in the refrigerator.

Makes 2 quarts

Bread-and-Butter Pickles *These are the sweet pickles that go so well with meat sandwiches. Once you get the hang of putting them up, you'll never spend your money on store-bought pickles again.*

30 small to medium (4-5 inches long) pickling cucumbers, unpeeled, sliced 1/4-inch thick

8 large yellow onions, halved lengthwise and cut crosswise into thin slices

1 medium red bell pepper, cored, seeded, and chopped

1/2 cup pickling salt

4 cups crushed ice

4 cups white vinegar

4 1/2 cups sugar

2 tablespoons mustard seed

2 teaspoons celery seed

1 tablespoon ground turmeric

1 teaspoon ground ginger

1 teaspoon black peppercorns

1. In a very large colander set over a larger bowl or Dutch oven, combine the cucumber slices, onions, and red bell pepper. Sprinkle the vegetable mixture with the pickling or kosher salt and toss well. Cover the vegetables with a 2-inch layer of crushed ice. Refrigerate for 3 to 4 hours, adding ice as needed.

2. In a large, heavy, nonreactive saucepan or Dutch oven over moderate heat, combine the vinegar, sugar, mustard seed, celery seed, turmeric, ginger, and peppercorns; bring the mixture to a boil and boil for 10 minutes. Stir in the cucumber mixture and return just to a boil.

3. Ladle the vegetables and liquid into sterilized 1-pint canning jars, leaving 1/4 inch of space between the top of the mixture and the rim of the jars (see Safe Canning with a Hot-Water Bath, page 72). Run a long, thin spatula around the inside of the jars to release any trapped air bubbles. Wipe the rims, cover, and process for 10 minutes in boiling water. Cool and test for airtight seals. Label, date, and store in a cool, dark place for 4 to 6 weeks. Once opened, store the pickles in the refrigerator.

Makes 8 pints

Pickled Gherkins *These are the tiny pickles that are served with pâtés and terrines.*

10 dozen French gherkins or tiny pickling cucumbers, well scrubbed

1 1/2 cups pickling or kosher salt

30 peppercorns, white, green, or multicolored

6 small bay leaves

18 sprigs fresh tarragon

4-6 cups white wine vinegar

4 1/2 cups sugar

1-2 tablespoons pickling or kosher salt, to taste

1. In a large, nonreactive bowl, place the gherkins or cucumbers and sprinkle with salt. Loosely cover and let stand 24 hours.

2. Drain the pickles and discard the brine. Pack the pickles, standing on end, into 6 sterilized 1-pint canning jars; leave a 1/4-inch space at the top of the jar. Add 5 peppercorns, 1 bay leaf, and 2 sprigs of tarragon to each jar.

3. Meanwhile, in a large, heavy, nonreactive saucepan or Dutch oven, combine the vinegar and sugar with the remaining 6 sprigs of tarragon. Over high heat, bring the mixture to a boil. Pour the mixture over the pickles in each jar to cover. Cover the jars and let stand overnight; the pickles will lose their color.

4. Drain and reserve the vinegar from the jars into a large, nonreactive saucepan. Stir in the salt, and over high heat, bring the mixture to a boil. Remove the pan from the heat and let the brine cool. Pour the cooled brine back over the pickles in the jar, dividing it evenly; the pickles should recover their color.

5. Wipe the rims, cover, and process for 15 minutes in boiling water (see Safe Canning with a Hot-Water Bath, page 72). Cool and test for airtight seals. Label, date, and store in a cool, dark place for 4 to 6 weeks. Once a jar has been opened, store the pickles in the refrigerator.

Makes about 6 half-pints

Pickled Baby Corn *These bright yellow mini corns add crunch to cold meat platters.*

1/2 cup sugar

2 cups cider vinegar

1 1/2 cups water

1 teaspoon kosher salt

1 teaspoon mixed whole pickling spices

3 cans (14 ounces each) baby corn, drained

1. In a nonreactive saucepan, combine the sugar, cider vinegar, water, and salt. Cut a square of cheesecloth. Place the pickling spices in the cloth, bring the corners together to make a bag, and secure with string. Add the bag to the brine. Bring the brine to a boil, stirring to dissolve the sugar; cook for 4 to 5 minutes. Remove and discard the spice bag.

2. Place the corn, divided equally, into 3 sterilized 1-pint canning jars, packing the corn so that they are standing on end; pour the hot brine over the corn, leaving a 1/4-inch space between the top of the liquid and the rim of the jar. Wipe the rims, cover, and process for 15 minutes in boiling water (see Safe Canning with a Hot-Water Bath, page 72). Cool and test for airtight seals. Label, date, and store in a cool, dark place for 4 to 6 weeks; the corn will be ready to eat in 1 week. Once a jar has been opened, store the corn in the refrigerator.

Makes 3 pints

Pickle Relish

The word "relish" says it all—savor the flavor—and put it on your hot dog or a ham sandwich. This luscious recipe is most inexpensive, and jars of pickle relish make fine gifts.

4 medium cucumbers, unpeeled and finely chopped

2 large red bell peppers, cored, seeded, and chopped

2 large green bell peppers, cored, seeded, and chopped

1 medium yellow onion, chopped

1 tablespoon ground turmeric

1/2 cup kosher salt

6 cups water

2 cinnamon sticks, broken in half

1 tablespoon mustard seed

2 teaspoons whole allspice

1 teaspoon whole cloves

2 cups sugar

2 cups cider vinegar

1. In a large, heavy, nonreactive saucepan or Dutch oven, combine the cucumbers, red and green bell peppers, and onion; sprinkle the turmeric over all the vegetables. In a large bowl, dissolve the salt in the water to make a brine. Pour the brine over the vegetables, loosely cover the saucepan, and let stand for 6 to 8 hours. Drain the vegetables, rinse well several times, and return the vegetables to the saucepan.

2. Cut a 4-inch square of cheesecloth. Place the cinnamon sticks, mustard seed, allspice, and cloves in the center of the cloth, bring the corners together to make a bag, and secure with kitchen string, Add the spice bag to the saucepan along with the sugar and cider vinegar. Over high heat, bring the mixture to a rolling boil and cook until the sugar is completely dissolved. Reduce the heat to moderate and boil gently, uncovered, for 10 minutes. Remove and discard the spice bag.

3. Spoon the relish into 8 warm, sterilized jars, leaving a 1/4-inch space between the top of the relish and the rim of the jar. Wipe the rims, cover, and process for 10 minutes in boiling water (see Safe Canning with a Hot-Water Bath, page 72). Cool and test for airtight seals. Label, date, and store in a cool, dark place for 4 to 6 weeks. Once a jar has been opened, store the relish in the refrigerator.

Makes 8 half-pints

Helpful Hint

In Canning, Acid Content Is a Crucial Factor

Jams, jellies, marmalades, chutneys, pickles—basically any fruit or mixture with a high enough acid content to inhibit the growth of microorganisms—can be safely canned with a hot-water bath. Low-acid vegetables—every type other than tomatoes, which are botanically a fruit—should be frozen for storage or canned with a pressure cooker unless you are pickling them. Pickling adds enough acidity to allow for safe hot-water processing.

Pickled, Preserved, and Frozen Foods

Pickled Cauliflower Florets *This is a traditional part of an antipasto plate.*

1 large head cauliflower, cut into florets, about 7 to 8 cups

White vinegar

1 tablespoon salt

1 tablespoon white peppercorns

1 tablespoon light brown sugar

1 medium red bell pepper, seed and finely sliced

6 small dried red chile peppers

1. In a large, nonreactive saucepan or Dutch oven, place the cauliflower florets and pour in enough vinegar to cover. Add the salt, peppercorns, and sugar.

2. Over high heat, bring the brine to a boil. Add the red bell pepper strips, and boil for 1 minute. Using a slotted spoon, transfer the vegetables to 2 warm, sterilized 1-quart jars with wide mouths. Pack the vegetables firmly, dividing the pepper strips evenly between the jars. Tuck 3 chile peppers into each jar.

3. Pour the hot brine over the vegetables in the jars until the cauliflower is completely covered, leaving a 1/4-inch space between the top of the brine and the rim of the jars. Wipe the rims, cover, and process for 20 minutes in boiling water (see Safe Canning with a Hot-Water Bath, page 72). Cool and test for airtight seals. Label, date, and store in a cool, dark place for 4 to 6 weeks; the cauliflower will be ready for eating in 2 weeks. Once a jar has been opened, store the cauliflower in the refrigerator.

Makes about 2 quarts

Pickled Onions *These yummy onions fit many a bill.*

Water to cover the onions

4 pounds small white pickling onions

1/2 cup salt

8 peppercorns

4 fresh red chiles (wear gloves when handling; they burn)

4 bay leaves

4 cups cider vinegar

1. In a large saucepan, bring water to a boil. Place the onions in a large, nonreactive bowl. Pour the hot water over the onions in the bowl and let stand for 5 minutes; drain. Trim the root end and the crowns; the peels should slip off easily. Do not remove too many layers of the onions.

2. Place the peeled onions in a large bowl and cover them with cold water. Add the salt and mix well. Let stand overnight.

3. Drain the onions. Using a large slotted spoon, transfer the onions to 4 warm, sterilized 1-pint jars with wide mouths. To each jar, add 2 peppercorns, 1 red chile, and 1 bay leaf.

4. In a large, nonreactive saucepan over high heat, bring the cider vinegar to a boil. Immediately pour the hot vinegar over the onions in the jars to cover them, leaving a 1/8-inch space between the top of the vinegar and the rim of the jars. Wipe the rims, cover, and process for 10 minutes in boiling water (see Safe Canning with a Hot-Water Bath, page 72). Cool and test for airtight seals. Label, date, and store in a cool, dark place; the onions will be ready to eat in 4 weeks. Once a jar has been opened, store the onions in the refrigerator.

Makes about 4 pints

Red Onion Relish

A noteworthy accompaniment to almost any variety of cheese, this red onion treat is cheaper and better made at home.

3 tablespoons olive oil

2 pounds red onions, peeled and sliced

1/2 cup sugar

1 teaspoon kosher salt

1/2 teaspoon black pepper, freshly ground

4 tablespoons balsamic or sherry vinegar

1 cup red wine

1. In a large, nonreactive saucepan over moderate heat, heat the olive oil. Add the onion slices and cook about 20 minutes, stirring occasionally.

2. Stir the sugar, salt, and pepper into the onion mixture. Reduce the heat to low, cover the saucepan, and cook very gently for 10 minutes; if the heat is too high, use a heat diffuser.

3. Add vinegar and the wine, and cook, uncovered, stirring at regular intervals, until the mixture has the consistency of chutney, about 20 to 30 minutes. Skim off and discard any scum that forms during cooking.

4. Ladle the onion relish into two hot, sterilized half-pint jars, leaving a 1/4-inch space between the top of the relish and the rim of the jar. Wipe the rims, cover, and process for 10 minutes in boiling water (see Safe Canning with a Hot-Water Bath, page 72). Cool and test for airtight seals. Label, date, and store in a cool, dark place; the onion relish will be ready to eat in 4 weeks. Once a jar has been opened, store the onion relish in the refrigerator.

Makes 2 half-pints

Pickled Spiced Plums

Enjoy the enticing spices of the Orient with these aromatic plums—the perfect partner to roast pork or lamb.

1 2/3 cups sugar

2 2/3 cups water

1 cup cider vinegar

4 cinnamon sticks, broken

1 tablespoon whole cloves

1 tablespoon black peppercorns

2-3 strips orange zest

2 pounds small, firm, ripe red or purple plums, well scrubbed

1. In a medium saucepan over moderately high heat, combine the sugar and water, and bring the mixture to a boil, stirring to dissolve the sugar. Reduce the heat and simmer for 10 minutes.

2. Add the cider vinegar, cinnamon sticks, cloves, peppercorns, and orange zest; stir to combine. Cover the pan and simmer the mixture gently for 15 minutes.

3. Using a sterilized skewer or ice pick, prick each plum in several places. Divide the plums equally between two 1-quart, warm, sterilized jars with wide mouths. Pour the hot spiced syrup over the plums to cover them, leaving a 1/4-inch space between the top of the syrup and the rim of the jars. Wipe the rims of the jars, cover, and process for 25 minutes in boiling water (see Safe Canning with a Hot-Water Bath, page 72). Cool and test for airtight seals. Label, date, and store in a cool, dark place; the plums will be ready to eat in 4 weeks. Once a jar has been opened, store the plums in the refrigerator.

Makes about 2 quarts

Learning to process your canned foods in a hot-water bath will remove any concerns about bacterial contamination. Safe canning includes processing foods at a high enough temperature for a long enough time—you'll find the recommended processing times in each recipe. You can purchase a hot-water bath set or put one together yourself out of things you probably already have or can purchase easily and cheaply (check out yard sales and resale stores for the best bargains).

You will need:

1 very large, deep, heavy, nonreactive saucepan or Dutch oven with a tight-fitting lid

1 wire rack or 1 basket to fit the saucepan

Glass canning jars and lids (the jars and metal screw bands to hold the lids in place can be reused; new lids must be used every time you can)

Canning tongs (these are designed to transfer jars)

Additional wire racks for cooling the jars

Here is how to proceed:

1. Start by sterilizing all the jars. Wash them in hot, soapy water, rinse thoroughly, and set in a saucepan of boiling water that covers the jars by 1 inch; boil for 10 minutes. Remove the saucepan from the heat but let the jars sit in the hot water until ready to use.

2. Prepare the lids following the manufacturer's directions.

3. Once the food is cooked, remove the cooking saucepan from the heat. Carefully remove the jars from the hot water. Ladle the food into the warm, clean jars, leaving a space between the top of the food and the rim of the jar as specified in the recipe (usually between 1/8 inch and 1/4 inch). Run a sterilized spatula around the inside of the jar to remove any large air bubbles.

4. Using a clean, damp cloth, wipe off the rims of each jar. Following the manufacturer's directions, apply the lids and screw bands.

5. Place the rack in the processing saucepan and fill halfway with hot water. Place the filled jars on the rack, then add boiling water (pour around the jars, not directly on the jars) until the jars are covered by at least 1 inch of boiling water.

Cover the saucepan. Set the saucepan over high heat and bring the water to a boil; begin timing when the water comes to a rolling boil. Process for the time specified in the recipe; at high altitudes, increase the boiling time by 1 minute for each 1,000 feet above sea level.

6. When the processing time has been reached, use the tongs to transfer the jars from the saucepan to a second wire rack and let the jars cool completely; be sure to leave space between the jars on the rack. Let the jars stand for 12 to 24 hours.

7. Gently press the center of each lid: if the depression in the center holds, the seal is good and you can remove the screw band and store the jar; if the depression does not hold, the seal is not good and you should store the jar in the refrigerator and use the food immediately.

8. Label and date each jar. Store canned foods in a cool (40°F to 60°F), dark storage space; check the seals periodically and just before opening. Any jar that leaks, or food that smells or looks questionable when opened, should be discarded. *Never* taste food to check for freshness.

Roasted Red Bell Peppers in Oil *Colorful and luscious, these are a must for any antipasto platter and make a superb snack on crusty bread.*

4 pounds (about 8 medium) firm red bell peppers

2 tablespoons coriander seed

1 tablespoon peppercorns

5 garlic cloves

5 bay leaves

1-2 cups virgin olive oil

1. Arrange the red bell peppers on a broiler pan or heavy-duty baking sheet. Set the pan 2 to 3 inches from a preheated broiler and broil 8 to 10 minutes, turning the peppers every few minutes so their skins blacken evenly. Transfer the peppers to a large heatproof bowl, cover with plastic wrap, and cool until safe to handle, about 10 minutes. The skins will loosen and slip right off the peppers. Cut the roasted peppers in thick slices, discarding the stalks and seeds.

2. Transfer the roasted peppers to 3 warm, sterilized half-pint jars, dividing the peppers evenly. Add some of the coriander seed, peppercorns, garlic, and bay leaves to each jar, dividing equally and arranging the peppers and spices attractively.

3. Pour olive oil into each jar to cover the peppers, leaving a 1/4-inch space between the top of the oil and the rim of the jars. Using a sterilized skewer, expel any air bubbles from the oil. Wipe the rims of the jars, cover, and store in the refrigerator for up to 1 month; the red peppers will be ready to eat within a few days.

Makes 3 half-pints

Oven-Dried Tomatoes *Oven drying is an easy, relatively quick way to preserve garden-fresh tomatoes.*

2 pounds ripe Italian plum or large cherry tomatoes, halved

1/4 cup kosher salt

1/4 teaspoon freshly ground pepper

2 tablespoons dried marjoram, crumbled

Olive oil, to cover

1. Preheat the oven to just below 200°F (warm).

2. Using a teaspoon, remove the seeds but not the fibrous tissue from the tomato halves. Line a baking sheet with foil. Place the tomatoes, cut side up, on the baking sheet and sprinkle them with salt, pepper, and marjoram. Place the baking sheet in the oven and bake for 12 to 24 hours; check periodically to be sure the tomatoes are drying, not cooking. If they are drying too quickly, prop open the oven door slightly. Drying tomatoes will slowly darken and wrinkle. Small tomatoes may take only 12 hours to dry; large tomatoes may take as long as 24 hours.

3. Spoon the tomatoes into 2 warm, sterilized, half-pint jars. Pour olive oil over the tomatoes, leaving a 1/4-inch space between the top of the oil and the rim of the jar. Wipe the rims of the jars, cover, and allow to cool. Label and date the jars, and store in the refrigerator for up to 1 month. Keep the tomatoes refrigerated once the jars are opened.

Makes 2 half-pints

chutneys

Mango Chutney
The pungent flavor of fresh ginger and the heat of red pepper lend dramatic appeal to this classic companion to spicy curries.

5 pounds green mangoes, peeled and chopped

1 teaspoon kosher salt

1 1/4 cups cider vinegar

1 1/4 cups apple cider

1 tablespoon chopped fresh ginger

2 teaspoons ground red pepper

1 large onion, chopped

1 1/2 cups firmly packed dark brown sugar

1. In a large, nonmetallic bowl, place the mangoes and sprinkle them with salt. Set aside the mangoes for 24 hours.

2. Rinse the mangoes under cold running water and drain them thoroughly. In a large, nonreactive saucepan, combine the mangoes, cider vinegar, apple cider, ginger, red pepper, onion, and sugar. Over low heat, simmer the mixture, uncovered, for 30 to 40 minutes.

3. Spoon the chutney into warm, sterilized jars, leaving a 1/4-inch space between the top of the chutney and the rim of the jar. Wipe the rims, cover, and process for 10 minutes in boiling water (see Safe Canning with a Hot-Water Bath, page 72). Place the jars of chutney in a cool, dark place to season; the chutney will be ready to eat in 4 weeks. Once a jar has been opened, store the chutney in the refrigerator.

Makes about 6 half-pint jars

Spicy Tomato Chutney
Turmeric, cumin, mustard seeds and powder, and red pepper all lend spicy notes to this intense chutney that is easy to make and a nice gift for kind neighbors. Stir a dollop into curry as it is cooking to add even more flavor, then serve the chutney alongside for a real eye-opener.

5 pounds ripe red tomatoes, quartered

5 medium yellow onions, chopped

3 garlic cloves, minced

2 tablespoons dry mustard

1 tablespoon salt

1 tablespoon chopped fresh ginger

1 tablespoon cumin seed

2 teaspoons ground turmeric

1 teaspoon mustard seed

1 teaspoon ground red pepper

1 cup cider vinegar

1. In a large, nonreactive saucepan, combine the tomatoes, onions, garlic, dry mustard, salt, ginger, cumin, turmeric, mustard seed, red pepper, and cider vinegar. Over moderately high heat, bring the mixture to a boil; reduce the heat to low and simmer gently, uncovered, stirring occasionally, until the chutney has thickened, about 50 to 60 minutes.

2. Spoon the chutney into warm, sterilized jars, leaving a 1/4-inch space between the top of the chutney and the rim of the jar. Wipe the rims, cover, and process for 10 minutes in boiling water (see Safe Canning with a Hot-Water Bath, page 72). Place the jars of chutney in a cool, dark place to season; the chutney will be ready to eat in 4 weeks. Once a jar has been opened, store the chutney in the refrigerator.

Makes about 8 half-pint jars

Green Tomato Chutney

Don't know how to use your tomato bonanza? Harvest some before they ripen and whip up some jars of this savory side dish. Give some as lovely, inexpensive house gifts.

4 pounds green tomatoes, chopped

2 medium onions, peeled and chopped

1 large green apple, peeled, cored, and chopped

3/4 cup golden raisins

1 teaspoon salt

1 teaspoon ground allspice

1 teaspoon curry powder

1/2 teaspoon ground red pepper

1 cup firmly packed brown sugar

2 cups cider vinegar

1. In a large, nonreactive saucepan, combine the tomatoes, onions, apple, raisins, salt, allspice, curry powder, red pepper, brown sugar, and cider vinegar. Over low heat, bring the mixture to a simmer, uncovered, and cook gently until the chutney has thickened, about 45 minutes. Stir occasionally to prevent the chutney from burning. Stop cooking if the chutney begins to dry out.

2. Spoon the chutney into warm, sterilized jars, leaving a 1/4-inch space between the top of the chutney and the rim of the jar. Wipe the rims, cover, and process for 10 minutes in boiling water (see Safe Canning with a Hot-Water Bath, page 72). Place the jars of chutney in a cool, dark place to season; the chutney will be ready to eat in 4 weeks. Once a jar has been opened, store the chutney in the refrigerator.

Makes about 6 half-pint jars

Lemon Lime Chutney

This citrus sensation is superb with mildly spiced couscous and lamb dishes. An expensive luxury from stores, it is easy to make at home.

4 large lemons

2 limes

2 medium yellow onions, chopped

1 teaspoon salt

2 1/2 cups cider vinegar

3/4 cup golden raisins

1 tablespoon mustard seed

1 teaspoon ground ginger

1/2 teaspoon ground red pepper

2 cups sugar

1. Wash and wipe the unpeeled lemons and limes. Chop them finely, removing any seeds. In a large bowl, combine the chopped lemons, limes, and onions. Sprinkle the mixture with the salt, and set aside for 12 hours.

2. Pour the lemon-lime mixture with the juices into a large, nonreactive saucepan. Bring the mixture to a simmer and cook gently, uncovered, until the fruit is soft. Stir in the cider vinegar, raisins, mustard seed, ginger, red pepper, and sugar. Increase the heat and bring the mixture to a boil; reduce the heat and simmer, uncovered, until the chutney thickens, about 45 minutes.

3. Spoon the chutney into warm, sterilized jars, leaving a 1/4-inch space between the top of the chutney and the rim of the jar. Wipe the rims, cover, and process for 10 minutes in boiling water (see Safe Canning with a Hot-Water Bath, page 72). Place the jars of chutney in a cool, dark place to season; the chutney will be ready to eat in 4 weeks. Once a jar has been opened, store the chutney in the refrigerator.

Makes about 5 half-pint jars

jams, jellies, and marmalades

Dried-Apricot Jam

Buy dried apricots in bulk at health food stores or look for them on sale and stock up. The dried apricots intensify the apricot flavor, giving you a superior jam at a reasonable price.

16 ounces dried apricots

3 1/2 cups orange juice

3/4 cup sugar

1 tablespoon lemon juice

1/2 teaspoon ground cinnamon

1/4 teaspoon ground ginger

1. In a large, nonreactive saucepan or Dutch oven, combine the apricots, orange juice, and sugar. Over moderately high heat, bring the mixture to a boil; reduce the heat, cover the saucepan, and simmer for 30 minutes.

2. Stir in the lemon juice, cinnamon, and ginger. Remove the saucepan from the heat and let the mixture cool to room temperature.

3. Transfer the mixture to the bowl of a food processor or blender. Whirl until the mixture is pureed. Spoon the puree into 4 widemouthed, warm, sterilized half-pint jars, leaving a 1/4-inch space between the top of the jam and the rim of the jar (see Safe Canning with a Hot-Water Bath, page 72). Wipe the rims, cover, label, and date. Store the jam in the refrigerator for up to 3 weeks or in the freezer for up to 1 year.

Makes 4 half-pint jars

the trio of good jamming ingredients

To make a great jam, jelly, or marmalade, you need three components to work in harmony: acid, pectin, and sugar. If the proportions of each or any one of these is off, you may not be happy with the results.

Acid: Added to the mixture as citrus juice (usually lemon) or tartaric acid, this improves both the taste and appearance of the finished product, and in conjunction with pectin, it helps the mixture to jell.

Pectin: Most fruits contain some amount of pectin naturally, and it is released when the fruit is boiled, but not all fruits are created equal. Apples are known for their pectin, and so are sometimes added in one form or another to fruits that are lower in pectin to help them jell. Currants and red plums are also high-pectin fruits; moderate-pectin fruits include apricots, blueberries, peaches, and raspberries. Pectin is also found in peels (particularly citrus) and seeds, so these are sometimes included in part of a recipe to release their pectin during cooking. Pectin is also available in liquid and powdered forms (check out health food stores and larger supermarkets). If you do canning regularly, it is prudent to keep some on hand, just in case your jam or marmalade or jelly is being uncooperative. Follow the manufacturer's directions carefully.

Sugar: Another factor in jelling, sugar (either beet or cane) also helps to preserve the fruit and really brings out its flavor in addition to adding sweetness and countering any bitter taste, such as lemon.

Lemony Fig Jam

The tartness of the lemons sets off the sweetness of the figs. Here is an unusual jam that makes a lovely gift and keeps you out of the expensive food specialty store.

1 pound dried figs

4 cups water

3 cups sugar

Zest and juice of 2 lemons

1/2 cup pine nuts, lightly toasted

1. Wash and roughly chop the figs. In a small bowl, combine the figs and the water. Cover the bowl and let stand for 12 hours or overnight.

2. In a heavy, nonreactive saucepan, combine the figs and soaking water. Over high heat, bring the mixture to a boil; reduce the heat to low and simmer for 35 minutes.

3. Add the sugar and the lemon zest and juice. Stir until the sugar is dissolved. Return the mixture to a boil; reduce the heat slightly, and cook until the jam thickens, for 10 to 15 minutes. Using a slotted spoon, skim off and discard any foam that rises to the surface. Add the pine nuts and stir until they are well incorporated.

4. Remove the saucepan from the heat and stir to distribute the fruit and nuts evenly. Spoon the hot jam into 3 widemouthed, warm, sterilized 1/2-pint jars, leaving a 1/4-inch space between the top of the jam and the rim of the jar. Wipe the rims, cover, and process for 10 minutes in boiling water (see Safe Canning with a Hot-Water Bath, page 72). Dry, label, and date. Store the jars of jam in a cool, dark place; the jam will be ready to eat in 2 weeks. Once a jar has been opened, store the jam in the refrigerator.

Makes about 3 half-pint jars

Pear Jam

Spiced up with cinnamon and cloves, this jam does not require pectin to thicken. It is a spicy jam that you can make for very little money without splurging at a gourmet shop.

8 cups (about 5 1/2 pounds) chopped or coarsely ground peeled, cored pears

4 cups sugar

1 teaspoon ground cinnamon

1/4 teaspoon ground cloves

1. In a large, nonreactive saucepan or Dutch oven, combine the pears, sugar, cinnamon, and cloves. Over moderately low heat, simmer the mixture, uncovered, until it becomes thick, about 1 1/2 to 2 hours. Stir the mixture occasionally while it cooks, and increase the frequency of stirring as the mixture thickens.

2. Remove the saucepan from the heat; skim off and discard any foam that rises to the surface. Spoon the hot jam into 6 widemouthed, warm, sterilized 1/2-pint jars, leaving a 1/4-inch space between the top of the jam and the rim of the jar. Wipe the rims, cover, and process for 10 minutes in boiling water (see Safe Canning with a Hot-Water Bath, page 72). Dry, label, and date. Store the jars of jam in a cool, dark place. Once a jar has been opened, store the jam in the refrigerator.

Makes about 6 half-pint jars

Quince Jam
Available in late winter, quinces have yellow skin and flesh, and are quite tart. They have a high pectin content, so they are perfect for jam.

5 pounds (about 5-7) firm
   quinces

8 cups water

Juice of 3 lemons

8 cups sugar

1. Wash and peel the quinces, then core and roughly chop them.

2. In a large, heavy saucepan, combine the quinces with the water. Bring to a boil; reduce the heat and simmer until the fruit is soft and pale pink, about 35 to 45 minutes.

3. Add the lemon juice and sugar, and stir until the sugar is dissolved. Increase the heat and bring to a boil again; boil rapidly until the jam thickens, about 10 minutes. Using a slotted spoon, skim off and discard any foam that rises to the surface.

4. Remove the saucepan from the heat. Spoon the hot jam into 8 widemouthed, warm, sterilized 1/2-pint jars, leaving a 1/4-inch space between the top of the jam and the rim of the jar. Wipe the rims, cover, and process for 10 minutes in boiling water (see Safe Canning with a Hot-Water Bath, page 72). Dry, label, and date. Store the jars of jam in a cool, dark place; the jam will be ready to eat in 2 weeks. Once a jar has been opened, store the jam in the refrigerator.

Makes about 8 half-pint jars

Peach Jam
The natural sweetness of peaches make this jam a low-sugar-added preserve. Plan to put up a slew when peaches are in season during the summer.

8-10 cups water

2 1/2 pounds ripe peaches

3 strips (1/2 x 2 inches)
   orange zest

2/3 cups fresh orange juice

2/3 cup unsweetened
   white grape juice

2/3 cup firmly packed light
   brown sugar

1 tablespoon fresh
   lemon juice

1/4 teaspoon ground ginger

1. In a large, heavy saucepan or Dutch oven over moderately high heat, bring water to a boil. Add the peaches, 2 or 3 at a time, and boil for 30 seconds. Using a slotted spoon, transfer the peaches to a colander and rinse with cold water; the peels should slide off easily. Peel, pit, and coarsely chop the peaches.

2. In a large, heavy saucepan or Dutch oven, combine the chopped peaches, orange zest and juice, grape juice, brown sugar, lemon juice, and ginger. Over moderate heat, slowly bring the mixture to a boil. Boil, stirring frequently, until the jam thickens, about 30 minutes.

3. Remove the saucepan from the heat and stir to distribute the fruit evenly; skim off and discard any foam that rises to the surface, and remove and discard the orange zest. Spoon the hot jam into 6 widemouthed, warm, sterilized 1/2-pint jars, leaving a 1/4-inch space between the top of the jam and the rim of the jar (see Safe Canning with a Hot-Water Bath, page 72). Wipe the rims, cover, label, and date. Store the jars of jam in the refrigerator for up to 2 months.

Makes about 6 half-pint jars

Strawberry Jam

Go strawberry wild in the early summer when the price of this dainty fruit goes way down. Look for the ripest, reddest berries for the greatest flavor. Making your own will be a bargain.

2 quarts fully ripe strawberries

1/4 cup lemon juice

7 cups sugar

3 ounces liquid fruit pectin

1. Wash and hull the strawberries, and place them in a medium bowl. Using a potato masher, crush the berries. You should have 4 cups of crushed berries.

2. In a heavy 6- or 9-quart, nonreactive saucepan or Dutch oven, combine the crushed berries, lemon juice, and sugar. Over high heat, bring the mixture to a boil, stirring constantly; boil, stirring, for 1 minute.

3. Add the liquid pectin; boil and stir for 1 minute longer. Remove the saucepan from the heat. Using a slotted spoon, skim off and discard any foam that rises to the surface.

4. Spoon the hot jam into 8 widemouthed, warm, sterilized 1/2-pint jars, leaving a 1/4-inch space between the top of the jam and the rim of the jar. Wipe the rims, cover, and process for 10 minutes in boiling water (see Safe Canning with a Hot-Water Bath, page 72). Dry, label, and date. Store the jars of jam in a cool, dark place; the jam will be ready to eat in 2 weeks. Once a jar has been opened, store the jam in the refrigerator.

Makes about 8 half-pints

Tri-Berry Jam

Make the most of berries in season with this salute to summer. Homemade will be better and cheaper than store-bought.

4 cups fresh or frozen blueberries

2 1/2 cups fresh of frozen red raspberries

2 1/2 cups fresh or frozen strawberries

1/4 cup lemon juice

2 packages (1 3/4 ounces each) powdered fruit pectin

11 cups sugar

1. In a large, nonreactive saucepan or Dutch oven, combine the blueberries, raspberries, strawberries, and lemon juice; using the back of a wooden spoon, slightly crush the fruit. Stir in the pectin. Over high heat, bring the mixture to a boil, stirring constantly.

2. Add the sugar and return the mixture to a boil; boil for 1 minute, stirring constantly. Remove the saucepan from the heat; skim off and discard any foam that rises to the surface.

3. Spoon the hot jam into 6 widemouthed, warm, sterilized 1-pint jars, leaving a 1/4-inch space between the top of the jam and the rim of the jar. Wipe the rims, cover, and process for 15 minutes in boiling water (see Safe Canning with a Hot-Water Bath, page 72). Dry, label, and date. Store the jars of jam in a cool, dark place. Once a jar has been opened, store the jam in the refrigerator.

Makes about 6 pint jars

Apple Ginger Jelly

Although you remove the solids later, the naturally rich pectin in the apple seeds negates the need to add pectin to this glowing orange-red jelly.

5 pounds (8-10) green apples

1/2 cup lemon juice

1 piece (1 inch) fresh ginger, peeled and bruised

6 cups water

3/4 cup sugar for every 1 cup juice

1. Wash and roughly chop the apples (do not peel or core). In a heavy, nonreactive saucepan or Dutch oven, combine the apples, lemon juice, ginger, and water. Over moderate heat, bring the mixture to a simmer; simmer until the fruit is very soft, about 25 to 30 minutes.

2. Strain the apple mixture through a wet jelly bag overnight (see A Bag to Give You Perfectly Clear Jelly, page 82).

3. Measure the juice left after the straining; this will determine how much sugar to add. In a large, nonreactive saucepan over moderately high heat, bring the apple juice to a boil; add the appropriate amount of sugar and stir until the sugar has dissolved. Slightly reduce the heat and gently boil the mixture until the jelly reaches the jelling point (see Has It Jelled Yet? below), about 5 to 10 minutes. Using a slotted spoon, skim off and discard any foam that rises to the surface.

4. Remove the saucepan from the heat. Spoon the hot jelly into 5 widemouthed, warm, sterilized 1/2-pint jars, leaving a 1/4-inch space between the top of the jelly and the rim of the jar. Wipe the rims, cover, and process for 10 minutes in boiling water (see Safe Canning with a Hot-Water Bath, page 72). Dry, label, and date. Store the jars of jelly in a cool, dark place; the jelly will be ready to eat in 2 weeks. Once a jar has been opened, store the jelly in the refrigerator.

Makes about 5 half-pint jars

has it jelled yet?

The crucial moment in jam- and jelly-making is the temperature at which the mixture jells and no longer needs to be cooked. To determine that "jelling point," most cooking experts highly recommend that you use a candy thermometer, but the plate test works pretty well too.

Thermometer: Determine the jelling point for your altitude. Hold a candy thermometer vertically in a pot of boiling water. Read the temperature at eye level and add 8°F for the jelling point. From sea level to about 1,000 feet above, the boiling point should be 212°F and the jelling point is 220°F.

Plate method: At the point indicated in the recipe, remove the saucepan from the heat and drop a teaspoonful of the jam or jelly onto a small, cold plate. Lightly press the jam or jelly with a fingertip—the surface should wrinkle, indicating that it has begun to jell. If the jam or jelly is still too liquid or does not pass the press test, return the saucepan to the heat and cook a few minutes longer, then retest.

Grape Jelly

Peanut butter's best friend, grape jelly is a childhood favorite. Look for Concord grapes in season (September and October).

3 pounds Concord grapes

3 1/4 cups water

3/4 cup sugar for every 1 cup juice

1. Wash the grapes and remove them from the stems. In a heavy, nonreactive saucepan, combine the grapes and water. Using a potato masher, crush the grapes. Over moderately high heat, bring the mixture to a boil; cover the saucepan, and cook for 10 to 15 minutes. Remove the saucepan from the heat and let the mixture cool to room temperature.

2. Strain the grape mixture through a wet jelly bag overnight (see A Bag to Give You Perfectly Clear Jelly, page 82).

3. Measure the juice left after the straining; this will determine how much sugar to add. In a large, nonreactive saucepan over moderately high heat, bring the grape juice to a boil; add the appropriate amount of sugar and stir until the sugar has dissolved. Increase the heat and boil rapidly until the jelly reaches the jelling point (see Has It Jelled Yet? opposite), about 12 to 16 minutes. Using a slotted spoon, skim off and discard any foam that rises to the surface.

4. Remove the saucepan from the heat. Spoon the hot jelly into 4 widemouthed, warm, sterilized 1/2-pint jars, leaving a 1/4-inch space between the top of the jelly and the rim of the jar. Wipe the rims, cover, and process for 10 minutes in boiling water (see Safe Canning with a Hot-Water Bath, page 72). Dry, label, and date. Store the jars of jelly in a cool, dark place; the jelly will be ready to eat in 2 weeks. Once a jar has been opened, store the jelly in the refrigerator.

Makes about 4 half-pint jars

a brief history of the concord grape

In 1849 Ephraim Wales Bull developed the Concord grape—after planting over 20,000 seedlings to get there. Descended from a wild grape native to the forbidding New England soil, the Concord grape ripens early (essential in a region of early killing frosts), is hardy, and boasts a rich, full, fruity flavor. It is named for the town in which Bull lived and worked. In 1853 Bull finally debuted this new grape—and won first prize at the Boston Horticultural Society Exhibition.

In 1869 a New Jersey dentist, with his wife and son, harvested 40 pounds of Concord grapes, cooked them, then squeezed the juice through cloth bags to remove the skins. They then decanted the juice into twelve 1-quart bottles, sealed them with wax, and processed them in a hot-water bath. This prevented fermentation into wine, and preserved the grape juice (which was used for Communion at the local Methodist church). The dentist's name: Dr. Thomas Welch. And Welch's Grape Juice is still making folks happy today. Nowadays more than 336,000 tons of Concord grapes are harvested every year.

Mint Jelly

The classic, emerald-green accompaniment to lamb, this jelly makes an eye-catching gift. You can make your own very inexpensively, particularly if you have a mint patch.

1 cup tightly packed fresh mint leaves

1 cup water

1/2 cup cider vinegar

3 1/2 cups sugar

5 drops green food coloring

3 ounces liquid pectin

1. Wash the mint, remove the stems, and coarsely chop the leaves. In a large, nonreactive saucepan, combine the mint, water, cider vinegar, and sugar. Over high heat, bring the mixture to a boil, stirring constantly. Remove the saucepan from the heat, and add the food coloring and pectin. Return the saucepan to the heat and return to a boil; boil for 30 seconds. Remove the saucepan from the heat, and strain the mixture through 2 layers of cheesecloth.

2. Spoon the hot jelly into 3 to 4 widemouthed, warm, sterilized 1/2-pint jars, leaving a 1/4-inch space between the top of the jelly and the rim of the jar. Wipe the rims, cover, and process for 10 minutes in boiling water (see Safe Canning with a Hot-Water Bath, page 72). Dry, label, and date. Store the jars of jelly in a cool, dark place. Once a jar has been opened, store the jelly in the refrigerator.

Makes about 3 to 4 half-pint jars

Helpful Hint

A Bag to Give You Perfectly Clear Jelly

Jelly is meant to be crystal clear, unlike jams and marmalades, so removing even the tiniest solid particles is crucial to achieving perfect results. Fortunately, there is equipment to facilitate the desired finished product: a jelly bag.

Cone-shaped with a hanging handle, a jelly bag forces the solids out of the jelly mixture over a period of time (generally 12 hours or overnight). After boiling the fruit with the liquid, dampen the jelly bag and hang it over a large, nonreactive bowl or saucepan. Pour the boiled fruit and liquid through and let stand for the specified amount of time. The weight of the fruit solids will press down and push out the liquid; don't squeeze the bag to extrude more liquid or you may make the jelly cloudy.

Seville Orange Marmalade

This is what most people think of when they hear the word "marmalade." If Seville oranges are difficult to find, substitute any firm, thin-skinned oranges, such as Valencias. Your homemade marmalade will cost less than store-bought and make you very proud.

2 pounds (4-6) Seville oranges

4 cups water

Juice of 3 lemons

8 cups sugar

1/4 cup Scotch whisky
(*optional*)

1. Wash the oranges and, using a sharp knife, cut them crosswise into thin slices, catching any juice and reserving the seeds. In a large bowl, combine the oranges with their juice and add the water. Tie the reserved seeds up in a bag of cheesecloth and add it to the bowl. Cover the bowl and let the orange mixture stand in a cool place for 18 hours.

2. In a heavy, nonreactive saucepan, combine the orange mixture and the lemon juice. Over moderately low heat, simmer the mixture, uncovered, until the orange rind is tender, about 20 to 30 minutes.

3. Add the sugar; stir until the sugar has dissolved. Bring the mixture to a boil and cook until the marmalade has reached the jelling point (see Has It Jelled Yet? page 80), about 30 to 40 minutes. Using a slotted spoon, skim off and discard any foam that rises to the surface.

4. Remove the saucepan from the heat; stir to distribute the fruit evenly. Spoon the hot marmalade into 8 widemouthed, warm, sterilized 1/2-pint jars, leaving a 1/4-inch space between the top of the marmalade and the rim of the jar. Wipe the rims, cover, and process for 10 minutes in boiling water (see Safe Canning with a Hot-Water Bath, page 72). Dry, label, and date. Store the jars of marmalade in a cool, dark place; the marmalade will be ready to eat in 2 weeks. Once a jar has been opened, store the marmalade in the refrigerator.

Makes about 8 half-pint jars

Helpful Hint

How to Make Marmalade

A dose of patience and careful attention to stirring are the two qualities needed to make marmalade—the first so you don't try to hurry the process, and the second to avoid scorching the fruit or syrup and tainting the finished taste. Unlike clear jelly, or thicker jam with pureed or chunks of fruit, marmalade is a thick syrup with bits of fruit cooked until they are almost translucent.

Citrus Marmalade

Popularity and tradition marry in this bright marmalade, composed of grapefruit, orange, and lemon. Be sure to plan ahead to make this gourmet treat: It requires two 12-hour (or overnight) standing times for the flavors to develop.

1 large grapefruit
1 large orange
1 large lemon
3 cups water
12 cups sugar

1. Wash the grapefruit, orange, and lemon. Using a sharp knife, cut each citrus fruit crosswise into thin slices, then cut each slice into quarters. Remove and tie the seeds up in a bag of cheesecloth.

2. In a heavy, nonreactive saucepan, combine the grapefruit, orange, and lemon pieces, water, and seeds. Bring the mixture to a boil and cook for 10 minutes. Remove the saucepan from the heat, cover, and let stand in a cool place for 12 hours.

3. Over high heat, return the mixture to a boil; reduce the heat to moderate and cook until the rinds are tender, about 40 minutes. Remove the pan from the heat, cover, and let stand in a cool place for 12 hours longer.

4. Over moderate heat, reheat the mixture and add the sugar; stir until the sugar has dissolved. Return the mixture to a boil and cook until the marmalade has reached the jelling point (see Has It Jelled Yet? page 80), about 20 to 30 minutes. Using a slotted spoon, skim off and discard any foam that rises to the surface.

5. Remove the saucepan from the heat; stir to distribute the fruit evenly. Spoon the hot marmalade into 8 widemouthed, warm, sterilized 1/2-pint jars, leaving a 1/4-inch space between the top of the marmalade and the rim of the jar. Wipe the rims, cover, and process for 10 minutes in boiling water (see Safe Canning with a Hot-Water Bath, page 72). Dry, label, and date. Store the jars of marmalade in a cool, dark place; the marmalade will be ready to eat in 2 weeks. Once a jar has been opened, store the marmalade in the refrigerator.

Makes about 8 half-pint jars

frozen vegetables

Freeze vegetables in self-sealing freezer bags that you have labeled and dated with a permanent marker; be sure to press out any excess air from the bag before sealing. Once the vegetable has thawed, do not refreeze.

Asparagus

2 1/2-3 pounds fresh yields 4 cups frozen

Wash, trim, and cut into 2-inch pieces. Sort asparagus according to the thickness of the stalks; water-blanch thin stalks for 2 minutes, thick stalks for 4 minutes. Rinse briefly under cold water and drain thoroughly. Pack, seal, label, date, and freeze.

Beets

2 1/2-3 pounds fresh yields 4 cups frozen

Wash and trim, leaving 1-inch stems (be careful not to pierce the skins). Sort according to size and cook small beets in boiling water for 25 to 30 minutes, large for 45 to 50 minutes or until tender when pierced with a fork. Drain and cool. Peel off the skins and slice or cube, as desired. Pack, seal, label, date, and freeze.

Bell Peppers

3 pounds fresh yields 4 cups frozen

Wipe firm bell peppers. Cut out stems and remove any seeds. Cut in halves, slices, or rings. Blanch halves for 2 minutes, slices and rings for 1 minute. Cool quickly and drain thoroughly. Pack, seal, label, date, and freeze.

Broad and Lima Beans

2 1/2 pounds fresh yields 4 cups frozen

Shell young, tender beans and discard any damaged ones. Water-blanch small beans for 1 minute, medium beans for 2 minutes, and large beans for 3 minutes. Cool quickly and drain thoroughly. Pack, seal, label, date, and freeze.

Broccoli and Cauliflower

2-2 1/2 pounds fresh yields 4 cups frozen

Wash and peel stalks if woody. Cut stalks and florets into 1 1/2-inch pieces. Steam-blanch for 5 minutes. Cool quickly and drain thoroughly. Pack, seal, label, date, and freeze.

Brussels Sprouts

2-2 1/2 pounds fresh yields
4 cups frozen

Trim off coarse leaves and stems and sort by size. Water-blanch small sprouts for 3 minutes, large sprouts for 5 minutes. Cool quickly and drain thoroughly. Pack, seal, label, date, and freeze.

Carrots

2 1/2-3 pounds fresh yields
4 cups frozen

Wash, trim, and cut into 2-inch pieces or 2-inch-thick slices, if desired. Blanch whole carrots 5 minutes, slices for 2 minutes. Rinse briefly under cold water and drain thoroughly. Pack, seal, label, date, and freeze.

Corn

2 1/2 pounds fresh kernels
yields 4 cups frozen

Ears: Use young cobs only. Remove the husks and silks. Water-blanch for 4 minutes. Cool quickly and drain well. Wrap each ear individually, airtight in freezer paper or foil, molding it to the shape of the ear. Pack several together in a freezer bag, expelling as much air as possible.

Kernels: Blanch the ears as above and cool completely. Using a very sharp knife, cut the kernels off the cobs and separate into meal-size portions. Pack, seal, label, date, and freeze.

Green Beans

1 1/2-2 1/2 pounds fresh
yields 4 cups frozen

Wash and trim off ends and any blemishes. Small green beans may be water-blanched whole, but cut larger beans into 2-inch pieces. Blanch whole beans for 3 minutes; pieces for 2 minutes. Cool quickly and drain thoroughly. Pack, seal, label, date, and freeze.

Mushrooms

1-2 1/2 pounds fresh yields
4 cups frozen

Wipe with a damp cloth to remove any dirt; do not peel or rinse.
Button varieties: Spread whole, raw mushrooms on a baking tray and place in the freezer. When hard, pack, seal, label, date, and freeze.
Wild mushrooms (portobello, shiitake): Slice and sauté in butter. Pour the mushrooms with the cooking liquid into individual bags. Seal, label, date, and freeze.

Peas

2 1/2 pounds fresh yields
4 cups frozen

Sweet peas: Shell sweet peas, discarding any damaged ones. Water-blanch for 1 1/2 minutes. Cool quickly and drain thoroughly. Pack, seal, label, date, and freeze.

Sugar snap or snow peas: De-string pods and water-blanch for 2 minutes. Cool quickly and drain thoroughly. Pack, seal, label, date, and freeze.

Pumpkin and Other Hard Squash

3 pounds fresh yields 4 cups
frozen puree

Wash, peel, and cut in half; remove any seeds and strings. Cut into slices or cubes. Steam-blanch until tender. Mash and let cool completely. Pack in plastic dishes (leaving a 1/2-inch space at the top), seal, label, date, and freeze.

Spinach and Other Dark Leafy Greens

2 1/2 pounds fresh yields
4 cups frozen

Wash leaves thoroughly; remove any thick stems and imperfect leaves. Water-blanch for 30 to 60 seconds, or until just wilted. Cool quickly by running cold water over the leaves. Drain thoroughly, pressing out excess moisture. Pack, seal, label, date, and freeze.

Mixed Vegetables

Chop larger vegetables or cut them into bite-size pieces. Blanch according to directions for each individual vegetable, remembering that a shorter blanching time may be required to compensate for the smaller piece size. When they are cool, mix your choice of vegetables and pack in plastic freezer bags in meal-size quantities. Seal, label, date, and freeze.

how to blanch vegetables

You can blanch vegetables with either boiling water or steam. Which method you use—and the time required to do it—depends on the vegetable involved.
Water-blanching: Bring at least 12 cups of water to a boil in a large saucepan. Place 1 pound prepared vegetable pieces in a wire-mesh basket and plunge into the boiling water. When the water returns to a boil, cook the vegetables for the time required. Lift the basket and place it into a large bowl of cold or ice water to cool; change the water as needed or add ice to keep the water cold. Drain completely.
Steam-blanching: Place prepared vegetables in a single layer inside a steamer basket in a large saucepan containing 2 inches of boiling water. Cover, and steam the vegetables for the time required. Cool, but don't rinse the vegetables.

frozen fruits

Use only unblemished fruit and keep the handling time to a minimum (fruit tends to brown when handled). Be sure to press out any excess air before sealing the freezer bags. Thaw frozen fruit in the bag in the refrigerator for several hours or place the bag in a bowl of cool water 30 minutes.

Apples

2 1/2-3 pounds fresh yields 4 cups prepared

Peel, core, and slice the apples. Dip and drain the slices thoroughly. Arrange in a single layer on a rimmed tray and freeze until just firm. Pack, seal, label, date, and freeze.

Apricots

1 1/4-1 1/2 pounds yields 4 cups prepared

Pit and slice or halve the apricots. Dip and drain the slices or halves thoroughly. Arrange in a single layer on a rimmed tray and freeze until just firm. Pack, seal, label, date, and freeze.

Blueberries

1-1 1/2 pound fresh yields 4 cups prepared

Remove any stems. Dip and drain the blueberries thoroughly. Arrange in a single layer on a rimmed tray and freeze until just firm. Pack, seal, label, date, and freeze.

Cherries

2-3 pounds fresh yields 4 cups prepared

Stem and pit the cherries. Dip and drain thoroughly. Arrange in a single layer on a rimmed tray and freeze until just firm. Pack, seal, label, date, and freeze.

Mangoes

2 1/2-3 pounds fresh yields 4 cups prepared

Pit and slice or halve the mangoes. Dip and drain the slices or halves thoroughly. Arrange in a single layer on a rimmed tray and freeze until just firm. Pack, seal, label, date, and freeze.

Peaches and Plums

2-3 pounds fresh yields 4 cups prepared

Pit and slice or halve the peaches or apricots. Dip and drain the slices or halves thoroughly. Arrange in a single layer on a rimmed tray and freeze until just firm. Pack, seal, label, date, and freeze.

Raspberries

1 pound fresh yields 4 cups prepared

Remove stems and leaves from the raspberries. Dip and drain the berries thoroughly. Arrange in a single layer on a rimmed tray and freeze until just firm. Pack, seal, label, date, and freeze.

Strawberries

1 1/4 pounds fresh yields 4 cups frozen

Remove leaves and hull strawberries. Strawberries can be sliced or left whole. Dip and drain the berries thoroughly. Arrange in a single layer on a rimmed tray and freeze until just firm. Pack, seal, label, date, and freeze.

how to dip fruits for freezing

While working, keep fresh fruit in a bowl of acidulated water (about 8 cups water with 1 1/2 tablespoons of lemon juice or mild vinegar added). This keeps the cut fruit from browning and is commonly refered to as dipping. After dipping, drain the fruit on paper towels to remove as much moisture as possible. This helps prevent ice from forming around the pieces and keeps them from sticking together.

inside this chapter

quick breads
Beer Bread
Cheese and Parsley Bread
Corn Bread
Zucchini and Cheese Bread
Irish Soda Bread
Olive and Sun-Dried Tomato Bread
Sesame Pumpkin Bread
Banana Nut Bread
Carrot Bread
Pecan Bread
Zucchini Bread

yeast breads
French Bread
Multigrain Bread
Oatmeal Bread
Focaccia
Challah
Cinnamon-Raisin Swirl Bread
Pita Bread
Sourdough Bread

muffins
Cranberry Cheddar Muffins
Herb Bacon Muffins
Apple and Raisin Muffins
Blueberry Muffins
Bran Muffins

rolls
Parker House Rolls
Soda Bread Rolls
Crescent Rolls
Cinnamon Rolls
Hot Cross Buns
Sticky Buns

cakes
Spice Cake
Chocolate Cake
Devil's Food Cake
White Cake
Broiled Brown Sugar-Coconut Icing
Buttercream Frosting
Chocolate Buttercream Frosting
Orange Buttercream Frosting
Angel Cake

Cheesecake with Strawberry Glaze
Chocolate Cheesecake
Pumpkin Cheesecake

pies and meringues
Basic Double Crust Pie Pastry
Basic Single Crust Pie Pastry
Pecan Pie
Perfect Apple Pie
Custard Pie
Meringue Shells
Strawberry Pavlova

cookies
Chocolate Chip Cookies
Oatmeal Cookies
Peanut Butter Cookies
Brownies
Blondies
Chocolate Sandwich Cookies
Coconut Macaroons
Gingersnaps
Graham Crackers
Sugar Cookies

chapter 3

Baked Goods You Can Make

Nothing can compare to the aroma—or taste—of freshly baked bread. But with the demise of the neighborhood bakery, it is not a pleasure that we

encounter very often these days, except maybe when it is artificially piped into the baked goods section of a fancy supermarket to whet your appetite and open your wallet. The sad truth of the matter is that most of those packaged and wrapped breads, rolls, muffins, cakes, pies, and cookies that you find in the typical supermarket are made from bleached flour—flour that has been stripped of most its healthful nutrients and fiber. And they have often been replaced with taste-diminishing additives and preservatives to give the product a longer shelf life.

If your baking has been limited to the occasional pie, birthday cake, or holiday cookies, you will be pleasantly surprised at how easy, fast, and economical it is to make your own everyday baked goods such as bread, rolls, and muffins. You will discover not only how much better and fresher they taste but also the enormous variety of both savory and sweet baked bread products you can serve up, fresh and additive-free, to your family. The same is true of the really sweet baked goodies—there's an ample selection of cakes, pies, and cookies on the following pages. Some of the cakes can be made in almost no time using the cake mix from Chapter 1, and handmade piecrust is flaky, with a rich flavor that complements any filling.

quick breads

Beer Bread
Use a light lager for a lighter taste or be bold with a stout for a richer, darker flavor—the beer's the limit! If you can find this savory bread at a grocery or bakery, it will cost at least twice as much.

2 1/2 cups all-purpose flour

2 tablespoons sugar

2 teaspoons baking powder

1 teaspoon salt

1 cup beer

1/4 cup plus 2 tablespoons butter, melted

1. Preheat the oven to 350°F. Lightly grease an 8 x 4-inch loaf pan and line the pan with baking paper.

2. In a large bowl, sift together the flour, sugar, baking powder, and salt. Add the beer and the 1/4 cup of melted butter, and stir until a soft dough forms.

3. Spoon the dough into the prepared pan and pour the remaining 2 tablespoons of melted butter over the top of the loaf. Bake until the loaf is golden brown and sounds hollow when tapped, 40 to 45 minutes. Remove the loaf from the pan to a wire rack to cool.

Makes 1 loaf

Cheese and Parsley Bread
Golden, crusty, savory—this loaf is essentially a big scone and totally irresistible. You may have trouble finding such a bread at the supermarket at any price. Luckily, you don't need to.

2 cups whole wheat flour

1 teaspoon baking powder

1 teaspoon baking soda

3/4 cup shredded cheddar or 1/4 cup grated Parmesan cheese

1/4 cup fresh parsley

1 teaspoon salt

3/4 cup milk or buttermilk

1. Preheat the oven to 450°F. In the bowl of a food processor, place the flour, baking powder, baking soda, all but 1 table-spoon of the cheese, parsley, and salt. Whirl until the cheese crumbles into the flour and the parsley is finely chopped.

2. Add the milk or buttermilk all at once, and whirl just until a soft dough forms, about 5 seconds.

3. Lightly flour a work surface and a baking sheet. Turn out the dough onto the work surface and knead gently. Transfer the dough to the baking sheet and form into a round loaf. Using a sharp knife, cut the dough almost through into 8 wedge-shaped pieces. Sprinkle the wedges with the remaining tablespoon of cheese.

4. Bake in the center of the oven until the loaf is puffed and brown, 20 to 25 minutes. Remove the loaf from the oven, wrap it in a lint-free towel, and let it cool slightly. Cut through the marked wedges of the bread to serve.

Makes 1 loaf (8 wedges)

Corn Bread

As tasty to the eye as to the palate, this beautiful yellow bread is a wholesome welcome addition to any meal.

1 1/2 cups all-purpose flour

1 1/4 cups yellow cornmeal

4 teaspoons baking powder

2 tablespoons sugar

1 teaspoon salt

1 egg

1 1/4 cups cold milk

1/4 cup vegetable oil

1. Preheat the oven to 400°F. Lightly grease an 8-inch square baking pan.

2. In a large bowl, sift together the dry ingredients. In a smaller bowl, combine the egg, milk, and oil; beat until the ingredients are well blended. Make a well in the center of the dry ingredients; pour in the milk mixture all at once and, using a fork, stir just until the wet and dry ingredients are blended—do not overmix.

3. Pour the batter into the prepared pan and bake until the bread pulls away slightly from the sides of the pan and is slightly browned, 20 to 25 minutes.

4. Remove the pan to a wire rack and let the bread cool for 10 minutes. Cut into large squares and serve warm.

Makes 1 loaf (about 9 squares)

variation:

Corn Muffins: Prepare the batter as above, but pour into well-greased or paper-lined muffin cups. Bake until the muffins are lightly browned and springy to the touch, 17 to 20 minutes.

Zucchini and Cheese Bread

Use this recipe to make a loaf or muffins—either is a splendid backdrop to cream cheese, smoked salmon, and a few capers. Toasted, slices of this bread are delicious with a hearty soup.

2 cups all-purpose flour

1 teaspoon baking powder

1 tablespoon sugar

1 teaspoon salt

6 tablespoons butter, cut up

1 cup shredded sharp cheddar cheese

1 cup milk

1 large egg

1 cup grated zucchini, squeezed dry in a towel to remove excess moisture

1 tablespoon grated onion

1 teaspoon Dijon mustard

1. Preheat the oven to 375°F. Lightly grease an 8 x 4-inch loaf pan.

2. In a large bowl, sift together the flour, baking powder, sugar, and salt. Using a pastry blender or 2 knives, cut in the butter until the mixture resembles coarse bread crumbs. Stir in the cheese.

3. In a medium bowl, combine the milk and egg, and beat until they are well blended. Stir in the zucchini, onion, and mustard. Add the milk mixture to the dry ingredients. Using a fork, stir just until all the ingredients are moistened and the dough holds together; do not overmix or the bread may be too heavy.

4. Spoon the dough into the prepared pan. Bake until the bread is well risen and brown, and a tester inserted into the center of the loaf comes out clean, 40 to 45 minutes.

5. Remove to a wire rack to cool in the pan 10 minutes, then remove the bread from the pan and let it cool completely.

Makes 1 loaf

Irish Soda Bread

St. Patrick's Day wouldn't be complete without a loaf of this traditional Irish bread, but don't wait until it's offered in the stores. This easy-to-make bread can be topped with a sprinkling of seeds or oatmeal, and is a wonderful accompaniment to stews and hearty soups.

4 cups all-purpose flour

3 tablespoons sugar

3 teaspoons baking powder

1 teaspoon salt

3/4 teaspoon baking soda

6 tablespoons cold butter or margarine

1 1/2 cups currants or raisins

1 tablespoon caraway seed

2 eggs, lightly beaten

1 1/2 cups low-fat buttermilk

1. In a large bowl, sift together the flour, sugar, baking powder, salt, and baking soda. Using a pastry blender or 2 knives, cut in butter until the mixture resembles coarse crumbs. Stir in the currants or raisins and caraway seed.

2. Set aside 1 tablespoon of the beaten egg. In a medium bowl, combine the buttermilk and remaining eggs, and stir until they are well blended. Make a well in the center of the flour mixture. Pour the buttermilk mixture into the well and stir just until the flour is moistened and a sticky dough forms.

3. Flour a work surface well. Turn out the dough onto the work surface and, using well-floured hands, knead the dough about 10 times. Shape the dough into a round loaf.

4. Lightly grease a 9-inch round baking pan. Place the loaf in the prepared pan. Using a sharp knife, cut a cross, 1/4-inch deep, in the top center of the loaf. Brush the loaf with the reserved egg.

5. Bake at 350°F until a toothpick inserted near the center of the loaf comes out clean, about 1 hour and 20 minutes. If the loaf top browns too quickly, tent loosely with foil for the final 20 minutes of baking time. Remove to a wire rack and cool in the pan for 10 minutes before removing the loaf from the pan to the rack to cool completely.

Makes 1 loaf

One-Minute Substitute

If You Run Out of Buttermilk

If a recipe calls for 1 cup buttermilk and you don't have any on hand, pour 1 tablespoon white vinegar or lemon juice in a 1-cup measure and add enough regular milk to make 1 cup. Or simply substitute 1 cup plain yogurt.

Olive and Sun-Dried Tomato Bread

You can almost taste the Mediterranean when you bite into this peasant-style bread, with its strong flavors and chewy texture. This recipe will save you money and add excitement to a bowl of soup.

2 eggs

2/3 cup milk

2 cups all-purpose flour

2 teaspoons baking powder

1 teaspoon kosher salt

3 tablespoons oil drained from sun-dried tomatoes or olive oil

1/2 cup black olives in oil, drained, pitted, and slivered

1/2 cup sun-dried tomatoes packed in oil, drained and sliced

1 tablespoon fresh minced basil or marjoram

1. Preheat the oven to 400°F. Lightly grease an 8-inch springform pan.

2. In the bowl of a food processor or blender, combine the eggs and milk. Whirl just until the ingredients are combined. Sift together the flour and baking powder, and add to the milk mixture. Whirl for 2 minutes; add the salt and oil, and whirl for 1 minute more. Using a spoon, stir in the olives, sun-dried tomatoes, and basil or marjoram.

3. Pour the batter into the prepared pan and bake until a tester inserted into the bread comes out clean, about 30 minutes.

4. Remove the pan to a wire rack and let the bread cool slightly. Remove the outer ring of the pan and serve the bread warm.

Makes 1 loaf

Sesame Pumpkin Bread

Wake up your taste buds with this unusual bread, experiencing autumn in every bite. You may find a similar loaf among the specialty breads at the market, but you can be sure it will be much more costly.

4 cups all-purpose flour

1/4 cup sugar

4 teaspoons baking powder

1 teaspoon salt

1 cup plus 2 tablespoons milk

1 egg

1 cup pumpkin puree

1/3 cup butter, melted

1 tablespoon sesame seed

1. Preheat the oven to 425°F. Lightly grease and flour a baking sheet. In a large bowl, sift together the flour, sugar, baking powder, and salt.

2. In a medium bowl, combine 1 cup of milk and the egg; beat until well blended. Stir in the pumpkin puree and butter. Make a well in the center of the dry ingredients; pour the pumpkin mixture and, using a fork, stir until all the ingredients are well blended.

3. Lightly flour a work surface. Turn out the dough onto the work surface and knead lightly until the dough is smooth, 4 to 5 minutes. Shape the dough into a round loaf and transfer to the prepared baking sheet. Using a sharp knife, cut a cross over the top of the loaf. Brush lightly with the remaining 2 tablespoons milk. Sprinkle with the sesame seeds.

4. Bake the loaf 25 minutes; reduce the heat to 375°F and bake until the loaf sounds hollow when tapped, about 15 minutes longer. Remove the loaf to a wire rack to cool.

Makes 1 loaf

Banana Nut Bread

Buy bananas in bulk from a price club or when they go on sale at the supermarket, and use some to make this luscious loaf. You can double or triple the recipe and freeze the extra loaves for later. Either way, you will save on a delicious bread for brunches or teatime.

1/2 cup walnuts or pecans

1 3/4 cups all-purpose flour

1 1/2 teaspoons baking powder

1/2 teaspoon baking soda

1/2 teaspoon salt

1/2 teaspoon ground cinnamon

1/4 teaspoon ground allspice

1/2 cup (1 stick) butter, at room temperature

1/3 cup firmly packed light brown sugar

1/2 cup granulated sugar

2 eggs

1 cup mashed ripe bananas

1/3 cup buttermilk

1/4 teaspoon almond extract

1 cup golden seedless raisins

1. Preheat the oven to 350°F. Lightly grease a 9 x 5-inch loaf pan; lightly dust the pan with flour.

2. Spread the walnuts or pecans in a pie plate and toast, uncovered, until the nuts are lightly browned, about 7 minutes. Let the nuts cool, then coarsely chop and set aside.

3. In a medium bowl, combine the flour, baking powder, baking soda, salt, cinnamon, and allspice; stir until all the ingredients are well blended.

4. In a large bowl with an electric mixer on moderate speed, beat the butter until it is creamed. Gradually add the brown and granulated sugars, beating well after each addition. Add the eggs, 1 at a time, beating well after each addition again. Add the flour mixture, a little at a time, beating after each addition only enough to incorporate the flour. The batter will not be smooth.

5. In a small bowl, combine the mashed bananas, buttermilk, and almond extract; stir until the ingredients are blended. Pour the banana mixture into the batter, stir, then fold in the raisins and reserved toasted nuts.

6. Pour and scrape the batter into the prepared pan. Bake the bread on the middle rack of the oven until a toothpick inserted into the center of the loaf comes out clean, 50 to 55 minutes. Remove the pan to a wire rack and let the bread cool in the pan for 10 minutes. Using a knife or spatula, loosen the edges of the bread from the sides of the pan and carefully remove the bread from the pan. Let the bread cool completely on the rack.

Makes 1 loaf

One-Minute Substitute

If You Run Out of Baking Powder
If a recipe calls for 1 teaspoon baking powder and you don't have any on hand, combine 1/4 teaspoon baking soda with 1/2 teaspoon cream of tartar.

Carrot Bread
Spicy goodness that will bring to mind carrot cake, without the high price. Serve with tea or coffee or as dessert.

1 3/4 cups all-purpose flour

2 1/2 teaspoons baking powder

1/2 teaspoon salt

1/4 teaspoon ground cardamom

1/4 teaspoon ground ginger

1/4 teaspoon ground allspice

1/2 cup (1 stick) butter, at room temperature

2/3 cup sugar

2 eggs

1 1/2 cups peeled shredded carrots

1/2 cup orange juice

1. Preheat the oven to 350°F. Lightly grease a 9 x 5-inch loaf pan; lightly dust the pan with flour.

2. In a medium bowl, combine the flour, baking powder, baking powder, salt, cardamom, ginger, and allspice; stir until all the ingredients are well blended.

3. In a large bowl with an electric mixer on moderate speed, beat the butter until it is creamed. Gradually add the sugar, beating well after each addition. Add the eggs, 1 at a time, beating well after each addition again. Add the flour mixture, a little at a time, beating after each addition only enough to incorporate the flour. The batter will not be smooth.

4. In a small bowl, combine the carrots and orange juice; stir until blended. Pour the carrot mixture into the batter and stir until all the ingredients are well blended.

5. Pour and scrape the batter into the prepared pan. Bake the bread on the middle rack of the oven until a toothpick inserted into the center of the loaf comes out clean, about 1 hour. Remove the pan to a wire rack and let the bread cool in the pan for 10 minutes. Using a knife or spatula, loosen the edges of the bread from the sides of the pan and carefully remove the bread from the pan. Let the bread cool completely on the rack.

Makes 1 loaf

Pecan Bread
Slice and serve this nutty Southern bread with fruit and soft cheeses. You can buy it, but you will pay much, much more.

2 cups all-purpose flour

2 teaspoons baking powder

1 teaspoon salt

3/4 cup coarsely chopped pecans

1/3 cup firmly packed light brown sugar

1 cup milk

1 egg

3 tablespoons butter, melted

1. Preheat the oven to 350°F. Lightly grease an 8 x 4-inch loaf pan.

2. In a large bowl, sift together the flour, baking powder, and salt. Stir in the pecans and brown sugar. In a medium bowl, combine the milk and egg, and beat well. Stir the melted butter into the milk mixture.

3. Make a well in the center of the flour mixture. Pour the milk mixture into the well and, using a fork, stir the ingredients just until they are all moistened and the dough holds together; do not overmix.

4. Spoon the dough into the prepared pan. Bake the bread until a tester inserted into the center of the loaf comes out clean, 45 to 50 minutes.

5. Remove the pan to a wire rack and let the bread cool 10 minutes, then remove the bread from the pan and let it cool completely.

Makes 1 loaf

Baked Goods You Can Make   **97**

Zucchini Bread

Every gardener we know always has excess zucchini during the summer— this is the delectable way to use it up while saving money on the cookies and desserts that zucchini bread replaces. You can make several loaves and freeze the extras.

1 cup chopped pecans

1 3/4 cups all-purpose flour

1 1/2 teaspoons baking powder

1/2 teaspoon baking soda

1/2 teaspoon salt

1 teaspoon ground cinnamon

1/2 cup (1 stick) butter, at room temperature

3/4 cup sugar

2 eggs

1 1/2 cups shredded zucchini, squeezed to remove excess moisture

1/3 cup buttermilk

1/4 teaspoon almond extract

1. Preheat the oven to 350°F. Lightly grease a 9 x 5-inch loaf pan; lightly dust the pan with flour.

2. Spread the pecans in a pie plate and toast, uncovered, until the nuts are lightly browned, about 7 minutes. Let the nuts cool, then coarsely chop and set aside.

3. In a medium bowl, combine the flour, baking powder, baking soda, salt, and cinnamon; stir until all the ingredients are well blended.

4. In a large bowl with an electric mixer on moderate speed, beat the butter until it is creamed. Gradually add the sugar, beating well after each addition. Add the eggs, 1 at a time, beating well after each addition again. Add the flour mixture, a little at a time, beating after each addition only enough to incorporate the flour. The batter will not be smooth.

5. In a small bowl, combine the zucchini, buttermilk, and almond extract; stir until blended. Pour the zucchini mixture into the batter, stir, then fold in the reserved toasted nuts.

6. Pour and scrape the batter into the prepared pan. Bake the bread on the middle rack of the oven until a toothpick inserted into the center of the loaf comes out clean, about 1 hour. Remove the pan to a wire rack and let the bread cool in the pan 10 minutes. Using a knife or spatula, loosen the edges of the bread from the sides of the pan and carefully remove the bread from the pan. Let the bread cool completely on the rack.

Makes 1 loaf

yeast breads

French Bread

Many meals are finished off with a loaf of French bread to sop up the gravy, hold the cheese, or complement the salad. Nothing is better, but unfortunately, nothing gets stale quicker, so making your own not only saves money but also ensures a fresh, crusty loaf. Surprisingly, this recipe doesn't require kneading.

1 package (1/4 ounce)
  active dry yeast

1 1/2 cups warm water
  (110°F-115°F), divided

1 tablespoon sugar

2 teaspoons salt

1 tablespoon butter, melted

4 cups all-purpose flour

Cornmeal

1. In a large bowl, combine the yeast with 1/2 cup of the water and stir until the yeast is dissolved.

2. Add the sugar, salt, butter, and remaining 1 cup water. Stir until all the ingredients are well blended and the powdered ingredients are dissolved. Add the flour and stir until the dough is smooth; do not knead. Cover the bowl and let the dough rise in a warm place until it is doubled in size, about 1 hour.

3. Lightly flour a work surface. Divide the dough in half; let the dough halves rest for 10 minutes. Using a lightly floured rolling pin, roll one dough half into a 10 x 8-inch rectangle. Beginning on a long side, roll up the dough, jelly-roll-fashion; pinch the edges to seal the loaf. Repeat with the remaining dough half.

4. Lightly grease a baking sheet and sprinkle it with cornmeal. Place the loaves, seam side down, on the prepared baking sheet; sprinkle the tops of the loaves with additional cornmeal. Cover the loaves and let rise until doubled in size, about 45 minutes.

5. Preheat the oven to 400°F. Using a sharp knife, make five diagonal cuts across the top of each loaf. Bake the loaves until they are lightly browned, 20 to 30 minutes. Remove the loaves to wire racks to cool.

Makes 2 loaves

Helpful Hint

Yeast Breads Are Easier to Make Than You Think
One of the absolute best aromas in the world—fresh baking bread. You may have shied away from yeast breads in the past, thinking the yeast would be difficult to work with. Not at all. Follow the directions and you'll be turning out perfect loaves in no time at all. If you enjoy the aroma and the price of homemade bread and time is a factor, you may want to invest in a bread machine. Most recipes can be converted for a machine.

Multigrain Bread

Whole wheat flour, rye flour, stone-ground cornmeal, wheat bran and germ, and buttermilk form a hearty, wholesome bread your family will rave about. So will your pocketbook.

2 teaspoons sugar

1/2 cup lukewarm water (105°F-115°F)

2 packets (1/4 ounce each) active dry yeast

1 1/4-1 1/2 cups all-purpose flour

1 cup whole wheat flour

1 cup rye flour

1/3 cup sifted stone-ground yellow or white cornmeal

1/4 cup wheat bran

1/4 cup wheat germ, plain, toasted, or honey crunch

1 cup buttermilk

3 tablespoons butter, melted

1 1/2 teaspoons salt

1. In a large bowl, combine the sugar, water, and yeast. Stir until the solids are dissolved. Let stand until the mixture is bubbly, about 10 minutes.

2. In another large bowl, combine 1 1/4 cups of the all-purpose flour, the whole wheat and rye flours, cornmeal, wheat bran, and wheat germ.

3. In a small saucepan over low heat, combine the buttermilk, butter, and salt, and cook until the mixture is lukewarm.

4. Pour the buttermilk mixture into the yeast mixture. Using a wooden spoon or an electric mixer with the dough hook attached, beat at moderate speed, adding the flour mixture 1 cup at a time, until the dough is soft but manageable; beat in the remaining 1/4 cup of all-purpose flour, if needed to reach the desired consistency. Continue to beat until the dough is smooth and elastic, 7 to 8 minutes. If mixing by hand, knead on a floured work surface for 8 to 10 minutes.

5. Butter a 5-quart bowl well. Shape the dough into a ball and place the ball in the prepared bowl, turning it until the dough surface is completely coated. Cover the bowl with a cloth and set in a warm, draft-free place until the dough is doubled in size, 1 1/2 to 2 hours.

6. Lightly grease a 9 x 5 x 3-inch loaf pan; lightly flour a work surface. Punch down the dough and turn out onto the work surface. Knead gently for 2 minutes. Shape the dough into a loaf, place it in the prepared pan, cover, and let rise until doubled in size, about 1 hour.

7. Preheat the oven to 375°F. Bake until the loaf is golden brown and sounds hollow when tapped, 40 to 45 minutes. Remove the pan to a wire rack and let the bread cool for 10 minutes. Using a knife, loose the edges of the bread from the sides of the pan, turn out the bread, and set it on the wire rack to cool completely.

Makes 1 loaf

Oatmeal Bread

The old-fashioned goodness of this nutty, crunchy bread makes it the ideal base for sandwiches, but try it toasted with homemade jam or apple butter too. Cooking the oats before using them to make bread results in a lighter, finer texture. Again, by making your own oatmeal bread, you will save money as well as benefit from the aroma of baking bread.

1 1/2 cups milk

1/4 cup (1/2 stick) butter or margarine plus
1 tablespoon, melted

1 cup plus 2 tablespoons quick-cooking oats

5 teaspoons firmly packed light brown sugar

1/4 cup lukewarm water (105°F-115°F)

2 packets (1/4 ounce each) active dry yeast

1 egg, beaten

2 teaspoons salt

1 cup whole wheat flour

2 1/2-3 cups all-purpose flour

Glaze

1 egg beaten with 1 tablespoon water

1. In a small saucepan over moderate heat, combine the milk and 1/4 cup of butter until the mixture is steaming. Add 1 cup oats and stir until the oats are evenly moistened, about 1 minute. Remove the saucepan from the heat and let cool to room temperature, 25 to 30 minutes.

2. In a large bowl, combine 1 teaspoon brown sugar, the water, and the yeast. Stir until the solids are dissolved. Let stand until the mixture is bubbly, about 10 minutes. Using a wooden spoon or an electric mixer with a dough hook attached, beat in the cooled oatmeal mixture, the remaining 4 teaspoons brown sugar, the egg, salt, whole wheat flour, and 2 1/2 cups all-purpose flour. Continue beating at moderate speed, until the dough is soft, but manageable, adding the remaining 1/4 to 1/2 cup flour as needed, 7 to 8 minutes. If mixing by hand, knead on a floured work surface 8 to 10 minutes.

3. Butter a 5-quart bowl well. Shape the dough into a ball and place the ball in the prepared bowl, turning it until the dough surface is completely coated. Cover the bowl with a cloth and set in a warm, draft-free place until the dough is doubled in size, about 1 hour.

4. Lightly grease a 9 x 5 x 3-inch loaf pan and sprinkle the bottom and sides of the pan with 1 tablespoon of the remaining oats; lightly flour a work surface. Punch down the dough, turn out onto the work surface, and knead gently for 2 minutes (the dough will be soft). Shape the dough into a loaf, place it in the prepared pan, cover, and let rise until doubled in size, 1 to 1 1/2 hours.

5. Preheat the oven to 375°F. Lightly brush the top of the loaf with the glaze, then sprinkle with the remaining tablespoon of oats. Bake until the loaf is golden brown and sounds hollow when tapped, 40 to 45 minutes. Remove the pan to a wire rack and let the bread cool 10 minutes. Using a knife, loosen the edges of the bread from the sides of the pan, turn out the bread, and set it on the wire rack to cool completely.

Makes 1 loaf

Focaccia

Thick and chewy, this Italian bread can be topped with grilled or marinated vegetables, grilled meats, cold cuts, cheese—or just drizzled with a little extra-virgin olive oil and enjoyed on its own. It has become popular, but you will find that homemade is better and cheaper than store-bought.

1 packet (1/4 ounce) active dry yeast

1/4 teaspoon sugar

2 cups warm water (105°F-110°F)

4 1/2-5 1/2 cups bread flour or all-purpose flour

1/4 cup olive oil plus additional

1 tablespoon salt

Tiny sprigs fresh rosemary

Kosher salt

1. In a small bowl, combine the yeast, sugar, and water. Stir rapidly to dissolve the solids. Set the bowl in a warm place until the mixture is activated and frothy, about 20 minutes.

2. In a large bowl, pour 4 1/2 cups flour and make a well in the center. Pour the yeast mixture, 1/4 cup oil, and salt into the well, then stir until the ingredients are well blended. Add additional flour as needed to reach the desired consistency.

3. Lightly flour a work surface and lightly coat a large bowl with olive oil. Turn the dough out onto the work surface, and knead until the dough is smooth, about 10 minutes. Place the dough in the prepared bowl, turning it once to coat the entire ball with oil. Cover the bowl with lightly oiled plastic wrap, and set to rise in a warm place for 1 hour.

4. Lightly grease 2 baking sheets. Divide the dough in half, and spread each half on a prepared baking sheet; with fingers, press down and out until each half is a round loaf about 1/2-inch thick. Cover the loaves with lightly oiled plastic wrap and let rise for 10 to 20 minutes.

5. With fingers, press the loaves down and out again. Recover and let the loaves rise for 30 minutes.

6. Preheat the oven to 425°F. With fingers, indent the loaves all over. Press a sprig of rosemary into each dent, drizzle the whole with oil, then sprinkle with salt. Bake until the loaves are firm and golden, about 25 minutes. Serve warm.

Makes 2 loaves

Make It a Gift

Take a Mix-and-Match Approach to Gift Baskets
When pondering gift giving with your own homemade items, take a tip from those high-end catalogs and pair natural partners in an attractive package—breads with jams, jellies, or marmalades; pasta with homemade sauces; cookies with hot cocoa, coffee or tea blends; granola with fresh-baked muffins; canned fruit with a dessert sauce; soup with hearty rolls; pita breads with hummus. Whenever you browse through a yard or rummage sale, look for baskets, saucepans, ceramic or porcelain bowls, and other fun packaging for personalized gifts.

Challah

The traditional bread of the Jewish Sabbath, this attractive loaf is braided and given a shiny coating of egg wash. Scrumptious the day it's baked, and you can use leftovers (if any) to make the best French toast you'll ever taste!

2 packages (1/4 ounce each)
  active dry yeast

1 cup warm water
  (110°F-115°F)

1/2 cup vegetable oil

1/3 cup sugar

1 tablespoon salt

5 eggs

6-6 1/2 cups
  all-purpose flour

1 teaspoon cold water

1 tablespoon sesame or
  poppy seed *(optional)*

1. In a large bowl, combine the yeast with the warm water and stir until the yeast is dissolved. Add the oil, sugar, salt, 4 eggs, and 4 cups flour. Beat until all the ingredients are well blended and the consistency is smooth. Stir in enough of the remaining flour to form a firm dough.

2. Lightly flour a work surface. Turn out the dough onto the work surface and knead until the dough is firm and elastic, 6 to 8 minutes. Lightly grease a bowl with butter or oil, place the dough in the bowl, and turn it once to coat the entire ball. Cover the bowl and let the dough rise in a warm place until it is doubled in size, about 1 hour.

3. Punch down the dough, turn in onto another floured work surface, and divide the dough in half. Divide each portion into thirds. Roll each piece into a 15-inch-long rope.

4. Lightly grease a baking sheet. Place 3 dough ropes on the sheet, pinching them together at one end. Braid the ropes together and pinch the opposite ends to seal them, then tuck the pinched ends under at both ends. Repeat with the remaining dough ropes to make a second loaf. Cover the loaves with a cloth and let rise until doubled in size, about 1 hour.

5. Preheat the oven to 350°F. In a small bowl, beat the remaining egg with the cold water. Brush the egg mixture over the loaves. If desired, sprinkle the loaves with the sesame or poppy seed. Bake the loaves until they are golden brown, 30 to 35 minutes. Remove the loaves from the baking sheet to wire racks and let cool completely.

Makes 2 loaves

Cinnamon-Raisin Swirl Bread

The ultimate morning treat, this beautiful bread, spiraled with cinnamon, thick with raisins, and drizzled with sugar icing, is a treat for all the senses. And store-bought doesn't fill your house with the same aroma!

6 teaspoons sugar

1 cup lukewarm whole or 2% milk (105°F-115°F)

2 packets (1/4 ounce each) active dry yeast

2 1/4 cups lukewarm water (105°F-115°F)

5 tablespoons butter or margarine, melted

2 teaspoons salt

6-6 1/2 cups all-purpose flour

1 cup dark seedless raisins, soaked in hot water 15-30 minutes, drained well

Cinnamon Swirl Filling

3 tablespoons butter or margarine, melted

1/2 cup sugar

1 tablespoon ground cinnamon

Icing

2 cups sifted confectioners' sugar

2 tablespoons water

1. In a large bowl, combine 1 teaspoon sugar with the milk and yeast, and stir until the solids are dissolved. Let stand until the mixture bubbles, 5 to 10 minutes. In a medium bowl, combine 1 1/4 cups warm water, 4 tablespoons butter, the salt, and the remaining 5 teaspoons sugar. Stir the butter mixture into the yeast mixture.

2. Using a wooden spoon or an electric mixer with a dough hook attached, beat in the flour, 1 cup at a time, until a soft dough forms. Continue to beat at moderate speed until the dough is elastic, 7 to 8 minutes. If mixing by hand, knead on a floured work surface for 8 to 10 minutes.

3. Pour the final 1 tablespoon butter into a 5-quart bowl. Shape the dough into a ball and place the ball in the prepared bowl, turning it until the dough surface is completely coated. Cover the bowl with a cloth and set in a warm, draft-free place until the dough is doubled in size, about 1 hour.

4. Lightly butter two 9 x 5 x 3-inch loaf pans. Lightly flour a work surface. Punch down the dough and turn out onto the work surface. Knead the dough gently for 2 minutes. Divide the dough in half, cover, and let rest for 5 to 10 minutes. Working with a half at a time and using a rolling pin, roll the dough into a 9 x 15-inch rectangle. Sprinkle 1/2 cup of the raisins over each portion of the dough and gently knead until the raisins are evenly distributed. Cover the dough and let rest for 10 minutes.

5. Prepare the filling: In a small bowl, combine 2 tablespoons butter, the sugar, and cinnamon; stir until the ingredients are well blended. Using a rolling pin on a floured surface, again roll each dough half into a 9 x 15-inch rectangle. Spread each half with half of the filling. Beginning on a short side, roll up the dough, jelly-roll-fashion, to make a loaf; repeat with the remaining half. Place each loaf, seam side down, in a prepared pan, cover with a cloth, and let rise for 1 hour.

6. Preheat the oven to 400°F. Brush the tops of the loaves with the remaining tablespoon of butter. Bake until the bread is brown and sounds hollow when tapped, 35 to 40 minutes. Remove the pans to wire racks and let the bread cool for 10 minutes. Using a knife, loosen the edges of the bread from the sides of the pans, turn out the bread, and set on wire racks to cool.

7. Prepare the icing: In a small bowl, combine the confectioners' sugar and water, and stir until the icing is smooth. Brush, pour or drizzle over the cooled loaves.

Makes 2 loaves

Pita Bread

This popular staple of Middle Eastern and Mediterranean cuisine is a wonderfully versatile bread. You can stuff the pockets with almost anything you can think of to make a sandwich; slice the bread into triangles, toast, and serve with any dip; even top with tomato paste, marinated vegetables, and mozzarella cheese for a variation on pizza. Fresh pita is better and cheaper than store-bought.

1 1/2 cups warm water (105°F-110°F)

1 teaspoon dry yeast

1 teaspoon sugar

3 cups bread flour or all-purpose flour

1 heaping teaspoon salt

1 1/2 teaspoons olive oil plus additional

1/4 cup minced fresh herbs, such as thyme, rosemary, cilantro, or parsley *(optional)*

1. In a large bowl, combine the water and yeast. Using a fork, stir rapidly to dissolve the yeast. Add the sugar and 1 1/2 cups flour. Using the paddle attachment of an electric mixer, stir until all the ingredients are well blended. Cover the bowl with lightly oiled plastic wrap and let stand in a warm place until the dough has doubled in size, about 2 hours.

2. Add the salt, 1 1/2 teaspoons oil, and the remaining 1 1/2 cups flour. Again using the paddle attachment, beat the mixture until it is smooth and elastic, 5 to 10 minutes.

3. Lightly flour a work surface and lightly oil a large bowl. Turn out the dough onto the work surface and knead until the dough is smooth and elastic, 10 to 12 minutes. Place the dough in the bowl and turn it until it is completely coated in the oil. Cover the bowl with lightly oiled plastic wrap and set in a warm place to let the dough rise, about 1 1/2 hours.

4. Preheat the oven to 475°F. Line a baking sheet with parchment paper or foil.

5. Lightly flour the work surface again and turn out the dough onto the surface. Divide the dough into 4 balls. Using a rolling pin, roll each ball into a 1/2-inch thick, 6-inch-diameter circle. Place the dough circles on the prepared baking sheet. Lightly brush each circle with oil and, if desired, sprinkle with herbs. Bake until the pita breads are golden, about 8 minutes. Remove the pita breads to wire racks to cool.

Makes 4 pita breads

Sourdough Bread

The starter, a combination of flour, sugar, and water left in a warm place to attract airborne yeast, is essential to the chewy texture and signature flavor of sourdough bread. Once you have a starter, you use some for each loaf you bake, but feed the starter to keep it going—an endless supply for a sensational bread. Our version uses a commercial yeast, so it takes less time to prepare, but developing your own starter is well worth the time. Yes, home-made is cheaper.

Starter

2 cups lukewarm water
(105°F-115°F)

1 packet (1/4 ounce) active
dry yeast

1 1/2 cups bread flour

Dough

1 1/2 cups starter

1 cup water

2 tablespoons sugar

1 tablespoon salt

5-6 cups bread flour

4 tablespoons (1/2 stick)
butter, melted

1. Prepare the starter: In a medium glass or ceramic bowl, combine the ingredients and whisk until well blended. Cover the bowl loosely with wax paper and set in a warm, draft-free place for 12 hours or overnight.

2. Prepare the dough: In a large bowl, combine the starter, water, sugar, salt, and 2 1/2 cups flour. Using a wooden spoon or the paddle attachment of an electric mixer, beat the dough at moderate speed until it is smooth, about 15 seconds.

3. If using an electric mixer, remove the paddle and attach a dough hook. Add 3 tablespoons butter and 2 1/2 cups of the remaining flour, 1/2 cup at a time. Continue beating about 10 minutes, adding an extra 1/2 to 1 cup of flour, if necessary, to make a smooth and elastic dough. (If mixing by hand, you will probably have to knead in the last of the flour.)

4. Butter a 5-quart bowl well. Using your hands, shape the dough into a ball and place in the prepared bowl, turning it to completely coat the surface of the dough with butter. Cover the bowl with a cloth and set in a warm, draft-free place to rise until doubled in size, 1 to 1 1/2 hours. Punch down the dough, cover again, and let rise 1 1/2 hours longer.

5. Lightly flour a work surface and lightly grease two 8-inch-round cake or springform pans. Punch down the dough again and turn out onto the work surface. Knead lightly until the dough is smooth, 2 to 3 minutes. Divide the dough in half and roll each half into a ball. Place each ball into a prepared pan, cover both with a cloth, and let rise until the dough is doubled in size, 45 minutes to 1 hour. Preheat the oven to 350°F.

6. Brush the loaves with the remaining 1 tablespoon of melted butter. Using a sharp knife, cut a diagonal slash across the top of each loaf. Bake until the loaves are richly golden and sound hollow when tapped, 45 to 50 minutes. Remove the loaves to a wire rack to cool.

Makes 2 loaves

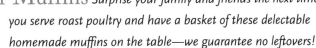

muffins

Cranberry Cheddar Muffins

Surprise your family and friends the next time you serve roast poultry and have a basket of these delectable homemade muffins on the table—we guarantee no leftovers!

2 cups all-purpose flour

2/3 cup firmly packed light brown sugar

1/2 cup finely shredded cheddar cheese

2 1/2 teaspoons baking powder

1/2 teaspoon baking soda

12 teaspoon salt

1/4 teaspoon ground allspice

1/8 teaspoon ground cayenne pepper

1 1/4 cups buttermilk

1/4 cup (1/2 stick) butter, melted

1 egg, separated

1 cup washed fresh or frozen cranberries (unthawed)

1. Preheat the oven to 400°F. Lightly grease or insert paper baking cups into 12 (2 1/2-inch) muffin cups.

2. In a large bowl, combine the first eight ingredients and whisk until well blended.

3. In a small bowl, combine the buttermilk, butter, and egg yolk and whisk until well blended. In a separate small bowl, beat the egg white until soft peaks form.

4. Make a well in the center of the dry ingredients. Pour the buttermilk mixture into the well and, using a fork, stir just until all the ingredients are blended; do not overmix. Fold in the egg white and the cranberries.

5. Spoon the muffin batter into the prepared muffin cups, filling each 3/4 full. Bake until a toothpick inserted in a muffin comes out clean, about 20 minutes. Remove the pan to a wire rack and let the muffins cool for 5 minutes. Using a knife, loosen the edges of each muffin from the sides of the cup, and turn out the muffins.

Makes 12 muffins

Helpful Hint

Muffins Are Not Just for Breakfast

Savory muffins—like the cranberry cheddar and the herb bacon ones here—are made to go with lunch and dinner. Try adding other herbs, cheeses, meats, and such to a muffin recipe to make a striking side for grilled meats, poultry, or seafood. Sweet muffins, on the other hand, are a toothsome treat anytime you serve them. They make a marvelous beginning to any day, a welcome addition to a brunch buffet, a comforting classic with afternoon tea. Either type is fresher, tastier, and cheaper when homemade.

Baked Goods You Can Make   **107**

Herb Bacon Muffins

You can add whatever herbs you fancy to this muffin recipe— fresh thyme, basil, or marjoram would be superb. You will be glad you made them yourself.

1 3/4 cups all-purpose flour

2 teaspoons baking powder

1/2 teaspoon salt

1/4 cup chopped fresh herbs

1/4 cups grated
Parmesan cheese

1 tablespoon sugar

1/3 cup cooked, crumbled
bacon

1 egg, beaten

1 cup milk

1/4 cup (1/2 stick) butter,
melted

1. Preheat the oven to 400°F. Lightly grease or insert paper baking cups into 12 (2 1/2-inch) muffin cups or 24 miniature muffin cups.

2. In a large bowl, sift together the flour, baking powder, and salt. Add the herbs, cheese, sugar, and bacon, and stir until the ingredients are well blended.

3. In a small bowl, combine the egg, milk, and butter. Stir until the ingredients are well blended. Make a well in the center of the dry ingredients. Pour the milk mixture into the well and, using a fork, stir just until the dry ingredients are moistened. Do not overmix; the batter should be lumpy.

4. Spoon the batter into the prepared muffin cups, filling them 2/3 full. Bake until the muffins are browned: 15 to 20 minutes for regular muffins, 12 to 15 minutes for mini muffins. Remove the pan to a wire rack and let the muffins cool for 5 minutes. Using a knife, loosen the edges of each muffin from the sides of the cup, and turn out the muffins. Serve the muffins warm.

Makes 12 regular muffins or 24 mini muffins

Apple and Raisin Muffins

Grated apple is the sweetener to these muffins, reducing the need for added sugar and letting flavor stand out.

2 cups all-purpose flour

3 teaspoons baking powder

1 teaspoon salt

1/2 teaspoon ground cinnamon

1/4 teaspoon ground nutmeg

3/4 cup peeled, grated apple

1/3 cup golden seedless raisins

2/3 cup firmly packed light
brown sugar

1/4 cup chopped walnuts or
pecans

2 eggs, well beaten

2/3 cups milk

1/4 cup vegetable oil

1 cup corn, bran, or
wheat flakes cereal

1. Preheat the oven to 400°F. Lightly grease or insert paper baking cups into 12 (2 1/2-inch) muffin cups.

2. In a large bowl, combine the flour, baking powder, salt, cinnamon, and nutmeg. Add the apple, raisins, sugar, and nuts. Stir until the dry ingredients are blended.

3. In a small bowl, combine the eggs, milk, and oil, and stir to blend them well. Make a well in the center of the dry ingredients. Pour the milk mixture into the well and, using a fork, stir just until the dry ingredients are moistened. Do not overmix; the batter should be lumpy. Fold in the cereal.

4. Spoon the batter into the prepared muffin cups, filling them 2/3 full. Bake until the muffins are puffed and browned, 15 to 20 minutes. Remove the pan to a wire rack and let the muffins cool for 5 minutes. Using a knife, loosen the edges of each muffin from the sides of the cup, and turn out the muffins. Serve the muffins warm.

Makes 12 muffins

Blueberry Muffins *When blueberries are in season, the flavor is out of this world!*

1 1/2 cups blueberries,
  fresh or thawed frozen

3 cups all-purpose flour

1 tablespoon baking powder

1/2 teaspoon baking soda

1 teaspoon salt

3/4 cup plus 2 tablespoons
  sugar

3 tablespoons butter, melted

2 eggs, lightly beaten

1 cup buttermilk

1 1/2 teaspoons vanilla
  extract

1. Preheat the oven to 400°F. Lightly grease or insert paper baking cups into 12 (2 1/2-inch) muffin cups. Rinse the blueberries and pat dry. In a bowl, combine the blueberries with 2 tablespoons flour, and toss to coat them.

2. In a large bowl, combine the remaining flour, baking powder, baking soda, salt, and 3/4 cup sugar. Stir to blend.

3. In a small bowl, combine the butter, eggs, buttermilk, and vanilla, and stir to blend them well. Make a well in the center of the dry ingredients. Pour the milk mixture into the well and, using a fork, stir just until the dry ingredients are moistened. Do not overmix; the batter should be lumpy. Fold in the blueberries.

4. Spoon the batter into the prepared muffin cups, filling them 2/3 full; sprinkle the muffin tops with 2 tablespoons sugar. Bake the muffins in the center of the oven until the muffins are golden, 20 to 25 minutes. Remove the pan to a wire rack and let the muffins cool for 5 minutes. Using a knife, loosen the edges of each muffin from the cup, and turn out the muffins.

Makes 12 muffins

Bran Muffins *Low in fat and high in fiber—plus an absolutely heavenly flavor when you make them yourself.*

1 cup raisins

1 1/4 cups all-purpose flour

1 tablespoon baking powder

1/3 cup sugar

1 teaspoon cinnamon

1/2 teaspoon salt

1 cup bran cereal (not flakes)

1 cup milk

1 egg

1/4 cup vegetable oil

1. Preheat the oven to 400°F. Lightly grease or insert paper baking cups into 12 (2 1/2-inch) muffin cups. In a small bowl, combine the raisins with 2 tablespoons flour, and toss to coat the raisins completely.

2. In a medium bowl, combine the remaining flour, baking powder, sugar, cinnamon, and salt. Stir until the dry ingredients are well blended.

3. In a large bowl, combine the bran cereal and milk; let the mixture stand 2 minutes. Add the egg and the oil, and stir until the bran mixture is well blended. Add the dry ingredients to the bran mixture and, using a fork, stir just until the dry ingredients are moistened; do not overmix. Fold in the raisins.

4. Spoon the batter into the prepared muffin cups, filling them 2/3 full. Bake until the muffins are golden brown, 18 to 20 minutes. Remove the pan to a wire rack and let the muffins cool for 5 minutes. Using a knife, loosen the edges of each muffin from the sides of the cup, and turn out the muffins.

Makes 12 muffins

rolls

Parker House Rolls

These classic homemade rolls will melt in your mouth. The secret may be the potato.

2 tablespoons sugar

1/2 cup lukewarm water
(105°F-115°F)

2 packets (1/4 ounce each)
active dry yeast

1 cup milk

1 cup water

2 teaspoons salt

1/2 cup (1 stick) plus
3 tablespoons butter,
melted

1 large all-purpose potato,
peeled, diced, boiled,
and riced

6 1/2-7 cups
all-purpose flour

1 egg, lightly beaten

1. In a small bowl, combine the sugar, water, and yeast; stir until the solids are completely dissolved. Let the yeast mixture stand until it is bubbly, about 10 minutes.

2. In a small saucepan over moderately high heat, combine the milk and water, and bring to a boil. Pour the hot liquid into a large bowl. Add the salt and 3 tablespoons butter, stir to blend, and let cool 10 minutes. Using a wooden spoon or electric mixer with a paddle at moderate speed, add the potato, 2 cups flour, and the egg, beating for 1 minute after each addition. Add the yeast mixture and beat 1 minute longer.

3. If using the mixer, remove the paddle and attach a dough hook. Add 4 1/2 cups flour and beat 3 to 5 minutes or until a soft, manageable dough forms, adding 1/4 to 1/2 cup of flour as needed to reach the desired consistency.

4. Butter a 5-quart bowl well. Using your hands, shape the dough into a ball and place in the prepared bowl, turning it to completely coat the surface of the dough with butter. Cover the bowl with a cloth and set in a warm, draft-free place to rise until doubled in size, about 50 minutes.

5. Lightly flour a work surface and lightly grease 6 baking sheets. Punch down the dough and turn out onto the work surface. Divide the dough into 4 equal portions, working with 1 portion at a time. Using a rolling pin, roll the dough portion into a 1/4-inch thick, 8 x 10-inch rectangle. Using a floured 2 1/2-inch biscuit cutter, cut the dough into 12 rounds. Gather the scraps together, and reroll; cut 4 more rounds.

6. Brush each dough round with melted butter. Using the blunt side of a knife, crease each circle along the diameter and fold, stretching the top half so it covers the bottom half. Pinch the edges to seal. Repeat with the remaining 3 portions of dough.

7. Arrange the rolls on the prepared baking sheets and brush the tops with the remaining butter. Cover the rolls with a cloth and let rise for 30 minutes. Preheat the oven to 350°F.

8. Bake until the rolls are golden brown, about 30 minutes. Serve immediately or cool on wire racks.

Makes 64 rolls

variations:

Cloverleaf Rolls: After the dough rises, on a floured work surface, pinch off 72 walnut-size pieces of dough and roll each into a 1-inch-diameter ball. Lightly grease muffin pan cups; place 3 dough balls in each cup to make a cloverleaf shape. Cover, let rise, and bake as above.

Fantans: Roll out the risen dough and cut all the rounds with a 2-inch biscuit cutter. Spread butter on top of 1 round, and place another on top; repeat to make a roll with 5 round layers with butter between each layer. Take one layered roll, slightly fold it up, and tuck it into a greased muffin pan cup so the folds are facing up. Cover, let rise, and bake as above.

Soda Bread Rolls

Sprinkle a little oatmeal or some caraway seeds over the tops of these rolls that are hard to find in stores after St. Patrick's Day. Make them yourself anytime.

2 cups all-purpose flour

2 teaspoons baking soda

1 1/2 teaspoons salt

1/3 cup vegetable shortening or margarine

2 cups whole wheat flour

1 2/3 cups buttermilk

1. Preheat the oven to 400°F. Lightly grease a baking sheet.

2. In a large bowl, sift together the all-purpose flour, baking soda, and salt. With a pastry blender or two knives, cut in the shortening until the mixture resembles coarse bread crumbs. Stir in the whole wheat flour. Add the buttermilk and stir to blend thoroughly and to form a soft dough.

3. Lightly flour a work surface. Turn out the dough onto the work surface and knead until the dough is smooth, 4 to 5 minutes. Divide the dough into 8 pieces and roll each into a ball. Place the dough balls, evenly spaced 2 to 3 inches apart, on the prepared baking sheet. Using a sharp knife, cut a cross in the top of each ball.

4. Bake until the rolls are crusty brown and sound hollow when tapped, about 20 minutes. Remove the rolls to a wire rack to cool slightly; serve the rolls warm.

Makes 8 rolls

Crescent Rolls

Don't spend your money on store-bought tubes. These homemade crescent rolls taste much better, have incredible texture, and are not at all difficult to prepare.

1 package (1/4 ounce) active dry yeast

1/4 cup warm water (110°F-115°F)

1 tablespoon plus 1/2 cup sugar

3/4 cup warm milk (110°F-115°F)

3 eggs, lightly beaten

1/2 cup (1 stick) butter or margarine, softened

1 teaspoon salt

5-5 1/2 cups all-purpose flour

Additional butter or margarine, melted

1. In a large bowl, combine the yeast and water, and stir until the yeast is dissolved. Add 1 tablespoon sugar, and let the mixture stand until bubbly, about 5 minutes.

2. Add the milk, eggs, butter or margarine, salt, and 1/2 cup sugar. Stir until all the ingredients are well blended. Add 5 cups flour, 1 cup at a time, stirring after each addition until the mixture forms a stiff dough; add as much of the remaining 1/2 cup of flour as you need to reach the desired consistency.

3. Butter a large bowl well; lightly flour a work surface. Turn out the dough onto the work surface and knead until the dough is smooth and elastic, 6 to 8 minutes. Using your hands, shape the dough into a ball and place in the prepared bowl, turning it to completely coat the surface of the dough with butter. Cover the bowl with a cloth and set in a warm, draft-free place to rise until doubled in size, about 1 1/2 hours.

4. Reflour the work surface and lightly grease 2 baking sheets. Punch down the dough and divide it into thirds; work with one portion at a time. Place 1 dough portion on the work surface. Using a rolling pin, roll out the dough into a 12-inch-diameter circle. Using a sharp knife or pizza cutter, cut the circle into 8 wedges. Brush the wedges with some melted butter. Starting at the wide end, roll up each wedge. Place each wedge on the baking sheet, 2 inches apart, with the small point tucked underneath and slightly bend the wedge to form a crescent shape. Repeat with the remaining dough. Cover the crescents with a cloth and let rise in a warm place until doubled in size, about 30 minutes.

5. Preheat the oven to 375°F. Bake until the crescents are golden brown, 10 to 12 minutes. Remove the crescents to wire racks and cool slightly.

Makes 24 rolls

Cinnamon Rolls

Your whole house will be infused with the aroma of these sweet delicacies as they're baking. Store-bought rolls can't do that. Cream cheese frosting is the perfect finishing touch.

1 package (1/4 ounce) active dry yeast

1 cup warm milk (110°F–115°F)

1/2 cup sugar

1/3 cup butter, melted

2 eggs

1 teaspoon salt

4-4 1/2 cups all-purpose flour

Cinnamon Filling

3/4 cup firmly packed brown sugar

2 tablespoons ground cinnamon

1/4 cup (1/2 stick) butter, melted

Cream Cheese Frosting

1/2 cup (1/2 stick) butter, softened

1 1/2 cups confectioners' sugar

1/4 cup cream cheese, softened

1/2 teaspoon vanilla extract

1/8 teaspoon salt

1. In a large bowl, combine the yeast and the milk; stir until the yeast is completely dissolved. Add the sugar, 1/3 cup butter, eggs, salt, and 2 cups flour. Beat until the ingredients are smooth. Stir in enough remaining flour to form a soft, sticky dough.

2. Lightly flour a work surface; lightly grease a large bowl. Turn out the dough onto the work surface and knead until the dough is smooth and elastic, 6 to 8 minutes. Place in the prepared bowl, turning it to completely coat the surface of the dough with butter. Cover the bowl with a cloth and set in a warm, draft-free place to rise until doubled in size, about 1 hour.

3. Prepare the filling: In a small bowl, combine the brown sugar and cinnamon until they are well blended. Lightly grease two 13 x 9 x 2-inch baking pans; reflour the work surface.

4. Punch down the dough and turn out onto the work surface. Divide the dough in half. Using a rolling pin, roll each half into an 11 x 8-inch rectangle. Brush each rectangle with some of the melted butter. Sprinkle half the filling over each rectangle, leaving a 1/2-inch border around all the edges. Starting from a long side, roll up each rectangle, jelly-roll-fashion, and pinch the seams together to seal. Using a sharp knife, cut each roll into 8 slices. Place the slices, cut side down, in the prepared baking pans. Cover the pans and let rise until doubled in size, about 1 hour.

5. Preheat the oven to 350°F. Bake the rolls until they are golden brown, 20 to 25 minutes. Remove the pans to wire racks and let the rolls cool for 5 to 10 minutes.

6. Prepare the frosting: In a small bowl, combine the ingredients and beat until the frosting is smooth. Frost the warm cinnamon rolls and serve immediately.

Makes 16 rolls

Hot Cross Buns

A traditional Easter morning bun, just sweet enough and loaded with dried fruit. Homemade hot cross buns can be had any time of year.

2 packages (1/4 ounce each) active dry yeast

2 cups warm milk (110°F-115°F)

1/3 cup butter or margarine, softened

2 eggs, lightly beaten

1/4 cup sugar

1 1/2 teaspoons salt

6-7 cups all-purpose flour

1/2 cup raisins

1/2 cup dried currants

1 teaspoon ground cinnamon

1/4 teaspoon ground allspice

2 tablespoons water

1 egg yolk

Icing

2 cups sifted confectioners' sugar

2 tablespoons water

1. In a large bowl, combine the yeast and milk and stir to dissolve the yeast. Add the butter, eggs, sugar, and salt; stir until the ingredients are well blended.

2. In a medium bowl, combine 3 cups flour, the raisins, currants, cinnamon, and allspice. Add the flour mixture to the yeast mixture, and stir until well blended. Add enough of the remaining flour to form a soft dough.

3. Lightly flour a work surface; butter a large bowl well. Turn out the dough onto the work surface and knead until the dough is smooth and elastic, 6 to 8 minutes. Place the dough in the prepared bowl, turning it to completely coat the surface of the dough with butter. Cover the bowl with a cloth and set in a warm, draft-free place to rise until doubled in size, about 1 hour.

4. Lightly grease 3 baking sheets. Punch down the dough. Pinch off enough to form a 1 1/2-inch to 2-inch-diameter ball. Repeat with the remaining dough, placing the dough balls 2 inches apart on the prepared baking sheets. Using a sharp knife, cut a cross on top of each dough ball. Cover the buns with a cloth and let rise until doubled in size, about 30 minutes.

5. Preheat the oven to 375°F. Meanwhile, combine the 2 tablespoons water with the yolk and whisk until they are well blended. Brush the egg-yolk mixture over the risen buns. Then bake until the buns are golden brown, 15 to 20 minutes. Remove the buns to wire racks to cool.

6. Prepare the icing: In a small bowl, combine the confectioners' sugar and water, and stir until the icing is smooth. Place the icing in a pastry bag or self-sealing plastic bag and snip off one corner. Pipe a cross in the cuts on top of each bun.

Makes 30 buns

Sticky Buns

A nutty variation on the cinnamon roll, these gooey, sticky, sensational treats will have them banging down the kitchen door for more.

2 tablespoons sugar

1/2 cup lukewarm water (105°F-115°F)

2 packets (1/4 ounce each) active dry yeast

1 cup milk

1 cup water

2 teaspoons salt

1/2 cup (1 stick) plus 3 tablespoons butter, melted

1 large all-purpose potato, peeled, diced, boiled, and riced

6 1/2-7 cups all-purpose flour

1 egg, lightly beaten

Filling

1/2 cup firmly packed light brown sugar

1/2 cup light corn syrup

2 teaspoons ground cinnamon

1 cup (2 sticks) softened butter

Additional melted butter

2 cups chopped pecans

1. In a small bowl, combine the sugar, warm water, and yeast; stir until the solids are completely dissolved. Let the yeast mixture stand until it is bubbly, about 10 minutes.

2. In a small saucepan over moderately high heat, combine the milk and water, and bring to a boil. Pour the hot liquid into a large bowl. Add the salt and 3 tablespoons of the melted butter, stir to blend, and let cool for 10 minutes. Using a wooden spoon or electric mixer with a paddle attached at moderate speed, add the potato, 2 cups of the flour, and the egg, beating for 1 minute after each addition. Add the yeast mixture to the flour mixture and beat for 1 minute longer.

3. If using the mixer, remove the paddle and attach a dough hook. Add 4 1/2 cups of the remaining flour and beat for 3 to 5 minutes or until a soft, manageable dough forms, adding 1/4 to 1/2 cup of flour as needed to reach the desired consistency.

4. Butter a 5-quart bowl well. Using your hands, shape the dough into a ball and place in the prepared bowl, turning it to completely coat the surface of the dough with butter. Cover the bowl with a cloth and set in a warm, draft-free place to rise until doubled in size, about 50 minutes.

5. Lightly flour a work surface and lightly grease 6 baking sheets. Punch down the dough and turn out onto the work surface. Divide the dough in half. Using a rolling pin, roll each dough half into a 1/4-inch thick, 15 x 12-inch rectangle.

6. Prepare the filling: In a small bowl, combine the brown sugar, corn syrup, cinnamon, and 1 cup of softened butter. Stir until the filling is well blended. Lightly grease a 15 x 10-inch jelly-roll pan.

7. Spread half of the filling over each rectangle, leaving a 1/2-inch-wide border around all the edges. Sprinkle each rectangle with 1 cup of the pecans. Starting from a long side, roll up each rectangle, jelly-roll-fashion, and pinch the seams together to seal; place seam side down. Using a sharp knife, cut each roll into fifteen 1-inch-thick slices. Arrange the slices, not touching, in the prepared jelly-roll pan. Cover the pan with a cloth and let rise about 20 minutes.

8. Preheat the oven to 350°F. Bake until the buns are golden brown, about 40 minutes; brush the buns with a little melted butter and bake for 5 minutes longer.

Makes 30 buns

cakes

Spice Cake
Inviting on its own, this spice-filled cake is also wonderful with Buttercream Frosting (page 119). Much less expensive than a bakery sheet cake, it is also tastier. This cake and the chocolate cake recipe that follows are also outstanding examples of what you can do with the Basic Cake Mix from Chapter 1.

5 cups Basic Cake Mix (page 61)

1 1/4 teaspoons ground nutmeg

1 1/4 teaspoons ground cinnamon

1/2 teaspoon ground cloves

1 cup water

1/4 cup butter or margarine

1/2 cup sour cream or plain nonfat yogurt

2 eggs, lightly beaten

1. Preheat the oven to 375°F. Generously grease a 13 x 9 x 2-inch baking pan.

2. In a large bowl, combine the cake mix, nutmeg, cinnamon, and cloves; stir to distribute the spices evenly.

3. In a small saucepan over moderately high heat, combine the water and butter or margarine. Bring the mixture to a boil. Remove the saucepan from the heat and pour the butter mixture into the bowl. Using a wooden spoon or an electric mixer, beat the batter until all the ingredients are well blended. Stir in the sour cream or yogurt and the eggs; beat until they are incorporated and no streaks of white remain.

4. Pour the batter into the prepared baking pan. Bake until a toothpick inserted into the center of the cake comes out clean and the top of the cake springs back when lightly touched, about 40 minutes. Remove the baking pan to a wire rack and let the cake cool completely.

Makes one 13 x 9 x 2-inch sheet cake

Chocolate Cake If you like chocolate, this cake is guaranteed to please your guests and your pocketbook.

3 1/3 cups Basic Cake Mix
(page 61)

9 tablespoons cocoa powder

1 cup milk

2 eggs, lightly beaten

3 tablespoons butter or
margarine, melted

1. Preheat the oven to 375°F. Lightly grease and flour two 8-inch round cake pans.

2. In a large bowl, combine the cake mix and cocoa. Add 1/2 cup of the milk. Using an electric mixer on medium speed, beat the batter for 2 minutes. Add the remaining 1/2 cup milk, the eggs, and butter or margarine; beat for 2 minutes longer.

3. Pour the batter into the prepared cake pans, dividing it equally. Bake the cake until a toothpick inserted into the center comes out clean and the top of the cake springs back after you touch it, about 25 minutes.

4. Remove the cake pans to wire racks and let stand for 10 minutes to cool slightly. Run a knife around the edges of the cake layers to loosen them from the sides of the pans, invert the pan and remove the cake layers. Set the cake layers on the wire racks and let them cool completely. Fill and frost as desired.

Makes 1 layer cake or 12 servings

Devil's Food Cake This is a one-bowl cake—meant to be beaten with an electric mixer so all the ingredients are in an order to prevent overmixing. Devil's food cake has a beguiling, bitter chocolate flavor that is moister and more distinctive in homemade versions.

1 tablespoon unsweetened
cocoa powder

2 cups sifted cake flour

1 1/2 teaspoons baking soda

1 teaspoon salt

1/2 teaspoon baking powder

1 1/2 cups sugar

1 cup buttermilk, at room
temperature

1/2 cup (1 stick) butter or
margarine, softened

1 teaspoon vanilla extract

3 eggs, at room temperature

3 ounces semisweet
chocolate, melted

1. Preheat the oven to 350°F. Lightly grease two 8-inch round cake pans, dust with the cocoa, divided equally; tap out any excess powder.

2. In a large bowl, combine the flour, baking soda, salt, baking powder, sugar, buttermilk, butter, vanilla, eggs, and chocolate, being careful to add the ingredients in the order listed. Using an electric mixer at low speed, beat all the ingredients for 1 minute, using a spatula to scrape down the sides of the bowl occasionally. Increase the speed to medium-high, and beat for 2 minutes longer, scraping the sides of the bowl twice.

3. Pour the batter into the prepared cake pans. Bake until a toothpick inserted into the center of the cake layers comes out clean, about 30 minutes. Remove the pans to wire racks and let the cake layers cool for 10 minutes. Turn each layer out of its cake pan, then set the layers back on the wire racks to cool completely. Fill and frost as desired.

Makes 1 layer cake or 12 servings

White Cake

Try this sheet cake, topped with Broiled Brown Sugar-Coconut Icing (below) for a terrific offering at a potluck picnic or barbecue. Or make it as a layer cake with Buttercream Frosting (opposite). Either way, it's a fresh, delectable cake for half the price.

2 1/2 cups sifted cake flour

3 teaspoons baking powder

1/2 teaspoon salt

2/3 cup butter or margarine, at room temperature

1 1/2 cups granulated sugar

1 teaspoon vanilla extract

1/2 teaspoon almond extract

3/4 cup milk

4 egg whites, at room temperature

1. Preheat the oven to 375°F. Grease and flour a 13 x 9 x 2-inch baking pan.

2. In a small bowl, sift together the flour, baking powder, and salt. In a large bowl, using an electric mixer at moderately high speed, beat the butter or margarine until it is light. Gradually add 1 1/4 cups of the flour, beating constantly until the mixture is fluffy. Reduce the mixer speed to low, and beat in the vanilla and almond extracts. Add the flour mixture to the bowl, alternating with the milk, beginning and ending with the flour mixture, and adding about 1/3 of the ingredients at a time.

3. In a medium bowl with the electric mixer with clean beaters attached, beat the egg whites until they are frothy. Begin adding the remaining 1/4 cup of sugar, a little at a time, until the mixture forms soft peaks. Fold the egg-white mixture into the batter just until the ingredients are blended and no white streaks remain.

4. Spoon the batter into the prepared pan and, using a spatula, smooth the top. Bake until the cake is lightly browned and springs back when lightly touched, 25 to 30 minutes. Remove the pan to a wire rack and let stand for 5 minutes. Frost as desired.

Makes 20 servings

Broiled Brown Sugar-Coconut Icing

2/3 cup firmly packed brown sugar

1/4 cup softened butter or margarine

1/4 cup heavy cream

1/2 cup flaked coconut

1. Preheat the broiler. In a large bowl using a wooden spoon, combine all the ingredients and beat until well blended.

2. Spread the icing over a warm cake and broil 5 inches from the heat source until the icing bubbles and browns slightly, 3 to 4 minutes. Remove the pan to the wire rack again, and cool the cake slightly before serving.

Makes enough to frost one 13 x 9 x 2-inch sheet cake

Buttercream Frosting
This classic cake frosting is easy and cheap to make and luscious to eat.

1/3 cup butter or margarine, softened

1 box (16 ounces) confectioners' sugar, sifted

1/4 cup light cream

2 teaspoons vanilla extract

1-2 drops food coloring (optional)

1. In a medium bowl with an electric mixer on moderately high speed, beat the butter or margarine until it is light and fluffy.
2. Reduce the speed to medium, and alternately add the sugar and the cream, a little at a time and beating constantly. Add the vanilla and beat until the frosting is creamy. If desired, add food coloring to tint the frosting.

Makes enough to fill and frost one 8- or 9-inch layer cake, 24 cupcakes, or one 13 x 9 x 2-inch sheet cake

Chocolate Buttercream Frosting
This is the icing that kids like to lick out of the bowl. Inexpensive and easy to make, it is delicious.

1/3 cup butter or margarine, softened

1 box (16 ounces) confectioners' sugar, sifted

1/4 cup light cream

2 teaspoons vanilla extract

3 ounces semisweet chocolate, melted, or 1/2 cup sifted unsweetened cocoa powder

1. In a medium bowl with an electric mixer on moderately high speed, beat the butter or margarine until it is light and fluffy.
2. Reduce the speed to medium, and alternately add the sugar and the cream, a little at a time and beating constantly. Add the vanilla and melted chocolate or cocoa powder; beat until the frosting is creamy.

Makes enough to fill and frost one 8- or 9-inch layer cake, 24 cupcakes, or one 13 x 9 x 2-inch sheet cake

Orange Buttercream Frosting
Lightly flavored with orange juice and zest, this homemade icing would be particularly tempting on a spice cake. Make it fresh and save money.

1/3 cup butter or margarine, softened

1 box (16 ounces) confectioners' sugar, sifted

1/4 cup fresh orange juice, strained

2 teaspoons vanilla extract

1 tablespoon grated orange zest

1-2 drops orange food coloring (optional)

1. In a medium bowl with an electric mixer on moderately high speed, beat the butter or margarine until it is light and fluffy.
2. Reduce the speed to medium, and alternately add the sugar and the orange juice, a little at a time and beating constantly. Add the vanilla and orange zest, and beat until the frosting is creamy. If desired, add orange food coloring to tint the frosting.

Makes enough to fill and frost one 8- or 9-inch layer cake, 24 cupcakes, or one 13 x 9 x 2-inch sheet cake

Angel Cake

Aptly named indeed, this cake is so light and airy that you'll swear it'll float away if you don't eat it quickly. It's also free of any fat, and can be the base for many a light, luscious dessert. It is not hard to make yourself, and the homemade one will be even lighter and airier.

1 1/2 cups egg whites (about 15 eggs)

1 1/2 teaspoons cream of tartar

1/4 teaspoon salt

1 1/2 cups sugar

1 cup sifted cake flour

2 teaspoons vanilla extract

1/4 teaspoon almond extract

1. Place the oven rack at the lowest possible position. Preheat the oven to 325°F; set out a 10-inch tube pan.

2. In a large bowl with an electric mixer at medium speed, combine the egg whites, cream of tartar, and salt, and beat until the mixture is frothy. Gradually add the sugar, 2 tablespoons at a time, beating constantly. Increase the speed to high and continue beating until the mixture forms very soft peaks.

3. Fold the flour, 1/4 cup at a time, into the egg whites, then fold in the vanilla and almond extracts.

4. Spoon the cake batter into the ungreased tube pan and gently smooth the top with a spatula. Cut the spatula through the batter once to break and release any large air bubbles.

5. Bake the cake until the top springs back when lightly touched, 50 to 60 minutes. Invert the tube pan with the central tube over the neck of a large bottle; let the cake cool completely. Using a knife, loosen the edges of the cake from the sides of the pan, and turn out the cake onto a cake plate.

Makes 12 servings

Cheesecake with Strawberry Glaze

You can substitute raspberries, blackberries, or blueberries in this recipe. Whatever you choose, you will have a dessert to rival very expensive bakery or deli cheesecake.

Crust

1 1/4 cups crumbled purchased or homemade Graham Crackers (page 132)

5 tablespoons butter or margarine, melted

1/4 cup sugar

Filling

3 packages (8 ounces each) cream cheese

1 cup sugar

3 eggs

1 cup sour cream

Strawberry Glaze

1/4 cup strawberry jelly

1 tablespoon water

1 pint fresh strawberries, hulled and thinly sliced

1. Prepare the crust: Preheat the oven to 325°F. In a medium bowl, using a fork, toss the crumbs, butter, and sugar until well blended. Press the crust mixture firmly over the bottom of a 9-inch springform pan.

2. Prepare the filling: In the bowl of a food processor or blender, combine the cream cheese and sugar, and pulse until they are well blended and smooth. With the motor running, add the eggs 1 at a time. Scrape down the sides of the bowl, add the sour cream, and whirl until the filling is smooth and well blended.

3. Pour the filling into the prepared pan and bake until the filling is only slightly loose in the center of the cheesecake, about 50 minutes. Transfer the pan to a wire rack and let the cheesecake cool to room temperature. Remove the sides of the pan before glazing the cheesecake.

4. Prepare the glaze: In a small saucepan over moderately high heat, combine the jelly and water, and bring the mixture to a boil. Remove the pan from the heat and let the glaze cool slightly. Brush the cheesecake with about 1/3 of the glaze. Beginning along an outside edge of the cake top, arrange the sliced strawberries in overlapping concentric circles. Brush the remaining glaze lightly over the strawberries.

Makes one 9-inch cheesecake or 6 to 8 servings

Chocolate Cheesecake

You love chocolate; you love cheesecake—now you can have your cheesecake and your chocolate too!

Crust

1 1/4 cups chocolate wafer cookie crumbs

5 tablespoons butter melted

1/4 cup sugar

Filling

3 packages (8 ounces each) cream cheese

1 cup sugar

3 eggs

1/4 cup unsweetened Dutch-process cocoa powder

1/4 cup boiling water

1 cup sour cream

Chocolate curls and/or chocolate-dipped nuts (*optional*)

1. Prepare the crust: Preheat the oven to 325°F. In a medium bowl using a fork, toss the crumbs, butter, and sugar until well blended. Press the crust mixture firmly over the bottom of a 9-inch springform pan.

2. Prepare the filling: In the bowl of a food processor or blender, combine the cream cheese and sugar, and pulse until they are well blended and smooth. With the motor running, add the eggs 1 at a time. Scrape down the sides of the bowl. In a small bowl or cup, combine the cocoa with the boiling water, stirring until the cocoa has completely dissolved. Add the liquid cocoa and the sour cream to the cream-cheese mixture, and whirl until the filling is smooth and well blended.

3. Pour the filling into the prepared pan and bake until the filling is only slightly loose in the center of the cheesecake, about 50 minutes. Transfer the pan to a wire rack and let the cheesecake cool to room temperature. Remove the sides of the pan before glazing the cheesecake and, if desired, garnish with chocolate curls and chocolate-dipped nuts before serving.

Makes one 9-inch cheesecake or 6 to 8 servings

Pumpkin Cheesecake

Surprise your family and friends this Thanksgiving with this spicy pumpkin cheesecake instead of the traditional pumpkin pie. It will be an inexpensive treat that they will think came from the bakery.

Crust

1 1/4 cups crumbled Gingersnaps (page 131)

5 tablespoons butter melted

1/4 cup sugar

Filling

3 packages (8 ounces each) cream cheese

1 1/2 cups firmly packed light brown sugar

3 eggs

1 can (29 ounces) unsweetened pumpkin puree

1/4 teaspoon ground cinnamon

1/4 teaspoon ground cloves

1/4 teaspoon ground nutmeg

1. Prepare the crust: Preheat the oven to 325°F. In a medium bowl, using a fork, toss the crumbs, butter, and sugar until well blended. Press the crust mixture firmly over the bottom of a 9-inch springform pan.

2. Prepare the filling: In the bowl of a food processor or blender, combine the cream cheese and sugar, and pulse until they are well blended and smooth. With the motor running, add the eggs 1 at a time. Scrape down the sides of the bowl. Add the pumpkin puree, cinnamon, cloves, and nutmeg, and whirl until the filling is smooth and well blended.

3. Pour the filling into the prepared pan and bake until the filling is only slightly loose in the center of the cheesecake, about 50 minutes. Transfer the pan to a wire rack and let the cheesecake cool to room temperature. Remove the sides of the pan before glazing the cheesecake.

Makes one 9-inch cheesecake or 6 to 8 servings

pies and meringues

Basic Double Crust Pie Pastry

Both savory (meat, cheese, and such) and sweet, pies are among the most popular items in the frozen food section of any grocery store. And sweet pies are featured in every bakery section. (You'll find recipes for main-dish pies starting on page 172 and ones for sweet pies on page 124.) When you have made your own, you will understand why homemade is best even before you add up your savings. Don't waste your cash on pre-made piecrust. Piecrust is easy to make, doesn't take very long, and if you know a few tricks, it will turn out light and flaky every time. Here is the basic recipe for a pie that has a top crust as well as a bottom one.

2 1/4 cups all-purpose flour
1/2 teaspoon salt
1/2 cup (1 stick) cold butter, cut up
1/4 cup vegetable shortening
5-6 tablespoons ice water

1. In a large bowl, sift together the flour and salt. Using a pastry blender or 2 knives, cut in the butter and shortening until the mixture resembles coarse bread crumbs.

2. Add the ice water, 1 tablespoon at a time, stirring the mixture with a fork to incorporate the water into the dough. Add water only until the dough begins to hold together. Handling the dough as little as possible, divide it in half, shape each half into a ball, and wrap each ball in plastic wrap. Chill the dough balls for at least 1 hour before using.

3. For the bottom crust, place 1 ball of dough on a lightly floured board or pastry cloth. Flatten the ball slightly; then, using a lightly floured or covered rolling pin, roll from the center of the ball outward in all directions. Make the dough circle large enough to cover the bottom and sides of a pie plate plus about 1 inch more.

4. For top crust, place the remaining ball of dough on the lightly floured surface and flatten slightly. Roll the dough from the center outward in all directions until the circle is large enough to cover the pie plate plus about a 1/2-inch margin.

Makes enough for a 8- or 9-inch double crust pie

Basic Single Crust Pie Pastry

Use this recipe when you are making an open-face pie or one with a meringue or crumb topping.

1 1/2 cups all-purpose flour

1/4 teaspoon salt

6 tablespoons cold butter, cut up

3 tablespoons vegetable shortening

3-4 tablespoons ice water

1. In a large bowl, sift together the flour and salt. Using a pastry blender or two knives, cut in the butter and shortening until the mixture resembles coarse bread crumbs.

2. Add the ice water, 1 tablespoon at a time, stirring the mixture with a fork to incorporate the water into the dough. Add water only until the dough begins to hold together. Handling the dough as little as possible, shape it into a ball, and wrap it in plastic wrap. Chill the dough ball for at least 1 hour before using.

3. Place the dough on a lightly floured board or pastry cloth. Flatten the ball slightly; then, using a lightly floured or covered rolling pin, roll from the center of the ball outward in all directions. Make the dough circle large enough to cover the bottom and sides of a pie plate plus about 1 inch more. Drape carefully over a pie plate and fold over the outer edge and crimp it with your fingers to make a decorative edge. Fill and bake according to the pie recipe.

4. For a prebaked pie shell, preheat the oven to 375°F. Place the pie shell on a baking sheet and prick the bottom. Line the bottom with two layers of foil and add dried beans or pastry beads to weight it down; otherwise the bottom will puff up during cooking. Bake 10 to 15 minutes or until golden brown.

Makes enough for a 8- or 9-inch single crust pie

Pecan Pie

Each bite is a bit of heaven in your mouth. And your pocketbook will be heavier for not having bought this easy-to-make delicacy.

Basic Single Crust Pie Pastry (above)

3 large eggs

1 cup light corn syrup

1/8 teaspoon salt

2/3 cups chopped pecans

1/3 cup melted butter

1 teaspoon vanilla extract

1 cup white or brown sugar (or half each)

10-20 large perfect pecan halves

1. Preheat the oven to 450°F. Line a 9-inch pie plate with the piecrust; turn under the edges of the dough and, if desired, form a decorative edge around the piecrust.

2. In a large bowl, beat the eggs slightly. Add the corn syrup, salt, chopped pecans, butter, vanilla, and sugar. Stir until all the ingredients are well blended. Pour the syrup mixture into the prepared piecrust. Arrange the pecan halves over the top of the pie, spacing them evenly, in concentric circles or as desired.

3. Bake the pie for 10 minutes; reduce the heat to 350°F and bake until a knife inserted in the center comes out clean, 45 to 55 minutes more. Do not open the oven door during the baking time. Let the pie cool for at least 20 minutes before serving.

Makes 6 to 8 servings

Perfect Apple Pie

You will win kudos for this pie, and you will never enjoy a store-bought apple pie again after you have tasted it.

Basic Double Crust Pie
  Pastry (page 123)

1 large egg, separated

4 tart apples, such as Granny
  Smith, Jonathan,
  Winesaps, or Northern Spy

4 sweet apples, such as
  Golden Delicious,
  Gravenstein, McIntosh, or
  York Imperial

2 tablespoons lemon juice

1/2 cup firmly packed light
  brown sugar

1/2 cup granulated sugar

1/3 cup sifted
  all-purpose flour

1/4 teaspoon ground cinnamon

1/8 teaspoon ground allspice

1/8 teaspoon grated nutmeg

2 tablespoons butter

1 tablespoon cold water

1. Preheat the oven to 425°F. Line a 9-inch pie plate with the bottom piecrust, letting the edges hang over about 1 inch. In a cup, whisk the egg white until frothy and brush over the bottom crust; reserve the egg yolk for the top crust glaze. Roll out the remaining piecrust. Cover the top crust with plastic wrap until ready to use.

2. Peel, core, and slice all the apples about 1/4-inch thick, placing them in a large bowl. Sprinkle the apple slices with the lemon juice as you work to prevent browning. In a small bowl, combine the sugars, flour, cinnamon, allspice, and nutmeg. Sprinkle the sugar mixture over the apple slices, tossing as you work to coat all the slices. Spoon the apple slices into the prepared bottom piecrust, mounding the slices higher in the center. Cut the butter into small pieces and scatter the pieces throughout the apple slices.

3. Using a pastry brush, moisten the edges of the bottom piecrust with a little water. Carefully transfer the top crust to cover the pie filling. Fold the top edges of the pastry over and under the bottom crust edges; pinch the edges together to seal. Cut slits or make decorative vents. If desired, form a decorative edge around the piecrust. In a small bowl, whisk together the reserved egg yolk and cold water. Brush the glaze over the top of the pie, avoiding the slits or decorative vents.

4. Bake the pie 15 minutes; reduce the temperature to 375°F and bake until the filling is bubbly and the piecrust is golden brown, about 35 minutes more. If the crust edges are browning too quickly, cover them with pieces of foil. Place the pie on a rack to cool for at least 20 minutes before serving.

Makes 8 servings

Custard Pie *This creamy pie is never so good from a store as it is from your kitchen.*

Basic Single Crust Pie
  Pastry (page 124)
4 eggs
2 1/2 cups milk
1/2 cup sugar
1 teaspoon vanilla extract
1 teaspoon almond extract
1 teaspoon salt
1 teaspoon ground nutmeg

1. Preheat the oven to 400°F. Line a 9-inch pie plate with the piecrust; turn under the edges of the dough and, if desired, form a decorative edge around the piecrust. Prick the bottom of the crust and bake it for 10 minutes.

2. Meanwhile, in a large bowl, beat the eggs. Add the remaining ingredients and stir to blend well. Pour the egg mixture into the piecrust. Cover the edges of the crust with pieces of foil and bake until a knife inserted near the center comes out clean, 20 to 25 minutes. Let the pie cool completely before serving; store in the refrigerator.

Makes 6 to 8 servings

Meringue Shells *Since these are cooked through, it is safe to use fresh egg whites. The finished appearance should be dry and crisp, but not browned.*

1 cup egg whites (10 large
  eggs)
3/4 cup granulated sugar
1/2 cup sifted confectioners'
  sugar

1. Preheat the oven to 250°F. Line a baking sheet with parchment paper.

2. In a large bowl with an electric mixer on low, slowly beat the egg whites until they are frothy. Continuing to beat on low, gradually add 1/2 cup of the granulated sugar until the egg whites are silvery in appearance. Increase the mixer speed to moderate, and slowly add the remaining 1/4 cup of granulated sugar, beating just until the egg whites form stiff peaks. Using a spatula, fold in the confectioners' sugar.

3. Fit a pastry bag with a number 6 star tip, and fill the bag with the meringue.

4. Pipe 6 coiled circles of meringue onto the prepared baking sheet. Pipe a second-tier ring of meringue along the outer edge of each of the first circles. Or, spoon 6 mounds of meringue onto the baking sheet and, using the back of the spoon, press a hollow in the center of each mound to make a shell.

5. Bake the meringues for 1 hour; turn off the oven but do not open the oven door. Let the meringues stand in the warm oven for 1 hour longer. Remove the meringues to wire racks to cool.

Makes 6 individual meringues or 1 meringue pie shell

Serving example:

Meringue Shells with Raspberry Sauce: Sweetly tart raspberries are the perfect foil for crispy sweet meringue shells. Make 3/4 cup Raspberry Sauce (page 58). Place each meringue shell on an individual serving plate or shallow bowl. Spoon some of the raspberry sauce into each shell and serve immediately.

Strawberry Pavlova

Legend has it that this resplendent sweet was concocted in honor of the celebrated ballerina Anna Pavlova. You can honor your own heroine or hero with this heart-shaped delicacy.

1/2 recipe Meringue Shells (opposite)

Filling

2 cups whipping cream

2 tablespoons sugar

1 quart fresh strawberries, trimmed and sliced

1. Preheat the oven to 250°F. Line a 14-inch pizza pan with parchment paper. Spoon the meringue onto the prepared pan, forming a 12-inch heart shape with slightly built-up edges. Bake the meringue shell for 1 hour; turn off the oven but do not open the oven door. Let the meringue shell stand in the warm oven for 1 hour longer. Remove the meringue shell to a wire rack to cool.

2. Prepare the filling: In a large bowl with an electric mixer on moderately high, beat the whipping cream until it forms soft peaks. Gradually add the sugar, beating constantly, until stiff peaks form.

3. Spoon the whipped cream into the meringue shell, mounding it decoratively. Arrange the strawberry slices on top of the whipped cream and serve immediately.

Makes 12 servings

cookies

Chocolate Chip Cookies

This American classic has been loved for generations and has never really been improved upon. Homemade are just better and less expensive.

1 cup butter or margarine, softened

3/4 cup sugar

3/4 cup firmly packed brown sugar

2 eggs

1 teaspoon vanilla extract

2 1/4 cups all-purpose flour

1 teaspoon salt

1 teaspoon baking soda

1 cups (6 ounces) semisweet chocolate chips

1 cup chopped walnuts or pecans *(optional)*

1. Preheat the oven to 350°F; lightly grease 2 or more baking sheets. In a medium bowl, combine the butter and sugars; beat until the mixture is well creamed. Add the eggs one at a time, beating well after each addition. Add the vanilla and stir until all the ingredients are well blended.

2. In a small bowl, combine the flour, salt, and baking soda. Add the flour mixture to the creamed mixture, stirring until all the ingredients are well blended. Add the chocolate chips and, if desired, the nuts, and stir until they are evenly distributed.

3. Using a tablespoon, drop the cookie dough onto the prepared sheets, spacing the cookies about 2 inches apart. Bake until the cookies are golden brown, about 10 minutes. Transfer the cookies to wire racks to cool.

Makes about 3 1/2 dozen

Oatmeal Cookies
Wholesome and wholly appealing, this is the cookie that says "home." Homemade are tastier and cheaper.

1 cup raisins

1 cup boiling water

3/4 cup shortening

1 cup firmly packed light
  brown sugar

1/2 cup granulated sugar

2 eggs

1 teaspoon vanilla extract

2 1/2 cups all-purpose flour

1 teaspoon baking soda

1 teaspoon salt

1 teaspoon ground cinnamon

1/2 teaspoon baking powder

1/4 teaspoon ground cloves

2 cups quick-cooking oats

1. Preheat the oven to 375°F; set out 2 or more baking sheets.

2. In a small bowl, combine the raisins and the boiling water. Let stand until the raisins are plump, about 15 minutes. Drain the raisins, reserving the liquid. Add enough water to the raisin liquid to equal 1/2 cup.

3. In a large bowl, combine the shortening, sugars, eggs, and vanilla, and beat until the mixture is well creamed. Stir in the raisin liquid. Add the flour, baking soda, salt, cinnamon, baking powder, and cloves, and stir until all the ingredients are well blended. Stir in the raisins and the oats.

4. Using a teaspoon, drop the dough onto the prepared sheets, spacing the cookies about 2 inches apart. Bake until the cookies are light brown, 10 to 12 minutes. Transfer the cookies to wire racks to cool completely.

Makes 5 dozen cookies

Peanut Butter Cookies
One of America's favorite flavors in one of its favorite cookies is a perfect home-bake success. It is easy and delectable.

1/2 cup butter or margarine,
  softened

1/2 cup granulated sugar

1/2 cup firmly packed
  brown sugar

1/2 cup Peanut Butter
  (page 33)

1 egg

1/2 teaspoon vanilla extract

1 1/4 cups all-purpose flour

1/2 teaspoon baking soda

1/2 teaspoon baking powder

Additional granulated sugar

1. In a large bowl, combine the butter or margarine and the sugars; beat until the mixture is well creamed. Add the peanut butter, egg, and vanilla; beat until the mixture is smooth.

2. In a small bowl, combine the flour, baking soda, and baking powder. Add the flour mixture to the creamed mixture, and beat until all the ingredients are well blended. Cover the bowl with plastic wrap and place in the refrigerator until the dough is chilled, about 1 hour.

3. Preheat the oven to 375°F; set out 2 or more baking sheets.

4. Pinch off a walnut-size portion of the chilled dough. Using your hands, roll the dough into a 1-inch-diameter ball and place the ball on one of the baking sheets. Repeat with the remaining dough, spacing the cookies about 2 inches apart. Using a fork dipped in granulated sugar, flatten each dough ball by pressing the tines in a crisscross pattern on each cookie.

5. Bake until the cookies are set and the bottoms are lightly browned, 10 to 12 minutes. Transfer the cookies to wire racks to cool completely.

Makes about 4 dozen cookies

Brownies

This recipe is studded with nuts, but you can substitute chocolate chips or just make a plain brownie. Bought ones are no match for warm brownies out of your oven, filling the air with the smell of chocolate and costing half as much.

5 squares (1 ounce each) unsweetened chocolate, coarsely chopped

1 1/2 cups all-purpose flour

1 teaspoon baking powder

1/2 teaspoon salt

3/4 cup (1 1/2 sticks) butter or margarine, softened

1 1/2 cups sugar

4 eggs

2 teaspoons vanilla extract

2 cups coarsely chopped walnuts or pecans

1. Preheat the oven to 350°F. Line a 13 x 9 x 2-inch baking pan with foil. Lightly grease and flour the foil, and set aside the pan.

2. In a small, heavy saucepan over the lowest heat, melt the chocolate, stirring occasionally. Remove the saucepan from the heat and let the chocolate cool.

3. In a small bowl or on a sheet of wax paper, combine the flour, baking powder, and salt.

4. In a large bowl with an electric mixer on medium speed, cream the butter or margarine for 2 minutes. Add the sugar and beat for 2 minutes longer. Add the eggs, 1 at a time, beating well after each addition. Beat in the vanilla and the cooled chocolate.

5. Using a wooden spoon, add the flour mixture to the chocolate mixture and stir until all the ingredients are well blended. Stir in the nuts. Pour the batter into the prepared pan. Bake the brownies until a toothpick inserted in the center comes out clean, about 35 minutes. Remove the baking pan to a wire rack and let the brownies cool before cutting.

Makes 24 (2 1/2-inch-square) brownies

One-Minute Substitute

If You Run Out of Chocolate

Unsweetened chocolate: If a recipe calls for 1 square (1 ounce) unsweetened chocolate and you don't have any on hand, combine 3 tablespoons unsweetened cocoa powder with 1 tablespoon butter, margarine, or vegetable shortening.

Semisweet chocolate: If 1 ounce semisweet chocolate is called for, combine 3 tablespoons unsweetened cocoa powder with 1 tablespoon butter, margarine, or vegetable shortening and 1 tablespoon sugar.

Blondies
The yin to brownies' yang, blondies are sold at many stores for a pretty penny, but they are not the same as fresh ones out of your oven.

3/4 cup butter, softened

1 1/2 cups sugar

3 eggs

2 teaspoons vanilla extract

1 3/4 cups all-purpose flour

1 teaspoon baking powder

1/2 teaspoon salt

2 cups coarsely chopped walnuts or pecans

1. Preheat the oven to 350°F. Line a 13 x 9 x 2-inch baking pan with foil. Lightly grease and flour the foil.

2. In a large bowl with an electric mixer on medium speed, cream the butter for 2 minutes. Add the sugar and beat for 2 minutes longer. Add the eggs and beat well; beat in the vanilla.

3. Using a wooden spoon, gradually add the flour, baking powder, and salt to the creamed mixture and stir until all the ingredients are well blended. Stir in the nuts. Pour the batter into the prepared pan. Bake the blondies until a toothpick inserted in the center comes out clean, about 35 minutes. Remove the baking pan to a wire rack and let the blondies cool before cutting.

Makes 24 (2 1/2-inch-square) blondies

Chocolate Sandwich Cookies
Try making your own version of this popular store-bought cookie. For a flavor sensation, replace the vanilla in the filling with 1/4 teaspoon peppermint extract.

3/4 cup butter, softened

1 cup sugar

1 egg

1/2 teaspoon vanilla extract

2 cups all-purpose flour

3/4 cup cocoa powder

1 teaspoon baking powder

1/2 teaspoon baking soda

1/2 teaspoon salt

1/4 cup milk

Filling

3 tablespoons butter, softened

1 1/2 cups confectioners' sugar

1 tablespoon milk

1 teaspoon vanilla extract

1. In a large bowl, combine the butter and sugar, and beat until they are well creamed. Add the egg and vanilla, and beat until all the ingredients are well blended.

2. In a small bowl, combine the flour, cocoa powder, baking powder, baking soda, and salt. Add the flour mixture and the milk, alternating, to the creamed mixture, and beat until each addition is well blended.

3. Divide the dough in half. Shape each dough half into a 10 1/2-inch-long roll. Wrap each dough roll in plastic wrap and refrigerate 12 hours or overnight.

4. Preheat the oven to 325°F; lightly grease 2 or more baking sheets. Unwrap 1 dough roll and, using a sharp knife, cut the dough into 1/8-inch-thick slices. Arrange the dough slices on the prepared cookie sheets, spacing them 2 inches apart. Bake until the edges of the cookies are set, 9 to 11 minutes. Transfer the cookies to wire racks to cool completely.

5. Prepare the filling: In a medium bowl, combine all the ingredients and, using an electric mixer, beat until smooth.

6. Using a knife or spatula, spread about 1 teaspoon of the filling on 1 cookie; top with a second cookie. Repeat with the remaining cookies and filling.

Makes 5 dozen sandwich cookies

Coconut Macaroons

Look in health food stores or the natural-foods section of your supermarket for desiccated coconut—it makes for a particularly delectable macaroon, which you can make better and more inexpensively than any manufacturer.

3 egg whites

1 cup sugar

2 1/2 cups desiccated coconut

1 cup macadamia nuts or almonds, finely chopped

1. Preheat the oven to 350°F; lightly grease 2 baking sheets.

2. In a medium bowl with an electric mixer on high, beat the egg whites until soft peaks form. Gradually add the sugar, beating after each addition, until stiff, glossy peaks form. Add the coconut and nuts, and fold until the ingredients are well blended.

3. Using a tablespoon, scoop out a portion of the dough. Using damp hands, roll the dough into a ball and place the ball on the prepared baking sheet. Repeat with the remaining dough.

4. Bake until the macaroons are lightly golden, 20 to 25 minutes. Transfer the macaroons to wire racks to cool completely. Store in an airtight container for 2 to 3 days.

Makes about 35 cookies.

Gingersnaps

The bright tang of ginger infuses each bite of these old-fashioned favorites. The spicy aroma of their baking will warm the kitchen and make you glad you are making your own for less cost and more taste.

3/4 cup shortening

1/2 cup sugar

1/2 cup firmly packed brown sugar

1 egg

1/4 cup molasses

2 cups all-purpose flour

2 teaspoons baking soda

1 1/2 teaspoons ground ginger

1 teaspoon ground cinnamon

1/2 teaspoon salt

Additional granulated sugar

1. Preheat the oven to 350°F; lightly grease 2 or more baking sheets.

2. In a large bowl, combine shortening and sugars and beat until well creamed. Add the egg and molasses, and beat until the ingredients are well blended.

3. In a small bowl, combine the flour, baking soda, ginger, cinnamon, and salt. Gradually add the flour mixture to the creamed mixture, beating after each addition, until the ingredients are well blended.

4. Place the additional granulated sugar in a small bowl. Pinch off a walnut-size portion of the dough. Using your hands, roll the portion into a ball, then roll the ball in the sugar and place it on the prepared baking sheet. Repeat with the remaining dough, spacing the cookies about 2 inches apart.

5. Bake until the cookies are lightly browned and crinkly, 12 to 15 minutes.

Makes 3 to 4 dozen cookies

Baked Goods You Can Make   **131**

Graham Crackers

Store-bought just won't taste the same after you enjoy your home-made graham crackers.

1 cup all-purpose flour

1 1/4 cups whole wheat flour plus additional

5 tablespoons sugar

1 teaspoon baking powder

1/2 teaspoon salt

1/2 teaspoon baking soda

1/4 teaspoon ground cinnamon

3 tablespoons chilled butter or margarine, cut into small pieces

1/4 cup solid vegetable shortening

2 tablespoons honey

1 tablespoon molasses

1/4 cup water

1 teaspoon vanilla extract

1. In a medium bowl, combine the flours, sugar, baking powder, salt, baking soda, and cinnamon. Using a pastry blender or 2 knives, cut in the butter and shortening until the mixture resembles coarse crumbs.

2. In a small bowl, combine the honey, molasses, water, and vanilla, and stir until well blended. Using a fork, gradually add the honey mixture to the flour mixture, tossing the ingredients together until they are well blended. Form the dough into a ball; the mixture may be crumbly, but do not add water. Cover the dough with plastic wrap and place in the refrigerator until the dough is chilled, for several hours.

3. Place the oven rack in the center of the oven and preheat to 350°F; set out 2 large baking sheets. Divide the dough in half and let it stand at room temperature for 15 minutes.

4. Spread wax paper over a work surface. Lightly sprinkle whole wheat flour over the wax paper. Place 1 dough half on the paper, and flatten the dough with a rolling pin. Sprinkle the dough with more whole wheat flour, and cover it with a second piece of wax paper. Using the rolling pin, roll out the dough to form a 7 x 15-inch rectangle; if the dough breaks, pinch the pieces together before continuing to roll.

5. Peel off the top piece of wax paper. Using a fork, mark dotted lines at 1/2- to 1-inch intervals, breaking the dough into 2 1/2-inch squares. Using a spatula, transfer the dough to a baking sheet, placing the squares close together. Repeat with the remaining dough and second baking sheet. Gather the scraps and reroll until all the dough is made into squares.

6. Bake until the crackers are lightly browned on the edges, about 15 minutes. Transfer the crackers to wire racks to cool. Store the graham crackers in an airtight container at room temperature for 1 month, or freeze the crackers in a freezer-safe container for up to 6 months.

Makes 24 to 28 crackers

Sugar Cookies
We include a recipe for frosting, but these sugar cookies are buttery tender and tasty on their own. These are the cookies you bake in holiday shapes with the children, and there is no store-bought equivalent to that.

1 1/2 cups sugar

1 1/2 cups butter, softened

2 eggs

2 tablespoons vanilla extract

4 cups all-purpose flour

1 teaspoon salt

1 teaspoon baking soda

1 teaspoon cream of tartar

Frosting

1 1/2 cups
  confectioners' sugar

3 tablespoons butter,
  softened

1 tablespoon vanilla extract

1 tablespoon milk

Food coloring, as desired

Colored sugar, as desired

1. In a large bowl, combine the sugar and butter, and beat until the mixture is well creamed. Add the eggs and vanilla, and beat until the mixture is smooth

2. In a small bowl, combine the flour, salt, baking soda, and cream of tartar. Add the flour mixture to the cream mixture, and beat until all the ingredients are well blended. Cover the bowl with plastic wrap and place in the refrigerator until the dough is chilled, about 30 minutes.

3. Preheat the oven to 350°F, set out 2 or more baking sheets, and lightly flour a work surface.

4. Turn out the dough onto the prepared work surface. Using a rolling pin, roll the dough out to a 1/4-inch thickness. Using cookie cutters dipped in flour, cut out as many cookies as possible. Carefully transfer the cookies to the ungreased baking sheets. Collect the dough scraps, reroll, and cut out additional cookies until there is no more dough left.

5. Bake until the cookies are just lightly browned on the edges, 10 to 12 minutes. Transfer the cookies to wire racks to cool completely.

6. Prepare the frosting: In a medium bowl, combine the ingredients and beat until creamy. Add a little additional milk as needed to reach the desired consistency. Add a few drops of food coloring as desired. Spread the frosting over the cooled cookies and sprinkle with colored sugar.

Makes 7 dozen cookies

chapter 4

Snacks, Nibbles and Drinks

When it comes to satisfying the afternoon munchies, the recipes in this chapter provide healthful alternatives to greasy fast food and those

bags of salty goodies from the vending machine. You'll find real honest-to-goodness homemade potato chips, pretzels, and French fries, even pizza. And when you taste them, you'll finally realize why these foods became so popular in the first place. You may even spoil yourself and never be able to settle for the commercial versions again. Your own pizza dough, you'll discover, is yeasty and delicious, inviting new and interesting toppings.

You'll also find recipes for those breakfast treats that we often go out for—or buy frozen and pay too much for. Homemade French toast, made quickly with day-old bread, costs about two-thirds less than heated frozen French toast—and with no preservatives or additives, it tastes a lot fresher and sweeter. In addition, there are recipes here that can be real money savers when you entertain. You'll discover how easy it is to make your own finger foods and dips, instead of hiring a caterer or buying out the local deli. These savory treats include an antipasto platter, pâté, and rich cheesy nibbles as well as several delicious easy-to-make dips.

And for that insatiable thirst or caffeine craving, the recipes here provide not only some pleasing summer quenchers but also some delightful and economical substitutes to the pricey products at your local coffee boutique.

fast foods and snacks

Potato Chips
We are a nation of snackers, so we might as well make our own and be sure they are as healthy as we can make them.

Vegetable oil or shortening for deep-fat frying (about 2 quarts)

1 pound Idaho potatoes, peeled

Salt to taste

1. Pour the oil or melt the shortening in a deep-fat fryer or large, heavy saucepan to a depth of 3 inches. Insert a deep-fat thermometer and heat the oil to 375°F.

2. Meanwhile, slice the potatoes into 1/8-inch-thick rounds. As you work, drop the rounds into ice water. When ready to fry, lift the rounds from the water and pat dry on paper towels.

3. Place the potato slices in the fryer in small batches to avoid affecting the temperature of the oil; fry until crisp and golden, 3 to 5 minutes per batch. Using a slotted spoon or fryer basket, transfer the chips to paper towels to drain. Allow the oil to reheat to the correct temperature before frying the next batch.

4. Lightly sprinkle the chips with salt.

Makes 4 Servings

Pretzels
Big, chewy, and oh, so satisfying! You may never get to taste these pretzels— if your family gets to them first!

1 1/2 teaspoons active dry yeast

3/4 cup warm (110°F-115°F) water

1 1/2 teaspoons sugar

3/4 teaspoon salt

1 1/2 cups all-purpose flour

2 tablespoons butter, melted

Coarse or kosher salt

1. In a large mixing bowl, combine the yeast and warm water, and stir to dissolve the yeast. Stir in the sugar and the salt. Add the flour, 1/2 cup at a time, to form a soft dough.

2. On a lightly floured surface, turn out the dough and knead until the dough is soft and elastic, about 5 minutes (the dough will be slightly sticky). Place the dough in a lightly oiled bowl, turning once to coat the top of the dough ball with oil. Cover the bowl and let the dough rise in a warm (70°F to 80°F) place until it is doubled in size, about 1 hour.

3. Preheat the oven to 425°F. Punch down the dough and divide it into 6 equal portions. On a lightly floured surface, roll 1 dough portion into a 14-inch-long rope; twist the rope into a pretzel shape—an oval with overlapping ends in the middle. Place the pretzel on a lightly greased baking sheet. Repeat with the remaining dough portions. Brush each pretzel with the melted butter and sprinkle with salt.

4. Bake the pretzels until they are golden brown, 15 to 20 minutes. Transfer the pretzels to wire racks to cool slightly.

Makes 6 pretzels

French Fries

Who can resist those hot, crisp-on-the-outside, creamy-on-the-inside potato delights! The good news is that you can make them easily yourself, and because you control the frying and can do it right, very little fat will remain on the fries—making them a whole lot healthier than the fast-food variety. Vegetable oil or vegetable shortening will both work for deep-fat frying.

2 quarts (about) vegetable oil or shortening

1 pound Idaho potatoes, peeled

Salt to taste

1. Pour the oil or melt the shortening in a deep-fat fryer or large, heavy saucepan to a depth of 3 inches. Insert a deep-fat thermometer and heat the oil to 375°F.

2. Meanwhile, cut the potatoes into 2 x 1/4 x 1/4-inch strips. As you work, drop the strips into a bowl of ice water. When ready to fry, lift the strips from the water and pat them completely dry on paper towels.

3. Place the potato strips in the fryer in small batches to avoid lowering the temperature of the oil; fry until brown and crisp, about 5 minutes per batch. Using a slotted spoon or fryer basket, transfer the fries to paper towels to drain. Keep warm on a hot tray or in a 200°F oven. Allow the oil in the fryer to reheat to the correct temperature before frying the next batch.

4. Sprinkle the fries with salt and serve hot.

Makes 4 servings

Oven-Baked French Fries

A healthier alternative to the perennial favorite, these fries are loaded with flavor but low in fat and contain no cholesterol.

2 tablespoons cornstarch

4 cups water

2 tablespoon reduced-sodium soy sauce

4 medium potatoes, peeled and cut into strips

4 teaspoons olive oil

1/4 teaspoon salt

1. In a large bowl, combine the cornstarch, water, and soy sauce, and whisk until well blended and smooth. Add the potatoes to the bowl; cover and refrigerate for 1 hour.

2. Preheat the oven to 375°F. Drain the potatoes and place on paper towels to drain; pat dry. In a large bowl, toss the potatoes with the olive oil and sprinkle with the salt. Coat a baking sheet with nonstick cooking spray. Arrange the potato strips in a single layer over the baking sheet. Bake for 15 minutes; turn the strips over and bake for 15 to 20 minutes longer or until the fries are tender and golden brown.

Makes 4 servings

Snacks, Nibbles and Drinks   **137**

Pizza

Making your own pizza is not only thrifty but an easy way to please everyone—let each family member choose the topping for his or her part of the finished pie. It will be easier if you have a baking stone or baking tiles for the bottom of the oven and a baker's paddle to put the pizza in and take it out of the oven. This recipe makes enough dough for a single family-size pizza, or you can divide it into four pieces to make individual pizzas—everyone can top his or her own!

Dough

1/4 cup warm (110°-115°F) water

1 packet (1/4 ounce) active dry yeast

1 1/2 cups unsifted all-purpose flour

1/4 cup water at room temperature

3 tablespoons olive oil

1/2 teaspoon salt

Topping

Cornmeal

1/2 cup tomato sauce or paste

Toppings as desired: shredded mozzarella cheese, sliced pepperoni, sliced mushrooms, bell pepper strips, sautéed Italian sausage, sliced olives, thinly sliced onions, Canadian bacon, pineapple, anchovies

1. In a small bowl, combine the warm water, yeast, and 1/4 cup of the flour. Stir to combine; this will form a sponge. Cover the bowl and let rise for 30 minutes.

2. Stir down the sponge; add the room-temperature water, the remaining 1 1/4 cups flour, olive oil, and salt. On a lightly floured surface, turn out the dough and knead for 10 minutes (or use the dough hook of an electric mixer and knead for 5 minutes). The dough is now ready to use.

3. For use within 1 day, wrap the dough tightly in plastic wrap and store in the refrigerator. Let it sit at room temperature for 1 to 2 hours before using. For future use, wrap the dough tightly in plastic wrap and place in a self-sealing freezer-safe plastic bag; squeeze out all the air before sealing. Freeze for up to 3 months. Thaw in the plastic wrap in the refrigerator for several hours, then bring the dough to room temperature before using.

4. Remove the oven racks and place a baking stone on the bottom of the oven. Preheat the oven to 450°F for about 20 minutes; it should be very hot. Dust a heavy upside-down baking sheet or a wooden baker's paddle with cornmeal. On a lightly floured surface using a lightly floured rolling pin, roll the dough into a 12-inch circle. Flop the dough over the rolling pin and unroll onto the cornmeal-covered baking sheet or paddle. (You can also sprinkle cornmeal on a regular baking pan and cook the pizza on an oven rack, but the crust may be soggier.)

5. Spread the tomato sauce or paste (or a mix of 1/4 cup of each) over the pizza dough, leaving a 1-inch margin. Scatter the toppings as desired.

6. Gently shake the pizza off the baking sheet or paddle onto the baking stone. Bake until the crust is golden brown, about 20 minutes. Serve immediately.

Makes a 12-inch pizza

Chicken Nuggets
For many parents, these morsels are a life- and time-saver, but the cost of buying them can really eat away at your budget.

1 1/2 pounds boneless skinless chicken breasts

2 large eggs

2 tablespoons water

1/2 cup Seasoned Coating Mix (page 44)

2 cups plain dry bread crumbs

1. Cut each chicken breast into 1-inch cubes. In a self-sealing bag, place the coating mix. In a pie plate, whisk together the eggs and water until frothy. In a large, shallow dish, place the bread crumbs.

2. Drop the chicken cubes, a few pieces at a time, into the bag of coating mix; seal and shake until the strips are well coated. Shake off any excess coating mix. Dip each cube into the beaten egg, then into the bread crumbs, gently pressing the crumbs onto the chicken until they stick. Arrange the coated cubes on a large, nonstick baking sheet. Once all the cubes are coated and on the baking sheet, place the sheet in the refrigerator to chill for 30 minutes.

3. Preheat the oven to 400°F. Bake the chicken nuggets until they are golden brown and crisp, about 15 minutes, turning them once or twice during the cooking time. Serve hot or at room temperature.

Makes about 6 servings

breakfast treats

Griddle French Toast
There are two methods for making French toast—this recipe is a quick fix in the morning; the following recipe can be prepared the night before for baking while the coffee brews.

4 eggs

1 cup milk

1 teaspoon vanilla

1/8 teaspoon ground nutmeg

1/8 teaspoon ground cinnamon

8 slices bread

1. In a medium bowl, lightly beat the eggs and the milk. Stir in the vanilla, nutmeg, and cinnamon. Pour the mixture into a large, shallow dish with a flat bottom.

2. Spray a griddle or large, flat skillet with nonstick baking spray. Heat the griddle to hot but not smoking. Dip each piece of bread into the egg mixture, completely soaking it, then place the slice on the griddle. Cook until the bread is brown on one side, flip it over, and grill the other side of the bread. Serve immediately or keep warm briefly in a 200°F oven.

Makes 4 servings

Snacks, Nibbles and Drinks **139**

Baked French Toast
You can make this the night before, then pop it into the oven in the morning.

3 eggs

1 1/2 cups milk

2 tablespoons unsalted butter or margarine, melted

3 tablespoons light or dark brown sugar

1/2 teaspoon finely grated lemon zest

1/8 teaspoon ground nutmeg

1/8 teaspoon ground cinnamon

14 slices French bread (about 3/4-inch thick)

1 tablespoon confectioners' sugar

1. In a medium bowl, beat the eggs, milk, butter, brown sugar, lemon zest, nutmeg, and cinnamon. Pour half the mixture into a greased 17 x 11 1/2 x 3-inch baking dish. Lay the bread slices on top in a single layer, pressing them as close together as possible. Pour the remaining mixture over the bread slices and cover the pan with aluminum foil. Refrigerate overnight or at least 2 hours.

2. Preheat the oven to 350°F. Bake, uncovered, until the toast is puffy and golden brown, 50 to 60 minutes. Sprinkle with the confectioners' sugar. Serve hot with maple or blueberry syrup, honey, or fresh fruit, nuts, and yogurt.

Makes 4 servings

Drop Biscuits
To add extra flavor, stir 1 teaspoon of your favorite herb into the dough.

2 cups Biscuit and Pancake Mix (page 61)

1/2 cup nonfat or 1% milk

1. Preheat the oven to 450°F. In a medium bowl, combine the mix and milk, and stir until just moistened.

2. Coat a baking sheet lightly with nonstick cooking spray. Drop the mixture by heaping tablespoons onto the baking sheet. Bake until lightly browned, 8 to 10 minutes.

Makes about 20 biscuits

Cutout Biscuits
For a savory addition, stir 1/2 cup finely shredded cheddar or grated Parmesan cheese into the dough.

2 cups Biscuit and Pancake Mix (page 61)

1/2 cup nonfat or 1% milk

1. Preheat the oven to 450°F. In a medium bowl, combine the mix and milk, and stir until just moistened.

2. On a lightly floured surface, turn out the dough and gently knead 10 times. Using a floured rolling pin, roll the dough out to a 1/2-inch thickness and, using a 2 1/2-inch floured cutter, cut out biscuit rounds. Reroll the scraps and cut out more biscuit rounds. Place the rounds on an ungreased baking sheet.

3. Bake the biscuits until they are lightly browned, 10 to 12 minutes.

Makes about 10 biscuits

Pancakes

Sliced bananas and strawberries, whole blueberries, or even chocolate chips can be added to pancake batter before cooking for a luscious breakfast treat.

2 cups Biscuit and Pancake Mix (page 61)

2 large eggs, lightly beaten

1 cup nonfat or 1% milk

1. In a large bowl, combine the mix with the eggs and milk. Stir until the batter is just blended. Don't overmix—the batter should be slightly lumpy.

2. Coat a griddle or large, flat skillet with nonstick cooking spray. Over moderate heat, bring the griddle or skillet to hot but not smoking. Spoon the batter onto the griddle, using about 1/4 cup per pancake, and cook until bubbles form across the top, about 2 minutes. Flip the pancakes and cook about 2 minutes more. Serve immediately or keep warm in a 200°F oven.

Makes about 10 to 12 pancakes

Scones

This treat from Scotland is essentially a sweet biscuit. You can add all sorts of things to scones, including currants, chopped dried apricots, or mini chocolate chips—experiment with gusto!

2 cups Biscuit and Pancake Mix (page 61)

1 tablespoon sugar

2 eggs

1/2 cup heavy cream

1 teaspoon vanilla extract

1. Preheat the oven to 425°F. In a large bowl, stir together the mix and sugar.

2. In a medium bowl, beat the eggs with the cream and the vanilla until well blended. Pour the egg mixture into the mix and stir until a soft dough forms.

3. On a lightly floured surface, turn out the dough and gently knead 5 to 6 times. Using a lightly floured rolling pin, roll out the dough to a 1/2-inch thickness and, using a floured 3-inch cutter, cut out scone rounds. Reroll the scraps as necessary (do not knead again).

4. Place the scones 2 inches apart on an ungreased baking sheet and bake until golden brown, 10 to 15 minutes.

Makes about 8 scones

variation:

Scone Wedges: Follow the above recipe through Step 2. Turn the dough onto a lightly greased baking sheet and pat into a large round (like a soda bread loaf). If desired, brush the top with additional cream and sprinkle with additional sugar or a combination of sugar and cinnamon. Using a floured knife, cut the dough round into 8 wedges, but don't separate the pieces. Bake in the preheated oven for about 12 minutes or until golden brown. Carefully separate the scone wedges and serve immediately.

Waffles

A classic breakfast or brunch dish for special occasions, waffles give maple syrup a good name, but also go deliciously with fresh fruit toppings.

2 large eggs, separated

1 3/4 cups Biscuit and Pancake Mix (page 61)

1 cup nonfat or 1% milk

3 tablespoons butter or margarine, melted

1 teaspoon vanilla extract *(optional)*

1. Following the manufacturer's directions, preheat a waffle iron.

2. In a large bowl, lightly beat the egg yolks. Add the mix, milk, melted butter or margarine, and vanilla, if desired; stir until the mixture is just moistened. In a medium bowl, beat the egg whites with an electric mixer until soft peaks form. Using a rubber spatula, gently fold the egg whites into the batter until no white streaks remain.

3. Cook the waffles following the manufacturer's directions.

Makes about 5 (4 x 8-inch) waffles

the origin of waffles

Surprisingly, waffles have been enjoyed for centuries. From the time of the ancient Greeks through the Middle Ages, flat cakes were baked between two metal plates. These were known as obleios, and were popular into the 13th century. At that time, an enterprising craftsman forged decorative plates to resemble honeycombs. The name "waffle" is derived from the Dutch *wafel*, which first appeared in print in 1620. And the Pilgrims, who took refuge in Holland before immigrating to America, introduced waffles to this country. Thomas Jefferson brought a waffle iron back with him after his years in Paris, and within a century, you could buy waffles from vendors on the streets. In the 20th century, an electric waffle iron made these breakfast treats even more popular and easy to make, and in 1953, Frank Dorsa debuted his Eggo waffles—the height of convenience.

appetizing nibbles

Antipasto Platter

The star of the buffet table is an antipasto ("before the meal") platter, which most people have catered by an Italian restaurant for a hefty price. This classic appetizer has colorful marinated vegetables, cheese, and sausage in an eye-catching arrangement. Accentuate the drama by placing contrasting colors or shapes next to each other—straight or diagonal patterns on a rectangular plate or concentric circles on a round or oval platter.

1 pound small new potatoes, quartered

3 tablespoons olive oil

1 teaspoon dried rosemary

1 teaspoon salt

1 large red bell pepper, cut into 1-inch strips

1 large green bell pepper, cut into 1-inch strips

1 medium zucchini, cut into 1-inch slices

1 medium summer squash, cut into 1-inch slices

2 small red onions, cut into thin wedges

8 ounces button mushrooms

2 garlic cloves, minced

8 ounces fresh mozzarella, sliced

1/2 pound prosciutto, sliced

1 cup oil-cured Greek black or green olives

Sprigs of rosemary or thyme

Marinade

3 tablespoons balsamic vinegar

1 tablespoon extra-virgin olive oil

1 tablespoon chopped parsley

1/4 teaspoon dried thyme

2 teaspoons Dijon mustard

1 small garlic clove, minced

1 teaspoon lemon zest

1/2 teaspoon salt

1/4 teaspoon ground pepper

1. Preheat the oven to 450°F. In a large, shallow baking pan, combine the potatoes with the olive oil, rosemary, and salt. Toss to coat the potatoes well. Bake the potatoes, uncovered, 15 minutes.

2. Add the red and green bell peppers, zucchini, summer squash, red onions, and mushrooms to the baking pan. Sprinkle the minced garlic over all the vegetables. Bake, uncovered, until the vegetables are lightly browned and tender, 35 to 45 minutes.

3. Meanwhile, prepare the marinade: In a small bowl, combine the ingredients and whisk until well blended and the marinade is a smooth consistency.

4. Pour the marinade over the cooked vegetables in the baking pan, and stir gently until they are thoroughly coated. Let the vegetables cool to room temperature.

5. Arrange the marinated vegetables, mozzarella cheese, prosciutto, and olives in an attractive pattern on a large serving platter. Garnish with rosemary or thyme.

Makes 6 to 8 servings

...iver Pâté

This smooth, rich paste is easy to make at home for your fanciest occasions. Serve it with toast points or water crackers.

...tter

...ken livers, ...ned, and

1 package (3 ounces) cream cheese, softened to room temperature

1-2 tablespoons brandy

1 teaspoon salt

1/8 teaspoon ground pepper

1/2 teaspoon dried thyme

1/8 teaspoon ground nutmeg

1. In a heavy skillet over moderately high heat, melt the butter. Add the chicken livers and cook until they are lightly browned, 4 to 5 minutes.

2. Transfer the livers to the bowl of a food processor or blender. Pour in the pan drippings, scraping up the browned bits in the skillet and adding them to the bowl. Add the cream cheese, brandy, salt, pepper, thyme, and nutmeg. Whirl until the mixture forms a smooth paste, 20 to 30 seconds. Taste and adjust the seasonings as desired.

3. Using a spatula, scrape the paste into a crock or serving bowl, smoothing the top. Cover the crock and refrigerate overnight.

Makes 4 servings

Ham, Pork, and Veal Terrine

A simple, classic baked terrine is perfect for a picnic in summer or sampling by a roaring fire in winter with pumpernickel or crusty French bread.

1 pound diced cooked ham

1 pound minced pork

1 pound minced veal

1 garlic clove, minced

1 teaspoon dried thyme

1/2 teaspoon dried marjoram

1/4 teaspoon ground nutmeg

1 teaspoon salt

1/8 teaspoon ground pepper

1/2 cup dry white wine

4 small bay leaves

6-8 slices bacon

1/4 pound fresh chicken livers, cleaned, trimmed, and halved

1. Preheat the oven to 300°F. In a large, nonreactive bowl, combine the ham, pork, and veal. Add the garlic, thyme, marjoram, nutmeg or mace, salt, and pepper. Using clean, damp hands, mix the ingredients until they are well blended. Mix in the wine, cover, and refrigerate for 1 hour.

2. On the bottom of a 9 x 5-inch loaf pan, arrange the bay leaves. Line the sides of the pan crosswise with half of the bacon slices, allowing the ends to hang over the edges of the pan. Pack half of the meat mixture into the loaf pan. Arrange the chicken livers along the center of the meat, then add the remaining meat mixture. Cover the meat loaf with the remaining bacon slices, tucking in the ends and folding the ends of the bottom slices over the top of the loaf.

3. Set the loaf pan in a baking dish. Add enough warm water to come halfway up the sides of the loaf pan. Bake the terrine until the loaf pulls away from the sides of the pan and the juices run clear when the loaf is pierced with a clean skewer or toothpick, 2 to 2 1/2 hours.

4. Set the loaf pan on a wire rack and let the terrine cool. Pour off any liquid. When the terrine is completely cool, turn in out onto a plate, cover with plastic wrap, and refrigerate overnight.

Makes about 10 servings

Country Pork Sausages

Needing no casings, these hearty and delicious homemade sausages are ready to star at your next brunch. Because you make them, you know what's in them and you can adjust the seasonings to suit your own tastes.

2 pounds lean pork, trimmed

1/4 pound uncooked pork fat

1 1/2 teaspoons kosher salt

1 1/2 teaspoons dried sage, crumbled

1/2 teaspoon dried thyme, crumbled

1/4 teaspoon crushed black peppercorns

1 small onion, finely chopped

1. Cut the pork and pork fat into 1/2-inch cubes. Place the cubes in a large bowl, cover, and refrigerate until the meat is chilled.

2. In a small bowl, combine the salt, sage, thyme, and peppercorns. Sprinkle the seasoning mixture over the meat, add the onion, and, using your hands, mix all the ingredients together thoroughly.

3. In the bowl of a food processor or blender, place half the sausage mixture. Whirl until the mixture is a medium-coarse consistency. Scrape the pureed mixture to another large bowl, and repeat with the second half of the sausage mixture. Cover the bowl and refrigerate 12 hours or overnight to let the texture firm up and the flavors develop fully.

4. Using damp hands, divide the sausage mixture into 10 to 12 equal portions, and roll each portion into a ball. Form each ball into a small sausage patty. Either cook immediately, or place the sausages on foil, with pieces of foil between any layers. Wrap the entire package of sausages in additional foil or a self-sealing plastic bag. Refrigerate the uncooked sausages for up to 2 days; store in the freezer for up to 3 weeks.

5. To cook: Preheat a large, heavy skillet over moderate heat. Add the sausages and cook, turning often, until they are browned on all sides and cooked through, 13 to 15 minutes. Drain off any fat as it accumulates, and transfer the cooked sausages to paper towels to drain completely before serving.

Makes 10 to 12 sausage patties

Deviled Eggs

Contrary to popular terminology, eggs should never actually be boiled; they should be "hard cooked" as in the recipe below. Although you can cook the eggs up to one day ahead, to avoid contamination they should not be stuffed until shortly before serving.

12 eggs

1/2 cup regular or reduced-fat mayonnaise

4 teaspoons yellow mustard

4 teaspoons white wine vinegar

1 teaspoon salt

1 teaspoon sugar

1 teaspoon ground white pepper

1/2 cup finely chopped celery

Paprika *(optional)*

1. In a large saucepan, place the eggs in a single layer. Add enough cold water to cover the eggs by 1 inch. Set the saucepan over high heat and bring to a full boil; immediately remove the saucepan from the heat, cover, and let stand for 15 minutes.

2. Drain the eggs and crack the wide end of each, then plunge into a large bowl of ice water. To peel, crack each shell all over by tapping it on a countertop. Hold each egg under cold running water while removing the shell. Set each shelled egg on a paper towel to drain as you peel them.

3. Using a small, sharp knife, cut each egg in half lengthwise. Using a small spoon, scoop out the yolks and put them in a sieve set over a medium bowl. Arrange the egg-white halves on a plate and refrigerate. Using the back of a spoon, press the egg yolks through the sieve into the bowl.

4. Add the mayonnaise, mustard, vinegar, salt, sugar, pepper, and celery to the sieved yolks. Using a fork, stir gently to combine all the ingredients well.

5. Using a small spoon or a pastry bag fitted with a number 6 star tip, fill each egg-white half with about 1 tablespoon of the egg-yolk mixture. If desired, sprinkle the eggs with a little paprika before serving.

Makes 12 servings

variations:

Caper-Dill Eggs: To the 1/2 cup mayonnaise, add 3 tablespoons drained and chopped capers, 3 tablespoons minced fresh dill, and 1/2 teaspoon ground white pepper.

Chili Eggs: To the 1/2 cup mayonnaise, add 4 teaspoons chili powder and 1 teaspoon ground cumin.

Curried Eggs: To the 1/2 cup mayonnaise, add 4 teaspoons curry powder and 3 tablespoons chopped chutney.

Spicy Eggs: To the 1/2 cup mayonnaise, add 1/4 cup prepared horseradish and 2 tablespoons minced fresh parsley.

Globe Artichokes in Olive Oil

End of winter, around February or March, is the time to find small, tender baby artichokes in the market. Use these seasoned artichokes in salads, serve them with strong-flavored cheeses, or just enjoy them on their own.

2 pounds (about 6 small) fresh young globe artichokes

1 large lemon, halved

4 cups white wine vinegar

1 tablespoon kosher salt

1 tablespoon dill seed

1 tablespoon black peppercorns

2 bay leaves

2 sprigs fresh herbs such as rosemary, dill, or marjoram

2 garlic cloves, sliced

2 small fresh red chiles

3-4 cups extra-virgin olive oil

1. Using scissors, cut off the outer, tough leaves of each artichoke; trim off the pointed tip of each remaining leaf. Using a sharp knife, cut each artichoke in half lengthwise and rub the cut halves with the lemon halves to prevent browning. Fill a medium bowl with cold water and place the artichoke halves in the bowl with any remaining juice in the lemons. Let stand for 1 hour.

2. In a large, nonreactive saucepan over moderately high heat, combine the vinegar, salt, dill seed, peppercorns, and bay leaves; bring the mixture to a boil.

3. Drain the artichokes and add them to the saucepan; reduce the heat to moderately low and simmer for 10 minutes.

4. Drain the artichokes again and let them dry; discard the cooking liquid. Transfer the artichokes to 2 warm, sterilized, wide-mouthed quart jars, dividing them equally (see Safe Canning with a Hot-Water Bath, page 72). Add 1 herb sprig, half the garlic slices, and 1 chile pepper to each jar. Pour the olive oil over the artichokes, leaving a 1/4-inch space between the top of the oil and the rim of the jar. Wipe the rims, cover, and store in the refrigerator for up to 1 month. The artichokes will be ready for eating in a few days.

Makes 2 quarts

Marinated Goat Cheese

How do you make a good thing even better? In the case of goat cheese, you marinate it yourself in herb-infused olive oil. You can buy marinated goat cheese, but this is easy and made to your own taste.

1 goat cheese (3-4 ounces)

1/4 teaspoon mixed peppercorns (black, white, green)

1/8 teaspoon coriander seed, crushed

Fresh thyme sprigs

Fresh rosemary sprigs

Fresh fennel sprigs

1 bay leaf

1 small red chile pepper

1 garlic clove

1/2 cup olive oil

1. In a warm, sterilized widemouthed jar, center the goat cheese. Tuck the peppercorns, coriander seed, thyme, rosemary and fennel sprigs, bay leaf, chile pepper, and garlic around the cheese.

2. Pour in the olive oil until the top of the oil is 1/4 inch from the rim of the jar. Wipe the rim, cover the jar, and label and date it. Store the cheese in the refrigerator for up to 1 month; the cheese will be ready for eating in 1 week.

Makes 1 cheese

Spinach-Feta Phyllo Triangles

It's true that phyllo, the multilayered Greek dough, is difficult and time-consuming to make. Purchased phyllo dough, however, is a wonderful base for appetizers, desserts, or other dishes that are very expensive to buy finished. Follow the package directions to thaw frozen dough; once opened, the dough will keep in the refrigerator for about 1 week.

4 tablespoons butter or margarine plus 2 teaspoons melted butter or margarine

1 small yellow onion, finely chopped

1 package (10 ounces) frozen chopped spinach, thawed and squeezed dry

1 tablespoon minced fresh dill or 1/4 teaspoon dried dill, crumbled

1/2 cup (4 ounces) crumbled feta cheese

1 egg, lightly beaten

6 sheets frozen phyllo pastry, thawed

1. Preheat the oven to 350°F. In a large skillet over moderate heat, melt the 4 tablespoons butter or margarine. Add the onion and sauté until translucent, 3 to 5 minutes. Add the spinach and cook for 2 minutes longer. Stir in the dill. Transfer the spinach mixture to a large bowl. Add the feta cheese and the egg, and stir until the mixture is well blended.

2. Lay 1 sheet of the phyllo pastry on a work surface and brush lightly with 1 teaspoon of the melted butter. Top with a second sheet of phyllo, brush with butter, repeat with a third sheet of phyllo.

3. Using a sharp knife or pizza cutter, and a ruler if you like, cut the stack of buttered phyllo sheets lengthwise into six 1 3/4-inch-wide strips. Cut the strips in half to make 12 strips. Place 1/2 teaspoon of the spinach-feta mixture at the end of each strip. Fold the end of each strip diagonally over the filling to form a triangle. Continue folding diagonally along the entire strip, alternating directions (like folding a flag), and ending with a triangle. When each triangle is complete, brush the top with some of the butter.

4. Repeat, using the remaining phyllo sheets, butter, and spinach-feta filling to make another 12 triangles.

5. Line a baking sheet with parchment paper. Arrange the filled triangles over the paper-lined sheet, and bake until the triangles are golden brown, about 25 minutes.

Makes 24 triangles

Quesadillas

You can serve a quesadilla as a lunch dish or use a pizza cutter to cut it into small triangles and arrange on a plate with sour cream and guacamole as an appetizer.

4 eight-inch flour tortillas

1 cup (4 ounces) shredded Monterey Jack cheese

1 large red bell pepper, cored, seeded, and cut into 1/4-inch slices

1/4 cup cooked fresh or thawed frozen corn kernels

3 scallions with tops, thinly sliced

1/4 cup chopped fresh cilantro

1/4 cup fresh or prepared salsa

Sour cream, plain yogurt, or guacamole *(optional)*

1. Preheat the oven to 425°F. Place each tortilla on a 12-inch square of foil. Sprinkle each tortilla with the cheese, bell pepper, corn, scallions, cilantro, and salsa, dividing the toppings equally. Moisten the edges of 1 tortilla and fold in half, encasing the toppings; press the edges together. Repeat with the remaining tortillas.

2. Move a folded tortilla so it is centered on the top half of the foil square. Fold in each side edge of the foil over the quesadilla. Fold the bottom half of the foil up and over the quesadilla until the top and bottom foil edges are even; fold the edges together twice to make a packet. Repeat with the remaining quesadillas. Arrange the foil-wrapped quesadillas on a baking sheet.

3. Bake the quesadillas until the cheese melts, about 7 minutes. Remove the baking sheet from the oven, unwrap each quesadilla, and arrange it on a plate or serving platter. If desired, garnish with a dollop of sour cream, plain yogurt, or guacamole.

Makes 4 servings

Zucchini Strips

Because it cooks quickly, zucchini is an ideal choice for batter frying.

2 quarts (about) vegetable oil or shortening for deep-fat frying

1 cup all-purpose flour

1/2 cup cold water or stale beer

1 pound firm, bright green zucchini, cut into 2 x 1/4 x 1/4-inch strips

Balsamic vinegar

1. Pour the oil or melt the shortening in a deep-fat fryer or large, heavy saucepan to a depth of 3 inches. Insert a deep-fat thermometer and heat the oil to 375°F.

2. Meanwhile, in a medium bowl, combine 1/2 cup of the flour and the water or beer. Whisk until the mixture is smooth and well blended. Pour the remaining 1/2 cup of flour into a shallow dish. Working in small batches, dredge the zucchini strips in the flour, shaking off any excess, then toss the coated strips in the batter, separating any that cling together.

3. Place the zucchini strips in the fryer in small batches to avoid affecting the temperature of the oil; fry until brown and crisp, about 5 minutes per batch. Using a slotted spoon or fryer basket, transfer the strips to paper towels to drain. Allow the oil in the fryer to reheat to the correct temperature before frying the next batch.

4. Lightly drizzle the zucchini strips with the balsamic vinegar before serving.

Makes 4 servings

dips

Baba Ghanoush

Much loved in the Middle East, this smoky favorite, available in supermarkets and delis for $4 to $5 for 4 ounces, gets its smoky flavor from charring the eggplant first. You can make this delicious dip yourself and serve it with pita triangles.

1 large (1 1/4 pounds) eggplant

1/4 cup lemon juice

1 tablespoon extra-virgin olive oil

2 garlic cloves, quartered

1/4 cup tahini (sesame paste)

Salt and ground black pepper, to taste

1. Preheat the broiler. Using a sharp fork or skewer, prick the eggplant all over. Place the eggplant in the broiler 6 inches from the heat source. Broil, turning every 5 minutes, until the skin is blackened and the eggplant is soft, about 20 minutes. Remove the eggplant and let stand until it is cool to the touch.

2. Using a sharp knife, remove the peel from the eggplant; discard the peel. Place the eggplant flesh in the bowl of a food processor or blender, cutting as needed to fit. Add the lemon juice, olive oil, garlic, and tahini. Pulse until the mixture is well blended and is a spreadable consistency. Taste and season as desired with the salt and pepper.

3. Scrape the baba ghanoush into a bowl, cover, and refrigerate for at least 2 hours before serving to allow the flavors to develop.

Makes about 2 cups

Guacamole

One of the greatest recipes ever, this creamy blend of avocados, tomato, red onion, and cilantro is a divine dip for chips, crudités, pretzels, and more. It can also be a memorable addition to taco salads, grilled poultry, or fish, and is a must for wraps. At $4 for 4 ounces at the grocery, it pays you to make your own, which also tastes fresher and better.

2 ripe Hass avocados, halved and pitted (reserve 1 pit)

1 medium tomato, cored, seeded, and finely chopped

1/2 cup finely chopped red onion

1/3 cup chopped fresh cilantro

2 tablespoons lime juice

3/4 teaspoon salt

3/4 teaspoon ground cumin *(optional)*

3/4 teaspoon jalapeño pepper sauce *(optional)*

1. Using a spoon, scoop out the avocado flesh into a medium, nonreactive bowl. Using a fork, mash the avocado until it is not quite smooth (there should be small chunks of avocado flesh).

2. Add the tomato, onion, cilantro, and lime juice, and stir with the fork until the ingredients are well blended but the consistency is still slightly rough. If desired, stir in the cumin and jalapeño sauce to add more heat to the guacamole.

3. Spoon the guacamole into a serving bowl and push the reserved pit down into the dip. The pit helps keep the guacamole from turning brown. Serve immediately or cover the bowl with plastic wrap and refrigerate until ready to serve.

Makes 2 1/2 cups

Green Goddess Dip

Making your own is not only easy and cheaper, you can lower the calories and fat of this delectable dip by using low- or nonfat sour cream and low- or nonfat mayonnaise.

1 cup sour cream

1 cup mayonnaise

1 small ripe avocado, peeled, pitted, and cut into chunks

2 large scallions, trimmed and sliced

1/3 cup fresh parsley leaves

2 tablespoons lemon juice

2 teaspoons anchovy paste

1 garlic clove

1 teaspoon dried tarragon, crumbled

1/2 teaspoon ground black pepper

1/4 teaspoon salt

Working in batches if necessary, in the bowl of a food processor or blender, whirl all the ingredients until they are blended and the dip is a smooth consistency, scraping down the bowl sides as needed. Serve with raw vegetables or chips.

Makes 3 1/2 cups

Hummus

Another staple of Middle Eastern cooking, hummus is excellent with pita triangles, crudités, or bagel chips, but it can be used as a spread in sandwiches too. Buying it from delis or specialty stores can cost $1 an ounce or more.

2 cups cooked chickpeas or 1 can (19 ounces) chickpeas, drained and rinsed

1 tablespoon extra-virgin olive oil

2 garlic cloves, quartered

1/2 teaspoon ground cumin

1/4 cup tahini (sesame paste)

1/4-1/2 cup freshly squeezed lemon juice

Salt and freshly ground pepper, to taste

Minced fresh parsley or paprika

1. In the bowl of a food processor or blender, combine the chickpeas, olive oil, garlic, cumin, and tahini. Whirl until the mixture is a rough consistency.

2. With the motor running, slowly pour in the lemon juice a little at a time until the desired consistency is reached. Taste the hummus and season with the salt and pepper. Before serving, sprinkle with fresh parsley or paprika.

Makes 1 1/2 cups

Skordalia

A mouthwatering blend of garlic roasted to nutty perfection, walnuts, and lemon juice, this dip has an unusual base: mashed potatoes. This is a Greek garlic sauce that you might buy in a Greek grocery. Use it with beet salad or as a dip for raw vegetables.

14 unpeeled garlic cloves

5 slices firm-textured white bread, preferably stale

1 1/2 cups mashed potatoes

1/2 cup shelled walnuts

1/4 cup fresh lemon juice

3/4 teaspoon salt

3/4 teaspoon ground black pepper

2/3 cup extra-virgin olive oil

Fresh parsley sprigs or lemon zest *(optional)*

1. Preheat the oven to 350°F. Place the garlic cloves on a large piece of foil. Bring the long edges together and fold under twice; fold each short end over twice to form a packet. Fill a small baking dish with 1/4 inch water and place the foil packet in the baking dish. Bake until the garlic is tender, about 45 minutes. Remove the garlic from the oven and let cool to the touch.

2. Meanwhile, in a large, shallow baking dish, arrange the bread slices in a single layer. Pour in enough water to cover the bread and let stand for 5 to 10 minutes.

3. Gently squeeze the bread to remove most of the water. In the bowl of a food processor or blender, place the bread. Squeeze each clove of garlic to extract the flesh and add it to the bowl; discard the peels. Add the mashed potatoes, walnuts, lemon juice, salt, and pepper. Pulse until the ingredients are just combined. With the motor running, slowly drizzle in the olive oil and continue whirling until the dip is well blended and smooth.

4. Spoon the dip into a serving bowl and, if desired, garnish with parsley sprigs or lemon zest.

Makes about 3 cups

Helpful Hint

Dips Are Not Just for Dipping

So much more than something to plunge crackers, chips, or crudités into, dips are a versatile performer in your culinary productions. Many can be used as condiments, toppings for various dishes, fillings for omelets, or spreads for sandwiches. Experiment!

Tapenade

Not for the faint of palate, this rich spread combines the heady taste of Mediterranean or Greek olives, anchovies, capers, and garlic. Available in more and more specialty departments of supermarkets, it is a pricey treat. Make your own and enjoy it on toasted slices of Italian bread, drizzled with extra-virgin olive oil. Tapenade also makes an exceptional spread for an Italian hard sausage sandwich.

1 cup oil-cured Mediterranean or Greek black olives, pitted

6-8 anchovy fillets

1/4 cup capers, drained

2 garlic cloves, halved

2 teaspoons lemon juice

3-4 tablespoons extra-virgin olive oil

Freshly ground black pepper, to taste

1. In the bowl of a food processor or blender, combine the olives, anchovy fillets, capers, garlic, and lemon juice. Whirl until the mixture is finely chopped.
2. Add 3 tablespoons of the olive oil, pulsing on and off, until the mixture is a spreadable, grainy paste; add additional olive oil as needed to reach the desired consistency. Taste the tapenade and season with the pepper.

Makes about 1 cup

Tzatziki

A creamy cucumber concoction to cool the fires of the spiciest dish, this quintessential Greek dip is a natural in summer, when cucumbers are plentiful. You can buy it in specialty shops, but it is easy to make your own. Serve it with crudités, chips, or pita triangles, as a dressing for Greek salad, or as a side for grilled kabobs or fish.

1 medium cucumber, peeled, sliced lengthwise, and seeded

2 cups plain, nonfat yogurt

1 garlic clove, minced

1 tablespoon minced fresh mint

2 tablespoons olive oil

Kosher salt and freshly ground black pepper, to taste

Additional olive oil

1. Cut the cucumber into small dice and place the pieces between layers of paper towels to dry well.
2. In a medium bowl, combine the yogurt, cucumber pieces, garlic, mint, and olive oil, and stir until all the ingredients are well blended. Taste the tzatziki and season with salt and pepper.
3. Spoon the tzatziki into a serving bowl and drizzle olive oil over the top.

Makes about 2 1/2 cups

cold drinks

Classic Iced Tea
An American original, iced tea made its debut at the St. Louis World's Fair in 1904—in reaction to muggy weather and the need for a cool pick-me-up. Always best when it is freshly made, iced tea is an economical thirst quencher.

1 quart cold water

2 tablespoons loose tea leaves or 6 regular-sized tea bags

Sugar Syrup (opposite) to taste

Lemon wedges or small fresh mint sprigs *(optional)*

1. In a large saucepan or teakettle over high heat, bring 2 cups of the cold water to a full, rolling boil.

2. Rinse a teapot with boiling water and discard the water. Place the tea in the pot and slowly pour the 2 cups of boiling water over the tea, cover the teapot, and let the tea steep for 3 to 5 minutes.

3. Stir the tea once, strain the tea leaves or remove and discard the tea bags. Pour the tea into a large pitcher, add the remaining 2 cups of cold water and sweeten to taste with the sugar syrup.

4. To serve, fill glasses with ice cubes and pour the cold tea over the ice; if desired, garnish each serving with a lemon wedge or sprig of fresh mint.

Makes 4 servings

Cranberry Iced Tea
A fruity twist on the American classic, this red tea is perfect for a special occasion. The fresh tea makes it delicious and economical.

2 cups cold water

4 tablespoons loose tea leaves or 6 regular-sized tea bags

2 cups cranberry juice cocktail

Sugar Syrup (opposite) to taste

Fresh or frozen whole cranberries or lime slices *(optional)*

1. In a large saucepan or teakettle over high heat, bring 2 cups of the cold water to a full, rolling boil.

2. Rinse a teapot with boiling water and discard the water. Place the tea in the pot and slowly pour the 2 cups of boiling water over the tea, cover the teapot, and let the tea steep for 3 to 5 minutes.

3. Stir the tea once, strain the tea leaves or remove and discard the tea bags. Pour the tea into a large pitcher, add the 2 cups of cranberry cocktail, and sweeten to taste with the sugar syrup.

4. To serve, fill glasses with ice cubes and pour the cold tea over the ice; if desired, garnish each serving with a few whole cranberries or a lime wedge.

Makes 4 servings

Helpful Hint

Make the Perfect Sweetener: Sugar Syrup

Keep a jar of this sugar syrup in your refrigerator to sweeten iced teas and coffees. Because the sugar is already dissolved, you'll get the ideal sweetness without any graininess added. Here's how to make it:

In a small saucepan over moderate heat, combine 2 cups sugar and 2 1/2 cups water. Cook, stirring frequently, until the mixture boils and the sugar has dissolved completely. Remove the saucepan from the heat, cover, and let stand for 1 to 2 minutes to allow the steam to dissolve any unmelted crystals on the sides of the saucepan. Pour the cooled syrup into a 1-quart jar, cover tightly, and store in the refrigerator.

Makes 3 cups

Raspberry Iced Tea

Raspberries are sweet-tart, so they are a good foil for tea in this popular variation of homemade iced tea, a rare treat for a reasonable price.

4 quarts water

1 1/2 cups sugar

1 package (12 ounces) frozen unsweetened raspberries

10 individual tea bags

1/4 cup lemon juice

1. In a large, nonreactive saucepan or Dutch oven over moderately high heat, combine the water and sugar; bring the mixture to a boil. Remove the saucepan from the heat and stir until the sugar has completely dissolved.
2. Add the raspberries, tea bags, and lemon juice to the saucepan. Cover the saucepan and steep the tea for 3 minutes. Set a large sieve over a heatproof pitcher. Pour the tea mixture through, straining and discarding the solids. Place the pitcher in the refrigerator until the tea is completely chilled. Serve the tea over ice.

Makes 4 quarts (about 16 servings)

Frosty Caramel Cappuccino

A gourmet-style coffee concoction that you can whip up for pennies without leaving home or standing in line.

1 cup half-and-half

1 cup 2% milk

3 tablespoons plus 2 teaspoons caramel sauce

2 teaspoons instant espresso powder

8-10 ice cubes

4 tablespoons whipped cream (fresh or canned)

1. In the bowl of a food processor or blender, combine the half-and-half, milk, 3 tablespoons of the caramel sauce, espresso powder, and ice cubes. Cover and whirl until the mixture is smooth.
2. Pour the cappuccino into two chilled glasses. Top with whipped cream and drizzle with the remaining 2 teaspoons of caramel sauce. Serve immediately.

Makes 2 servings

Iced Coffee Slush

Ah, iced coffee without diluted flavor—because you freeze the coffee itself. This chilly delight will take the heat out of summer without making a hole in your purse or requiring a trip to a coffee emporium.

3 cups hot strong brewed coffee

1/2-1 cup sugar

4 cups milk

2 cups half-and-half

1 1/2 teaspoons vanilla extract

1. In a freezer-safe bowl, combine the coffee and the amount of sugar desired. Stir until the sugar has completely dissolved. Cover the bowl and refrigerate until the coffee mixture is thoroughly chilled. Stir in the milk, half-and-half, and vanilla. Re-cover the bowl and place in the freezer until the coffee mixture is solid.

2. Transfer the bowl from the freezer to the refrigerator several hours before serving. Using a mallet, break up the coffee mixture. Transfer the mixture to the bowl of a food processor or blender, and whirl until the coffee mixture is slushy. Serve immediately.

Makes 2 1/4 quarts (about 12 servings)

Lemonade Syrup

Whip up a batch of this syrup whenever you see lemons on sale, then keep it on hand to make the best homemade lemonade you've ever tasted—in a flash! This makes a much less expensive and better-tasting lemonade than anything you can buy.

3 cups sugar

1 cup boiling water

3 cups fresh lemon juice (about 16 lemons)

2 tablespoons grated lemon zest

1. In a 1 1/2-quart, heatproof container, place the sugar. Add the boiling water, stirring constantly, until the sugar has completely dissolved. Let the sugar mixture stand until it is cool.

2. Add the lemon juice and zest, and stir until all the ingredients are well blended. Cover the container, and store in the refrigerator for up to 1 week.

Makes 5 1/2 cups syrup

variation:

Limeade Syrup: Substitute 3 cups fresh lime juice and 2 tablespoons grated lime zest and proceed as above.

Lemonade

Tart, sweet, and oh, so refreshing, this syrup-based lemonade is quick, delicious, and cheap.

1/4-1/3 cups Lemonade Syrup (opposite)

3/4 cup cold water

Ice cubes

Lemon wedge or fresh mint sprig *(optional)*

In a tall glass, combine the desired amount of syrup and cold water, and stir until they are well blended. Add ice cubes and, if desired, garnish with a lemon wedge or mint sprig.

Makes 1 glass

Lemon Squash

This is the fizzy version of economical lemonade, loaded with bright lemon taste and bubbles.

4 strips (3 inches each) lemon zest, cut into thin slices

1 cup Lemonade Syrup (opposite)

3 cups chilled club soda, seltzer, or sparkling water

Lemon slices or small fresh mint sprigs *(optional)*

1. In a 2-quart pitcher, combine the lemon zest, and syrup to taste. Stir until all the ingredients are well blended.

2. Just before serving, pour in the club soda, seltzer, or sparkling water; stir gently to blend the ingredients. Fill glasses with ice cubes, pour the lemon squash over the ice, and if desired, garnish each serving with a lemon wedge or small sprig of fresh mint.

Makes 4 servings

variation:

Lime Squash: Prepare as directed above, substituting lime zest and Limeade Syrup (opposite) for the lemon zest and Lemonade Syrup or to taste. Garnish with lime wedges or fresh strawberries.

Orange Blossom

For a nonalcoholic version of this festive drink, substitute sparkling water for the gin and add it after shaking the orange juice and sugar. This is a popular cocktail that is easy and inexpensive to make at home.

1 large piece orange zest

1 teaspoon superfine sugar plus small saucer for dipping

2 ounces gin

1 ounce orange juice

1 orange slice

1. Rub the orange zest around the rim of a chilled martini glass. Dip the rim into the saucer of sugar.

2. In a cocktail shaker, combine the remaining superfine sugar, gin, and orange juice. Cover and shake until the mixture is well blended. Place a strainer over the glass, and pour the mixture through. Garnish with the orange slice.

Makes 1 serving

Berry Orange Shrub

Wonderfully fizzy and full of taste, this drink can be its own dessert, a soda fountain kind of concoction that would cost a fortune at an ice-cream store.

1 quart cran-raspberry juice

1/2 cup sugar

Zest of 1 orange, cut into thin strips

2/3 cup orange juice

4 cups club soda

Orange sherbet

1. In a medium, nonreactive saucepan over low heat, combine the cran-raspberry juice, sugar, and orange zest; slowly bring the mixture to a boil. Reduce the heat and simmer, stirring occasionally, 10 minutes. Remove the saucepan from the heat.

2. Stir in the orange juice and let the mixture cool to room temperature. Pour the mixture into a 2-quart pitcher, cover, and refrigerate until the mixture is chilled.

3. Before serving, remove and discard the orange zest. Pour 1/2 cup of the shrub mixture into punch cups or glasses, add 1/2 cup of the club soda, and top with a scoop of the orange sherbet.

Makes 8 servings

Sparkling Fruit Bowl

Beautifully colored, with essence of raspberries, strawberries, and oranges, this is a spicy, fizzy fruit punch for parties.

1 package (10 ounces) dry-pack frozen raspberries

1 package (10 ounces) dry-pack frozen strawberries

6 cups water

1 1/2 cups sugar

10 whole cloves

1/2 teaspoon ground cardamom

6 strips (3 x 1/2 inch each) orange zest

1 vanilla bean, split

2 cups orange juice

2 cups club soda

1. In a large, nonreactive saucepan or Dutch oven over moderately high heat, combine the first eight ingredients and bring to a boil. Reduce the heat to moderately low and simmer, uncovered, stirring occasionally, about 10 minutes.

2. Place a large sieve over a large pitcher. Pour the berry mixture through, straining out the solids; do not press the solids. Let the berry mixture cool to room temperature. Stir in the orange juice.

3. Just before serving, stir in the club soda. Serve the punch over ice.

Makes 10 servings

Fruit Juice Spritzer

Here is a lovely, light, and fizzy cooler that you can customize to suit your taste and your menu—try cran-raspberry juice, pineapple juice, Concord grape juice, pink grapefruit juice, tangerine juice, or anything else that tickles your fancy. If you don't use wine, you can blend 2 juices instead. A wonderful start to a summer party that won't break the bank.

3 cups chilled dry white wine or fruit juice of choice

1 1/2 cups chilled fruit juice of choice or complementary juice

1 1/2 cups chilled carbonated beverage (soda, seltzer, or ginger ale)

Fresh mint leaves or citrus wedges *(optional)*

1. In a 2-quart pitcher, combine the wine or fruit juice, additional or complementary juice, and carbonated beverage.
2. Serve straight or over ice cubes. If desired, garnish individual glasses with mint leaves or citrus wedges.

Makes 8 servings

Bloody Mary Mix

Keep this mix ready to go in the refrigerator and you can whip up fantastic Bloody Marys in a flash—or just serve it over ice as a spicy tomato juice treat. You can buy Bloody Mary mixes, but the homemade version is livelier and much, much cheaper.

2 1/4 cups tomato juice

1/4 cup lemon juice

1/2 teaspoon black pepper

1/2 teaspoon salt

1/2 teaspoon celery seed

1 teaspoon Worcestershire sauce

1/2 teaspoon hot red pepper sauce

In a 1-quart jar with a tight-fitting lid, combine the ingredients. Cover the jar tightly and shake to blend well. Refrigerate for up to 1 week; shake well before using.

Makes 2 1/2 cups

Bloody Mary

An eye-opener for breakfast or brunch, this spicy drink stands up to even the most flavorful foods. Homemade with your own mix, it's a treat without being a threat to your pocketbook.

1/2 cup cracked ice

2 1/2 ounces vodka

5 ounces Bloody Mary Mix (above)

1 celery stalk

In a tall glass, place the cracked ice. Pour the vodka and Bloody Mary mix over the ice. Garnish with the celery stalk.

Makes 1 serving

Snacks, Nibbles and Drinks   **159**

Sangria

The color of garnets, full of fruit, and always welcome regardless of the season, sangria is an easy-to-make, delightful wine punch that is served at Spanish restaurants. Homemade is fresher-tasting and a lot less pricey.

2 oranges, sliced

2 lemons, sliced

2 cinnamon sticks

3/4 cup brandy

1 bottle (750 milliliters) red wine of choice

1 bottle (750 milliliters) sparkling cider, chilled

Ice cubes

1. In a large punch bowl or glass pitcher, combine the first four ingredients.
2. Pour the red wine and sparkling cider over the fruit mixture, gently stirring until the punch is well blended. Just before serving, add ice cubes as desired.

Makes about 1 3/4 quarts

hot drinks

Caffe Latte

Why pay $3 to $5 for a cup of special coffee when you can so easily make it yourself—and at a fraction of the price?

1 1/2 cups skim or low-fat milk

2/3 cup freshly brewed espresso

Ground cinnamon or sweetened cocoa powder *(optional)*

1. In a small saucepan over low heat, cook the milk just until tiny bubbles begin to form around the edges of the saucepan, 10 to 15 minutes; do not let the milk come to a boil. If a skin forms on the surface of the milk, remove it with a spoon and discard.
2. Divide the espresso between two 8-ounce cups. Add 1/3 cup of the hot milk to each cup.
3. Using an electric mixer or wire whisk, beat the remaining hot milk until it is frothy. Spoon the milk froth into the coffee cups, dividing it equally. If desired, sprinkle a little cinnamon or sweetened cocoa powder over the foam before serving.

Makes 2 servings

variations:

Chocolate Mint Latte: Prepare as directed above, adding a finely chopped 1/2-ounce chocolate-covered peppermint patty to each cup along with the espresso.

Caffe Latte à l'Orange: Prepare as directed above, adding 1 tablespoon Grand Marnier or other orange-flavored liqueur to each cup along with the espresso.

Cappuccino Mix

Love the convenience of instant special coffees to keep at the office or to brew a fast cup for an afternoon pick-me-up? Make your own and you'll save a bundle.

1 cup instant coffee creamer

1 cup instant chocolate milk powder

2/3 cup instant coffee crystals or espresso powder

1/2 cup sugar

1/2 teaspoon ground cinnamon

1/4 teaspoon ground nutmeg

In an airtight container, combine the ingredients. Cover and shake until they are well blended. For 1 cup of instant cappuccino, place 3 tablespoons in a mug or coffee cup. Add 6 ounces boiling water and stir until the mix has completely dissolved.

Makes 3 cups dry mix

Cocoa

On a cold, blustery day, there's nothing quite like cocoa made the good, old-fashioned way.

2 tablespoons sugar

1 tablespoon unsweetened cocoa

1/4 cup water

3/4 cup 1% milk

Miniature marshmallows *(optional)*

1 cinnamon stick, 4 inches long *(optional)*

1. In a small saucepan, combine the sugar and cocoa. Add the water. Over moderate heat, bring the mixture to a boil, stirring constantly until the sugar has dissolved. Lower the heat and simmer 2 minutes, whisking constantly.

2. Stir in the milk. Increase the heat to moderate and cook until the cocoa is heated through; do not allow the mixture to boil.

3. To serve, pour the cocoa into a mug or cup. If desired, top with several marshmallows and use the cinnamon stick as a stirrer.

Makes 1 serving

Hot Chocolate Viennese

Chocolate, coffee, and hot milk—triple yum! This is a coffeehouse treat that you can enjoy for much less at home.

1/3 cup unsweetened cocoa powder

1/3 cup sugar

2 1/2 cups milk

1 1/2 cups freshly brewed strong coffee or espresso

1. In a medium saucepan, combine the cocoa powder and sugar, pressing out any lumps. Stirring constantly, pour in enough of the milk to moisten the dry mixture, about 1/2 cup; whisk in the coffee and the remaining 2 cups milk.

2. Over moderately low heat, cook, stirring occasionally, until the mixture steams but does not boil, 8 to 10 minutes. Pour the hot chocolate into mugs or coffee cups and serve.

Makes 4 servings

Chai
The spicy, creamy tea drink that has shot up in popularity, chai is a lovely afternoon soother or stimulator. It is convenient and economical to make your own.

2 cups water

2 individual tea bags

1 cinnamon stick

6 cardamom pods, crushed

1 whole clove

1/4 teaspoon ground ginger

2 1/2 cups milk

1/3 cup sugar

Whipped cream, ground cinnamon, and cinnamon sticks *(optional)*

1. In a small saucepan over moderately high heat, combine the first six ingredients; bring the mixture to a boil. Reduce the heat, cover the saucepan, and simmer 5 minutes.

2. Stir in the milk. Increase the heat and return the mixture to a boil; boil 1 minute. Remove the saucepan from the heat, place a sieve over a warmed teapot, and pour the mixture through; discard the solids. Add the sugar and stir until dissolved.

3. To serve, pour into 4 mugs or cups and, if desired, top with a dollop of whipped cream, sprinkle with cinnamon, and tuck a cinnamon stick along the side.

Makes 4 servings

Hot Spiced Tea
Give extra zest to hot tea with this inviting spice mixture—it will make your kitchen smell fabulous while it warms you to your toes. No mix can match this hot spiced tea at any price. It's the perfect drink for a winter afternoon.

2 cinnamon sticks

6-12 whole allspice

1 teaspoon whole cloves

12 cups water

12 individual tea bags

1 cup packed brown sugar

1 cup cranberry juice

1/2 cup orange juice

1/4 cup lemon juice

1. Cut a 4-inch square of double-thickness cheesecloth. Combine the cinnamon sticks, allspice, and cloves in the center. Bring together the corners of the cheesecloth to form a bag; secure with a piece of kitchen string.

2. In a large, nonreactive saucepan or Dutch oven over high heat, combine the water and the spice bag; bring the water to a boil. Remove the saucepan from the heat and add the tea bags; cover the saucepan and let the tea steep 5 minutes. Remove and discard the tea bags and spice bag.

3. Stir in the brown sugar until it has completely dissolved. Add the juices, stirring until the ingredients are well blended. Return the saucepan to low heat, and gently heat the spiced tea through.

Makes 3 quarts

Hot Mulled Cider

One of the best warm-me-ups, this cider has some surprises in its spice. You don't have to go to a ski lodge to enjoy it.

4 cups apple cider
10 whole cloves
10 black peppercorns
4 strips (3 x 1/2 inch each) orange zest
1 cinnamon stick, cracked
1 vanilla bean, split

1. In a medium saucepan over moderate heat, combine the ingredients; bring the mixture to a boil. Remove the saucepan from the heat and let stand 30 minutes to steep. Remove and discard the spices.

2. Return the saucepan to low heat and slowly cook until the cider begins to steam. Ladle the cider into mugs, wait 3 to 5 minutes, and serve.

Makes 4 servings

Holiday Wassail

A traditional holiday punch served warm or cool, this wassail is festive for parties and quite economical when you make it up fresh.

1 quart hot brewed tea
1 cup sugar
1 bottle (32 ounces) cranberry juice
1 bottle (32 ounces) apple juice
2 cups orange juice
3/4 cup lemon juice
24 whole cloves
2 cinnamon sticks
1 orange, sliced

1. In a large, nonreactive saucepan or Dutch oven over moderately high heat, combine the hot tea and sugar, stirring until the sugar has dissolved. Add the juices, 12 cloves, and the cinnamon sticks. Bring the mixture to a boil and boil 2 minutes.

2. Remove the saucepan from the heat. Pour the wassail into a heatproof punch bowl. Insert the remaining cloves into the orange slices and float them on the wassail as garnish. Serve the wassail warm or cooled to room temperature.

Makes 12 to 16 servings

chapter 5

Make Your Own Take-Out Food

Have you ever noticed how the prepared-food sections are taking up more and more of your supermarket? That's because we are quickly becoming a nation

addicted to ready-made dishes, and the supermarket is only responding to the demand. The only problem is that those eat-as-they-are or pop-in-the-microwave dishes carry an enormous price premium for the little extra convenience that they provide. This chapter is dedicated to the true convenience foods that you can make fresh in your own kitchen. Most make minimal demands on your time. And many are foods that you can make ahead—or leave simmering in a slow cooker—for a meal later.

On the following pages, you'll find tasty meat, egg, and bean dishes and satisfying savory pies of the type that you might pick up at the deli counter or from the freezer case. A homemade turkey potpie is great way to use up leftover Thanksgiving meat. You'll also find a nice selection of delicious easy-to-make pasta dishes. (For a special treat, try them with fresh pastas from Chapter 1.) There are hearty soups that will fill your kitchen with good smells, delight your family, and use up leftovers. And unlike the bland canned versions, homemade soups can provide more flavor with less salt. There is also a wide selection of deli-style salads that you can make without a lot of fuss, ranging from sides like coleslaw to main dishes like Cobb salad—and, unlike some deli salads, they will never have too much mayonnaise.

deli-style dishes

Savory Meat Mix

The base for many a dish, this can be made with either ground beef or ground turkey. Two recipes that use this mix follow, and there is another at the beginning of the Pasta Dishes section (page 175).

2 tablespoons olive or canola oil

2 medium onions, chopped

2 garlic cloves, minced

1 celery stalk, chopped

2 carrots, chopped

2 1/2 pounds lean ground beef or turkey

2 teaspoons dried basil

1 teaspoon dried oregano

1 teaspoon salt

1/2 teaspoon ground pepper

Large pinch sugar

1 tablespoon Worcestershire sauce

1 can (14 1/2 ounces) diced tomatoes in sauce

1. In a large, deep skillet or Dutch oven over moderate heat, heat the oil. Add the onions, garlic, celery, and carrots to the skillet and sauté until softened, about 5 minutes, stirring occasionally. Crumble the beef or turkey into the skillet, breaking it up with a large spoon; cook, stirring occasionally, until the meat is no longer pink. Drain off as much fat as possible

2. Add the basil, oregano, salt, pepper, sugar, Worcestershire sauce, and the tomatoes with their sauce; stir until all the ingredients are well mixed. Reduce the heat, cover the skillet, and simmer 20 to 25 minutes.

3. Remove the skillet from the heat and let the mixture cool completely. Spoon off any visible fat and then divide the mixture among 3 to 4 (1 pint) self-sealing, freezer-safe plastic bags. Seal, label, date, and freeze. The mix will keep up to three months in the freezer.

Makes 3 1/2 to 4 pints of mix

Skillet Noodle Supper

This is a favorite family dinner that takes only 20 minutes or so to bring to the table.

1 package (10 ounces) frozen mixed vegetables

1 pint Savory Meat Mix (above), thawed

2 cups cooked egg noodles

1 can (8 ounces) tomato sauce

1 cup shredded cheddar cheese

1. Cook the vegetables following the package directions on the stovetop or in the microwave.

2. In a large skillet over moderate heat, combine the vegetables, meat mix, noodles, and tomato sauce, and gently stir to combine the ingredients. Cover the skillet and cook about 10 minutes, stirring occasionally; add a few sprinkles of water as needed to prevent the mixture from sticking.

3. Sprinkle the cheese over the top of the mixture in the skillet; do *not* stir. Cover the skillet again and heat just until the cheese is melted. Serve from the skillet.

Makes 4 to 6 servings

Chili Con Carne
This will be the fastest chili you ever put together with fresh meat.

1 pint Savory Meat Mix
(opposite), thawed

2 teaspoons to 1 tablespoon
or more chili powder

1 teaspoon cumin

2 cans (15 1/2 ounces each)
red kidney beans, drained
and rinsed

Hot pepper sauce, to taste

Hot cooked rice, tortilla
chips, shredded cheddar or
Monterey Jack cheese,
sour cream or plain yogurt
(optional)

1. In a medium saucepan, combine the meat mix, chili powder,
cumin, and kidney beans. Cover and cook over moderately
high heat until the chili is heated through, about 10 minutes.
Add hot pepper sauce to the desired level of spiciness.

2. Serve the chili over rice or with tortilla chips, if desired.
Sprinkle a little cheese over each serving or top with a dollop of
sour cream or yogurt, if desired.

Makes 6 servings

Tomato Herb Tarts
*Frozen puff pastry makes these individual tarts easy to whip up
in a jiffy. Tarts you buy at the grocery are never as fresh-tasting or
as inexpensive.*

1 sheet frozen puff pastry

1/2 cup finely shredded
cheddar cheese

2 tablespoons grated
Parmesan cheese

1 pound ripe tomatoes,
peeled and sliced

2 tablespoons minced
fresh parsley

2 tablespoons minced
fresh basil

2 tablespoons minced
fresh thyme

1 tablespoon virgin olive oil

Freshly ground black pepper

1. Preheat the oven to 400°F.

2. Place the sheet of puff pastry on a work surface. Using a large,
round cutter, cut 4 to 6 circles from the pastry. Place the pastry
circles on a baking sheet, and bake until puffed and golden brown,
10 to 12 minutes. Remove baking sheet; do not turn off the oven.

3. Sprinkle some of the cheddar and Parmesan cheeses, divided
equally, over each pastry circle, leaving a small border around
the edges. Layer tomato slices, divided equally, on top of the
cheese on each circle. Sprinkle some of the parsley, basil, and
thyme over the tomatoes. Drizzle each circle with some of the
olive oil, then sprinkle pepper as desired.

4. Return the baking sheet to the oven and bake until the cheeses
are completely melted, about 5 minutes. Turn off the oven and
let the tarts stand for a few minutes before removing them
from the oven. Serve immediately or at room temperature.

Makes 4 to 6 tarts

Make Your Own Take-Out Food   **167**

Texas-Style Barbecue Sauce

Meant for spareribs (see Barbecued Spareribs, below), this tangy taste of the Lone Star State can also be used on chicken. Again, you can adjust ingredients to your own taste and save money at the same time.

1 1/2 cups ketchup

1 cup cider vinegar

2/3 cup peanut or safflower oil

1/3 cup Worcestershire sauce

1/2 cup firmly packed dark brown sugar

3 tablespoons mild yellow mustard

1/2 teaspoon freshly ground black pepper

Juice of 1 large lemon

1-2 fresh red chile peppers, minced *(optional)*; wear gloves when handling; they burn

In a medium saucepan over moderate heat, combine the ingredients. Bring the mixture to a boil; immediately reduce the heat to low, cover, and simmer until the sugar has completely dissolved and the sauce has thickened slightly, about 20 minutes.

Makes about 3 cups

One-Minute Substitute

If You Run Out of Brown Sugar

If a recipe calls for 1/2 cup brown sugar and you don't have any on hand, stir 1 tablespoon molasses into 1/2 cup regular granulated sugar.

Barbecued Spareribs

You get the best results when you make your own ribs; you also save money.

5 pounds pork spareribs in slab of 6-8 ribs

3 cups Texas-Style Barbecue Sauce (above)

1. Place the ribs in a large self-sealing bag, glass baking dish, or nonreactive bowl. Pour 2 cups of the barbecue sauce over the ribs, cover, and refrigerate overnight.

2. On a covered kettle-style grill, following the manufacturer's directions, prepare the coals for the indirect method of cooking. Add the ribs and cook 1 to 1 1/2 hours, basting frequently with the marinating sauce. In a small saucepan over low heat, warm the reserved barbecue sauce and serve on the side with the ribs.

Makes 6 servings

Baked Beans

A staple of the Puritans, baked beans solved a religious dilemma for these hardworking people. The tenets of their faith forbade working on the Sabbath, including cooking. Beans could be baked slowly on Saturday, then reheated or served cold for Sunday breakfast or lunch.

1 pound dried peas or navy beans, sorted and rinsed

1/3 cup molasses

1 teaspoon dry mustard

1 teaspoon salt

1/2 teaspoon ground black pepper

1/4 pound salt pork

1 medium onion, peeled

1. Place the beans in a 4-quart Dutch oven and add enough water to cover plus 2 inches. Bring the water to a boil and boil 2 minutes. Remove the saucepan from the heat, cover, and let stand 1 hour.

2. Add more water to cover the beans and return the pan to the heat. Bring to a boil, reduce the heat, and simmer until the beans are tender, about 1 hour, adding more water as necessary to keep the beans covered. Drain the beans, reserving the cooking liquid.

3. Place the drained beans in a 2-quart bean pot or casserole dish. In a bowl, combine the molasses, mustard, salt, and pepper, and pour the mixture over the beans. Cut the pork into 1/2-inch slices up to but not through the rind. Add the pork and the onion to the bean mixture, pressing them down until they are buried. If needed, add the reserved cooking liquid until the beans are completely covered.

4. Place the bean pot or casserole in a 250°F oven and cook, covered, 5 hours, adding additional reserved cooking liquid or water to prevent the bean mixture from drying out. Remove the cover for the last hour of cooking time.

Makes 6 servings

Helpful Hint

Always Have Beans on Hand

Any pantry should be well stocked with a variety of beans. Dried will cost less but must be soaked before cooking. Canned beans don't always hold their shape and are often very high in salt. Always rinse canned beans under cold running water to reduce the sodium content by as much as 40 percent before using them. Many bean dishes are simple, delicious, filling, and very nutritious, but the best ones are made at home.

Classic Refried Beans

One of the mainstays of Mexican cooking, refried beans can be used in dips, tacos, tortillas, burritos—and just about any other dish too! They are traditionally served as a side dish with rice and are very mild in flavor, although you can spice them up easily.

1 pound (approximately 2 cups) dried pinto or red kidney beans, sorted and rinsed

1 large yellow onion, quartered

3 garlic cloves, unpeeled

1/2 teaspoon ground cumin

3-4 drops hot pepper sauce

1/4 cup vegetable shortening, lard, vegetable oil, or bacon drippings

Chopped fresh cilantro leaves, shredded cheddar or Monterey Jack cheese, or homemade Spicy Tomato Salsa (page 31)

1. In a 4-quart Dutch oven, place the beans and the onion, and add water to cover plus 2 inches. Bring the mixture to a boil and boil 2 minutes. Remove the saucepan from the heat, cover, and let stand for 1 hour. Drain the beans and discard the soaking liquid.

2. Return the beans to the saucepan and add enough water to cover. Add the onion and garlic, and bring the mixture to a boil. Reduce the heat to low, cover the saucepan, and simmer until the beans are very tender, about 2 hours, adding water as needed to keep the beans covered. Remove and discard the onion and garlic.

3. Using a potato masher, mash the beans to the desired consistency. Stir in the cumin and hot pepper sauce.

4. To fry: In a heavy skillet over moderate heat, melt the shortening or lard, or heat the oil or bacon drippings. Add the mashed bean mixture and cook, stirring occasionally, until the mixture forms a smooth paste and begins to pull away from the sides of the pan, 5 to 10 minutes. Continue to cook, scraping the mixture from the bottom of the pan and turning it over until the bean mixture is thick and has a creamy texture.

5. Serve the beans with sprinkled cilantro, cheese, or salsa on top.

Makes about 9 servings

Refritos Rapido

Still want homemade refried beans but crunched for time? That's not a problem with this recipe.

2 tablespoons vegetable oil

1 large onion, chopped

2 cans (15 ounces each) pinto, kidney, or black beans, drained and rinsed

1 teaspoon ground cumin

Salt, to taste

Chili powder, to taste *(optional)*

1. In a large, heavy skillet over moderate heat, heat the oil. Add the onion and sauté until just softened. Add the beans, cumin, salt, and chili powder, if desired. Cook, stirring, until heated through, 5 to 10 minutes. Remove the pan from the heat.

2. Using a potato masher, mash the bean mixture to the desired consistency. Return the skillet to moderate heat and cook until the mixture is thick and creamy in texture, about 15 minutes.

Makes 4 to 6 servings

Basic Rice Pilaf

Once you learn how to make pilaf (seasoned rice or other grains), you have the base for an almost infinite variety of dishes. Try using brown rice, wild rice, bulgur, or barley instead of white rice; stir in cooked meats, seafood, or vegetables; add a handful of toasted pine nuts, pistachios, or pecans—you've got a gourmet meal in minutes.

1 tablespoon virgin olive oil or vegetable oil

1 cup long-grain white rice

2 cups Chicken Stock (page 50)

1. In a medium, heavy saucepan over moderately high heat, heat the oil until it is very hot. Add the rice; cook, stirring constantly, until the oil is absorbed and the rice is translucent, about 5 minutes.

2. Add the stock, raise the heat to high, and bring the mixture to a boil. Stir once, lower the heat, and cover the pan tightly. Simmer until the broth is absorbed and the rice is tender, 15 to 20 minutes.

Makes about 3 cups (4 to 6 servings)

Curry with Rice

Flavorful, economical, and easy to prepare, curry is one of the most adaptable recipes you'll ever make. It's a fast and easy way to use up leftovers. Meat, poultry, seafood, vegetables—just about anything can be used to make curry.

1/4 cup all-purpose flour

1/2 teaspoon salt

1/4 teaspoon ground black pepper

1 1/2 pounds skinless, boneless chicken or turkey breasts or thighs, or lamb, cut into 1-inch cubes

3 tablespoons vegetable oil

1 large yellow onion, chopped

2 garlic cloves, minced

2 small celery stalks, chopped

1-2 tablespoons Curry Powder (page 46)

1 3/4 cups Chicken Stock (page 50) or reduced-sodium canned chicken broth

4 medium carrots, peeled and cut crosswise into 1/2-inch slices

2 cups cauliflower florets (about 1/2 head medium cauliflower)

1 1/4 cups basmati rice

1. In a large, self-sealing bag, combine the flour, salt, and pepper. Working in small batches, add the chicken, turkey, or lamb to the bag, seal, and shake to coat the meat with the flour mixture.

2. In a large skillet with a tight-fitting lid over moderately high heat, heat the oil 1 minute. Divide the meat into 2 batches. Add one batch to the skillet and sauté until lightly brown, about 5 minutes. Remove the meat to paper towels to drain. Repeat with the remaining meat.

3. In the drippings left in the skillet, sauté the onion, garlic, and celery, stirring occasionally, until soft, about 5 minutes. Add the curry powder, stock, carrots, cauliflower, and reserved meat to the skillet. Reduce the heat to low, cover, and simmer until the cauliflower is just tender, 20 to 30 minutes.

4. Meanwhile, in a large saucepan over high heat, cook the basmati rice following the package directions. Transfer the cooked rice to a large, heated serving bowl. Spoon the curry over the rice and serve immediately.

Makes 4 servings

Make Your Own Take-Out Food **171**

main-dish pies

Classic Chicken Potpie
Frozen chicken potpies can't hold a candle to this lovely dish that uses up the leftovers from Sunday's roast chicken. The pie can be made ahead and frozen, tightly covered with freezer-safe foil, for up to 3 months.

1 cup chopped peeled potatoes

1 cup sliced carrots

1/3 cup chopped yellow onion

1/2 cup butter or margarine

1/2 cup all-purpose flour

3/4 teaspoon salt

1/2 teaspoon dried thyme, crumbled

1/2 teaspoon ground black pepper

1 1/2 cups Chicken Stock (page 50) or reduced-sodium canned chicken broth

3/4 cup milk

2 cups chopped cooked chicken

1/2 cup frozen peas

1/2 cup frozen corn

Basic Double Crust Pie Pastry (page 123)

1. In a large saucepan, combine the potatoes and carrots, and cover them with water. Bring the water to a boil; reduce the heat, cover, and simmer until crisp-tender, 8 to 10 minutes. Drain the potato-carrot mixture and set aside.

2. In a large skillet over moderate heat, sauté the onion in the butter or margarine until tender. Stir in the flour, salt, thyme, and pepper until well blended. Gradually add the stock and milk, stirring constantly. Bring the mixture to a boil; cook, stirring constantly, until the mixture is thickened. Stir in the chicken, peas, corn, and the potato-carrot mixture. Remove the skillet from the heat.

3. Preheat the oven to 425°F. Line a 9-inch pie plate with the bottom piecrust; trim the edges of the dough even with the edges of the plate. Spoon the pie filling into the bottom crust. Roll out the remaining piecrust; cut slits or decorative vents in the crust. Carefully transfer the crust to cover the pie filling. Fold the top edges of the pastry over and under the bottom crust edges; pinch the edges together to seal. If desired, form a decorative edge around the piecrust with a fork or with your fingers.

4. Bake the pie until the crust is golden brown, 35 to 40 minutes. Let the pie stand for 15 minutes before serving. To bake a frozen pie, cover the edges with pieces of foil and set on a baking sheet. Bake in a 425°F oven 30 minutes. Reduce the heat to 350°F and bake for an additional 70 to 80 minutes or until the crust is golden brown.

Makes 6 servings

Turkey Potpie

This is a very tasty way to use up Thanksgiving leftovers. If you don't want turkey again so soon, make the pie and freeze it in freezer-safe foil for up to 3 months.

1/4 cup chopped yellow onion

1 tablespoon butter or margarine

2 cans (10 3/4 ounces each) condensed cream soup (chicken, mushroom, asparagus)

3 cups chopped cooked turkey

1 large unpeeled tart apple, chopped

1/3 cup golden raisins

1 teaspoon lemon juice

1/4 teaspoon ground nutmeg

Basic Single Crust Pie Pastry (page 124)

1. In a large saucepan over moderate heat, sauté the onion in the butter or margarine until tender. Stir in the soup, turkey, apple, raisins, lemon juice, and nutmeg. Spoon the turkey mixture into an ungreased 11 x 7 x 2-inch baking dish.

2. Preheat the oven to 425°F. On a lightly floured surface with a lightly floured rolling pin, roll out the pastry to fit the top of the baking dish. Carefully transfer the crust to cover the pie filling; press the edges of the crust to the edges of the baking dish to seal, and flute the crust edges. Cut slits in the piecrust.

3. Bake the pie until the crust is golden brown and the filling is bubbly, 25 to 30 minutes.

Makes 6 servings

Savory Beef Pie

A toothsome array of spices makes this potpie a spicy and delicious meal.

2 medium potatoes, peeled and quartered

1 pound lean ground beef

3/4 cup sliced scallions

1 large carrot, finely chopped

1 garlic clove, minced

1/2 teaspoon dried thyme

1/2 teaspoon dried sage

1/2 teaspoon salt

1/2 teaspoon black pepper

1/4 teaspoon celery salt

Pinch ground cinnamon

1/4 cup minced fresh parsley

1/4 cup prepared chili sauce

Basic Double Crust Pie Pastry (page 123)

1 tablespoon Dijon mustard

1 tablespoon milk

1. In a large saucepan over high heat, cook the potatoes in boiling water until tender. Drain and mash the potatoes; set aside.

2. Meanwhile, in a large skillet over moderate heat, brown the beef until no pink remains; drain the liquid from the skillet and return the pan to the heat. Stir in the scallions, carrot, garlic, thyme, sage, salt, pepper, celery salt, and cinnamon. Simmer the mixture 4 to 5 minutes. Stir in the reserved potatoes, parsley, and chili sauce. Remove the skillet from the heat.

3. Preheat the oven to 450°F. Line a 9-inch pie plate with the bottom piecrust; trim the edges of the dough even with the edges of the plate. Brush the bottom crust with the mustard. Spoon the pie filling into the bottom crust. Roll out the remaining piecrust; cut slits or decorative vents in the crust. Carefully transfer the crust to cover the pie filling. Fold the top edges of the pastry over and under the bottom crust edges; pinch the edges together to seal. If desired, form a decorative edge around the piecrust. Brush the top of the crust with the milk.

4. Bake the pie 10 minutes. Reduce the heat to 350°F and bake until the crust is golden brown, about 25 minutes.

Makes 6 servings

Quiche Lorraine

One of the best-known quiches, this yummy custard pie takes its name from the Lorraine region in France. It was originally made just from cream and bacon, but now includes cheese—either a good Gruyère or other Swiss cheese. You can buy a quiche from the grocery for $8 to $12, but it will never taste as good as your own fresh out of the oven.

Basic Single Crust Pie
  Pastry (page 124)

6 slices good-quality bacon,
  diced and lightly fried

1 1/2 cups shredded
  Gruyère cheese

1 1/2 cups light cream

4 eggs

1/2 teaspoon salt

Small pinch ground
  red pepper

Small pinch ground nutmeg

1. Preheat the oven to 400°F.

2. Line a 9-inch pie plate with the prepared pastry and flute the edges. Place in the refrigerator and chill 15 to 20 minutes. Fill the crust with pie weights or beans and bake 10 minutes. Remove the piecrust and remove the weights or beans; do not turn off the oven.

3. Sprinkle the cooked bacon over the bottom of the piecrust. Sprinkle the cheese over the bacon. In a large bowl, combine the cream, eggs, salt, red pepper, and nutmeg. Beat until the ingredients are well blended. Carefully pour the cream mixture over the cheese and bacon in the piecrust.

4. Bake, uncovered, 15 minutes at 400°F; reduce the heat to 350°F and bake until the filling is set in the center, 15 to 20 minutes longer. Let the quiche stand for 10 minutes before serving to allow the custard to set.

Makes 6 main course or 12 appetizer servings

One-Minute Substitute

If You Run Out of Cream

Heavy cream: If a recipe calls for 1 cup heavy cream (not for whipping) and you don't have any on hand, combine 3/4 cup milk with 1/3 cup melted butter in a 2-cup measure and whisk until the mixture is well blended.

Light cream: If a recipe calls for 1 cup light cream and you don't have any on hand, combine 3/4 cup milk with 1/4 cup melted butter in a 2-cup measure and whisk until the mixture is well blended.

Half-and-half: If a recipe calls for 1 cup half-and-half and you don't have any on hand, combine 7/8 cup milk with 1 1/2 tablespoons melted butter in a 2-cup measure and whisk until the mixture is well blended.

Spinach-Wild Rice Pie
Here is a quiche-like pie that will delight everyone in the family, including the vegetarians.

Basic Single Crust Pie
Pastry (page 124)

3 eggs

1 cup half-and-half

1 cup cooked wild rice

1 cup (4 ounces) shredded
Swiss cheese

1/2 cup frozen chopped
spinach, thawed

1. Preheat the oven to 450°F. Line a 9-inch pie plate with the piecrust; turn under the edges of the dough and, if desired, form a decorative edge around the piecrust. Line the piecrust with a double thickness of foil. Bake the piecrust 5 minutes; remove the foil and bake 5 minutes more. Remove the piecrust from the oven and reduce the heat to 350°F.

2. In a large bowl, beat the eggs with the half-and-half. Add the wild rice, cheese, and spinach, and blend well. Pour the egg mixture into the piecrust. Cover the edges of the crust with pieces of foil and bake until a knife inserted near the center comes out clean, 30 to 35 minutes.

Makes 6 to 8 servings

pasta dishes

Spaghetti with Meat Sauce
Please a crowd in 30 minutes with this classic spaghetti recipe.

1 pint Savory Meat Mix
(page 166), thawed

1 can (14 1/2 ounces) diced
tomatoes in sauce

1 can (6 ounces)
tomato paste

1/2 cup dry red wine or
water

2 teaspoons dried basil,
crumbled

1 teaspoon dried oregano,
crumbled

1 package (16 ounces)
spaghetti or homemade
spaghetti

Freshly grated
Parmesan cheese

1. In a large saucepan or Dutch oven over moderate heat, combine the meat mix, tomatoes, tomato paste, wine or water, basil, and oregano. Stir until all the ingredients are well mixed. Bring the mixture to a boil over high heat, reduce the heat to low, and simmer, uncovered, stirring occasionally, about 30 minutes.

2. Meanwhile, cook the spaghetti following the package directions, and drain. Serve the spaghetti topped with the meat sauce and sprinkle Parmesan cheese over each serving.

Makes 6 to 8 servings

Spaghetti with Speedy Tomato Sauce *Never buy bottled sauce again!*

This tasty sauce can be whipped up in no time at all, and all the ingredients can be kept on hand for whenever you wish. During the summer, when fresh tomatoes are plentiful and cheap, substitute 3 pounds fresh, chopped tomatoes for the canned.

1 can (16 ounces) Italian plum tomatoes

1 can (6 ounces) tomato paste

1 teaspoon dried oregano, crumbled

1 teaspoon dried basil, crumbled

1 teaspoon sugar

1/2 teaspoon salt

1/4 teaspoon black pepper

1 batch homemade spaghetti or 1 pound purchased spaghetti

Freshly grated Parmesan cheese

1. In a large saucepan over moderate heat, combine the tomatoes and their liquid, tomato paste, oregano, basil, sugar, salt, and black pepper. Bring the mixture to a boil; reduce the heat and simmer, uncovered, 15 to 20 minutes.

2. Meanwhile, cook the homemade spaghetti until just tender or follow the package directions for commercial spaghetti.

3. Serve the sauce over the spaghetti and sprinkle with Parmesan cheese.

Makes about 6 servings

Pasta with Fresh Tomato Sauce *Incomparable on its own, bursting with the*

flavor of fresh, vine-ripened tomatoes, this classic also forms the base for many other pasta sauces. Overripe tomatoes can be used in this recipe, and impart an especially intense flavor. If tomatoes are not in season, you can substitute canned Italian plum tomatoes. But fresh tomato sauce just can't come in a can.

3 pounds ripe fresh tomatoes or 1 can (35 ounces) Italian plum tomatoes, chopped

2 tablespoons olive oil

3 garlic cloves

2 tablespoons tomato paste

2-3 tablespoons chopped fresh basil leaves, or 2 teaspoons dried basil, crumbled

1 teaspoon sugar

1 teaspoon salt

1/4 teaspoon freshly ground black pepper

1 pound hot cooked pasta, such as spaghetti, vermicelli, or linguine

Freshly grated Parmesan cheese

1. If using fresh tomatoes, in a large, nonreactive saucepan or Dutch oven, bring water to a boil. Place the tomatoes in the boiling water for 1 minute to loosen the skins, then transfer the tomatoes to a bowl of cold water. Using a slotted spoon, transfer the tomatoes to paper towels to drain. Peel the tomatoes, cut them in half, and squeeze gently to expel the seeds; chop the tomato flesh.

2. In a large, heavy, nonreactive saucepan or Dutch oven over moderate heat, heat the oil. Add the garlic and cook 1 minute. Add the tomatoes, tomato paste, basil, and sugar, and bring the mixture to a boil, stirring constantly. Reduce the heat to low and simmer until the sauce thickens, 12 to 15 minutes.

3. Stir in the salt and pepper. Serve over the hot cooked pasta with a little Parmesan cheese sprinkled over all.

Makes 3 cups

Pasta Puttanesca
Put some spice in your tomato sauce with some real Mediterranean ingredients!

2 tablespoons olive oil

2 garlic cloves, minced

1 cup halved, pitted, large black Greek olives

1/4 cup drained capers

8 chopped anchovies

1/8-1/4 teaspoon crushed red pepper flakes

3 cups Fresh Tomato Sauce (opposite)

1 pound hot cooked pasta

1. In a large skillet over moderately low heat, heat the oil. Add the garlic and sauté, stirring occasionally, until soft, about 2 minutes. Add the olives, capers, anchovies, red pepper flakes to desired spiciness, and tomato sauce.

2. Increase the heat to moderately high. Simmer the sauce, uncovered, 15 minutes, stirring often. Serve over the hot cooked pasta.

Makes 6 servings

One-Minute Substitute

If You Run Out of Tomato Sauce

If a recipe calls for 2 cups tomato sauce and you don't have any on hand, combine 3/4 cup tomato paste and 1 cup water in a 2-cup measure and whisk until the mixture is well blended.

Fettuccine Alfredo
The king of cream sauces, Alfredo has a rich flavor that is entirely dependent on the quality of the cheese, so indulge in the best. You will still pay less than restaurant prices. There is no comparison with prepared Alfredo sauces.

3 tablespoons butter

1/3 cup minced shallots

1 1/4 cups heavy cream

1 cup light cream

1/2 teaspoon salt

Pinch ground nutmeg

3/4 cup grated Parmesan cheese

1 pound fettuccine, cooked and drained

1. In a medium saucepan over moderate heat, melt the butter. Add the shallots and sauté until they are soft, 3 to 4 minutes. Stir in the heavy cream, light cream, salt, and nutmeg. Increase the heat to high and bring the mixture to a boil, stirring constantly. Reduce the heat to low and simmer, uncovered, until the sauce thickens, 4 to 5 minutes. Stir in the Parmesan cheese.

2. Place the fettuccine in a large, heated serving bowl and pour the Alfredo sauce over the pasta. Toss before serving.

Makes 4 servings

Penne with Four-Cheese Sauce

If you love cheese, this sauce is for you— not one, but four intriguing cheeses combine to make a superb pasta sauce. You can buy frozen lasagna made with this sauce for a considerable price that doesn't hold a candle to this savory homemade version.

3 tablespoons butter

2 garlic cloves, minced

2 tablespoons all-purpose flour

1 cup light cream

1 cup milk

1 cup shredded fontina cheese

1 cup shredded provolone cheese

1/2 cup shredded mozzarella cheese

1/2 cup grated Parmesan cheese

1/2 teaspoon salt

1/4 teaspoon ground pepper

1 pound hot cooked penne or other pasta, such as farfalle or rotini

1. In a large, nonstick saucepan over moderate heat, melt the butter. Add the garlic and cook until soft, about 2 minutes. Stir in the flour and cook until bubbly, about 1 minute. Remove the saucepan from the heat and gradually whisk in the cream and milk. Return the saucepan to moderate heat and cook, stirring often, until the sauce just boils and thickens, 3 to 5 minutes.

2. Add the cheeses, salt, and pepper, and cook, stirring constantly, until the cheeses melt and the sauce is smooth, 1 to 2 minutes.

3. Transfer the pasta to a heated serving bowl. Pour the cheese sauce over all and toss to mix well.

Makes 4 servings

Linguine with Red Clam Sauce

The secret is to sauté the garlic in the oil very gently so you don't burn the garlic and make it bitter. Properly cooked garlic has a light, nutty flavor that really brings out the flavor of the clams. No canned or frozen sauce can match the freshly made one.

1/4 cup olive oil

1 large yellow onion

3 garlic cloves, minced

1 can (28 ounces) Italian plum tomatoes, drained and chopped

1 teaspoon dried basil, crumbled

1/2 teaspoon sugar

1/4 teaspoon dried thyme

1/4 teaspoon salt

1/8-1/4 teaspoon crushed red pepper flakes

2 cans (6 1/2 ounces each) minced clams, with liquid

1/4 cup minced flat-leaf parsley

1 pound linguine, cooked and drained

1. In a large skillet over moderate heat, heat the oil for 1 minute. Add the onion and garlic, and sauté until soft, about 5 minutes. Add the tomatoes, basil, sugar, thyme, salt, and red pepper flakes. Simmer, uncovered, 3 minutes.

2. Stir in the clams and their liquid, and cook 1 minute more. Stir in the parsley.

3. Place the linguine in a large, hot serving bowl. Pour the clam sauce over the pasta, and toss well.

Makes 4 servings

Linguine with White Clam Sauce *One of the best pasta sauces, and so easy and inexpensive to make from scratch!*

1/4 cup olive oil

1 large yellow onion

3 garlic cloves, minced

1/3 cup dry vermouth or dry white wine

1/2 teaspoon salt

1/8-1/4 teaspoon crushed red pepper flakes

2 cans (6 1/2 ounces each) minced clams, with their liquid

1/4 cup minced flat-leaf parsley

1 pound linguine, cooked and drained

1. In a large skillet over moderate heat, heat the oil for 1 minute. Add the onion and garlic, and sauté until soft, about 5 minutes. Add the vermouth or wine, salt, and red pepper flakes. Simmer, uncovered, 3 minutes.

2. Stir in the clams and their liquid, and cook 1 minute more. Stir in the parsley.

3. Place the linguine in a large, hot serving bowl. Pour the clam sauce over the pasta, and toss well.

Makes 4 servings

Pasta with Classic Basil Pesto *It pays to use extra-virgin olive oil in this sauce, because it is not cooked. The intense flavor of the oil marries beautifully with the basil, garlic, and Parmesan cheese. Homemade is fresher and much tastier than any packaged pesto sauce.*

6 1/2 cups (about 2 bunches) firmly packed fresh basil

2 garlic cloves

1/4 cup extra-virgin olive oil

2 tablespoons butter, softened

1/2 cup grated Parmesan cheese

3/4 cup pine nuts

1/2 teaspoon grated lemon zest

1 teaspoon salt

1/4 teaspoon freshly ground pepper

1 pound hot cooked pasta

1. Pack the basil along with the garlic into the bowl of a food processor or blender. Whirl at high speed until all the leaves are pureed, about 2 minutes, scraping down the sides of the bowl as needed. With the motor still running, pour in the oil in a slow, steady stream.

2. Add the butter, cheese, pine nuts, lemon zest, salt, and pepper. Puree, scraping down the sides of the bowl 2 or 3 times, until the mixture forms a paste, about 3 minutes. Add a tablespoon or two of water if the mixture seems too stiff.

3. While the pasta is still very hot, add the pesto, about 1/2 cup at a time, tossing thoroughly after each addition to evenly distribute the sauce in the pasta; if the pesto is too sticky, add 1 tablespoon hot water to thin it slightly.

Makes 1 1/2 cups or 4 servings

Pesto Is More Than Green Basil Sauce

Pestare means "to pound" in Italian, and that is the technique used to make this simple, classic sauce. Most people are familiar with the green sauce made from pulverized basil leaves, but not all pestos are made from basil—they're not even all green. The technique is what makes it pesto.

Pasta with Mushroom Pesto *An earthy variation on the theme that would be quite costly if you had to buy it.*

2 tablespoons butter

1 garlic clove, minced

10 ounces fresh mushrooms, thinly sliced

2 tablespoons butter, softened

2 tablespoons snipped chives or scallion tops

1/2 cup grated Parmesan cheese

3/4 teaspoon salt

1/4 teaspoon freshly ground black pepper

1 pound hot cooked pasta

1. In a large skillet over moderately high heat, melt the butter. Add the garlic and mushrooms, and sauté until golden, 2 to 3 minutes.

2. Transfer the mushroom mixture to the bowl of a food processor or blender. Add the butter, chives or scallions, cheese, salt, and pepper. Whirl until the mixture is a smooth puree.

3. While the pasta is still very hot, add the mushroom pesto, about 1/2 cup at a time, tossing thoroughly after each addition to evenly distribute the sauce in the pasta; if the pesto is too sticky, add 1 tablespoon of hot water to thin it slightly.

Makes 3/4 cup or 4 servings

Pasta with Sun-Dried Tomato Pesto *Intense tomato flavors are enhanced by walnuts in another pesto that is always better when it is freshly made.*

1 cup tightly packed fresh basil leaves

1/2 cup sun-dried tomatoes in oil, undrained

1/4 cup chopped walnuts, raw or lightly toasted

1 small red chile pepper, seeded and chopped *(optional)*; wear gloves when handling; they burn

1/2 cup olive oil

1/3 cup freshly grated Parmesan cheese

1 pound hot cooked pasta

1. Pack the basil into the bowl of a food processor or blender. Whirl at high speed until all the leaves are pureed, about 2 minutes, scraping down the sides of the bowl as needed. Add the tomatoes with their liquid, walnuts, and if using, red chile pepper. Whirl again to puree all the ingredients. With the motor still running, pour in the oil in a slow, steady stream.

2. Scrape the tomato-basil mixture into a large bowl. Fold in the cheese until it is incorporated.

3. While the pasta is still very hot, add the pesto, about 1/2 cup at a time, tossing thoroughly after each addition to evenly distribute the sauce in the pasta; if the pesto is too sticky, add 1 tablespoon of hot water to thin it slightly.

Makes about 1 cup or 4 servings

Ravioli *You can fill these tasty morsels with just about anything you like plus a soft cheese of some kind, such as the ricotta used below.*

1 batch pasta dough

Prosciutto-Ricotta Filling

2 teaspoons olive oil

1 ounce prosciutto, coarsely chopped

3 garlic cloves, minced

1 cup part-skim ricotta cheese

1/2 cup grated Parmesan cheese

1 egg yolk

1/2 cup minced fresh basil

1/2 teaspoon salt

1/4 teaspoon black pepper

Tomato Sauce

2 teaspoons olive oil

1 small yellow onion, chopped

2 garlic cloves, minced

1 can (28 ounces) Italian plum tomatoes, chopped with their juice

1/2 teaspoon salt

Freshly grated or shaved Parmesan cheese

1. Prepare the pasta dough. Cover the dough and let sit for 1 hour.

2. Meanwhile, prepare the prosciutto-ricotta filling: In a large nonstick skillet over moderate heat, heat the oil for 1 minute. Add the prosciutto and garlic and cook until the garlic is soft, about 2 minutes. Transfer the prosciutto mixture to a medium bowl and let cool to room temperature. Add the ricotta and Parmesan cheeses, egg yolk, basil, salt, and pepper, and stir gently to blend; set aside the prosciutto-ricotta filling.

3. Divide the dough into 2 equal portions. Re-cover 1 portion. On a lightly floured surface, roll out the second portion into a 9 x 12-inch rectangle, about 1/16-inch thick. Using a sharp knife or pastry wheel, cut the rectangle into 4 strips 3 inches wide and 9 inches long.

4. On 2 of the dough strips, drop 3 equal mounds of the filling, spacing the mounds about 1 inch apart and leaving a 1/2-inch margin all around the edges of the strip. Using a pastry brush, brush the margins around each mound with water. Carefully place 1 of the remaining dough strips on top of 1 mound-covered strip; repeat. Firmly press the dough along the margins and around each mound to seal the strips firmly. Slice each strip crosswise into 3 ravioli. Repeat with the remaining portion of the dough.

5. Prepare the tomato sauce: In a large, nonstick skillet over moderate heat, heat the oil for 1 minute. Add the onion and sauté, stirring occasionally, until soft, about 5 minutes. Add the garlic and cook 2 minutes more. Add the tomatoes and their juice, and the salt; bring the mixture to a boil over moderate heat; reduce the heat to a bubbling simmer, and cook, uncovered, stirring often, until the sauce thickens slightly, about 10 minutes.

6. Meanwhile, in a large pot of boiling water, cook the ravioli until firm-tender, about 6 minutes. Drain well, divide among 4 heated serving plates, and top with some of the tomato sauce. Serve with Parmesan cheese.

Makes 12 ravioli, about 4 servings

Lasagna

Homemade lasagna is a wonderfully welcoming dish that is better than anything you can buy. And you can make it with just the ingredients you like best. Homemade pasta offers a subtle base to the other ingredients.

1 batch homemade pasta or
1 pound lasagna noodles,
cooked until almost tender
and drained

1/2 cup grated
Parmesan cheese

1 cup shredded
mozzarella cheese

Sauce

2 cans (28 ounces each)
Italian plum tomatoes,
undrained

1 medium yellow onion,
finely chopped

4 garlic cloves, minced

1/4 cup chopped fresh basil

1/2 teaspoon dried thyme,
crumbled

1/2 teaspoon salt

1/2 teaspoon ground
black pepper

2 tablespoons all-purpose
flour mixed with 1/4 cup
cold water

Sausage Filling

1 tablespoon butter or
olive oil

1 medium yellow onion,
finely chopped

4 garlic cloves, minced

1 pound bulk Italian sausage,
mild or spicy as desired

2 tablespoons butter or
olive oil

10 ounces mushrooms,
coarsely chopped

1. Prepare the sauce: In a large Dutch oven over moderately high heat, combine the tomatoes and their juice, the onion, garlic, basil, thyme, salt, and pepper; bring the mixture to a boil. Reduce the heat to moderately low, and simmer, uncovered, stirring occasionally to break up the tomatoes, 15 minutes. Slowly whisk in the flour-water paste and simmer, stirring constantly, until the sauce thickens, about 2 minutes.

2. Prepare the sausage filling: In a large skillet over high heat, melt 1 tablespoon butter or heat the oil. Add the onion and garlic, and sauté until the onion is golden, about 3 minutes. Add the sausage and cook, stirring occasionally to break up any lumps, until no pink remains, about 10 minutes. Transfer the sausage mixture to a large bowl.

3. In the same skillet over high heat, melt 2 tablespoons butter or heat the oil. Add the mushrooms and cook until light brown, about 5 minutes. Add the mushrooms to the sausage mixture along with 4 cups of the sauce.

4. Cover the bottom of an ungreased 9 x 13-inch baking dish with 1/2 of the remaining sauce. Top with a single layer of slightly overlapping lasagna noodles, 3 cups of the sausage filling, and 1/4 cup of the Parmesan cheese. Repeat the layers, beginning with the noodles. Scatter the mozzarella cheese over the top of the lasagna.

5. Cover the dish with foil, shiny side down, set the dish on a baking sheet, and bake until bubbly, 45 to 55 minutes. Let the lasagna stand for 10 minutes before serving.

Makes 6 servings

soups

Beef Barley Soup

The culinary use of barley can be traced back to the Stone Age. Pearl barley is the type most often used for soups—it is polished and the bran has been removed. Homemade beef barley soup is filling and delicious, a bargain all around.

1 tablespoon butter

1/2 cup chopped carrot

1/2 cup chopped celery

1/2 cup chopped onion

4 cups Beef Stock (page 49) or reduced-sodium canned beef broth

4 cups water

2 cups chopped cooked roast beef

1 can (14 1/2 ounces) diced tomatoes, undrained

1 cup quick-cooking barley

1 1/2 teaspoons salt

1/2 teaspoon dried basil, crumbled

1/2 teaspoon dried oregano, crumbled

1/2 teaspoon ground pepper

1/2 cup frozen peas

1. In a large saucepan or Dutch oven over moderate heat, melt the butter. Add the carrot, celery, and onion, and sauté until the vegetables are tender, about 5 minutes.

2. Add the stock, water, roast beef, tomatoes and their liquid, barley, salt, basil, oregano, and pepper; bring the mixture to a boil. Reduce the heat, cover the saucepan, and simmer for 20 minutes, stirring occasionally. Stir in the peas. Simmer, uncovered, 5 minutes longer.

Makes 8 servings

Helpful Hint

Make the Most of Soup

One of the all-time, soul-satisfying comfort foods, homemade soup is easy to make, nutritious and very tasty to eat, and usually extremely economical. It is a wonderful way to use up leftovers, from vegetable peelings to pot roast. Best of all, it is a filling meal you can make in a single pot. Add a tossed green salad and crusty bread or rolls, and you're ready to eat!

Black Bean Soup

Southwestern flavor fills every bowl of this stick-to-your-ribs favorite. Black beans are loaded with fiber, are a good source of iron, and contain lots of B vitamins. Homemade black bean soup can feed a crowd for practically pennies. There is no canned or dried equivalent.

1 pound dried black beans, sorted and rinsed

Water, as needed to cover

8 thick slices bacon

2 large yellow onions, chopped

2 celery stalks, chopped

2 medium carrots, chopped

2 garlic cloves, minced

2 bay leaves

1 teaspoon dried thyme, crumbled

8 cups water

1/2 teaspoon hot red pepper sauce

1/4 cup chopped fresh cilantro

2 tablespoons lemon juice

Sour cream or plain yogurt *(optional)*

8 fresh cilantro sprigs *(optional)*

1. Place the black beans in a 5-quart, heavy saucepan or Dutch oven; add enough cold water to cover the beans. Over high heat, bring the mixture to a boil; cook 2 minutes. Remove the saucepan from the heat, cover, and let the beans stand for 1 hour. Drain the beans and discard the cooking liquid; set aside the beans.

2. Using sharp kitchen shears, stack the bacon slices and cut them crosswise into 1/2-inch strips. (Place the bacon in the freezer for 1/2 hour before cutting.) Return the saucepan to moderately high heat and add the bacon strips. Cook, stirring occasionally, until the bacon is crisp, 5 to 8 minutes. Using a slotted spoon, transfer the bacon to paper towels to drain.

3. In the bacon drippings in the saucepan over moderate heat, sauté the onions, celery, carrots, garlic, bay leaves, and thyme, stirring occasionally, until the vegetables are tender, 8 to 10 minutes.

4. Add the water and reserved beans, and return to a boil; reduce the heat to moderately low, cover the saucepan, and simmer 45 minutes. Remove and discard the bay leaves.

5. In the bowl of a food processor or blender, place 1 cup of the black bean mixture and whirl until it is a smooth puree. Pour the bean puree back into the saucepan, add the reserved bacon, hot red pepper sauce, cilantro, and lemon juice, and stir until all the ingredients are well blended. Ladle the soup into individual soup bowls. If desired, garnish each serving with a dollop of sour cream or plain yogurt and a cilantro sprig.

Makes 8 servings

Chicken Noodle Soup

The medicinal mainstay of grandmothers and a childhood favorite of many, this yummy soup is full of vegetables, chunks of chicken, and egg noodles. Homemade is tastier and cheaper than canned or dried, and this version is quick and easy to make.

1 teaspoon butter

1 medium carrot, chopped

1 celery stalk, chopped

1/4 cup chopped onion

6 cups Chicken Stock (page 50) or canned broth

1 1/2 cups chopped cooked chicken

1 teaspoon salt

1/2 teaspoon dried marjoram

1/2 teaspoon dried thyme

1/8 teaspoon ground pepper

1 1/4 cups uncooked medium egg noodles

1 tablespoon minced parsley

1. In a large saucepan or Dutch oven over moderate heat, melt the butter. Add the carrot, celery, and onion, and sauté until the vegetables are tender, 8 to 10 minutes.

2. Add the stock, chicken, salt, marjoram, thyme, and pepper. Bring the mixture to a boil; reduce the heat and stir in the noodles. Cook until the noodles are tender, about 10 minutes. Stir in the parsley.

Makes 6 servings

Manhattan Clam Chowder

Big, bold, tomato taste is the trademark of this clam chowder. This easy home recipe tastes wonderful and costs very little.

2 tablespoons butter

1 large onion, chopped

1 large celery stalk, chopped

2 teaspoons chopped green bell pepper

1 garlic clove, minced

2 cups hot water

1 large potato, cubed

1 can (28 ounces) diced tomatoes, undrained

2 cans (6 1/2 ounces each) minced clams, undrained

1 teaspoon salt

1/2 teaspoon dried thyme

1/4 teaspoon ground pepper

Dash ground cayenne pepper

2 teaspoons minced parsley

1. In a 3-quart saucepan or Dutch oven over low heat, melt the butter. Add the onion, celery, bell pepper, and garlic, and cook, stirring frequently, until the vegetables are very soft, about 20 minutes.

2. Add the water and potato. Increase the heat to moderately high and bring the mixture to a boil; reduce the heat, cover, and simmer until the potato is tender, about 15 minutes.

3. Stir in the tomatoes with their liquid, clams with their liquid, salt, thyme, pepper, and cayenne. Cook until the chowder is heated through; stir in the parsley.

Makes 6 to 8 servings

New England Clam Chowder

This creamy, rich soup is how New Englanders like their clam chowder. You won't find anything like it in a can at any price.

24 cherrystone or chowder clams (about 2 pounds), scrubbed

4 slices turkey bacon, cut into 1/2-inch pieces

1 large onion, chopped

2 tablespoons all-purpose flour

1 pound all-purpose potatoes, peeled and cut into 1/2-inch cubes

2 cups reduced-fat (2%) milk

2 teaspoons fresh thyme leaves

1 bay leaf

Pinch ground red pepper

1/4 cup chopped flat-leaf parsley

1. Bring clams and 2 cups water to boil in a large saucepan over high heat. Reduce heat, cover, and simmer 5 minutes. Uncover and transfer clams with tongs or a slotted spoon to bowl as they open. Strain clam broth, adding enough water to equal 1 1/2 cups; set aside. Wipe out saucepan.

2. Lightly coat saucepan with nonstick cooking spray and set over medium heat. Sauté bacon and onion until onion is golden, about 7 minutes. Sprinkle in flour and cook, stirring constantly, just until bubbling but not browned, about 1 minute.

3. Add potatoes, milk, reserved clam broth, thyme, bay leaf, and pepper. Bring to a simmer over medium heat and cook, stirring occasionally, until potatoes are tender, about 10 minutes (do not boil).

4. Meanwhile, remove clams from shells and cut into bite-size pieces if necessary. Stir in clams and cook until heated through, about 2 minutes longer. Discard bay leaf. Ladle into bowls and sprinkle with parsley.

Makes 4 servings

Cream of Tomato Soup

Pair this with a grilled cheese sandwich and you've got the ultimate comfort meal. If you have eaten canned tomato soup all your life, you are in for a big treat!

2 1/2 cups diced peeled tomatoes, fresh or canned

1/4 cup diced celery

1/4 cup diced onion

1 tablespoon vegetable oil

2 tablespoons all-purpose flour

1 cup cream

1 teaspoon salt *(optional)*

1/8 teaspoon ground black pepper

3 tablespoons sour cream *(optional)*

3 teaspoons minced fresh parsley *(optional)*

1. In a medium saucepan over moderately high heat, combine the tomatoes, celery, and onion, and bring the mixture to a boil. Reduce the heat to low, cover the saucepan, and simmer 15 minutes, stirring often. Remove the saucepan from the heat and let the mixture cool for 10 minutes.

2. Pour the tomato mixture into the bowl of a food processor or blender. Whirl until the tomato mixture is a smooth puree.

3. In a large saucepan over moderate heat, heat the oil. Add the flour and stir until the mixture is smooth. Gradually add the cream, stirring constantly. Bring the cream mixture to a boil and cook for 2 minutes. Gradually add the tomato mixture, stirring constantly. Add the salt, if desired, and the pepper. Continue to cook until the soup is heated through. Ladle the soup into individual bowls and garnish each with a dollop of the sour cream and a sprinkle of the parsley, if desired.

Makes 3 servings

Gumbo

Is it soup or is it stew? We just know it's delicious if you whip it up yourself from scratch. This good Cajun flavor doesn't come in a can.

1/4 cup olive oil

1 pound beef brisket or chuck steak, cut into 1/2-inch chunks

6 ounces baked ham, cut into 1/2-inch chunks

1 large yellow onion, chopped

6 scallions, including green tops, thinly sliced

1 large red bell pepper, cored, seeded, and diced

3 tablespoons all-purpose flour

1 cup thinly sliced fresh okra or 1/2 package (10 ounces) frozen okra

4 cups Chicken Stock (page 50) or reduced-sodium canned chicken broth

8 ounces cabbage, cored and cut into 1/2-inch chunks

4 cups thinly sliced mustard greens

3 cups thinly sliced turnip greens

1/2 teaspoon salt

1/4 teaspoon ground black pepper

1 bay leaf

1/2 teaspoon dried thyme, crumbled

1/2 teaspoon dried marjoram, crumbled

4 whole allspice

2 whole cloves

1/8 teaspoon ground cayenne pepper

6 cups trimmed, washed, and chopped spinach

1 bunch watercress, tough stems removed and leaves chopped

1. In a large saucepan or an 8-quart Dutch oven over moderate heat, heat the olive oil about 2 minutes. Add the brisket or chuck steak and ham, and cook, stirring frequently, until the meat is lightly browned, about 5 minutes. Using a slotted spoon, transfer the meat to a bowl and set aside.

2. Add the onion and scallions to the Dutch oven and cook, stirring frequently, until the vegetables are softened, about 5 minutes. Add the red bell pepper and cook, stirring frequently, until it is crisp-tender, about 4 minutes. Stir in the flour until the vegetables are well coated. Add the okra and cook, stirring constantly, until all the ingredients are well combined. Gradually pour in the stock, stirring until well blended.

3. Add the cabbage, mustard greens, turnip greens, salt, pepper, bay leaf, thyme, marjoram, allspice, cloves, cayenne, and reserved meats. Bring the mixture to a boil, reduce the heat to moderately low, and simmer, stirring occasionally, until the gumbo is thickened and the beef is tender, about 1 1/2 hours.

4. Add the spinach and watercress. Cover the Dutch oven and cook until tender, about 15 minutes longer. Remove and discard the bay leaf.

Makes 4 servings

Lentil Soup

Long a staple of both Indian and Middle Eastern cooking, lentils are an excellent source of fiber, protein, folate, and iron. That's why lentil soup is so good for you. It tastes so good because you made it yourself—a low-cost one-dish dinner.

1 cup dried lentils, sorted and rinsed

6 cups Chicken Stock (page 50) or canned broth

1 tablespoon vegetable oil

2 cups chopped onion

1 garlic clove, minced

2 1/2 cups chopped fresh tomatoes

1 cup sliced carrots

1/2 teaspoon dried thyme

1/4 teaspoon dried marjoram

1. In a large saucepan over moderately high heat, combine the lentils and the stock, and bring the mixture to a boil. Reduce the heat to low and simmer 30 minutes.

2. Meanwhile, in a large skillet over moderately high heat, heat the oil. Add the onions and garlic, and sauté until tender, about 5 minutes. Pour the onion mixture into the saucepan with the lentils.

3. Add the tomatoes, carrots, thyme, and marjoram to the lentil mixture. Cook the mixture until the lentils and vegetables are tender, about 30 minutes.

Makes 8 servings

Minestrone

Italian cooks have no definite rules for what goes into minestrone. It just has to be a hearty mix of vegetables, white beans, and pasta or rice. To make it vegetarian, substitute vegetable broth for the beef broth. Nothing in a can tastes as good as this simple, homemade inexpensive soup.

1 tablespoon olive oil

1 large yellow onion, chopped

2 garlic cloves, minced

3 1/2 cups beef broth

1 can (15 ounces) great northern beans, drained

1 3/4 cups chopped tomatoes or 1 can (14 1/2 ounces) Italian-style tomatoes, undrained, cut up

2 cups coarsely shredded cabbage

2 large carrots, thinly sliced

1 teaspoon dried oregano

1 teaspoon dried basil

1/2 teaspoon salt

1/2 teaspoon ground pepper

2 ounces vermicelli, broken

1 small zucchini, sliced

Grated Parmesan cheese

1. In a large, nonstick saucepan over medium-high heat, heat oil. Add onion and garlic and sauté 5 minutes or until onion is tender. Stir in broth, beans, tomatoes, cabbage, carrots, oregano, basil, salt, and pepper.

2. Bring to a boil and stir in vermicelli. Reduce heat, cover, and simmer, 15 minutes or until vegetables and pasta are tender. Stir in zucchini and cook, uncovered, 3 minutes. Serve with cheese.

Makes 8 servings

Onion Soup

Easier to make than you may think, this classic of French cooking is mostly a matter of slicing onions! Nothing in a can or a packet compares.

- 2 tablespoons butter
- 5 medium yellow onions, thinly sliced
- 2 tablespoons sugar
- 3 1/2 cups Beef Stock (page 49) or canned broth
- 5 cups water
- 1/4 cup brandy *(optional)*
- 1/2 teaspoon salt
- 1/2 teaspoon ground pepper
- 4 slices (1/2-inch thick) French bread, toasted
- 4 tablespoons shredded Gruyère cheese

1. Preheat the oven to 400°F. In a large saucepan or 5-quart Dutch oven over moderately high heat, melt the butter. Add the onions and sugar, increase the heat to high, and sauté until the onions are lightly golden, about 10 minutes. Reduce the heat to moderately low and sauté 10 minutes longer, stirring occasionally.

2. Add the stock and water, increase the heat to high, and bring to a boil; reduce the heat to moderately low and simmer, uncovered, 20 minutes. Add the brandy, if desired, and the salt and pepper, and increase the heat to high; return the soup to a boil.

3. Place four 8-ounce ovenproof ramekins or soup bowls on a heavy-duty baking sheet or ovenproof metal tray. Ladle the soup into the bowls, dividing it equally. Place 1 slice French bread and 1 tablespoon of the cheese on top of each portion of soup.

4. Bake, uncovered, until the cheese is melted, about 5 minutes.

Makes 4 servings

Vegetable Soup

The best vegetable soup is made with the freshest produce, and it doesn't come from a can. You make it yourself from what's ripe in the garden or at the farmers' market.

- 3 tablespoons olive oil
- 1 large red onion, diced
- 5 garlic cloves, minced
- 2 large carrots, thinly sliced
- 4 medium squashes, diced
- 2 medium zucchini, diced
- 1/2 pound green beans, sliced
- 2 pounds tomatoes, peeled and chopped
- 5 cups Vegetable Stock (page 51) or canned broth
- 1 pound new potatoes, diced
- 3/4 teaspoon salt
- 3/4 teaspoon dried marjoram
- 1/2 teaspoon ground pepper

1. In a large saucepan or 5-quart Dutch oven over moderate heat, heat the oil. Add the onion and garlic, and cook until soft, about 5 minutes. Add the carrots and cook, stirring frequently, until the vegetables are soft, about 5 minutes.

2. Add the squashes, zucchini, green beans, tomatoes, stock, potatoes, salt, marjoram, and pepper. Increase the heat to high and bring the mixture to a boil; reduce the heat to moderately low, cover, and simmer until the vegetables are tender, 40 to 50 minutes.

Makes 4 servings

Split Pea Soup

This is a great winter soup to make when you have a ham bone in the house. You can make this soup to feed a crowd for pennies.

1 package (16 ounces) dried green split peas

2 1/2 quarts water, plus additional soaking water

1 ham bone

1 large onion, chopped

1 teaspoon salt

1/2 teaspoon ground black pepper

1/2 teaspoon dried thyme, crumbled

1 bay leaf

1 cup diced carrots

1 cup diced celery

1. In a large saucepan or Dutch oven, combine the split peas and enough water to cover the peas by 2 inches. Over high heat, bring the mixture to a boil; boil for 2 minutes. Remove the pan from the heat, cover, and let stand 1 hour. Drain and rinse the peas, discarding the soaking liquid. Return the peas to the saucepan.

2. Add the 2 1/2 quarts of water, the ham bone, onion, salt, pepper, thyme, and bay leaf to the saucepan. Over high heat, bring the mixture to a boil; reduce the heat to low, cover, and simmer 1 1/2 hours, stirring occasionally.

3. Using a slotted spoon, transfer the ham bone to a cutting board; let cool. Remove the meat from the bone; discard the bone. Cut the meat into dice, and return to the saucepan.

4. Add the carrots and celery to the saucepan. Over moderately low heat, simmer the soup, uncovered, until it reaches the desired consistency and the vegetables are tender, 45 to 60 minutes. Remove and discard the bay leaf before serving.

Makes 10 servings

Gazpacho

A great joy of summer is fresh tomatoes—and this chilled soup is the most refreshing way to use that bounty. Whip up a batch and keep it in the refrigerator in a pitcher for a quick, refreshing snack, lunch, or start to a grilled dinner. It's a treat you can make better than groceries or delis can, adapting it to your own taste.

3 cups chopped tomatoes

2 celery stalks, chopped

1 medium green pepper, chopped

1 medium cucumber, chopped

1/4 cup parsley, minced

1 tablespoon chives, minced

1 scallion, thinly sliced

1 garlic clove, minced

1 can (46 ounces) tomato juice

1/3 cup red wine vinegar

1/4 cup olive oil

1 teaspoon salt

1/2 teaspoon Worcestershire sauce

1/2 teaspoon ground pepper

Seasoned croutons *(optional)*

In a large, nonreactive bowl, combine all the ingredients, except croutons, and stir until well blended. Cover the bowl and refrigerate the soup for several hours or overnight. If desired, top each serving with a few croutons.

Makes 10 servings

salads

Classic Coleslaw
The quintessential side for a perfect picnic, tangy slaw offers crunchy texture and good nutrition. No deli slaw—at any price—can compare with your own.

1 small head green cabbage, shredded and immersed in ice water for 1 hour

3 medium carrots, shredded

1 cup Mayonnaise (page 29)

1/3 cup sugar

1/4 cup cider vinegar

1. Drain the cabbage and transfer it to paper towels. Blot the cabbage with additional towels until it is completely dry. In a large bowl, combine the cabbage and carrots, and toss to mix them thoroughly.

2. In a small bowl, combine the mayonnaise, sugar, and cider vinegar; stir until the mixture is well blended and a smooth consistency.

3. Pour the dressing over the cabbage mixture and toss until all the ingredients are well blended.

Makes 10 to 12 servings

Sweet-and-Sour Coleslaw
A tasty variation on a theme with lots of color— for even more color, substitute red cabbage for the green. Again, you can't match this recipe with one from a grocery or a deli.

8 cups shredded cabbage (about 1 small green cabbage)

2 carrots, peeled and grated

1 red bell pepper, cored, seeded, and finely chopped

1/3 cup corn oil

1 medium red onion, finely chopped

2 tablespoons firmly packed brown sugar

1/3 cup cider vinegar

1 tablespoon sweet pickle relish

1 teaspoon Dijon mustard

1 teaspoon salt

1/4 teaspoon ground black pepper

1. In a large, heatproof bowl, combine the cabbage, carrots, and red bell pepper.

2. In a large skillet over moderately high heat, heat the oil for 1 minute. Add the onion and sauté 2 to 3 minutes. Stir in the sugar and sauté 2 minutes longer. Stir in the vinegar, pickle relish, mustard, salt, and pepper.

3. Pour the hot dressing over the vegetables in the bowl, and toss to combine all the ingredients well. Let the coleslaw cool to room temperature before serving.

Makes 8 servings

Potato Salad

What would a picnic or barbecue be without this stalwart standby adding its creamy goodness and rib-sticking potatoes? Make your own for less money and better flavor. "Waxy" potatoes, such as new potatoes, red new potatoes, and California long whites, are ideal for salad making, since they have a firmer texture when cooked.

1 1/2 pounds potatoes, cut into same-size chunks

1 tablespoon cider vinegar

1 teaspoon sugar

1/2 cup chopped celery

1/2 cup chopped red onion

1/4 cup chopped stuffed olives

1/2 teaspoon salt

1/2 teaspoon celery seed

3/4 cup Mayonnaise (page 29) or salad dressing

2 hard-cooked eggs, chopped

1. In a large, nonreactive saucepan, combine the potatoes with enough water to cover. Over high heat, bring the water to a boil; boil until the potatoes are tender, 20 to 30 minutes. Drain the potatoes and remove the peels. When the potatoes are cool enough to handle, cut them into cubes and place in a medium bowl.

2. Drizzle the cider vinegar over the potatoes, then sprinkle with the sugar. Add the celery, onion, olives, salt, and celery seed. Add the mayonnaise and eggs, and fold gently until all the ingredients are well blended. Cover the bowl and refrigerate for at least 1 hour before serving.

Makes 4 servings

Hot German Potato Salad

A wonderful warm variation, this potato salad uses a cooked vinegar dressing with bacon for an enticing side dish to grilled or roasted meats. Make your own to save money and serve it warm.

4 thick slices bacon, diced

1/2 cup finely chopped yellow onion

1 tablespoon all-purpose flour

1/2 cup Beef Stock (page 49) or reduced-sodium canned beef broth

1/2 cup cider vinegar

2 tablespoons sugar

1 teaspoon salt

1/4 teaspoon ground black pepper

3 pounds small red- or white-skinned new potatoes, boiled, peeled, and cut into 1/4-inch-thick slices

1 cup sliced scallions

1/4 cup minced fresh parsley

1. In a medium skillet over moderately low heat, cook the bacon until it is crisp, about 5 minutes. Transfer the bacon to paper towels to drain completely.

2. Return the skillet to the heat and add the onion; sauté until the onion is soft, about 5 minutes. Stir in the flour until it is well blended; remove the skillet from the heat. Slowly add the stock, stirring constantly; stir in the vinegar, sugar, salt, and pepper. Return the skillet to the heat and bring the mixture to a boil, stirring constantly. Cook the dressing for 1 minute longer, reduce the heat to low, and keep the dressing warm.

3. Place the potatoes in a heatproof serving bowl. Add the scallions, parsley, and reserved bacon. Pour the hot dressing over the potato mixture and toss gently until all the ingredients are well blended.

Makes 6 servings

Pasta Salad
This salad uses roasted bell peppers for a colorful combination, but this basic pasta salad is also a good place to use whatever vegetables are in season—just blanch or sauté the vegetables before adding to the pasta. Made at home, it will be cheaper and tastier.

- 8 ounces pasta, such as fusilli, farfalle, or penne
- 1 medium red bell pepper, cored, seeded, and cut into 1/4-inch-thick strips
- 1 medium yellow bell pepper, cored, seeded, and cut into 1/4-inch-thick strips
- 2 tablespoons olive oil
- 2 tablespoons red wine vinegar
- 1/2 teaspoon salt
- 1/4 teaspoon ground black pepper
- 2 tablespoons minced fresh parsley
- 2 tablespoons minced fresh basil
- 2 tablespoons drained capers
- 2 garlic cloves, minced
- 1/2 cup diced red onion
- 1 cup peeled, seeded, and chopped tomatoes

1. Cook the pasta following the package directions until it is firm but tender. Drain the pasta and place it in a large serving bowl.

2. Add the remaining ingredients and toss gently until well blended.

3. Let the salad stand at room temperature for 30 minutes for the flavors to develop. Toss gently again before serving.

Makes 4 servings

Egg Salad
Dark pumpernickel or a flavorful rye sets off the creamy texture and taste of this old favorite—cheaper and better when you make it yourself with the ingredients you like best.

- 4 hard-cooked eggs, chopped
- 1/4 cup chopped green olives
- 1/4 cup Mayonnaise (page 29) or salad dressing

In a medium bowl, combine all the ingredients and gently fold until well blended.

Makes 4 servings

Ham Salad

A zesty addition to a picnic or buffet, serve on a crusty roll or with buttery crackers. Again, you can economize and customize by making this salad at home.

1 cup minced ham

1/4 cup Mayonnaise (page 29) or salad dressing

2 tablespoons sweet pickle relish

2 teaspoons mustard

1 teaspoon drained prepared horseradish

In a medium bowl, combine the ingredients and gently fold until well blended.

Makes 4 servings

Creamy Chicken Salad

Serve this old favorite on a bed of lettuce, with fruit, or as a filling for sandwiches. Chicken salad costs $8 a pound and up at the deli and isn't nearly as good as homemade, particularly if you use homemade mayonnaise.

2 cups Mayonnaise (page 29)

3/4 cup chopped celery

1 tablespoon mustard

1 1/4 teaspoons poppy seed

1/2 teaspoon salt

10 cups cubed cooked chicken

Chopped pecans

1. In a large bowl, combine the mayonnaise, celery, mustard, poppy seed, and salt. Stir until the ingredients are well blended.

2. Add the cooked chicken and gently fold to coat. Cover the bowl and place in the refrigerator for 3 to 4 hours until the salad is chilled. Sprinkle with the pecans before serving.

Makes about 12 servings

Curried Chicken Salad

A piquant filling for pita bread, this salad is also sensational served with tropical fruit or cooked rice. It's as good as any you can buy and costs much less.

1/2 cup Mayonnaise (page 29) or salad dressing

1/2 cup chutney

1-3 tablespoons curry powder

6 cups cubed cooked chicken

1. In a large bowl, combine the mayonnaise, chutney, and desired amount of curry powder. Stir until the ingredients are well blended.

2. Add the cooked chicken and gently fold to coat. Cover the bowl and place in the refrigerator for 3 to 4 hours until the salad is chilled and the flavors have developed.

Makes about 12 servings

Turkey Salad

A great way to use up leftover turkey, this recipe will allow you to make wonderful sandwiches for next to nothing. Serve on whole wheat rolls with lettuce.

1 cup finely chopped cooked turkey

1/4 cup Mayonnaise (page 29) or salad dressing

1/4 cup minced celery

1 tablespoon chili sauce

In a medium bowl, combine the ingredients and gently fold until well blended.

Makes 4 servings

Tuna Salad

An ingenious variation on the plain mayonnaise-tuna mixture, this special salad adds capers, red onion, and dill. And you can make it better and cheaper than what you would buy at the deli.

1/4 cup plus 1 tablespoon Mayonnaise (page 29)

3 tablespoons finely chopped red onion

3 tablespoons sweet pickle relish

2 tablespoons chopped celery

2 tablespoons lemon juice

1 tablespoon drained capers

1 tablespoon minced fresh dill

1/4 teaspoon salt

2 cans (6 1/2 ounces each) solid light tuna, drained

1. In a medium bowl, combine the mayonnaise, onion, pickle relish, celery, lemon juice, capers, dill, and salt. Stir until the dressing is well blended and smooth.
2. Add the tuna and gently fold until all the ingredients are well blended.

Makes 4 servings

Crab Salad

Though this salad is fabulous in a sandwich or served on whole-grain crackers, for a eye-catching buffet table, mound it in wedges of fresh papaya and sprinkle with a little chopped fresh parsley. Crab salad is a special treat—always pricey—so put the money into more and better crab and make your own.

1/4 cup Mayonnaise (page 29)

1/4 cup finely chopped celery

1/4 cup minced fresh parsley

2 tablespoons lemon juice

1/4 teaspoon salt

Pinch ground cayenne pepper

1 pound lump crabmeat, chopped

1/4 cup diced red bell pepper

1. In a medium bowl, combine the mayonnaise, celery, parsley, lemon juice, salt, and cayenne pepper. Stir until the dressing is well blended and smooth.
2. Add the crabmeat and red bell pepper, and gently fold until all the ingredients are well blended.

Makes 4 servings

Shrimp Salad

For some reason, shrimp seems to signal a party! This luscious salad is lovely served on a bed of mixed greens, as a filling for soft rolls, or with flatbreads. Make it yourself with shrimp you know are fresh and your own mayonnaise, and your less expensive version will be the best.

1/4 cup Mayonnaise (page 29)

1/4 cup finely chopped celery

2 tablespoons lemon juice

2 tablespoons minced fresh tarragon

1/4 teaspoon salt

Pinch ground cayenne pepper

1 pound diced cooked shrimp or tiny cocktail shrimp

1. In a medium bowl, combine the mayonnaise, celery, lemon juice, tarragon, salt, and cayenne pepper. Stir until the dressing is well blended and smooth.

2. Add the shrimp and gently fold until all the ingredients are well blended.

Makes 4 servings

Cobb Salad

Created at Hollywood's famed Brown Derby restaurant in 1936 by the owner, Robert Cobb, this noteworthy salad always features cooked chicken or turkey, bacon, eggs, avocado, and tomato in an eye-pleasing arrangement. Your own will be less expensive than any restaurant version.

1 large shallot, minced

1 tablespoon Dijon mustard

1 tablespoon red wine vinegar

3 tablespoons olive oil

1 medium head romaine lettuce, but into 2-inch-long pieces

2 hard-cooked eggs, peeled and coarsely chopped

1/2 cup drained, Roasted Bell Peppers in Oil (page 73) or bottled red bell peppers, cut into 2 x 1/4-inch strips

3 plum tomatoes, cut length-wise into 8 wedges

1 peeled, pitted, and sliced avocado

2 cups cooked chicken, cubed

24 niçoise olives

1/2 cup crisp-cooked, crumbled bacon

1/2 cup crumbled blue cheese

1. In a large bowl, combine the shallot, mustard, vinegar, and oil. Whisk until the dressing is well blended. Pour 1/2 of the dressing into a small bowl and set aside.

2. Add the romaine lettuce to the bowl and toss to coat with the remaining dressing. Divide the lettuce equally between 4 individual serving plates.

3. Arrange the eggs, bell pepper strips, tomatoes, avocado slices, chicken, and olives, divided equally, on top of the lettuce on each plate. Drizzle some of the reserved dressing over each salad and sprinkle with 1/8 cup of the bacon and 1/8 cup of the blue cheese.

Makes 4 servings

Salade Niçoise

A gorgeous and appetizing array of tuna, eggs, and vegetables, this great classic from the South of France is a picture-perfect composed salad. Delight your family and friends with your own version—fresh and custom made. No restaurant can match that or your costs.

1 large shallot, minced

1 tablespoon Dijon mustard

1 tablespoon drained capers

1 tablespoon red wine vinegar

3 tablespoons olive oil

1 medium head romaine lettuce, cut into 2-inch-long pieces

2 hard-cooked eggs, peeled and halved lengthwise

1/2 cup drained, Roasted Bell Peppers in Oil (page 73) or bottled red bell peppers, cut into 2 x 1/4-inch strips

3 plum tomatoes, cut lengthwise into 8 wedges

2 carrots, peeled, parboiled, and thinly sliced

1/2 pound green beans, trimmed, blanched, and halved crosswise

1 pound small red new potatoes, boiled and cut into 1/4-inch-thick slices

24 niçoise olives

1 can (6 1/2 ounces) oil-packed tuna, drained

1. In a large bowl, combine the shallot, mustard, capers, vinegar, and oil. Whisk until the dressing is well blended. Pour 1/2 of the dressing into a small bowl and set aside.

2. Add the romaine lettuce to the bowl and toss to coat with the remaining dressing. Divide the lettuce equally between 4 individual serving plates.

3. Arrange the egg halves, bell pepper strips, tomatoes, carrots, beans, potatoes, olives, and tuna, divided equally, on top of the lettuce on each plate. Drizzle some of the reserved dressing over each salad or serve the dressing on the side.

Makes 4 servings

chapter 6

Easy-to-Make Sweet Treats

We are a country with a sweet tooth. Collected in this chapter are recipes for all kinds of sweet delicacies—candy, custards, fresh fruit mixtures,

ice creams, frozen yogurts, and ices—that will more than satisfy that yen for sweetness. What all these recipes have in common is that they are made with all-natural ingredients, with none of the fillers, stabilizers, or artificial sweeteners that often give store-bought sweets that faintly sawdust texture and slightly off taste. As a matter of fact, you'll find that sweets such as these are so good when you make them yourself that you may never venture into a candy shop or ice-cream parlor again—and certainly never buy a stale, boxed supermarket sweet again. And the treats you make at home won't cost you nearly as much as those pricey specialty store products do.

Some people may be surprised that you can make your own candies, but our grandparents thought nothing of making them, and it's really no more difficult than making cookies—and sometimes easier. And whether you make dinner mints, lollipops, or peanut brittle, they taste incredibly better than the wrapped products you grew up with. On the following pages, you'll find hot and cold fruit desserts, along with custards and puddings and even a cappuccino mousse. And when summer comes, you have a full assortment of ice creams, frozen yogurts, ices, granitas, sorbets, and sherbets that you can try—topped perhaps with one of the dessert sauces from Chapter 1.

candy

Gumdrops

These chewy goodies can be tailored to the occasion: For Christmas, use red and green food coloring and peppermint extract; for spring, try yellow and orange coloring and lemon or orange extract. Children will want to help make them.

3 envelopes unflavored gelatin

1 1/4 cups water

1 1/2 cups sugar

1/4-1/2 teaspoon flavoring extract of choice

2 food colorings of choice

Additional sugar

1. In a small bowl, sprinkle the gelatin over 1/2 cup of the water; let the mixture stand for 5 minutes.

2. In a small saucepan over moderate heat, combine the sugar and the remaining water; bring the mixture to a boil, stirring constantly. Add the gelatin mixture and reduce the heat. Simmer the mixture, stirring constantly, for 5 minutes. Remove the saucepan from the heat and stir in the flavoring extract.

3. Divide the mixture, placing each half into a small bowl for the desired color; add 2 to 4 drops of the desired color into each bowl and stir until the color is even.

4. Lightly grease two 8 x 4 x 2-inch loaf pans. Pour from 1 bowl into 1 prepared pan; repeat with the remaining bowl and pan. Place the loaf pans in the refrigerator and chill until the mixture is firm, about 3 hours.

5. Lightly coat a work surface with sugar and fill a small saucer with sugar; cover a baking sheet with wax paper. Using a sharp knife, loosen the edges of the gumdrop mixture from the sides of the pans, then turn the mixture out onto the prepared surface. Cut the gumdrops into 1/2-inch cubes. Roll each cube in the sugar in the saucer until the gumdrop is completely coated. Place the gumdrops on the prepared baking sheet and let them stand at room temperature, uncovered, until they are dry on all sides, 3 to 4 hours; turn the gumdrops every hour to allow each side to dry. Cover the gumdrops with plastic wrap and store in the refrigerator until ready to serve.

Makes about 1 pound candy

Helpful Hint

Checking the Candy Thermometer

The one crucial item needed for candy making is a good-quality candy thermometer—which you should test before each use: Bring water to a boil and dip in the thermometer. It should read 212°F. Adjust your recipe temperature up or down based on your test.

Lollipops

Few goodies are as evocative of childhood as these brightly colored sweets on a stick. Flavoring oils can be purchased at health food stores—the flavor is more intense, and since, unlike extracts, they are not alcohol-based, the flavor won't evaporate either.

12 lollipop sticks

1 cup sugar

1/2 cup water

2 tablespoons light corn syrup

4-8 drops food coloring of choice

2-3 drops flavoring oil of choice

1. Line a large baking sheet with foil. Arrange the lollipop sticks on the prepared pan, spacing the sticks 4 inches apart.

2. In a heavy saucepan over moderate heat, combine the sugar, water, and corn syrup; cook, stirring, until the sugar has dissolved. Cover the saucepan, increase the heat to high, and boil the mixture for 1 minute to wash down any sugar crystals. Remove the cover, and boil the syrup until it registers 310°F on a candy thermometer. Immediately remove the saucepan from the heat and set it on a wire rack.

3. Let the syrup cool for 5 minutes, then add the food coloring and flavoring oil of choice; stir until the color is even.

4. Spoon the colored syrup over the top end of each lollipop stick, making a puddle about 2 to 3 inches in diameter. Let the lollipops stand until they are completely cool and the candy has hardened. Wrap each lollipop in plastic wrap and secure below the candy.

Makes about 12 lollipops

Butterscotch

Buttery good, this recipe calls for rum extract to create its distinctive flavor. This homemade candy is rich and delicious and very inexpensive.

1 teaspoon plus 1 cup butter cut into cubes

2 1/2 cups firmly packed light brown sugar

3/4 cup water

1/2 cup light corn syrup

1/4 cup honey

1/2 teaspoon salt

1/2 teaspoon rum extract

1. Use the 1 teaspoon of butter to coat a 15 x 10 x 1-inch baking pan; set aside.

2. In a heavy saucepan over moderate heat, combine the sugar, water, and corn syrup. Cover the saucepan and bring the mixture to a boil; do not stir. Uncover the saucepan and continue to cook the mixture until a candy thermometer reads 270°F (soft-crack stage).

3. Add the honey, salt, and butter cubes. Cook, stirring constantly, until the mixture reaches 300°F (hard-crack stage). Remove the saucepan from the heat. Stir in the rum extract.

4. Pour the butterscotch into the prepared pan without scraping; do not spread. Let the butterscotch cool until the candy is almost set, 1 to 2 minutes. Using a sharp knife, score the butterscotch into 1-inch squares and let the candy cool completely. Break the candy squares along the scored lines. Store the butterscotch in an airtight container.

Makes 1 1/2 pounds candy

Easy-to-Make Sweet Treats   **201**

Caramels

Chewy, gooey, and irresistible, these candies save money and make great treats for Christmas stockings or birthday favor baskets.

1 cup sugar

1 cup dark corn syrup

1 cup butter or margarine

1 can (14 ounces) sweetened condensed milk

1 teaspoon vanilla extract

1. Line an 8-inch square baking pan with foil and grease the foil with butter; set aside.

2. In a 3-quart saucepan over moderate heat, combine the sugar, corn syrup, and butter or margarine. Bring the mixture to a boil, stirring constantly; reduce the heat slightly and boil slowly for 4 minutes without stirring.

3. Remove the saucepan from the heat and stir in the condensed milk. Return the saucepan to the heat, reducing the heat to moderately low. Cook the mixture until a candy thermometer reads 238°F (soft-ball stage), stirring constantly. Remove the saucepan from the heat and stir in vanilla.

4. Pour the candy into the prepared pan and let stand until the caramels are cool. Remove the caramels from the pan and cut them into 1-inch squares. Wrap each caramel individually in wax paper or plastic wrap, twisting the ends to seal.

Makes 64 caramels

Fudge

Using not one, but three kinds of chocolate, plus pecans and marshmallows, makes this a deep, rich, chocolaty dream of a fudge that will match any you can buy.

3 1/3 cups sugar

1 cup butter or margarine

1 cup firmly packed dark brown sugar

1 can (12 ounces) evaporated milk

32 large Marshmallows, halved (page 207)

2 cups (12 ounces) semisweet chocolate chips

2 milk chocolate candy bars (7 ounces each), broken into pieces

2 squares (1 ounce each) semisweet baking chocolate, chopped

1 teaspoon vanilla extract

2 cups chopped pecans

1. Grease a 15 x 10 x 1-inch baking pan.

2. In a large saucepan over moderate heat, combine the sugar, butter or margarine, brown sugar, and evaporated milk. Cook, stirring, until the sugar has completely dissolved. Increase the heat to high and bring the mixture to a boil; boil for 5 minutes, stirring constantly.

3. Remove the saucepan from the heat and add the marshmallows, stirring until they are melted. Add the chocolate chips and pieces and stir until they are melted. Fold in the vanilla and pecans until the mixture is well blended.

4. Pour the mixture into the prepared baking pan, spreading it evenly. Place the baking pan in the refrigerator and chill the fudge until it is firm. Using a sharp knife, cut the fudge into squares.

Makes 5 1/2 pounds

Peppermint Patties *These patties provide a burst of peppermint in your mouth.*

3 3/4 cups confectioners' sugar

3 tablespoons butter, softened

2-3 teaspoons peppermint extract

1/2 teaspoon vanilla extract

1/4 cup evaporated milk

2 cups (12 ounces) semisweet chocolate chips

2 tablespoons shortening

1. In a medium bowl, combine the sugar, butter, peppermint, and vanilla. Pour in the milk and beat until the ingredients are well blended.

2. Cover 2 to 3 baking sheets with wax paper. Pinch off some of the peppermint mixture and roll it into a 1-inch-diameter ball. Place the peppermint ball on the prepared baking sheet and press with the bottom of a glass to flatten the ball into a 1/4-inch-thick patty. Repeat with the remaining peppermint mixture. Cover the patties with plastic wrap and place the baking sheet in the freezer for 30 minutes.

3. In a heavy saucepan over low heat or a microwave-safe bowl following the manufacturer's directions, melt the chocolate chips and shortening; stir until the mixture is smooth.

4. Dip each peppermint patty into the melted chocolate to coat the patty completely. Place the coated patty back on the wax-paper-covered baking sheet. Repeat to coat all the patties with chocolate. Let the coated patties stand at room temperature until the chocolate is set. Store in an airtight container.

Makes 5 dozen patties

Pastel Mint Patties *Pretty confections perfect for a wedding or baby shower buffet.*

1/4 cup butter, softened

1/3 cup light corn syrup

4 cups confectioners' sugar

1/2-1 teaspoon peppermint extract

3 food colorings of choice

About 1 cup granulated sugar

1. In a small bowl, combine the butter and corn syrup. Add 2 cups sugar and the peppermint. Beat the mixture until it is well blended. Add another cup of sugar and beat well.

2. Lightly coat a work surface with the remaining sugar. Turn out the mixture onto the surface. Knead until the sugar is completely absorbed and the mixture is smooth.

3. Divide the peppermint mixture into three portions. Set aside one portion to remain white; tint the remaining portions the color desired by adding 1 to 2 drops of food coloring and kneading until the portion is the desired color.

4. Cover a baking sheet with wax paper. Place the granulated sugar in a shallow bowl or saucer. Pinch off a walnut-size piece of mixture. Using your hands, roll the piece into a ball, then roll the ball in the granulated sugar. Place the ball on the prepared baking sheet and, using a fork, flatten into a patty. Repeat with the remaining peppermint mixture and sugar. Let the patties stand, uncovered, at room temperature for 1 day. Store the patties in an airtight container.

Makes about 7 1/2 dozen patties

Pralines

This Southern confection is loaded with pecans—for the best-tasting pralines, select the freshest, best-quality pecans you can find. Homemade pralines are an easy, inexpensive treat that you can share with friends.

1 cup sugar

1 cup firmly packed brown sugar

1 cup milk

8 large purchased or homemade Marshmallows (page 207)

2 cups coarsely chopped pecans

2 tablespoons butter

1/2 teaspoon vanilla extract

Dash ground cinnamon

1. Lightly grease 2 baking sheets with butter; set aside.

2. In a medium, heavy saucepan over low heat, combine the granulated and brown sugars, milk, and marshmallows. Cook, stirring constantly, until the marshmallows are completely melted. Increase the heat to moderate and cook, stirring occasionally, until a candy thermometer reads 234°F to 240°F (soft-ball stage). Without stirring or scraping, pour the hot mixture into a second heavy saucepan. Add the pecans, butter, vanilla, and cinnamon. Stir rapidly until the mixture is thickened and creamy, about 3 minutes.

3. Using a tablespoon, drop the mixture onto the prepared baking sheets, placing the pralines about 1 inch apart; flatten the pralines slightly. Let stand until the pralines are set. Store in an airtight container.

Makes about 2 dozen pralines

Peanut Brittle

Crunchy with peanuts, melt-in-your-mouth delicious, this is a true classic candy that the whole family can help to make and package as gifts. It's not nearly as much fun to buy it.

2 3/4 cups sugar

1/2 stick unsalted butter

2/3 cup water

1 1/2 cups lightly salted peanuts

1. Grease a 9 x 13-inch baking pan, then line the pan with foil.

2. In a large, heavy saucepan over moderate heat with a wooden spoon, combine the sugar, butter, and water; simmer, stirring occasionally, until the mixture becomes a golden-brown syrup, about 25 minutes. Once the darkened mixture begins to bubble, remove the saucepan from the heat to a cool surface.

3. Add the peanuts to the syrup and stir until the nuts are evenly distributed. Pour the mixture into the prepared pan, spreading it evenly and ensuring that the peanuts are distributed equally.

4. Let the peanut brittle stand until it is cool and set completely, about 30 minutes. Using a knife handle, break the peanut brittle into bite-size pieces; store in an airtight container in a cool, dry place for up to 1 month.

Makes about 45 pieces

candy

Peanut Butter Cups *This is a tantalizing combination of chocolate and peanut butter.*

1 milk or dark chocolate candy bar (7 ounces), broken into pieces

1/4 cup butter

1 tablespoon shortening

1/4 cup creamy Peanut Butter (page 33)

1. Line the cups in a miniature muffin pan with paper or foil baking cups.

2. In a heavy saucepan over low heat or in a microwave-safe bowl following the manufacturer's directions, combine the chocolate, butter, and shortening. Stir until the mixture is smooth.

3. In a second heavy saucepan over low heat or in a microwave-safe bowl following the manufacturer's directions, heat the peanut butter until it has melted.

4. Pour 1 tablespoon of the chocolate into each of the prepared cups. Drop 1 tablespoon of peanut butter onto the chocolate in each cup. Pour the remaining chocolate, divided equally, into the cups, covering the peanut butter.

5. Place the muffin pan in the refrigerator until the cups are set, about 30 minutes. Store in airtight container in refrigerator.

Makes 1 dozen cups

Toffee Bars *These candy bars are a crunchy confection sure to delight.*

1 tablespoon plus 1 3/4 cups butter, softened

2 cups sugar

1 tablespoon light corn syrup

1 cup chopped pecans

1/4 teaspoon salt

1 pound milk chocolate candy coating

1. Use the 1 tablespoon of butter to grease a 15 x 10 x 1-inch baking pan; set aside.

2. In a heavy 3-quart saucepan over moderate heat, melt the remaining butter. Add the sugar and corn syrup; cook and stir until a candy thermometer reads 295°F (soft-crack stage). Remove the saucepan from the heat; stir in the pecans and salt.

3. Quickly pour the toffee mixture into the prepared pan. Let the toffee mixture stand for 5 minutes. Using a sharp knife, score the top of the toffee into the desired-size bars. Let the toffee stand at room temperature until cool. Break or cut the toffee into bars along the score lines.

4. Cover 1 or 2 baking sheets with wax paper. In a heavy saucepan over low heat or in a microwave-safe bowl following the manufacturer's directions, melt the chocolate candy coating, stirring often. Dip each toffee bar into the chocolate coating until it is completely covered. Then place the coated bar on the prepared baking sheet. Let the coated bars stand at room temperature until the chocolate has set.

Makes 2 1/4 pounds candy bars

Cow Pies

A silly name for a scrumptious sweet, full of almonds and raisins, with chocolate holding it all together.

2 cups (12 ounces) semisweet or milk chocolate chips

1 tablespoon shortening

1/2 cup raisins

1/2 cup chopped slivered almonds

1. In a heavy saucepan over low heat or a microwave-safe bowl following the manufacturer's directions, combine and melt the chocolate chips and the shortening; stir until the mixture is smooth. Remove the saucepan from the heat and stir in the raisins and almonds.

2. Line 2 baking sheets with wax paper. Using a tablespoon, scoop up the chocolate mixture and drop it onto the prepared sheets. Place the baking sheets in the refrigerator and chill the cow pies until ready to serve.

Makes 2 dozen candies

Fruit and Nut Truffles

Serve these sumptuous sweets with after-dinner espresso.

9 ounces bittersweet chocolate

2 tablespoons heavy cream

2 tablespoons cognac or rum

1 1/4 cups apricots, finely chopped

1/2 cup hazelnuts, finely chopped

2 tablespoons crystallized ginger, minced

2 tablespoons confectioners' sugar, sifted

30 hazelnut halves

1. Line a large baking sheet with baking parchment or foil. Lay a large piece of wax paper on a work surface.

2. In the top of a double boiler over low heat, cook 4 ounces of the chocolate, stirring, until it is melted. Remove the top saucepan from the heat and add the cream and cognac, beating until the mixture is well blended. Add the apricots, hazelnuts, ginger, and sugar, and stir until all the ingredients are well blended. Set the saucepan in the refrigerator and chill the mixture until it is firm enough to handle.

3. Using a spoon, scoop up a walnut-size portion of the mixture. Using your hand, roll the portion into a 1-inch-diameter ball, and place the ball on the prepared work surface. Repeat with the remaining mixture.

4. In the top of the double boiler over low heat, cook the remaining 5 ounces of chocolate, stirring, until it is melted. Remove the double boiler from the heat.

5. Using a fork, spear 1 fruit and nut ball. Dip the ball into the melted chocolate until the ball is completely coated; allow any excess chocolate to run back into the saucepan. Place the coated ball on the prepared baking sheet and top with 1 hazelnut half. Repeat with the remaining fruit and nut balls, chocolate, and hazelnut halves. Place the baking sheet in the refrigerator until the truffles are chilled and the chocolate has set.

6. Store the truffles in an airtight container in the refrigerator for up to 1 month.

Makes 30 truffles

Marshmallows

An electric stand mixer makes these homemade marshmallows quick and easy to whip up. They cost less than the commercial ones, and your children will love the process.

3 tablespoons confectioners' sugar

3 tablespoons cornstarch

1 1/2 tablespoons unflavored gelatin

1/3 cup water

1/2 cup granulated sugar

2/3 cup light corn syrup

1. Line a 13 x 9 x 2-inch baking pan with wax paper. In a small sieve, combine 1 tablespoon of the confectioners' sugar and 1 tablespoon of the cornstarch, and sift the mixture over the prepared pan.

2. In a medium bowl, combine the gelatin and water; let stand until the gelatin has softened, about 5 minutes.

3. Place the bowl in a large saucepan or deep skillet of simmering water. Stir until the gelatin has dissolved. Add the granulated sugar and continue to stir until the sugar has dissolved. Remove the bowl from the water and add the corn syrup. Using an electric mixer, beat the mixture until it is creamy and thick, 10 to 15 minutes. Let the mixture stand until it is cool.

4. Using a wet spatula, spread the mixture in the prepared pan, smoothing the top evenly. Let the mixture sit until it is cool and set, about 20 minutes.

5. Carefully lift the marshmallow mixture onto a cutting board. Following Step 1, lightly dust the marshmallow with 1 tablespoon of the remaining confectioners' sugar and cornstarch. Using a sharp knife, cut the marshmallow into small squares. In a cup, combine the remaining 1 tablespoon of confectioners' sugar and the cornstarch. Dip each marshmallow into the mixture until it is completely coated. Store the marshmallows in an airtight container in a cool, dry place for 1 to 2 weeks.

Makes about 36 marshmallows

One-Minute Substitute

If You Run Out of Corn Syrup

If a recipe calls for 1 cup corn syrup and you don't have any on hand, combine 1 cup regular granulated sugar and 1/4 additional cup of the liquid used in the recipe in a 2-cup measure. Stir until the mixture is blended.

Candied Citrus Peels

Dip these zesty treats in chocolate for an easy confection, or use them for decorations on cakes, ice cream, and other desserts.

3 firm, ripe lemons or oranges
1/4 cup granulated sugar
1/2 cup water

1. Using a swivel-bladed vegetable peeler, remove the peel from the citrus fruit, leaving the bitter white pith. Using a sharp knife, cut the peel into strips. For decorations, cut it into matchstick-thin strips; for dipping in chocolate, cut it into larger strips.

2. In a small saucepan, combine the citrus strips and add enough cold water to cover the strips. Over high heat, bring the water to a boil. Immediately drain the strips and rinse them under cold running water.

3. Return the strips to the saucepan; add the sugar and the 1/2 cup of water. Over moderate heat, cook the mixture until the liquid has evaporated and the peel is bright and shiny.

4. Spread a sheet of foil over a work surface. Transfer the candied peel to the foil to cool, keeping the strips separate. Store in an airtight container in the refrigerator for up to 6 months.

Makes about 1 cup

custards, mousses, and puddings

Vanilla Pudding

Marvelously satisfying on its own, vanilla pudding can also be the base for toasted nuts or coconut, miniature chocolate chips, or fresh berries. Or spoon some over Dried Fruit Compote (page 214).

3/4 cup sugar
1 1/2 tablespoons cornstarch
Pinch salt
2 cups milk
1 egg
2 tablespoons butter
1 teaspoon vanilla extract

1. In a medium saucepan, combine the sugar, cornstarch, and salt. Add the milk and stir until the mixture is smooth. Over moderate heat, cook the mixture, stirring constantly, until it boils and thickens; reduce the heat and simmer, stirring constantly, for 2 minutes. Remove the saucepan from the heat.

2. In a medium bowl using an electric mixer, beat the egg until it is foamy. Gradually stir in about 1/2 cup of the hot milk mixture. Stirring constantly, pour the egg mixture back into the remaining hot milk mixture. Cook over low heat, stirring constantly, for 2 minutes longer.

3. Remove the saucepan from the heat, stir in the butter and vanilla. Immediately pour the pudding into a large serving bowl or individual dessert dishes. Let the pudding cool to room temperature, then refrigerate.

Makes 4 to 6 servings

Chocolate Pudding

Like a grilled cheese sandwich, chocolate pudding is pure comfort food. You can make it from a packet or take a few more minutes and make it much better from scratch.

3/4 cup sugar

1 1/2 tablespoons cornstarch

Pinch salt

2 cups milk

2 ounces semisweet chocolate, chopped

1 egg

2 tablespoons butter

1 teaspoon vanilla extract

1. In a medium saucepan, combine the sugar, cornstarch, and salt. Add the milk and stir until the mixture is smooth; add the chocolate. Over moderate heat, cook the mixture, stirring constantly, until it boils and thickens; reduce the heat and simmer, stirring constantly, for 2 minutes. Remove the saucepan from the heat.

2. In a medium bowl using an electric mixer, beat the egg until it is foamy. Gradually stir in about 1/2 cup of the hot milk mixture. Pour the egg mixture back into the remaining hot milk mixture. Cook over low heat, stirring constantly, for 2 minutes longer.

3. Remove the saucepan from the heat, stir in the butter and vanilla. Immediately pour the pudding into a bowl or individual dessert dishes. Let the pudding cool to room temperature, then refrigerate.

Makes 4 to 6 servings

Rice Pudding

This is an old favorite that you can buy at any deli or grocery store. Once you have made your own—with or without raisins—you will save your money for other things.

3 1/2 cups milk

1/2 cup uncooked long-grain rice

1/3 cup sugar

1/2 teaspoon salt *(optional)*

1/2 cup raisins

1 teaspoon vanilla extract

Ground cinnamon *(optional)*

1. Preheat the oven to 325°F; lightly butter a 1 1/2-quart baking dish.

2. In a medium saucepan, combine the milk, rice, sugar, and if desired, the salt. Over moderate heat and stirring constantly, bring the mixture to a boil. Pour the hot mixture into the prepared baking dish, cover, and bake 45 minutes, stirring every 15 minutes.

3. Stir in the raisins and vanilla, re-cover, and bake 15 minutes longer. Remove the baking dish from the oven. If desired, sprinkle the top of the pudding with cinnamon before serving; serve warm or chilled.

Makes about 6 servings

Orange Rice Pudding

A new twist on an old favorite, this pudding uses a custard base for a very creamy rice pudding.

1/2 cup short-grain rice

2/3 cup water

1/8 teaspoon salt

1 cup milk

1 cup heavy cream

1/3 cup sugar

2 eggs

1 teaspoon grated
orange zest

1/8 teaspoon ground nutmeg

1. Preheat oven to 325°F; butter a 6-cup ovenproof dish.

2. In a medium saucepan over moderate heat, combine the rice, water, and salt; bring the mixture to a boil. Reduce the heat, cover the saucepan, and simmer 12 minutes. Remove the saucepan from the heat and add the remaining ingredients. Stir vigorously until well blended.

3. Pour the rice mixture into the prepared baking dish. Bake until the pudding is set, about 50 minutes. Serve warm or chilled.

Makes 6 servings

Crème Brûlée

This classic French custard is as tasty and exotic as its name.

Custard

3 cups milk

3/4 cup sugar

1 vanilla bean, split
lengthwise

4 strips (3 x 1/2 inch each)
orange zest

3 strips (2 x 1/2 inch each)
lemon zest

3 strips (2 x 1/2 inch each)
lime zest

1/4 teaspoon salt

3 eggs plus 3 egg yolks

Topping

3/4 cup firmly packed light
or dark brown sugar

1. Set 8 ungreased 6-ounce flameproof ramekins, spaced apart, on a folded kitchen towel in a large baking pan.

2. Prepare the custard: In a medium nonreactive saucepan over moderate heat, combine the milk, 1/4 cup of the sugar, vanilla bean, orange, lemon, and lime zests, and salt. Bring to a simmer; remove from heat, cover, and let stand for 30 minutes.

3. Preheat the oven to 325°F. In a large bowl using a whisk, combine the eggs and additional yolks and the remaining 1/2 cup sugar; beat until just blended. Set a large sieve over the bowl, and pour the milk mixture through into the egg mixture. Whisk until the ingredients are blended.

4. Spoon the custard into the ramekins. Pour enough water into the baking pan to come halfway up the sides of the ramekins. Bake, uncovered, until a knife inserted into the center of a custard comes out clean, about 45 minutes.

5. Remove the ramekins from the baking pan to wire racks. Preheat the broiler. Sprinkle 1 1/2 teaspoons of the brown sugar over the top of each custard. Place the ramekins in the broiler, 6 to 8 inches from the heat source, and broil until the sugar melts, about 45 seconds.

6. Remove the ramekins to wire racks and let cool to room temperature. Serve at room temperature or slightly chilled; do not refrigerate too long or the crust will begin to soften.

Makes 8 servings

Crème Caramel

You can make this popular restaurant dessert yourself for pennies.

To make a lower-fat version, substitute 3 cups evaporated skim milk for the whole milk, 1 1/2 cups egg substitute for the whole eggs and yolks, and reduce the sugar to 2/3 cup.

Caramel

1/2 cup sugar

1/2 cup water

Custard

3 cups milk

3/4 cup sugar

1 vanilla bean, split lengthwise

4 strips (3 x 1/2 inch each) orange zest

3 strips (2 x 1/2 inch each) lemon zest

3 strips (2 x 1/2 inch each) lime zest

1/4 teaspoon salt

3 eggs plus 3 egg yolks

1. Prepare the caramel: In a small saucepan over moderately high heat, combine the sugar and water, and bring the mixture to a boil. Continue to boil until the sugar turns amber in color, about 5 minutes. Pour the caramel into the bottoms of 8 ungreased 6-ounce ramekins. Tilt each ramekin to coat the bottom and about 1 inch of the sides. Place the ramekins on a folded kitchen towel in a baking pan large enough to hold them without touching.

2. Prepare the custard: In a medium nonreactive saucepan over moderate heat, combine the milk, 1/4 cup of the sugar, vanilla bean, orange, lemon, and lime zests, and salt. Bring the mixture to a simmer; remove the saucepan from the heat, cover, and let stand for 30 minutes.

3. Preheat the oven to 325°F. In a large bowl using a whisk, combine the eggs and additional yolks and the remaining 1/2 cup sugar; beat until just blended. Set a large sieve over the bowl, and pour the milk mixture through into the egg mixture. Whisk until the ingredients are blended.

4. Spoon the custard into the caramel-coated ramekins. Pour enough water into the baking pan to come halfway up the sides of the ramekins. Bake, uncovered, until a knife inserted into the center of a custard comes out clean, about 45 minutes.

5. Remove the ramekins from the baking pan to wire racks and let the custard cool to room temperature; refrigerate until ready to serve.

6. To serve, run a knife around the edges of the custards to loosen them, then invert the ramekins onto rimmed dessert plates or shallow dessert bowls. Allow the caramel to run down the custards and form a pool around them.

Makes 8 servings

Helpful Hint

Take Extra Care When Making Custard

Although it is surprisingly easy to make, custard requires a bit of cooking know-how: Don't overmix the eggs; more yolks mean smoother texture means slower cooking time; the container used for baking will determine the time, and it's safest to stick to the one specified in the recipe. You can do it, and it will be better than any you buy (and cheaper too).

Easy-to-Make Sweet Treats   **211**

Chocolate Mousse

The ultimate mousse experience—and the higher quality the chocolate you use, the more outstanding the final result. Expensive at a gourmet shop or restaurant, chocolate mousse can be made at home for much less and tastes even better.

8 ounces semisweet chocolate, coarsely chopped

3 eggs, separated

3/4 cup heavy cream

1/2 cup sugar

1/4 cup water

1 teaspoon vanilla extract

1. In the top of a double boiler over simmering water, melt the chocolate. Meanwhile, in a medium bowl with an electric mixer, beat the egg yolks until they are thick. Pour a little of the melted chocolate into the egg yolks, whisking constantly, then whisk all the egg yolk mixture back into the double boiler. Add 1/4 cup of the cream and whisk until well blended. Cook, stirring constantly, until the mixture thickens and reaches 160°F, about 4 minutes. Remove the top of the double boiler and let the chocolate mixture cool to room temperature, whisking often.

2. In a small saucepan over moderate heat, combine the sugar and water, and bring the mixture to a boil. Using a pastry brush dipped in water, brush down the sides of the saucepan, then cook the syrup without stirring until it reaches 238°F on a candy thermometer, about 5 minutes.

3. In a medium heatproof bowl with an electric mixer on medium speed, beat the egg whites until they are frothy. Place the bowl in a larger saucepan of boiling water (double-boiler style). With the mixer on low speed, gradually beat the boiling sugar syrup into the egg whites until the meringue peaks stiffly and a candy thermometer inserted at the center reaches 160°F. Whisk 1/3 cup of the hot meringue into the chocolate mixture, then fold in the remaining meringue.

4. In a small bowl with an electric mixer on high, beat the remaining 1/2 cup of cream until it forms soft peaks; beat in the vanilla. Fold the whipped cream into the chocolate mixture until no white streaks remain. Spoon into individual serving dishes or glasses, cover, and refrigerate for at least 1 hour or until serving time.

Makes 8 servings

Cappuccino Mousse

The aroma and flavor of cappuccino in a mousse is seductive. Make your own cappuccino mousse and serve it with espresso on the side. You'll save money and delight friends.

8 ounces semisweet chocolate, coarsely chopped

1/2 teaspoon ground cinnamon

3 eggs, separated

3/4 cup heavy cream

1/2 cup sugar

1/4 cup freshly brewed espresso

1 teaspoon vanilla extract

1. In the top of a double boiler over simmering water, melt the chocolate; stir in the cinnamon. Meanwhile, in a medium bowl with an electric mixer, beat the egg yolks until they are thick. Pour a little of the melted chocolate into the egg yolks, whisking constantly, then whisk all the egg yolk mixture back into the double boiler. Add 1/4 cup of the cream and whisk until well blended. Cook, stirring constantly, until the mixture thickens and reaches 160°F, about 4 minutes. Remove the top of the double boiler and let the chocolate mixture cool to room temperature, whisking often.

2. In a small saucepan over moderate heat, combine the sugar and espresso, and bring the mixture to a boil. Using a pastry brush dipped in water, brush down the sides of the saucepan, then cook the syrup without stirring until it reaches 238°F on a candy thermometer, about 5 minutes.

3. In a medium heatproof bowl with an electric mixer on medium speed, beat the egg whites until they are frothy. Place the bowl in a larger saucepan of boiling water (double-boiler style). With the mixer on low speed, gradually beat the boiling sugar syrup into the egg whites until the meringue peaks stiffly and a candy thermometer inserted at the center reaches 160°F. Whisk 1/3 cup of the hot meringue into the chocolate mixture, then fold in the remaining meringue.

4. In a small bowl with an electric mixer on high, beat the remaining 1/2 cup of cream until it forms soft peaks; beat in the vanilla. Fold the whipped cream into the chocolate mixture until no white streaks remain. Spoon into individual serving dishes or glasses, cover, and refrigerate for at least 1 hour or until serving time.

Makes 8 servings

fruit desserts

Brandied Peaches
You can buy brandied peaches in jars at gourmet stores, but you can just as easily—and much more cheaply—make your own fresh brandied peaches.

3 cups water

2 cups sugar

1/2 cup brandy

1 tablespoon whole cloves

2 cinnamon sticks

Zest of 1 lemon, slivered

Zest of 1 orange, slivered

4 peaches, peeled, pitted, and halved

1. In a large, heavy saucepan over high heat, combine the first seven ingredients and bring to a strong boil. Reduce the heat to moderate, prick the peach halves several times with the tines of a fork, and add them to the saucepan.

2. Cover the saucepan and reduce the heat to the lowest simmer; poach until the peaches are just cooked but still firm, about 20 minutes. Serve the peaches hot or warm, or chill and serve the peaches cold.

Makes 4 servings

Dried Fruit Compote
Keep ready-to-use self-sealing bags of these dried fruits on hand, then quickly poach them for a fast and fantastic dessert. You can buy dried fruit compotes in specialty stores, but your own will be better.

1 1/4 cups dried pitted prunes

2/3 cup golden raisins

1/2 cup dried figs

1/2 cup dried apricots

1 1/2 cups orange juice

1/3 cup water

1/4 cup sugar

1 cinnamon stick, broken

1/4 teaspoon ground ginger

1/8 teaspoon ground cloves

Pinch black pepper

3/4 teaspoon vanilla extract (optional)

1. In a medium nonreactive saucepan over high heat, combine all the ingredients except the vanilla; bring the mixture to a boil. Reduce the heat to low, cover the saucepan, and simmer until the fruit is tender, 25 to 30 minutes.

2. Remove the saucepan from the heat. Remove and discard the cinnamon stick pieces. Let the mixture stand until it is room temperature. If desired, stir in the vanilla. Serve at room temperature or chilled; store in an airtight container in the refrigerator for up to 3 days.

Makes 6 servings

Hot Curried Tropical Fruit

Intriguing hints of fresh ginger and curry lend pizzazz to mango, pineapple, and papaya. Try sprinkling with a little toasted coconut before serving. This is a take-out favorite that you can make at home for much less cash and much more flavor.

4 cups water

2 cups sugar

1/4 cup thinly sliced
fresh ginger

1 tablespoon curry powder

1 tablespoon whole cloves

2 cinnamon sticks

Zest of 1 lemon, slivered

Zest of 1 orange, slivered

1 firm, medium mango,
peeled, pitted, and sliced

1 medium pineapple, peeled,
cored, and thinly sliced

1 papaya, peeled, seeded,
and sliced

1. In a large, heavy saucepan over high heat, combine the first eight ingredients and bring to a strong boil. Reduce the heat to moderate, and add the mango, pineapple, and papaya.

2. Cover the saucepan and reduce the heat to the lowest simmer; poach the fruit until it is just cooked but still firm, about 15 minutes. Serve the fruit hot or warm, or chill and serve the fruit cold.

Makes 4 servings

Wine Poached Pears with Strawberries

Since Seckel pears hold up well through cooking, serve them standing with a drizzle of Custard Sauce (page 59). This is a restaurant dessert you can make at home for a modest sum and enjoy extravagantly.

4 cups red wine

1 cup sugar

1/4 cup thinly sliced
fresh ginger

2 cinnamon sticks

Zest of 1 lemon, slivered

Zest of 1 orange, slivered

4 Seckel pears, peeled and
cored with stems intact

2 cups strawberries, hulled

1. In a large, heavy saucepan over high heat, combine the first six ingredients and bring the mixture to a strong boil. Reduce the heat to moderate, and add the pears.

2. Cover the saucepan and reduce the heat to the lowest simmer; poach until the pears are just cooked but still firm, about 15 minutes. Remove the saucepan from the heat and let stand to cool for 5 minutes; stir in the strawberries.

3. Using a slotted spoon, remove the pears and strawberries to a serving platter or individual bowls. Return the saucepan to high heat, and bring the poaching liquid to a boil; boil until the liquid is reduced to about 1 1/2 cups. Pour the hot poaching liquid over the pears and strawberries before serving.

Makes 4 servings

ice cream

French Vanilla Ice Cream
This is the real thing—rich, creamy, and full of the strong, wonderful flavor of vanilla.

1 3/4 cups milk

2 1/2 cups heavy cream

1 cup sugar

1 vanilla bean, split
lengthwise

1/4 teaspoon salt

6 egg yolks

1. In a large saucepan over moderate heat, combine the milk and cream, 1/2 cup of the sugar, the vanilla bean, and salt. Scald the mixture just until small bubbles appear.

2. In a medium bowl, combine the egg yolks and remaining 1/2 cup sugar. Whisk until they are well blended. Gradually whisk a little milk mixture into the egg mixture, then pour the combined mixtures into the saucepan. Over low heat, cook, whisking constantly, until the custard mixture coats the back of a spoon, about 15 minutes.

3. Remove the saucepan from the heat and let the custard cool to room temperature. Remove the vanilla bean and scrape the seeds into the custard; discard the pod. Cover the saucepan and refrigerate until the custard is cold, 1 to 2 hours.

4. Transfer the custard to an ice-cream maker and, following the manufacturer's directions, freeze the ice cream.

Makes 1 quart

churn it yourself: ice-cream makers

Few pleasures in life compare with homemade ice cream—or frozen yogurt. But to make it, you will need an ice-cream maker. As a general rule, homemade ice cream costs half as much as commercial. You'll pay for an ice-cream maker in the first 10 to 12 quarts you make. To minimize costs, keep an eye out at yard or rummage sales, at resale or thrift shops, or at discount or oversale stores.

Old-fashioned crank churns: These use a combination of rock salt and ice packed around the churn to freeze the cream mixture. As the handle is cranked, the interior paddles stir the cream mixture while it is freezing. Naturally, the harder the ice cream gets, the harder it is to turn the handle, so you get a good workout before the delicious reward. This machine works particularly well for family gatherings or parties, where folks can trade off on the cranking but everyone enjoys the results.

Electric ice-cream makers: These handy machines are more costly but much easier on you, so you are likely to end up using them more frequently than a hand-churned model. Larger electric makers both freeze and churn for you. A less costly version requires a freezer or for the insert to be frozen ahead of time, but still does the arm-tiring churning for you. Less expensive 1-quart models from major manufacturers can be purchased for $30 to $40. (Most of the recipes here are for 1 quart.)

Blueberry Ice Cream

When blueberries come into season, toward the end of summer, indulge in this glorious concoction served in glass bowls so everyone can admire the color as well as the taste.

2 cups blueberries,
  washed and stemmed

1 1/3 cups sugar

4 strips (2 x 1/2-inch)
  lemon zest

1/2 teaspoon ground
  white pepper

1/2 teaspoon ground ginger

1 3/4 cups milk

2 1/2 cups heavy cream

1 vanilla bean,
  split lengthwise

1/4 teaspoon salt

6 egg yolks

1. In a medium saucepan over moderate heat, combine the blueberries, 1/3 cup of the sugar, and lemon zest. Cook, stirring very frequently, until the blueberries are very soft, 4 to 5 minutes. Place a fine sieve over a medium bowl. Pour the blueberry mixture through the sieve, pressing with the back of a wooden spoon to extract all the juice; discard the solids. Stir in the pepper and ginger. Set aside the blueberry mixture.

2. In a large saucepan over moderate heat, combine the milk and cream, 1/2 cup of the sugar, the vanilla bean, and salt. Scald the mixture just until small bubbles appear.

3. In a medium bowl, combine the egg yolks and remaining 1/2 cup sugar. Whisk until they are well blended. Gradually whisk a little milk mixture into the egg mixture, then pour the combined mixtures into the saucepan. Over low heat, cook, whisking constantly, until the custard mixture coats the back of a spoon, about 15 minutes.

4. Remove the saucepan from the heat and let the custard cool to room temperature. Remove the vanilla bean and scrape the seeds into the custard; discard the pod. Cover the saucepan and refrigerate until the custard is cold, 1 to 2 hours.

5. Pour the reserved blueberry mixture into the custard and stir until all the ingredients are well blended. Transfer the custard to an ice-cream maker and, following the manufacturer's directions, freeze the ice cream.

Makes 1 quart

Helpful Hint

Lowering the Fat in Homemade Ice Cream

We love the richness and texture of full-fat ice cream, but our bellies and thighs are not always so appreciative. Fortunately, it is not hard to lower the fat on homemade ice cream, and since it is home-churned as well, you should still have satisfyingly creamy results. The trick is to substitute an equal amount of evaporated skim milk for the whole milk and 3/4 cup egg substitute for the egg yolks when making a 1-quart batch.

Peach Ice Cream
Ripe, juicy peaches are a true taste of summer, so how could they be any better? In a luscious ice cream that you make yourself.

2 large, ripe peaches

1/3 cup firmly packed
   light brown sugar

1 tablespoon lemon juice

1/4 teaspoon ground ginger

1 3/4 cups milk

2 1/2 cups heavy cream

1 cup sugar

1 vanilla bean,
   split lengthwise

1/4 teaspoon salt

6 egg yolks

1. Blanch, peel, and pit the peaches, then finely chop them. In a medium bowl, combine the peach pieces, brown sugar, lemon juice, and ginger. Toss the ingredients together until they are well blended. Set aside the peach mixture.

2. In a large saucepan over moderate heat, combine the milk and cream, 1/2 cup of the sugar, the vanilla bean, and salt. Scald the mixture just until small bubbles appear.

3. In a medium bowl, combine the egg yolks and remaining 1/2 cup sugar. Whisk until they are well blended. Gradually whisk a little milk mixture into the egg mixture, then pour the combined mixtures into the saucepan. Over low heat, cook, whisking constantly, until the custard mixture coats the back of a spoon, about 15 minutes.

4. Remove the saucepan from the heat and let the custard cool to room temperature. Remove the vanilla bean and scrape the seeds into the custard; discard the pod. Cover the saucepan and refrigerate until the custard is cold, 1 to 2 hours.

5. Pour the reserved peach mixture into the custard, and stir until all the ingredients are well blended. Transfer the custard to an ice-cream maker and, following the manufacturer's directions, freeze the ice cream.

Makes 1 quart

Citrus Ice Cream
Tangy citrus combines with cream to create a refreshingly unusual treat, ideal for pairing with fresh fruit salad.

1/2 cup fresh citrus juice of
   choice

1 egg

1 cup sugar

1 cup heavy cream

1 1/2 cups milk

1 tablespoon grated zest of
   citrus fruit of choice

Pinch salt

1. In a heavy saucepan over low heat, combine the citrus juice, egg, and sugar, and cook, whisking constantly, until the sugar has dissolved and the mixture registers 170°F on a candy thermometer. Stir in the cream, milk, zest, and salt.

2. Remove the saucepan from the heat and let the mixture cool to room temperature. Cover the saucepan and refrigerate until the custard is cold, about 1 hour.

3. Transfer the custard to an ice-cream maker and, following the manufacturer's directions, freeze the ice cream.

Makes 5 to 6 cups

Strawberry Ice Cream

Celebrate the beginning of summer with homemade ice cream bursting with fresh strawberries.

1 3/4 cups milk

2 1/2 cups heavy cream

1 1/3 cups sugar

1 vanilla bean,
   split lengthwise

1/4 teaspoon salt

6 egg yolks

4 strips (3 x 1/2-inch)
   orange zest

2 cups strawberries

1. In a large saucepan over moderate heat, combine the milk and cream, 1/2 cup of the sugar, the vanilla bean, and salt. Scald the mixture just until small bubbles appear.

2. In a medium bowl, combine the egg yolks and another 1/2 cup sugar. Whisk until they are well blended. Gradually whisk a little milk mixture into the egg mixture, then pour the combined mixtures into the saucepan; add the orange zest. Over low heat, cook, whisking constantly, until the custard mixture coats the back of a spoon, about 15 minutes.

3. Remove the saucepan from the heat and let the custard cool to room temperature. Remove the vanilla bean and scrape the seeds into the custard; discard the pod. Remove and discard the orange zest. Cover the saucepan and refrigerate until the custard is cold, 1 to 2 hours.

4. Meanwhile, rinse and hull the strawberries. In the bowl of a food processor or blender, combine the strawberries with the remaining 1/3 cup sugar. Whirl until the mixture is pureed to the desired consistency.

5. Remove the saucepan from the refrigerator and stir the strawberries into the custard until they are well blended. Transfer the custard to an ice-cream maker and, following the manufacturer's directions, freeze the ice cream.

Makes 1 quart

Honey Banana Ice Cream

Gingersnaps (page 131) make a perfect partner for this homemade delight.

6 egg yolks

2 cups milk

1/2 cup honey

2 teaspoons vanilla extract

2 cups heavy cream

1 cup (3 ripe) bananas,
   mashed

1. In the top of a double boiler set over simmering water, combine the egg yolks and milk, and whisk until they are well blended. Add the honey and vanilla extract. Over moderate heat, cook, stirring constantly, until the mixture coats the back of a spoon and registers 170°F on a candy thermometer.

2. Pour the mixture into a large bowl, cover, and refrigerate until the mixture is chilled, about 1 hour.

3. Add the cream and mashed bananas to the egg mixture, and stir until the ingredients are well blended. Transfer the custard to an ice-cream maker and, following the manufacturer's directions, freeze the ice cream.

Makes 5 to 6 cups

Hawaiian Ice Cream

A taste of the tropics in every bite, this coconut-pineapple ice cream is rich and cooling and not too extravagant because you make it yourself.

1 1/3 cups milk

3 eggs

1 cup sugar

1/2 cup sweetened, flaked coconut

2 teaspoons vanilla extract

1 can (1 pound) crushed pineapple, drained

1 1/3 cups heavy cream

1. In a small, heavy saucepan over moderately high heat, scald the milk just until tiny bubbles appear.

2. In a medium heavy saucepan over low heat, combine the eggs and sugar. Pour the scalded milk into the egg mixture, whisking constantly. Cook, whisking constantly, until the custard thickens and registers 170°F on a candy thermometer.

3. Set a fine sieve over a large bowl. Pour the custard through the sieve; discard the solids. Add the coconut and vanilla; whisk until well blended. Stir in the pineapple and cream. Cover the bowl and refrigerate until the custard is cold, 1 to 2 hours.

4. Transfer the custard to an ice-cream maker and, following the manufacturer's directions, freeze the ice cream.

Makes about 1 quart

Chocolate Chocolate Chip Ice Cream

What is better than chocolate? More chocolate! Remember, however, that just because homemade is cheaper, it doesn't have fewer calories.

1 3/4 cups milk

2 1/2 cups heavy cream

1 cup firmly packed light brown sugar

1/4 teaspoon salt

6 egg yolks

1/4 cup unsweetened Dutch-process cocoa powder

1 teaspoon vanilla extract

1/2 cup mini chocolate chips

1. In a large saucepan over moderate heat, combine the milk and cream, 1/2 cup of the sugar, and salt. Scald the mixture just until small bubbles appear.

2. In a medium bowl, combine the egg yolks and remaining 1/2 cup sugar. Whisk until they are well blended. Whisk in the cocoa until it is well blended. Gradually whisk a little milk mixture into the egg mixture, then pour the combined mixtures into the saucepan. Over low heat, cook, whisking constantly, until the custard mixture coats the back of a spoon, about 15 minutes.

3. Remove the saucepan from the heat and let the custard cool to room temperature. Whisk in the vanilla. Cover the saucepan and refrigerate until the custard is cold, for 1 to 2 hours.

4. Add the mini chocolate chips and stir until they are evenly distributed. Transfer the custard to an ice-cream maker and, following the manufacturer's directions, freeze the ice cream.

Makes 1 quart

Chocolate Silk Ice Cream *A rich, chocolate custard is the base for this decadent delight.*

1 1/4 cups milk

3 eggs

3/4 cup sugar

2 ounces unsweetened chocolate, chopped

2 teaspoons vanilla extract

1/4 teaspoon salt

2 cups heavy cream

1. In a small, heavy saucepan over moderately high heat, scald the milk just until tiny bubbles appear.

2. In a medium heavy saucepan over low heat, combine the eggs and sugar. Pour the scalded milk into the egg mixture, whisking constantly. Cook, whisking constantly, until the custard thickens and registers 170°F on a candy thermometer.

3. Set a fine sieve over a large bowl. Pour the custard through the sieve; discard the solids. Add the chocolate, vanilla, and salt; whisk until well blended. Stir in the cream. Cover the bowl and refrigerate until the custard is cold, 1 to 2 hours.

4. Transfer the custard to an ice-cream maker and, following the manufacturer's directions, freeze the ice cream.

Makes about 1 quart

Rocky Road Ice Cream *Chocolate chips, marshmallows, and pecans make up this popular ice cream flavor. Once you've made your own, you'll wonder how you could have spent so much money on commercial ice cream.*

3 cups milk

3 cups half-and-half

9 squares (1 ounce each) semisweet chocolate

2 3/4 cups sugar

3/4 teaspoon salt

6 cups heavy cream

3 cups miniature marshmallows

2 1/4 cups mini chocolate chips

1 1/2 cups chopped pecans

6 teaspoons vanilla extract

1. In a large, heavy saucepan over moderately high heat, combine the milk and half-and-half. Cook, stirring constantly, until the mixture registers 175°F on a candy thermometer. Add the semisweet chocolate, sugar, and salt; stir until the chocolate has melted and the sugar has completely dissolved.

2. Remove the saucepan from the heat and place it in a large bowl of ice water to cool the mixture quickly; stir and chill for 2 minutes. Remove the saucepan and let the mixture cool completely.

3. Pour the mixture into a large bowl. Add the cream, marshmallows, chocolate chips, pecans, and vanilla. Stir until all the ingredients are well blended. Cover the bowl and refrigerate until the mixture is cold, 30 minutes.

4. Working in batches, transfer the mixture to an ice-cream maker and, following the manufacturer's directions, freeze the ice cream. Keep the remaining mixture refrigerated until ready to freeze; stir well before adding to the ice-cream maker.

5. Let stand in the ice-cream maker or place in the freezer to firm for 2 to 4 hours before serving.

Makes about 4 1/2 quarts

Mint Chocolate Chip Ice Cream

Mint and chocolate are a natural combination, and this is a popular flavor for ice cream, which you can make better and cheaper at home.

1 3/4 cups milk

2 1/2 cups heavy cream

1 cup pureed fresh mint leaves

1 cup sugar

1/4 teaspoon salt

6 egg yolks

1 teaspoon vanilla extract

1/2 cup mini chocolate chips

1. In a large saucepan over moderate heat, combine the milk and cream, mint leaves, 1/2 cup of the sugar, and salt. Scald the mixture just until small bubbles appear.

2. In a medium bowl, combine the egg yolks and remaining 1/2 cup sugar. Whisk until they are well blended. Gradually whisk a little milk mixture into the egg mixture, then pour the combined mixtures into the saucepan. Over low heat, cook, whisking constantly, until the custard mixture coats the back of a spoon, about 15 minutes.

3. Remove the saucepan from the heat and let the custard cool to room temperature. Whisk in the vanilla. Cover the saucepan and refrigerate until the custard is cold, 1 to 2 hours.

4. Add the mini chocolate chips and stir until they are evenly distributed. Transfer the custard to an ice-cream maker and, following the manufacturer's directions, freeze the ice cream.

Makes 1 quart

Peppermint Ice Cream

A feast for the eyes, this mouthwatering concoction of crushed peppermint candies in a creamy base is a natural holiday sweet. You can't always find it in the stores, but you can always make it at home—for much less.

4 egg yolks

1 1/2 cups half-and-half

3/4 cup sugar

1/4 teaspoon salt

2 cups heavy cream

4 1/2-6 teaspoons vanilla extract

1-1 1/4 cups crushed peppermint candy

1. In a large, heavy saucepan over low heat, combine the egg yolks, half-and-half, sugar, and salt. Cook, stirring constantly, until the mixture coats the back of a spoon and registers 160°F on a candy thermometer.

2. Remove the saucepan from the heat and place it in a large bowl of ice water to cool the mixture quickly; stir and chill for 2 minutes. Stir in the heavy cream and vanilla. Remove the saucepan and let the mixture cool completely.

3. Cover the saucepan with plastic wrap and refrigerate for several hours or overnight until the mixture is very cold.

4. Stir in the peppermint candy until it is evenly distributed. Transfer the mixture to an ice-cream maker and, following the manufacturer's directions, freeze the ice cream.

5. Let stand in the ice-cream maker or place in the freezer to firm for 2 to 4 hours before serving.

Makes 1 quart

Butter Pecan Ice Cream
Toasting the pecans really brings out their flavor in this old favorite.

3/4 cup chopped pecans

3 tablespoons butter, melted

1/8 teaspoon salt

1/4 cup plus 1 tablespoon sugar

1/2 cup firmly packed brown sugar

2 tablespoons cornstarch

2 eggs, beaten

1/3 cup maple-flavored pancake syrup

2 1/2 cups milk

1 cup heavy cream

2 teaspoons vanilla extract

1. Preheat the oven to 350°F. On a rimmed baking sheet, spread the pecans in a single layer. Drizzle the pecans with the butter and sprinkle with the salt and 1 tablespoon of the sugar; toss to coat the nuts. Toast the pecans for 15 minutes, stir, and toast for 15 minutes longer. Remove the baking sheet from the oven and let the pecans cool completely.

2. In the top of a double boiler set over simmering water, combine the remaining 1/4 cup of sugar, brown sugar, cornstarch, eggs, and pancake syrup. Stir until the ingredients are well blended. Gradually stir in the milk. Increase the heat to high and cook, stirring constantly, until the mixture thickens and coats the back of a spoon.

3. Remove the saucepan from the heat and let the custard cool to room temperature. Cover the saucepan and refrigerate until the custard is cold, for several hours or overnight.

4. Add the toasted pecans, cream, and vanilla, and stir until they are evenly distributed. Transfer the custard to an ice-cream maker and, following the manufacturer's directions, freeze the ice cream.

5. Let stand in the ice-cream maker or place in the freezer to firm for 2 to 4 hours before serving.

Makes about 2 quarts

Ice Cream Cake

This frozen cake is perfect for a summer birthday—or any time you need an easy but sensational dessert. Use whatever combination of ice cream pleases your fancy.

1 1/2 cups crumbled Chocolate Sandwich (page 130) or Oreo cookies

2 tablespoons butter, melted

1 1/2 pints first flavor ice cream, softened

3/4 cup Hot Chocolate Sauce (page 60), cooked then cooled but still liquid

1 1/2 pints second flavor ice cream, softened

1/2 cup grated chocolate or sliced, toasted almonds

1. In a small bowl, combine the cookie crumbs with the butter and toss until well blended. In an 8-inch springform pan, press the cookie mixture over the bottom and halfway up the sides. Place the pan in the freezer for 30 minutes.

2. Spoon the first-flavor ice cream into the prepared springform pan, spreading it in an even layer over the cookie crust. Return the pan to the freezer until the ice cream is firm, about 30 minutes. Pour the chocolate sauce into the pan, spreading it evenly over the ice-cream layer; freeze until firm, about 15 minutes. Spoon the second-flavor ice cream into the pan, spreading it in an even layer over the hardened chocolate sauce. Using a knife or spatula dipped in hot water, smooth the top of the cake, then sprinkle with either the grated chocolate or toasted almond slices. Cover the cake with plastic wrap and return to the freezer for at least 1 hour.

3. To serve, wipe the bottom of the springform pan with a hot, damp cloth, then carefully remove the sides of the pan. Dip a sharp knife in hot water before cutting the cake.

Makes 8 to 10 servings

frozen yogurt

Lemon Frozen Yogurt

Light and refreshing, the lemon flavor really comes through in this homemade frozen yogurt. Try a scoop with fresh berries.

1 carton (32 ounces) nonfat, plain yogurt

1 2/3 cups sugar

1/3 cup lemon juice

1 tablespoon grated lemon zest

4 drops yellow food coloring *(optional)*

1. In a medium bowl, combine the yogurt, sugar, lemon juice and zest. Stir until all the ingredients are well blended. If a brighter yellow color is desired, stir in the food coloring.

2. Transfer the mixture to an ice-cream maker and, following the manufacturer's directions, freeze the yogurt. Let stand in the ice-cream maker or place in the freezer to firm for 2 to 4 hours before serving.

Makes 5 cups

Strawberry Frozen Yogurt

The fresh strawberries add just the right sweet note to this simple, speedy homemade frozen yogurt.

- 2 cups (16 ounces) nonfat plain yogurt
- 2 cups pureed fresh strawberries
- 1 can (14 ounces) fat-free sweetened condensed milk
- 1 cup nonfat milk
- 3 teaspoons vanilla extract

1. In a large bowl, combine all the ingredients and stir until well blended.

2. Working in batches if needed, pour the mixture into an ice-cream maker, filling it two-thirds full; store the remaining yogurt in the refrigerator until ready to freeze. Following the manufacturer's directions, freeze the yogurt. Let stand in the ice-cream maker or place in the freezer to firm for 2 to 4 hours before serving. Remove from the freezer 30 to 45 minutes before serving to soften slightly.

Makes 1 1/2 quarts

Mocha Chip Frozen Yogurt

Coffee and chocolate marry divinely in this rich dessert that you can put together quickly and inexpensively for your family's enjoyment.

- 3 cups regular or low-fat plain yogurt
- 1 1/2 tablespoons instant espresso powder
- 3/4 cup sugar
- 1 cup heavy cream
- 2 ounces bittersweet chocolate, chopped
- 1 teaspoon vanilla extract

1. Set a large fine sieve over a large bowl. Add the yogurt and place in the refrigerator for 1 hour to drain.

2. In another large bowl, combine the espresso powder, sugar, and cream; stir until the sugar has completely dissolved. Beat the mixture until it holds soft peaks. Add the drained yogurt, chocolate, and vanilla, stirring until all the ingredients are well blended and no streaks of white remain.

3. Pour the mixture into an ice-cream maker and, following the manufacturer's directions, freeze the yogurt.

Makes 5 to 6 cups

Helpful Hint

Frozen Yogurt: An Alternative to Ice Cream

Once the province of health food aficionados, frozen yogurt has spread widely and grown wildly in popularity. Generally lower in fat and calories (though not always) than ice cream, frozen yogurt combines the slight tanginess associated with yogurt with the cool creaminess of ice cream. For the most healthful results, use nonfat yogurt when making it. It is made much like ice cream, and you need an ice-cream maker to make it.

ices, granitas, sherbets, and sorbets

Orange Ice *This treat requires only five ingredients and no ice-cream maker.*

3 cups water

1 cup sugar

1 can (12 ounces) frozen orange juice concentrate, thawed

2 tablespoons lemon juice

1/2 cup half-and-half

1. In a medium saucepan over high heat, combine 1 cup of the water and the sugar. Boil, stirring frequently, until the sugar has completely dissolved, about 1 minute.

2. Remove the saucepan from the heat and stir in the orange juice concentrate, lemon juice, and the remaining 2 cups of water. Stir until all the ingredients are well blended.

3. Pour the orange mixture into a large, freezer-safe bowl, cover, and freeze until firm.

4. Remove the bowl from the freezer and, using an electric mixer, beat the orange mixture until smooth. Add the half-and-half and beat again until well blended. Re-cover the bowl and return the orange mixture to the freezer.

5. Let the orange ice stand at room temperature for 20 minutes before serving.

Makes 10 to 12 servings

Blood-Orange Champagne Granita *If blood oranges are unavailable, substitute ruby red or pink grapefruit.*

1 1/2 cups sugar

1 cup water

2 cups freshly squeezed blood-orange juice

2 cups champagne

Pinch salt

1. In a medium saucepan over moderate heat, combine the sugar and water, stirring constantly until the sugar has dissolved. Bring the mixture to a boil, reduce the heat, and simmer for 3 minutes. Remove the saucepan from the heat and let stand until the syrup is cool, about 1 hour.

2. In a large bowl, combine the syrup, juice, champagne, and salt. Stir until all the ingredients are well blended.

3. Pour the mixture into ice-cube trays or a large, shallow pan. Cover with plastic wrap and place in the freezer. As the granita freezes, stir it with a fork, every 45 minutes, two or three times, to break up the ice and create an icy, flaky texture. Cover with plastic wrap and freeze for 8 hours or overnight.

4. When ready to serve, place the granita in the refrigerator for 15 minutes to soften; then, using an ice-cream scoop or large spoon, scrape across the top to bring up the granita in thin shavings. Serve in chilled glasses or bowls.

Makes 12 servings

Cappuccino Granita

An Italian specialty, this granita goes well with a few chocolate-covered coffee beans.

1 1/4 cups brewed strong black coffee or espresso

1/4 cup granulated sugar

5 tablespoons Kahlúa or other coffee-flavored liqueur

1 cup heavy cream

1 tablespoon confectioners' sugar

Unsweetened cocoa powder

1. In a small bowl, combine the coffee, sugar, and 3 tablespoons of the Kahlúa.

2. Pour the coffee mixture into ice-cube trays or a large, shallow pan. Cover with plastic wrap and place in the freezer. As the granita freezes, stir it with a fork, every 45 minutes, two or three times, to break up the ice and create an icy, flaky texture. Cover the granita with plastic wrap and freeze 8 hours or overnight.

3. In a medium bowl with an electric mixer, beat the cream with the remaining Kahlúa and confectioners' sugar until soft peaks form.

4. To serve, roughly break up the granita. Using an ice-cream scoop or large spoon, scrape across the top to bring up the granita in thin shavings. Place the granita in individual chilled serving bowls and top each with a dollop of the Kahlúa whipped cream. Sprinkle a dusting of cocoa powder over each serving.

Makes 6 to 8 servings

Kiwi Granita

A lovely green with a lively, tart taste, this homemade granita would be a fitting finale to a rich meal.

1 cup water

2 cups sugar

Juice of 2 lemons

6 large, ripe kiwis, peeled and coarsely chopped

1. In a small saucepan over moderate heat, combine the water, sugar, and half the lemon juice. Cook, stirring constantly, until the sugar has dissolved. Bring the syrup to a boil, reduce the heat, and simmer 3 minutes. Remove the saucepan from the heat and let stand until the syrup is just warm.

2. In the bowl of a food processor or blender, place the kiwis and whirl until they are pureed. Add the remaining lemon juice and whirl to blend. Pour the kiwi puree into the syrup.

3. Pour the kiwi mixture into ice-cube trays or a large, shallow pan. Cover with plastic wrap and place in the freezer. As the granita freezes, stir it with a fork every 45 minutes, two or three times, to break up the ice and create an icy, flaky texture. Cover the granita with plastic wrap and freeze 6 hours or until solid.

4. When ready to serve, place the granita in the refrigerator for 15 minutes to soften; then, using an ice-cream scoop or large spoon, scrape across the top to bring up the granita in thin shavings. Serve in chilled glasses or bowls.

Makes about 4 cups

Easy-to-Make Sweet Treats   **227**

Peach Granita
An out-of-this-world cooler for a hot summer's day, this granita is an easy home project.

1 cup water

1/2 cup sugar

4 ripe peaches, peeled, pitted and coarsely chopped

1 tablespoon peach schnapps or other fruit liqueur

1. In a small saucepan over moderate heat, combine the water and sugar, and stir until the sugar has completely dissolved. Bring the mixture to a boil, reduce the heat, and simmer 3 minutes. Remove the saucepan from the heat and let stand until the syrup is cool, about 1 hour.

2. In the bowl of a food processor or blender, place the peach pieces and whirl until they are pureed. Add the syrup and schnapps, and whirl until all the ingredients are well blended.

3. Pour the peach mixture into ice-cube trays or a large, shallow pan. Cover with plastic wrap and place in the freezer. As the granita freezes, stir it with a fork every 45 minutes, two or three times, to break up the ice and create an icy, flaky texture. Cover the granita with plastic wrap and freeze 6 hours or until solid.

4. When ready to serve, place the granita in the refrigerator for 15 minutes to soften; then, using an ice-cream scoop or large spoon, scrape across the top to bring up the granita in thin shavings. Serve in chilled glasses or bowls.

Makes about 4 cups

Lime Sherbet
Refreshingly tart, this homemade sherbet is better than any you can buy and costs lots less.

4 1/4 cups sugar

1 1/2 cups lime juice

3 tablespoons lemon juice

2 tablespoons grated lime zest

7 1/2 cups milk

1/2 cup buttermilk

1 drop green food coloring *(optional)*

1. In a large bowl, combine the first four ingredients and stir until well blended. Gradually stir in the milk and buttermilk. If a brighter green color is desired, stir in the green food coloring.

2. Working in batches if needed, pour the lime mixture into an ice-cream maker, filling it two-thirds full; store the remaining mixture in the refrigerator until ready to freeze. Following the manufacturer's directions, freeze the sherbet. Let stand in the ice-cream maker or place in the freezer to firm for 2 to 4 hours before serving. Remove from the freezer 10 minutes before serving to soften slightly.

Makes about 2 1/2 quarts

Strawberry Milk Sherbet

Smooth as ice cream but made with milk for a lighter treat, this sherbet is easy to make at home and an inexpensive treat whenever you want it.

1 pint strawberries, rinsed and hulled

1 cup milk

1 cup sugar

1. In the bowl of a food processor or blender, place the strawberries and whirl until they are pureed and a smooth consistency.

2. In a medium saucepan over high heat, combine the milk and sugar, and bring the mixture to a boil. Remove the saucepan from the heat and let stand until the milk mixture is just warm.

3. In a medium bowl, combine the strawberry puree and milk mixture, and whisk until they are well blended.

4. Pour the strawberry-milk mixture into an ice-cream maker. Following the manufacturer's directions, freeze the sherbet.

Makes 1 pint

Cassis Sorbet

A black-currant liqueur, cassis has a smooth, strong flavor that makes this sorbet particularly delicious as a formal dinner dessert that makes guests and your pocketbook happy.

1 1/2 cups water

1/2 cup sugar

1 cup cassis (black-currant liqueur)

1. In a medium saucepan over high heat, combine the water and sugar, and bring the mixture to a boil, stirring constantly until the sugar has dissolved. Remove the saucepan from the heat and let stand until the syrup is just warm.

2. In a medium bowl, combine the syrup and cassis, and stir until they are well blended.

3. Pour the cassis mixture into an ice-cream maker. Following the manufacturer's directions, freeze the sorbet.

Makes 1 pint

Citrus Sorbet

Oranges, lemons, and limes all lend their distinctive notes to this refreshing sorbet that you make at home for pennies.

1 cup water

1/2 cup sugar

1 1/4 cups orange juice

1/4 cup lemon juice

3 tablespoons lime juice

1. In a medium saucepan over high heat, combine the water and sugar, and bring the mixture to a boil, stirring constantly until the sugar has dissolved. Remove the saucepan from the heat and let stand until the syrup is just warm.

2. In a medium bowl, combine the syrup and the juices, and stir until they are well blended.

3. Pour the citrus mixture into an ice-cream maker. Following the manufacturer's directions, freeze the sorbet.

Makes 1 pint

Honeydew Sorbet

Serve a scoop of this delicate sorbet in a wedge of fresh honeydew. Or try substituting cantaloupe for the honeydew. Either way, you don't have to wait for your ice-cream parlor to feature this delicious flavor once a year.

6 cups honeydew melon cubes
3/4 cup sugar
3 tablespoons Midori or other melon-flavored liqueur

1. In the bowl of a food processor or blender, place all the ingredients. Whirl until the melon is pureed, and the ingredients are blended into a smooth consistency. Place the bowl in the refrigerator until the melon mixture is completely chilled.
2. Pour the melon mixture into an ice-cream maker. Following the manufacturer's directions, freeze the sorbet.

Makes 1 pint

Lemon Sorbet

Wonderfully tart, this classic sorbet works either as a dessert or as a palate cleanser between courses. As a variation, add 1/2 cup fresh mint leaves to the syrup before it cools, then strain before freezing. Make it better and cheaper yourself.

3 cups water
1 1/2 cups sugar
1 1/2 cups lemon juice
1 tablespoon grated lemon zest

1. In a medium saucepan over high heat, combine the water and sugar. Bring the mixture to a boil and cook, stirring constantly, until the sugar has completely dissolved, about 5 minutes. Remove the saucepan from the heat and let the syrup cool.
2. Add the lemon juice and zest to the syrup. Stir until all the ingredients are well blended.
3. Pour the lemon mixture into an ice-cream maker. Following the manufacturer's directions, freeze the sorbet. Let stand in the ice-cream maker or place in the freezer to firm for 2 to 4 hours before serving. Remove from the freezer 10 minutes before serving to soften slightly.

Makes about 1 quart

Raspberry Sorbet

Since it uses frozen raspberries, you can make this sorbet any time of the year. Try drizzling with a little Chocolate Sauce (page 60) before serving. Homemade is cheaper and better.

1 package (10 ounces) frozen raspberries, thawed

1 cup water

1 cup sugar

1 tablespoon lemon juice

1. In the bowl of a food processor or blender, place the raspberries and whirl until they are pureed and a smooth consistency.

2. In a medium saucepan over high heat, combine the water and sugar, and bring the mixture to a boil, stirring constantly until the sugar has dissolved. Remove the saucepan from the heat and let stand until the syrup is just warm.

3. In a medium bowl, combine the syrup, raspberry puree, and lemon juice, and stir until they are well blended.

4. Pour the raspberry mixture into an ice-cream maker. Following the manufacturer's directions, freeze the sorbet.

Makes 1 pint

Strawberry Sorbet

Look for really ripe, firm, red strawberries for extraordinary flavor and ravishing color. This sorbet is another treat you can make better and more frugally at home.

6 cups strawberries

1 3/4 cups sugar

2 cups fresh orange juice, strained

2 tablespoons Grand Marnier or other orange-flavored liqueur

1. Wash and hull the strawberries, drain well, and cut them in half. In a small bowl, combine the strawberry halves, sugar, and orange juice. Let the strawberry mixture stand for 1 hour.

2. In the bowl of a food processor or blender, whirl the strawberry mixture until it is a smooth puree. Add the Grand Marnier and pulse until well blended.

3. Pour the mixture into ice-cube trays or a large, shallow pan and freeze until just firm but not hard, 1 to 2 hours.

4. Spoon the mixture back into the bowl of the food processor and pulse until the mixture becomes slushy. Repeat to refreeze, then break up the sorbet. Return the mixture to the pan and freeze until solid.

5. Before serving, place the pan in the refrigerator and let the sorbet soften slightly, about 15 minutes.

Makes about 1 1/2 pints

ices, granitas, sherbets, and sorbets

frozen pops

Frozen Fruit Pops
Any flavor of gelatin will do to make these cool treats that you can keep in the freezer all summer.

1 package (3 ounces) fruit-flavored gelatin

1/2 cup sugar

2 cups boiling water

1 1/2 cups cold water

10-12 frozen pop molds or 3-ounce paper cups

10-12 frozen pop sticks or plastic spoons

1. In a medium bowl, combine the gelatin and sugar. Pour in the boiling water, stirring until the gelatin and sugar are completely dissolved. Stir in the cold water.

2. Pour the gelatin mixture into the frozen pop molds or paper cups, and place in the freezer until the pops are almost firm, about 2 hours. Insert a frozen pop stick or plastic spoon into the center of each pop. Return to the freezer until the pops are firm, 4 to 8 hours. To serve, unmold or tear away the paper cup from the pop.

Makes 10 to 12 pops

Fudge Pops
Cold, chocolaty, and oh, so satisfying, these treats are easy to make at home and taste much better than the commercial ones.

1 package (3.4 ounces) cook-and-serve chocolate fudge pudding mix

3 cups milk

1/4 cup sugar

1/2 cup whipping cream

12-13 frozen pop molds or 3-ounce paper cups

12-13 frozen pop sticks or plastic spoons

1. In a medium saucepan over moderate heat, combine the pudding mix, milk, and sugar. Bring the mixture to a boil; cook, stirring constantly, for 2 minutes. Remove the saucepan from the heat and let the pudding stand for 30 minutes, stirring the mixture several times, until it is cool.

2. In a small bowl using an electric mixer, whip the cream until soft peaks form. Fold the whipped cream into the pudding mixture until all the ingredients are well blended and no streaks of white remain.

3. Pour the pudding mixture into the frozen pop molds or paper cups, and place in the freezer until the pops are almost firm, about 2 hours. Insert a frozen pop stick or plastic spoon into the center of each pop. Return to the freezer until firm, 3 to 4 hours. To serve, unmold or tear away the paper cup from the pop.

Makes 12 to 13 pops

Orange Cream Pops

Yum! Creamy orange-flavored pops that you make at home go down very well on a hot day.

1 package (3 ounces) orange gelatin

1 cup boiling water

1 cup (8 ounces) low-fat vanilla yogurt

1/2 cup reduced-fat (2%) milk

1/2 teaspoon vanilla extract

10 frozen pop molds or 3-ounce plastic cups

10 frozen pop sticks or plastic spoons

1. In a large bowl, combine the gelatin and boiling water, and stir until the gelatin has completely dissolved. Let stand until the gelatin is room temperature.

2. Add the yogurt, milk, and vanilla, and stir until all the ingredients are well blended.

3. Pour the gelatin mixture into the frozen pop molds or paper cups, and place in the freezer until the pops are almost firm, about 2 hours. Insert a frozen pop stick or plastic spoon into the center of each pop. Return to the freezer until the pops are firm, 4 to 8 hours. To serve, unmold or tear away the paper cup from the pop.

Makes 10 pops

Strawberry Ice Pops

Fresh strawberries make these pops extra special—tasting like the pricey, high-end pops from the ice-cream store.

2 pints fresh strawberries, washed and hulled

1/2 cup apple juice concentrate

8 frozen pop molds or 3-ounce plastic cups

8 frozen pop sticks or plastic spoons

1. In a large bowl, using a potato masher, mash the strawberries roughly, leaving some chunks of strawberry intact. Add the apple juice concentrate and stir until the ingredients are well blended.

2. Spoon or pour the strawberry mixture into the frozen pop molds or paper cups, and place in the freezer until the pops are almost firm, about 2 hours. Insert a frozen pop stick or plastic spoon into the center of each pop. Return to the freezer until the pops are firm, 4 to 8 hours. To serve, unmold or tear away the paper cup from the pop.

Makes 8 pops

Tropical Pops

If you can't be sipping tropical drinks, you can at least keep your cool with these inexpensive, homemade tropical pops.

12 large or 24 small frozen pop molds or 1-cup or 1/2-cup plastic cups

12-24 frozen pop sticks or plastic spoons

6 cups fresh tropical fruit, such as pineapples, papayas, and/or mangoes, peeled and cored as needed, cut into bite-size pieces, reserving any juices

3 cups mixed tropical fruit punch or orange or pineapple juice

1. In a large bowl, combine the fresh fruit with any juices collected during their preparation. Stir the fruits well to distribute them equally.

2. Spoon the fruit mixture into the frozen pop molds or plastic cups, filling each three-quarters full.

3. Pour some of the fruit punch or juice into each mold or cup, leaving room at the top for the liquid to expand. Place in the freezer until the pops are almost firm, about 2 hours. Insert a frozen pop stick or plastic spoon into the center of each pop. Return to the freezer until the pops are firm, 4 to 8 hours. To serve, unmold or tear away the paper cup from the pop.

Makes 12 (1-cup) pops or 24 (1/2-cup) pops

Chocolate-Nut Frozen Bananas

Bananas are one of those fruits that can be frozen and eaten out of hand. But for a special treat, try dipping them in chocolate and nuts!

8 wooden skewers, sharp ends cut off

8 small bananas

8 ounces dark chocolate

3 tablespoons vegetable shortening

1 cup coarsely chopped walnuts, toasted

1 cup coarsely chopped macadamia nuts, toasted

1. Line a baking sheet with plastic wrap.

2. Insert 1 skewer into each banana, pushing it so the end is about halfway along the length of the fruit. Place each skewered banana on the prepared baking sheet. Cover the baking sheet with plastic wrap and place in the freezer until the bananas are frozen solid, about 8 hours.

3. In a small bowl placed over simmering water, combine the chocolate and shortening, and melt, stirring occasionally. Remove the bowl from the heat. In a shallow plate, combine the walnuts and macadamia nuts, and toss to mix well.

4. Remove the sheet of bananas from the freezer. Holding one banana pop by the stick end over the bowl, spoon chocolate over the banana, coating it completely. Then hold the banana over the nuts and scoop up and sprinkle nuts over the chocolate-covered banana. Return the banana to the baking sheet. Repeat to coat all the bananas with chocolate and nuts. Return the baking sheet to the freezer until the chocolate hardens and is frozen. Wrap each banana separately in plastic wrap, then place them all in a large, self-sealing freezer-safe plastic bag and store in the freezer.

Makes 8 servings

Part 2:

health and beauty care for you and yours

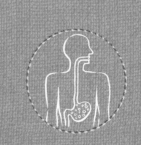

chapter 7

Your Own Beauty Products

Some of the loveliest and most seductive ads on television and in magazines are for cosmetics—makeup, scents, and skin care products in beautiful packages. They are all very intriguing and inviting until you read the small print and realize that you don't know what all those ingredients are or what they are designed to do. And, although you may feel, as one cosmetics company suggests, that the price doesn't matter because "you're worth it," you just might want to know what is going onto your skin.

Making your own beauty products is neither difficult nor mystifying. These recipes have all been thoroughly reviewed by experts. For not much more than a little time and effort, you can even give yourself spa treatments that will benefit your spirits as well as your skin—with face masks, exfoliants, and wrinkle fighters. Your pocketbook will barely be involved. You might even want to involve friends in the making and using of these recipes for special spa hours.

For everyday use, you can make cleansers, moisturizers, and toners; toothpaste and gargles; shampoos and hair rinses; shaving gels and refreshing splashes—with or without scent. For your bath, you can prepare lovely bath gels from soap slivers, almond rose or cinnamon soap, and several bath scrubs and milk baths. For hands and feet, there are special creams and soaks. There is also a selection of recipes for homemade men's toiletries: shaving soap, aftershaves, a shaving cut lotion, and a muscle rub.

face care products

Anti-Wrinkle Eye Cream

Apply this cream with a gentle touch around the eye, using light, circular strokes. It is especially geared for the soft tissue under and around the eyes—and it works just as well as, if not better than, the pricey versions sold in stores.

2 tablespoons elder flower water (available through mail order)

1/4 cup avocado oil

2 tablespoons almond oil

4 teaspoons wheat germ oil

2 tablespoons lanolin

2 tablespoons glycerin

2 drops geranium essential oil

1 vitamin E capsule, 400 IU

1. Warm the elder flower water in a nonreactive saucepan over low heat.

2. In the top of a double boiler, set over simmering water, warm the avocado, almond, and wheat germ oils. Stir in the lanolin until melted. Remove from heat.

3. Gradually beat in the warmed elder flower water. Stir in the glycerin and geranium essential oil. Pierce the vitamin E capsule with a needle, squeeze out the contents, and stir in.

4. Pour mixture into a clean widemouthed 6-ounce glass jar with a tight-fitting lid. Store in a cool, dark place.

Tired Eye Remedy

Here's a simple soak you can apply to soothe irritated or inflamed eyes. The price is a few rose petals from your garden.

8 ounces boiling water

2-3 rose petals

1. Pour the boiling water over the rose petals into a bowl. Steep for about 10 minutes. Cool and strain the petals out.

2. Soak two large cotton balls in the rose tea and apply over closed eyelids. Rest and relax.

One-Minute Substitute

Fast Relief with Witch Hazel Eye Compresses

We give our eyes a workout reading, watching TV, and staring at the computer screen. Here's a basic eye care remedy that costs no more than a few cents and provides a very valuable service. Just keep a small jar of witch hazel in the refrigerator. Soak two cotton pads in the chilled liquid, lie down, cover both eyelids, and relax for 5 minutes.

Rich Neck Moisturizer

In your beauty regimen, don't forget the neck, which can show the first signs of aging. Products like this often sell at beauty counters for $12 to $25 or more, but you can make it for just a few dollars with all-natural ingredients. This recipe uses oils to keep the skin supple. Use a small amount and massage from the neckline all the way to the chin.

1 teaspoon dried chamomile

1 1/8 cups boiling water

3 tablespoons avocado oil

3 tablespoons almond oil

2 teaspoons jojoba oil

1 ounce shaved or grated beeswax

2 teaspoons glycerin

20 drops lemon essential oil

1. Place the chamomile in a large cup, and add the boiling water. Cover and allow to steep for 15 minutes. Strain the liquid into another cup.

2. In the top of a double boiler, set over simmering water, warm the avocado, almond, and jojoba oils. Add the beeswax. Stir until melted. Remove from heat and beat in 1 ounce (2 tablespoons) of the warmed chamomile infusion, drop by drop until the mixture thickens and cools. Thoroughly mix in the glycerin and lemon essential oil.

3. Spoon into a sterilized, widemouthed, 6-ounce glass or ceramic jar with a tight-fitting lid. Store in a cool, dark place.

know your skin type

To pick the best products for your skin, you need to know your skin type. Most people have a combination of skin types—particularly on the face—where oily areas around the chin, nose, and forehead are different from the normal or dry skin around the eyes and on the cheeks.

There are four basic skin types:

Normal skin is clear, supple, and soft. It is neither too dry nor too oily, and it is not overly sensitive to sun, humidity, or the environment.

Dry skin looks dull, feels tight after washing, and needs sun protection and frequent moisturizing to prevent flaking.

Oily skin feels soft and supple, but it looks shiny and needs cleaning several times a day. Oily skin tends to support large pores and is more prone to pimples and blackheads than dry or normal skin.

Sensitive skin is easily burned by the sun and irritated by chemicals found in many commercial skin products that may cause rashes or blotching.

Peachy Keen Complexion Cream

This wonderful rich combination is easily made. You'll find it helps give your complexion that fabled glow. And you can't find anything like it in the stores.

1 ripe peach

Heavy cream

1. Mash the peach by hand or puree it in a food processor.

2. Add enough cream to the pulp to give you a soft, creamy mixture. Spoon into a clean glass jar with a tight-fitting lid and store in the refrigerator.

3. Once a day, apply the mixture to your face and massage in.

Artichoke Facial

Artichoke conditions dry or damaged skin. It reduces flaking and restores suppleness. Enjoy making this recipe in your kitchen laboratory, but watch out for the "choke!"

1 fresh artichoke heart, well cooked, or canned hearts in water, not oil

2 teaspoons light oil (avocado, olive, or canola)

1 teaspoon vinegar or fresh lemon juice

1. Mash artichoke heart in a ceramic bowl. Mix in oil and vinegar or lemon juice. Stir well until a smooth paste is formed.

2. Massage on face and neck. Let sit 10 to 15 minutes. Rinse off with warm water and pat dry.

Basic Skin Toner

A gentle cleanser or first step in your daily ritual. You can custom-design this basic skin toner to suit your skin type. See the box on page 254 to choose the essential oils that are right for you.

1 teaspoon dried chamomile

1/3 cup boiling water

2 drops essential oil

1. Place the chamomile and boiling water in a cup. Cover and allow to steep for 15 minutes. Strain the liquid through a fine sieve into a sterile 4-ounce glass bottle that has a tight-fitting lid. When cool, add the essential oil and shake well to mix. Allow to stand for 48 hours, shaking periodically.

2. Pour the liquid through a paper coffee filter into a sterile glass bottle. Cap the bottle and store in a cool, dark place.

3. Apply daily with a cotton ball.

fixed oil vs. essential oil

Olive oil, almond oil, and vegetable oils are all derived primarily from seeds. They are "fixed oils" that are nonvolatile. Essential oils, distilled from leaves or flowers, are volatile and flammable. They evaporate even at low temperatures, and they are potentially toxic if they are inhaled or if they are used incorrectly.

Most essential oils must be diluted in a fixed, or "carrier," oil before they are applied to the skin. The exceptions are lavender and tea tree essential oils, but even they should be used sparingly.

Cucumber Astringent

Straight from your garden or the grocer's counter, you can make this skin bracer in a jiffy. In summer you'll find this a refreshing and light treat for your skin. But any time of year, a simple cucumber astringent will perk you up.

1 cucumber

1. Peel the cucumber and puree it in a food processor. Apply the puree to your skin using a cotton pad, gently swathing your face. Rinse off with cool water.

2. Refrigerate any leftovers in a clean, covered container. It should keep for a day or two.

Egg-White Toner

For the price of an egg, you can make this one-ingredient toner that leaves your skin feeling tight and silky smooth.

1 egg white

1. Clean your face thoroughly using any natural cleanser.
2. Whisk the egg white just before applying it to your face. Leave it on for about 15 minutes.
3. Wash off with tepid water and pat skin dry.

Lemon Skin Toner

You can toss this toner together in just a few seconds from items you have in your pantry. Total cost: just pennies. Most toners purchased at the cosmetics counter run more than $6 a bottle.

2 ounces lemon juice
4 ounces distilled water
3 ounces witch hazel

1. Combine all ingredients. Pour into a clean bottle or decorative cosmetics container. Shake well before using. Apply with a clean cotton ball.
2. Keep in the refrigerator indefinitely.

One-Minute Substitute

Instant Grape Cleanser for Your Face

Here's a sweet way to clean and refresh your skin. Split 3 or 4 large green or red grapes, remove any seeds, and rub the fleshy interior on your face and neck. The grapes condition your skin and reduce dryness, restoring suppleness. Rinse with cool water and gently pat skin dry.

Facial Cleansing Mask

This simple recipe is aimed at deep cleansing and is especially suited for young faces and the treatment of oily skin.

1 packet dry yeast
3 drops lemon juice
2 teaspoons water

1. In a small bowl, mix the yeast, lemon juice, and water vigorously until a thick paste forms. If necessary, add more water to achieve the correct consistency for applying to the face.
2. Pat the mixture on the face, avoiding the eyes. Allow to sit for 10 to 15 minutes. Rinse off with warm water. Pat skin dry.

Green Clay Purifying Face Mask

Green clay—also known as bentonite— is the most commonly used clay in face masks. It can absorb large quantities of water. In this mask, it is used to draw out excess sebum and dirt from deep down, making the mask suited to oily complexions. Green clay powder can be purchased online or in health food stores for about $5 for 8 ounces, which would be enough clay for 16 masks. Palmarosa is an essential oil available at health food or "new age" shops.

1 teaspoon apricot kernel oil
2 drops palmarosa
1 tablespoon green clay
Warm water

1. Clean your face thoroughly using any natural cleanser. In a small dish, mix the apricot oil and the palmarosa together. Put the green clay in a small bowl and stir in the apricot oil mixture. Add just enough warm water to make a spreadable paste. With your fingers, work the mixture thoroughly to incorporate all the ingredients.

2. Apply the mask immediately, avoiding the eyes. Let it sit for 10 to 15 minutes. As the moisture evaporates, you will feel the mask tighten.

3. Rinse the mask off with warm water, pat skin dry, and follow with an application of toner and then of moisturizer.

Yogurt and Oatmeal Deep-Cleansing Facial

Imagine! You can mix up this deep-cleansing face mask for less than 50 cents. Your face and your pocketbook will thank you.

1 tablespoon finely ground oatmeal
1 tablespoon yogurt (any kind)
1/2 teaspoon honey

1. Before starting, clean your face thoroughly with any natural cleanser so that you can immediately apply the deep-cleansing facial mixture when it has been stirred together.

2. In a clean bowl, combine the yogurt and oatmeal and mix to a spreadable consistency. In a small glass bowl sitting in a larger bowl of hot water, warm the honey and pour it into the yogurt and oatmeal mixture. Using a spoon, blend the ingredients thoroughly.

3. Immediately apply the mask to your face, avoiding the eyes, and let it stay on for 10 to 15 minutes. Wash it off with warm water. Pat skin dry and apply a toner and moisturizer to your face.

Almond Mayonnaise Scrub

Don't be afraid of this one, but keep in mind that it is for very dry skin. Mayonnaise, which contains eggs, oil, and lemon juice, will nourish the face. The almonds will provide a mild exfoliation/dermabrasion.

1/4 cup almonds

1/8 teaspoon mayonnaise

1 teaspoon red-wine or cider vinegar

1/2 cup water

1. Clean your face thoroughly with any natural cleanser. Grind almonds in a blender or food processor until they form a meal. Whirl in mayonnaise. Set aside.

2. In a small bowl, combine the vinegar and water. Rinse your face with this mixture.

3. Now gently and thoroughly massage your face with the almond-mayonnaise scrub. Leave it on your skin for 10 minutes. Rinse off with warm water and pat skin dry.

Honey Mask

The ingredients in this mask would make up a solid breakfast, but they're nourishing for your skin too. Costing under a dollar, it's a good deal for a meal or a mask.

1/2 cup hot water

10 tablespoons quick oats

1/2 apple, cored but with peel on

2 heaping tablespoons plain yogurt

2 tablespoons honey

1 egg white

1. Clean your face thoroughly with any natural cleanser. In a small bowl, stir the oats into the hot water until you have a smooth mixture. Let stand for about 5 minutes or until the mixture thickens to a paste.

2. Put the apple, yogurt, honey, and egg white in a blender or food processor and pulse for 45 seconds just to mix. Now add oatmeal mixture and pulse for 20 seconds more.

3. Apply this mask evenly to the face, avoiding the eyes, and let sit for 15 minutes or until skin feels tight. Rinse thoroughly with warm water and pat skin dry.

Banana, Sour Cream, and Honey Face Mask

Although this sounds like the beginning of a rich dessert, it's actually an enriching mask for your face. The banana is an astringent, the honey conditions, and the sour cream allows them to work together in a mask. You could travel to a fancy spa for a treatment like this, but making it at home will cost you just a few cents. Enjoy!

1/2 banana

1 tablespoon honey

2 tablespoons sour cream

1. Clean your face thoroughly with any natural cleanser. In a small bowl, mash the half-banana. Stir in the honey and sour cream.

2. Apply to your face, avoiding the eyes, and let set for 10 minutes. Gently wipe off with a damp washcloth. Rinse clean with warm water. Pat your skin dry.

Youthful Skin Face Mask

In this variation of the banana facial mask, banana is again the astringent. It induces a tightening or tingling sensation and thereby gives the effect of decreasing the appearance of wrinkles.

1/4 cup heavy whipping cream

1 medium banana

1 vitamin E capsule, 400 IU

1. Clean your face thoroughly with any natural cleanser. In a small bowl, mash together the cream and banana. Pierce the vitamin E capsule with a needle, squeeze out the contents, and stir in.

2. Smooth onto face and neck. Leave on for 10 to 15 minutes. Remove with damp cloth. Rinse clean with warm water. Pat your skin dry.

Helpful Hint

When Vitamin E Is Called For

Several of the recipes on in this part of the book call for using vitamin E. You can buy vitamin E oil as a liquid at most drugstores, but if you only need a small amount, it's sometimes more practical to use a 400 IU vitamin E capsule. Just pierce the capsule with a needle and squeeze out the contents.

Oatmeal Exfoliant

Here's a treat for your face that might be part of a spa regimen. You can mix this up in a jiffy to use as a cleanser anytime you're in the mood. Cost to you: less than 25 cents.

2 heaping teaspoons fine oatmeal

1 teaspoon baking soda

Lukewarm water

1. Clean your face thoroughly with any natural cleanser.

2. In a small bowl, stir together oatmeal and baking soda. (The oatmeal needs to be fine; if necessary, first pulse it in a food processor or blender.) Add enough lukewarm water to make a paste. Apply to face and rub gently. Rinse and gently pat the skin dry.

One-Minute Substitute

A Quick Banana Wrinkle Fighter

Peel away the years with this easy facial treatment. Banana is an astringent that induces a tightening or tingling sensation on the skin, which decreases the appearance of wrinkles. With bananas usually selling for less than 50 cents a pound, this is a very reasonable facial treatment. Clean your face thoroughly with any natural cleanser. Mash 1/4 of a ripe banana until very creamy and spread it all over your face, avoiding the eyes. Leave on for 15 to 20 minutes. Rinse with warm water and then splash cold water on your face. Gently pat your skin dry.

Mask for Oily Skin

1 teaspoon brewer's yeast
1/3 cup yogurt or as needed

This combination of brewer's yeast and yogurt deep-cleanses oily skin without over-drying. The inexpensive homemade mask leaves skin feeling fresh and revitalized, just as a $30 salon mask treatment does.

1. Clean your face thoroughly with any natural cleanser. In a small bowl, mix the brewer's yeast with the yogurt to make a thin paste. Pat this mixture onto the oily areas of your face. Allow the mask to dry for 15 to 20 minutes.
2. Rinse with warm water. Splash with cool water. Gently pat dry.

Strawberry Yogurt Mask

1 handful ripe strawberries
1 tablespoon ground almonds
2 tablespoons yogurt

If you grow strawberries in your garden, pluck a few to use in this treatment. Your face will thank you for this gentle, delicious treat that leaves the skin smooth and refreshed.

1. Clean your face thoroughly with any natural cleanser. In a small bowl, mash the strawberries and almonds until completely blended together. Stir in the yogurt to make a spreadable paste.
2. Apply immediately or refrigerate and use within 1 day on a clean face.

how to apply a face mask

Women have used face masks for centuries to clean and tone the skin and give it a glowing vitality. Face masks give their best results if used regularly—once a week is not too often.

1. To make the process easier, sit or stand in front of a mirror. Cover your shoulders with a clean towel and have a damp washrag or hand towel ready for wiping up any drips.

2. Apply the mask with a clean cotton ball or with your fingers. The mask should cover your face from the hairline to the chin, missing only the area around the eyes.

3. Leave the mask on for 15 minutes the first few times you use it. Later, if your skin is not irritated and you like the mask's effects, you can slowly increase the time to 30 minutes. To best enjoy the facial mask, lie down, shut your eyes, and relax while the mask is working.

4. When the time is up, remove the mask with your fingers over a basin. If the mask has dried, splash warm water on your face and try again to remove the mask with your fingers. Then use a wet washcloth to remove the last residue of the mask. Finally, splash your face with cool water, pat the skin dry, and apply a toner.

Galen's Cold Cream

As old as the hills, this recipe for cold cream is believed to have been devised by the Greek philosopher and doctor Galen in the 2nd century C.E. It is still every bit as effective today and will cost you pennies compared to the name brands at cosmetics counters. A 1-ounce bar of beeswax can be bought online for as little as 85 cents.

1 ounce beeswax, grated or shaved

1/3 cup light olive oil

2 tablespoons distilled water or rose water

3 drops geranium essential oil

1. In the top of a double boiler, over simmering water, melt the beeswax.

2. In a small saucepan over low heat, heat the oil slightly and then pour it into the melted wax. Using a fork, beat this mixture until combined.

3. Now heat the water or rose water in the saucepan and then stir it into the oil and wax mixture, one drop at a time. Remove from heat and stir until the mixture is cooled and thick. Stir in the essential oil.

4. Using a wooden spoon, put the mixture into a clean 5-ounce widemouthed jar with a tight-fitting lid. Store in a cool, dark place for several months.

care for lips and mouth

Honey Lip Balm

You'll get a kick out of making lip balm at home. You'll feel a little bit like a mad scientist, and a little bit like a truly creative cook. The following three formulations will cost about a dollar or so each, and provide a lot of lip gloss or balm for the buck. Consider dividing the lip balm mixture into several small containers, so that you can carry some with you.

4 ounces extra-virgin olive oil

3 ounces grated or shaved beeswax

1 ounce honey

1/2 capsule vitamin E, 400 IU

1. In a microwave or the top of a double boiler, melt the beeswax and oil together. *Do not boil.* If the mixture starts to boil, remove from heat and allow it to cool. Once the beeswax and oil are blended, stir in the honey. Then pierce the vitamin E capsule with a needle, squeeze out half the contents, and stir in. Pour the resulting mixture into clean containers with tops.

2. Let the lip balm sit at room temperature for 48 hours until it arrives at the proper consistency for spreading. You can carry a small container of lip balm around with you during the day, but you may find it keeps better in the refrigerator overnight.

Cocoa Lip Balm

Remember, although this concoction smells sweet, it is not a food product. If you plan to give it to a child, label it accordingly and explain how to use it.

4 ounces extra-virgin olive oil

3 ounces beeswax, grated or shaved

1/2 teaspoon cocoa powder

1/2 capsule vitamin E, 400 IU

1. In a microwave or the top of a double boiler, melt the beeswax and oil together. *Do not boil.* If the mixture starts to boil, remove from the heat and allow it to cool. Once the beeswax and oil are blended, stir in the cocoa powder. Pierce the vitamin E capsule with a needle, squeeze out half the contents, and stir it in. Pour the resulting mixture into clean containers with tops.

2. Let the lip balm sit for 48 hours at room temperature until it arrives at the proper consistency for spreading. You can carry a small container of lip balm around with you during the day, but you may find it keeps better in the refrigerator overnight.

Chocolate Chip Lip Balm for Kids

When you cook up this little treat in your kitchen, you may be tempted to eat it, but this yummy-smelling lip balm is not edible. Be sure to label it as lip balm and explain to young children what it is.

4 ounces extra-virgin olive oil

3 ounces beeswax, grated or shaved

1/2 capsule vitamin E, 400 IU

3-6 chocolate chips

1. In a microwave or the top of a double boiler, melt the beeswax and oil together. *Do not boil.* If the mixture starts to boil, remove from the heat and allow it to cool. Once the beeswax and oil are blended, pierce the vitamin E capsule with a needle, squeeze out half the contents, and stir in. Stir in the chocolate chips and pour the resulting mixture into clean containers with tops.

2. Let the lip balm sit for 48 hours at room temperature until it arrives at the proper consistency for spreading. You can carry a small container of lip balm around with you during the day, but you may find it keeps better in the refrigerator overnight.

One-Minute Substitute

A Fast, Hard-Working Mouthwash

For fighting bacteria and removing food particles caught in your teeth, this inexpensive recipe is about as effective a mouthwash as you can get. It uses the standard 3% hydrogen peroxide sold in drugstores. Hydrogen peroxide, however, may irritate sensitive teeth or delicate tissue in the mouth, so this rinse should not be used more than three times a week. In a cup, mix 2 tablespoons of hydrogen peroxide solution with 2 tablespoons of water. Swish the mixture in your mouth for 30 seconds, then spit it out—don't swallow it.

Refreshing Mouthwash

For just a few cents you can cook up a potful of this rinse that tastes good and can be safely used as often as you like. Unlike more expensive commercial mouthwashes, it has no alcohol.

1 cup water

2 tablespoons angelica seeds

Dash of peppermint oil or lemon verbena

1. In a small saucepan over medium heat, bring the water to a boil. Remove from the heat. Stir in the angelica seeds and peppermint oil or lemon verbena. Let the mixture sit for 10 minutes. Strain off and discard the solids.

2. Store the liquid in a clean, covered container in the refrigerator and use every day. It should keep indefinitely.

Spicy, Minty Mouthwash

This simple recipe offers a kick that will make your mouth feel wonderful for hours. Use it as often as you like—it's very inexpensive and doesn't burn like commercial mouthwashes with alcohol in them.

1 cup water

1 teaspoon whole cloves

1 teaspoon ground cinnamon

1 teaspoon peppermint extract

2 teaspoons parsley

1. In a small saucepan, bring the water to a boil over medium heat. Remove the pan from the stove and stir in the cloves, cinnamon, peppermint extract, and parsley. Let mixture sit for 10 minutes. Strain off the solids.

2. Pour the liquid into a clean, tightly covered container and store in the refrigerator, where it will keep indefinitely. Use as a gargle and mouthwash.

Bacteria-Fighting Citrus Mouthwash

Fight the damaging bacteria that dwell in your mouth with this lemon-tasting mouthwash with an alcohol base that acts as a disinfectant. It is as effective as any mouthwash you can buy and much less expensive. Rinse and swish or gargle, but don't swallow the liquid.

3/4 cup vodka

30 drops lemon essential oil

25 drops bergamot essential oil

1 1/4 cups distilled water

1. Place the vodka and the lemon and bergamot essential oils in a sterilized 16-ounce glass bottle with a tight-fitting lid. Shake the mixture vigorously to combine.

2. Add the distilled water and shake until well blended. Leave in the refrigerator for 1 week to mature, shaking from time to time.

3. To use, shake the bottle and mix 1 part of the mixture with 3 parts lukewarm distilled water in a small drinking glass. Rinse, but do not swallow the mouthwash.

Toothpaste

We've grown accustomed to some highly sweetened commercial toothpastes. And at $3 or $4 a tube, that acquired taste can add up to a nice chunk of change over the course of a year. Once you perfect your own homemade toothpaste recipe by adjusting the ingredients to your liking, you should be able to keep a family of four in toothpaste for less than $2 a year.

1/2 cup baking soda
2 teaspoons salt
3 teaspoons glycerin
10 or more drops peppermint or wintergreen flavoring
1 drop food coloring *(optional)*
Warm water

1. In a small bowl, mix the baking soda and salt. Add the glycerin, flavoring, and if desired, 1 drop blue or green food coloring. Add warm water, a drop at a time, until the texture and consistency seem right. Spoon the mixture into a clean squeeze bottle or any convenient, clean container with a tight lid.

2. You may have to adjust the amount of glycerin to arrive at a consistency that suits you. This toothpaste will keep indefinitely in a covered container.

shampoos, conditioners, and rinses

Beer Shampoo

This concoction will leave your hair with wonderful body. The proteins from the malt and hops in the beer coat the hair and build it up, helping to repair damage.

3/4 cup beer
1 cup shampoo (any kind)

1. In a nonreactive pan, boil the beer until it reduces to 1/4 cup. Cool the beer and add it to the 1 cup of shampoo in a clean bottle with a tight cap.

2. Wash your hair as usual.

One-Minute Substitute

A Quick, Sweet-Smelling Vinegar Hair Rinse

Pick up a bottle of raspberry or plum vinegar the next time you go shopping. Expect to pay about $2.50 for an 8-ounce bottle. It can do double duty in the kitchen. Use a few tablespoons for this recipe and the rest for salad dressings.

Rather than prepare ahead of time, simply bring a clean 1- or 2-cup measuring cup with 2 to 3 tablespoons of scented vinegar into the shower. After shampooing, add water, and rinse your hair with the solution. You can use this every time you shampoo, if you like.

Vinegar restores the proper acidic pH balance to hair. This rinse will remove remnants of shampoo and give your hair more shine.

Dandruff Treatment

Over-the-counter dandruff treatments can be very costly, starting at about $6 for a 10-ounce bottle. You can create this herbal remedy for less than a dollar.

2 teaspoons dried rosemary

2 teaspoons dried thyme

2/3 cup boiling water

2/3 cup cider vinegar

1. Place the herbs in a heatproof ceramic bowl. Pour in the boiling water. Cover and allow to steep for 15 to 20 minutes.

2. Strain the liquid into a clean, 10-ounce bottle that has a tight-fitting lid. Add the vinegar and shake. Store in a cool, dark place.

3. After shampooing, rinse hair thoroughly and then massage a small amount of the herbal treatment into the scalp. Between shampoos, massage a small amount into the scalp before going to bed.

Sun-Streaking Rinse

This is a rich hair dressing that provides sheen and elegance to tired hair. People with light-colored hair will find it helps them get clean, honest-looking highlights that they might otherwise pay $30 to $40 for at a salon. It can also be used as a pressing oil for hair straightening.

Juice of 1 lemon

2 teaspoons chamomile tea

1. In a small bowl, mix the lemon juice and tea. To achieve blond highlights, use an inexpensive straw hat with lots of holes in it. Pull strands of hair you would like to lighten through the holes with a crochet hook or pencil.

2. Douse the strands with the rinse. Sit in the sun for 1 1/2 hours.

what herbs in hair rinses do		
	Catnip	Believed to promote hair growth
	Chamomile	Keeps scalp and hair follicles healthy
	Comfrey	Soothes and heals scalp irritations
	Elder berries	Traditionally used to add color to gray hair
	Lemongrass	Tones the scalp
	Nettle	An astringent that helps relieve skin irritations and itching
	Parsley	Helps relieve skin irritations
	Rosemary	Believed to enhance color of dark hair and help control dandruff
	Sage	An astringent for oily hair and a benefit for damaged or fragile hair
	Thyme	Has antiseptic, tonic, and astringent properties
	Yarrow	Acts as a tonic for the hair

Chamomile Shampoo

This mild shampoo leaves your hair clean and healthy. The recipe gives you a chance to use those leftover slivers of soap you wonder why you save. Forget the well-advertised shampoos that cost $4 or $5 a bottle. You need only one tablespoon of this inexpensive shampoo per washing.

1 handful fresh or dried chamomile flowers

1 1/4 cups boiling water

3 tablespoons pure soap flakes or leftover slivers of soap

1 tablespoon glycerin

5 drops yellow food coloring

1. Place the flowers in a heatproof bowl and add the boiling water. Let stand for 15 minutes, then strain into another heatproof bowl.

2. Clean out the first bowl. Combine in it the soap flakes and the chamomile mixture and let them stand until the soap softens—a few minutes. Beat in the glycerin and food coloring until well blended.

3. Pour the mixture into a clean 14-ounce bottle with a tight-fitting lid. Keep in a cool, dark place.

Thick Hair Conditioner for Everyone

This two-ingredient conditioner offers a protein boost for your hair that in turn will make it feel thicker and more luxuriant. You don't need to go to an expensive hair salon to revitalize your hair.

1/2 ripe avocado

1/4 cup coconut milk, or as needed

1. In a small bowl, mash the avocado with a spoon. Mix in the coconut milk to form a thick gel-like substance.

2. Apply the entire recipe to clean hair and comb through. Leave the conditioner on the hair for 10 to 15 minutes. Rinse thoroughly.

Salad Dressing Conditioner

This treatment will leave your hair feeling cleansed and enriched. The conditioner will perform as well as drugstore conditioners that cost many times more.

2 tablespoons olive oil

1 tablespoon lemon juice

1/2 teaspoon apple cider vinegar

1 egg

1. In the container of a blender, combine the oil, lemon juice, vinegar, and egg and whirl until blended. Alternatively, whisk vigorously until combined.

2. Use the entire batch to condition hair after a regular shampoo. Leave the conditioner on the hair for 10 to 15 minutes. Rinse clean.

Shampoo Residue Remover for Blond Hair

Mix up this cleansing rinse that will leave your blond hair shining for just pennies.

1 part lemon juice
4 parts water

1. Combine lemon juice and water in a clean container. Shake to mix.
2. Use as a final rinse after a regular shampoo. Don't rinse it out.

Instant Dry Shampoo

This homey, penny-pinching recipe is tailor-made for that moment when you need a quick pick-me-up or you haven't got time to wash your hair.

1 tablespoon cornstarch or finely ground oatmeal

1. Sprinkle small amounts of cornstarch or oatmeal onto the hair, lifting it up in sections to let the powder get to the scalp. Rub the shampoo through the hair to absorb excess oil.
2. Comb the hair to remove tangles, then spend 5 to 10 minutes brushing (depending on the length and thickness of the hair) to remove all traces of the powder and prevent the suggestion of dandruff. Shake and blow on your hairbrush to clean it while you brush your hair.

body care treatments

Warm Herbal Body Treatment

This warm, scented spa-style treatment will relax and rejuvenate you—for the cost of a few tea bags!

8 cups water
4 chamomile tea bags or other gentle herbal tea
3 peppermint tea bags
Sprigs of fresh rosemary or sage *(optional)*

1. In a large saucepan, bring the water to a boil. Remove it from the heat and add the tea bags and herbs. Cover the pan and steep the tea for 10 to 15 minutes. Once the tea has cooled to a comfortably warm temperature, remove the tea bags and herbs.
2. Drop several clean but dispensable hand towels into the tea (the towels will be stained). Let them soak up the mixture, and then wring them out. Wrap your upper arms and legs with the tea-soaked towels. You may also place a soaked towel on your torso, but don't put one on your face.
3. Lie down on a protected bed, couch, or pad and rest for 10 to 15 minutes. Remove the towels and relax while cooling off for another 10 to 15 minutes. Shower off the residue.

Caution: Heat treatments such as this are not recommended for people with high blood pressure or heart problems.

Creamy Citrus Moisturizer

This creamy moisturizer will leave your skin soft and silky for less than a dollar. You can't buy a commercial moisturizer for anywhere near that.

1 egg yolk
2 tablespoons lemon juice
1 cup olive oil

1. In a medium bowl, whisk the egg yolk, lemon juice, and olive oil together until the mixture reaches a creamy consistency. Thin with more lemon juice as desired.

2. Massage into your skin as an intense moisturizing treatment before a shower or bath. Apply a light coating on your hands, arms, legs, and face. Gently massage into nails and cuticles. Apply about a tablespoon to each foot. Gently massage your toes, one by one, and then the arch of your foot, moving to the heel. Relax and allow the moisturizer to soak in for 10 to 15 minutes. Wipe away the excess and then step into the shower or tub to complete the treatment.

3. Store any leftovers in the refrigerator for a day or two.

Glorious Green Aloe Moisturizing Lotion

For about $1.50 you can cook up this delightful body lotion that has aloe vera, an antioxidant, as its primary ingredient. You scoop the gel out of aloe vera leaves or you can buy it at a health food store.

1 cup aloe vera gel
1 teaspoon vitamin E oil (if necessary, break several capsules)
5-10 drops essential oil of your choosing
3/4 ounce cosmetic-grade beeswax, grated or shaved
1/2 cup vegetable oil

1. In a medium bowl, stir together the aloe vera gel, vitamin E, and essential oil. Set aside.

2. In the top of a double boiler over simmering water, melt together the beeswax and vegetable oil. Stir until smooth and well blended. Remove from heat.

3. Slowly and continuously pour the melted mixture into the bowl with the aloe vera mixture, using a handheld electric mixer at slow speed to combine. Run a clean rubber spatula around the rim of the bowl to incorporate all the ingredients. Continue mixing until all the ingredients are blended.

4. Pour the final mixture into one sterilized 13-ounce jar or two sterilized 6-ounce jars with tight-fitting lids. You can use sterilized canning jars, if you have them. Keep the lotion in the refrigerator for up to 6 weeks.

the best body oil for your skin type

To make body oil, put 4 teaspoons almond oil in a sterile glass jar with a tight-fitting top. Add the appropriate drops of essential oils listed below for your skin type, shake, and pour a little into your palm, so that you can apply it to the rest of your body. Each blend will give you four body rubs.

Normal skin: 8 drops lavender
            6 drops geranium
            2 drops chamomile
Dry skin: 8 drops patchouli
            4 drops geranium
            2 drops carrot
Oily skin: 10 drops lemon
            6 drops geranium
            4 drops sandalwood
Sensitive skin: 3 drops geranium
            2 drops patchouli

Shaving Gel for Women

Using just four ingredients you probably already have at home in ample supply, you can make your very own shaving gel that is just right for shaving legs and underarms. It's a good recipe to make in a pinch, but it will also help you cut one more expense from your weekly shopping bill.

2 tablespoons conditioner (preferably the same brand as the shampoo used)
2 tablespoons shampoo
1/2–1 teaspoon baby oil
1 teaspoon hand cream

1. Start with a clean bottle with a secure cap. Pour 2 tablespoons conditioner into the bottle, then add 2 tablespoons shampoo. Mix together. Add the baby oil and then the hand cream. Secure top and shake until all the ingredients are well blended. Let mixture sit for about an hour before using.

2. Lather legs or underarms with the gel, shave, and rinse skin thoroughly. The shaving gel should keep for about a month in the bathroom. If the mixture separates, just shake it up before you use it.

Summer Body Splash

Refresh yourself with a splash of this delicate mixture of fruit and flower scents just perfect for hot summer days and nights.

1/3 cup vodka

10 drops lavender essential oil

5 drops lime essential oil

5 drops lemon essential oil

5 drops lemongrass essential oil

2 cups distilled or boiled water

1. Pour the vodka and essential oils into a sterilized 20-ounce bottle with a tight-fitting stopper. Stopper the bottle and shake for several minutes. Add the distilled or boiled water and shake for several minutes more. Set aside for at least 48 hours or up to 3 weeks.

2. Place a paper coffee filter in a sieve and drip the liquid through the filter into a ceramic or glass bowl. Now pour the liquid back into the large bottle or into a few smaller sterilized bottles. Keep one bottle in the refrigerator and store the others in a cool, dark place until needed.

Helpful Hint

What Is a Cool, Dark Place?

When you make home remedies and beauty products, you are usually told to store them in a cool, dark, dry place. Where is that? If you seal things in amber or opaque containers, that takes care of dark (most homemade potions are weakened by exposure to sunlight). A cool, dry place could be the linen closet or a shelf in a clothes closet that is not near any heat pipes, or a basement cupboard if the basement is dry. A safe last resort is the refrigerator.

Simple Fragrant Body Splash

If you have a favorite perfume oil that you'd like to wear in a lighter concentration, you'll love this easy recipe. Keep this spritzer in your purse for a pick-me-up on a warm day.

1 cup water

5-7 drops perfume oil

1. Have on hand a clean 8-ounce spray bottle. Pour the water into the bottle and drip the perfume oil drops into the water. Cover the top with your thumb and shake well.

2. Screw the top on and your body splash is ready.

Citrus Cologne Splash

Make this cooling scent at home for a few cents.

1 lime

1/2 cup rubbing alcohol

3 teaspoons lemon extract or orange extract

1. Juice the lime. Strain out the pulp. Combine the alcohol, lime juice, and lemon or orange extract in a clean bottle with a tight-fitting lid. Shake well.

2. Dab on pulse points. You may transfer the splash to a spray bottle. Store the splash in the refrigerator.

Cellulite Massage Oil

Include this massage oil—along with regular exercise and a healthy diet—in your tool kit to help lessen cellulite. A regular massage with this oil may help increase circulation and break down fatty deposits.

2 tablespoons almond oil

1/2 teaspoon jojoba oil

1/2 teaspoon carrot oil, available through mail order

14 drops geranium essential oil

6 drops lemongrass essential oil

4 drops cypress essential oil (available through mail order)

1. Combine all ingredients in a 1 1/2- to 2-ounce sterilized glass jar with a tight-fitting lid. Shake vigorously.

2. After a bath or shower, pat your skin dry and massage a small amount of the oil on cellulite-affected areas, using circular movements. Use 1/4 to 1/2 teaspoon, depending on the size of the area you are treating. Apply only once a day.

Almond Exfoliating Body Scrub

Scented, gritty body scrubs are all the rage. Here's a recipe you can make at home for about 50 cents.

1/4 cup coarse sea salt

1/4 cup baby oil

1/2 teaspoon almond extract, vanilla extract, or lightly scented perfume oil

1. In a small bowl, stir the salt and baby oil together until the oil is thoroughly incorporated into the salt. Add the extract and stir until it, too, is incorporated.

2. Use in the shower, after you are thoroughly wet. Apply with your hands, a washcloth, or a body puff scrubber. Massage in and rinse off.

Simple Sugar Scrub for Dry Skin

Here's another yummy body scrub that costs less than a dollar for three to four uses. For dry skin, this cannot be duplicated without spending at least 10 times as much.

1 cup brown sugar, white sugar, or a mix

1/2 cup olive, grapeseed, or other oil

2 drops vanilla or almond extract *(optional)*

1. In a medium bowl, combine the sugar and oil. Mix with a wooden spoon until you achieve a pastelike blend. Add extract if desired and stir until incorporated.

2. Transfer to a clean, airtight glass container to slow breakdown of the oil.

3. In the shower, massage this mixture gently over damp skin. It will exfoliate and moisturize at the same time. Do not use on broken, irritated, or scarred skin. Avoid the eyes. This is an especially oily mixture, so it is really best for dry skin.

4. Store mixture in the refrigerator for 6 months to a year.

Cranberry Sugar Scrub

The beauty of sugar scrub recipes is the way they offer up scent while managing to exfoliate, nourish, and polish the skin. Here is another spa-quality product you can make in your own kitchen.

1/2 cup frozen cranberries

1 teaspoon vegetable glycerin

1/4 cup sweet almond oil

1/4 cup sugar

2 drops orange essential oil

2 tablespoons oat powder (whirl oatmeal in blender if needed)

1. In the container of a food processor, combine cranberries, glycerin, and almond oil and whirl for 30 seconds—just enough to blend the ingredients without turning the berries to pulp. You want to keep the mixture thick.

2. Transfer mixture to a bowl and stir in the sugar. Stir in the essential oil. Add just enough of the oat powder to create a cohesive mixture that you can apply to your skin.

3. In the shower, rub the mixture on your skin. Massage in and remove with warm water.

Body Powder

This is a fresh-smelling and silky after-shower powder that you can use every day for a pittance. For a more feminine product, use just lavender and rose essential oils.

1/2 cup arrowroot

2 tablespoons white cosmetic clay

7 drops lavender essential oil

5 drops clary sage essential oil

2 drops patchouli essential oil

1. In a medium bowl, mix the arrowroot with the white cosmetic clay. Add the essential oils and mix well with your fingers.

2. Store in a tightly covered container for a couple of days to allow the powder to absorb the oils, then use all over your body as desired.

Body Spray

You can't buy a more refreshing body spray than this citrusy mixture that smells good, tones the skin, and feels delightfully cool.

1 tablespoon finely chopped orange peel

1 tablespoon finely chopped lemon peel

3 tablespoons plain vodka

1 tablespoon witch hazel

1 cup water

5 drops lemon verbena essential oil

10 drops bergamot essential oil

10 drops orange essential oil

1. In a small jar with a tight top, add orange and lemon peels to the vodka. Cover and leave for a week in a cool, dark place.

2. Strain the liquid into a clean spray bottle. Add the witch hazel, water, and the essential oils. Shake well and use as needed. Store in the refrigerator for up to two weeks.

Deodorant

Here's a serious homemade underarm deodorant that won't stain your clothes or strain your pocketbook.

2 ounces distilled witch hazel

1 ounce sage alcohol-based herbal extract

10 drops grapefruit-seed extract

10 drops clary sage essential oil

5 drops patchouli essential oil

1. In a small spray bottle, combine all the ingredients.

2. Shake well and spray under arms as needed.

bath products

Bubble Bath for Kids

This simple recipe provides a scented, bubbly bathful of suds you know are safe for your child and, as a bonus, helps you recycle extra shampoo. As always, parents should supervise children's use of such products. Beware of slippery tubs. Bubble baths are fun, but children shouldn't use them daily. Too much of a good thing could irritate sensitive skin.

1/2 cup shampoo

3/4 cup water

1/4 teaspoon table salt

1. In a medium bowl, mix shampoo and water. Gently stir until blended. Add salt. Stir until mixture thickens.

2. Pour through a funnel into a clean bottle with a tight cap. This bubble bath will keep safely for months in the bathroom.

Bubble Bath or Conditioning Bath

For an inexpensive, fun, and squeaky-clean bubble bath, this recipe gives you lots of bubbles and cleans up the tub as well. To be extra safe, test the solution on your child's inner arm to make sure he or she is not allergic to the solution. As always, parents should handle bubble bath products. Keep out of children's reach.

2 ounces gentle dishwashing solution

5-6 cups water

1 ounce glycerin

1. In a small bucket, swish all the ingredients together, altering the balance as you see fit. Pour into a bathtub of warm water for long-lasting bubbles. You may want to bring a bubble wand to the tub.

2. Keep an eye on children in the tub, which may be extra slippery with the bubble bath. Infants and very young children should not take bubble baths.

Bath Gel

This recipe is especially suited for children or adults with sensitive skin. It's easy to make and costs only about 50 cents for an 8-ounce jar. Wrap a grosgrain ribbon around the jar and you've got a delightful homemade gift.

1/2 cup distilled or bottled water, not tap water

1 packet unflavored gelatin

1/2 cup baby shampoo

1. In a small saucepan, bring the water to a boil. Add gelatin and stir until it is dissolved. Remove from heat. Slowly stir in the baby shampoo. Let this mixture cool until it's tepid enough to put in a clean, decorative widemouthed jar with a tight-fitting top.
2. Place jar in the refrigerator to set the gel.
3. Use a few teaspoons of gel per bath. Bath gel should keep up to a month in the refrigerator.

Liquid or Gel Soap

This bath or hand soap is easy to cook up and is a good way to use up old slivers of bar soap. Transfer the liquid soap to an empty pump container and you can supply your bathroom for just a portion of the price you'd pay at the store.

2 cups soap flakes or grated bar soap

1/2 gallon water

2 tablespoons glycerin

1. In a large pot or Dutch oven, combine all the ingredients. Cook over low heat, stirring occasionally, until the soap flakes have dissolved.
2. Transfer the mixture to a clean 1/2-gallon container and cover tightly. For a thinner gel soap, increase the water to 1 gallon.

Almond Rose Soap

Here's a simple method of soap-making using just a few basic tools. You'll create a fragrant soap that gently cleans.

2 tablespoons dried red rose petals

8 ounces pure soap flakes

2/3 cup boiling water

1/2 cup rose water

2 tablespoons ground almonds

9 drops geranium essential oil

1. Pound the rose petals with a mortar and pestle. In a large bowl, combine the ground petals, soap, and water and stir until smooth. If the soap starts to solidify, place the bowl over near-boiling water.
2. Stir in the rose water and ground almonds. Allow to cool. Stir in the essential oil.
3. Shape mixture into six balls and flatten them slightly. Allow the soap to harden between sheets of wax paper. Keep unused soap in a cool, dark place until needed.

Cinnamon Soap

You'll enjoy making this rich, spicy soap, which gives you another opportunity to use up leftover soap scraps.

2 pounds leftover soap

1 tablespoon spring water

1 teaspoon glycerin

1/2 teaspoon cinnamon essential oil

1 tablespoon sweet orange essential oil

10 drops clove bud essential oil *(optional)*

1. Coarsely grate the scraps of soap into a large mixing bowl. Add the spring water, glycerin, and essential oils. Mix well.

2. Cover the bowl with a clean cloth and allow it to stand for about 15 minutes, until the soap is slightly soft and pliable. (If your soap scraps are fairly new, they may be soft and not need much softening time.)

3. Scoop the mixture up by the handful and press or roll it into small balls. Compress it tightly. Place on wax paper. Allow the soap balls to dry and harden for a day or two.

Strawberries and Cream Bath Bags

Here's a charming idea you can make for about a dollar that provides a relaxing and soothing bath. The oatmeal mixture may help relieve dry or itching skin. For extra-sensitive skin, reduce or eliminate the essential oil. Dress up this bath product by scooping it into attractive cloth bags bought at a crafts store to create your own inexpensive version of high-end bath goodies.

1/2 cup oatmeal (regular or quick)

1/2 cup powdered milk

4 tablespoons almond meal (if necessary, whirl almonds in blender, coffee grinder, or food processor)

16 drops strawberry essential oil

1. In a small bowl, combine oatmeal, powdered milk, and almond meal, stirring to mix well. Stir in essential oil until blended. Divide mixture among three pretty cloth bags, and tie them at the top. Tie a generous loop of string or ribbon to the top of each bag.

2. When ready to use, hang the bag from the tub faucet by its loop. When you fill the tub, the water will run over the mixture inside the bag, dispersing it into the tub.

3. Keep bags in a cool, dark place until ready to use.

Bath Bag

This is a most inexpensive luxury for your bath. It makes you smell good afterward, but it is also delightful while you soak.

1 large handful mixed herbs (rosemary, lovage, lavender, lemongrass, sage, parsley, or peppermint)

Cheesecloth

1. Place the herbs of your choice in a doubled square of cheesecloth. Gather up the corners of the cheesecloth and tie securely.

2. Toss herb bag into a hot bath to soften and scent the water. Once you're in the bath, rub it all over your skin, paying particular attention to areas where odor is a problem.

Cinnamon Oatmeal Milk Bath

Mixing up this pleasantly scented bath will give you a double benefit. You'll gain as much pleasure making the concoction as you will from soaking in it. The combination of powdered milk, oatmeal, and cornstarch will leave you feeling silky and soft. The cinnamon will gently warm you and offer up a soothing aroma.

1 cup powdered milk

1/2 cup baking soda

1/2 cup finely ground oatmeal

2 teaspoon cornstarch

1 teaspoon cream of tartar

1 teaspoon cinnamon

1. Place all ingredients in a food processor and whirl to combine. Transfer into a clean, tightly covered, moisture-proof container, where it will keep indefinitely.

2. Add about 1/2 cup of the Cinnamon Oatmeal Milk Bath to a full tub of warm water and enjoy the soak.

Make It a Gift

Women's Bath Basket

Buy four brightly colored washcloths. Use each to wrap a home-made bath product: Almond Rose Soap, Delicately Scented Bath Powder, Bath Cookies, and Eucalyptus Foot Lotion, for example. Be sure each is labeled with ingredients and storage instructions. Nestle the bath treats in a nice basket that could hold extraneous bath supplies and attach a card with a large bow.

Gentle Milk Bath

You can shake up a soothing milk bath anytime you want to escape into a warm tub. Milk will leave your skin smooth and silky.

1/3 cup powdered milk

3 tablespoons cornstarch

1-2 drops essential oil of your choice

1. Pour the powdered milk and cornstarch into a clean jar with a tight top. Shake well. Add the essential oil and shake to thoroughly incorporate. If the mixture clumps, use your fingers to dissolve the lumps.

2. For a bath, put the mixture under the running water. Splash around with your hand to disperse it in the tub.

Note: You may double or triple this recipe and store it indefinitely by omitting the oil. Store the combined powdered milk and cornstarch in an airtight container; use 1/2 cup for each bath. Add the essential oil to the tub separately after swishing in the combined powders.

Magic Fruity Bath Salts

For about $1.35 you can mix up a quart of colorful, soothing bath salts. They're every bit as good as any you'd find in boutiques or on pharmacy shelves selling for anywhere from $3 to $12.

4 cups Epsom salts

1 envelope unsweetened Kool-Aid or equivalent, any flavor

1. Pour half the Epsom salts into a clean one-quart container. Empty the pouch of soft drink into the salts. Cover and shake until combined.

2. Add the rest of the salts and continue shaking. Your mixture will be subtly colored, but the "magic" colors will appear as you toss the salts into the warm tub.

3. Use up to a half-cup of bath salts per bath. Water will be scented and colorful. For a more dramatic appearing display, double or triple the recipe, but use several different-colored (flavored) packets of drink mix and layer the crystals and salt in a clear glass jar. Don't shake to mix. (Be sure to purchase the unsweetened drink mix.)

Store in a covered container. Keeps indefinitely.

Bath Cookies

If you like experimenting with recipes in the kitchen, you'll get a real kick out of making these "cookies" for the tub. Bakers will recognize the steps in dough-making, rolling, and baking, but there's a twist! Make one batch for yourself and another for friends.

2 cups fine sea salt

1/2 cup cornstarch, plus more for rolling dough

1/2 cup baking soda

1 tablespoon dried, chopped lavender or sage *(optional)*

2 eggs

2 tablespoons vegetable oil

1 teaspoon vitamin E oil (if necessary, break open several capsules)

8 drops essential oil or perfume oil of your choosing

1. Preheat oven to 350°F. In a large bowl, combine salt, cornstarch, and baking soda. Stir in chopped herbs, if using. Stir in eggs, vegetable oil, vitamin E oil, and essential oil and keep stirring until you form a dough.

2. Rub cornstarch on a rolling pin and spread some on a work surface. Roll the dough out to about 3/4 inch. Cut into shapes with cookie cutters or a biscuit cutter. Place your "cookies" on an ungreased cookie sheet about 1 inch apart. Bake for 10 to 12 minutes. Cool and store in a tight-topped cookie tin in a cool, dry place.

3. When ready to use, place one or two of your bath cookies into the tub as the water runs.

Easy Bath Powder

This simple combination creates a refreshing finish to the shower or bath and costs just pennies to make.

1 cup powdered arrowroot

1 cup cornstarch

1/4 cup baking soda

In a medium bowl, stir together all the ingredients. Store in an airtight container. Should keep indefinitely.

Basic Bath Powder

For an after-bath or after-shower touch, this fragrance-free home-made powder is so natural, it's a safe bet your great-grandmother used it. Keep a container of this mixture in your bathroom. Apply with a powder puff or sprinkle it on from a shaker-top jar.

1/2 cup baking soda
1/2 cup cornstarch

In a small bowl, stir both ingredients to combine. Store in a wide-mouthed glass jar or plastic container or keep in a shaker-top jar. Should keep indefinitely.

Delicately Scented Bath Powder

This variation provides a lightly scented powder suitable for adults. While alum is used as an antiperspirant and deodorant for adults, it is best to use a simple sprinkle of cornstarch on baby's skin.

2 tablespoons crumbled dried chamomile flowers
1/4 cup cornstarch
1 tablespoon orrisroot
1/2 teaspoon alum

1. Combine ingredients in a bowl and mix well. Let stand a few days.
2. Sift mixture through a flour sifter. Pour into a powder shaker or other container. Should keep indefinitely.

nail, hand, and foot care

Gardener's Hand Cream

This hand cream is especially good for those hard-working hands. You will spend just a dollar or so to make the entire recipe, but because you are using unpreserved vegetable oils, if you don't have a cool, dark place to store the hand cream or a friend to share with, consider making only half this recipe at a time. To make calendula tea, pour a cup of boiling water over half a teaspoon of dried calendula flower petals and let it steep until cool.

3 tablespoons beeswax, grated or shaved
1/2 cup sesame oil
1 tablespoon coconut oil
1 teaspoon honey
2 tablespoons calendula tea
3 drops lavender essential oil
1/2 teaspoon baking soda

1. In a small microwave-safe bowl, mix all the ingredients. Set the microwave to a medium heat and cook 30 seconds or until beeswax is melted. Remove from oven with hot pads and allow to cool.
2. Pour mixture into a widemouthed, sterilized jar with a tight top. Store in cool, dark place until ready to use.

Cuticle Cream
Here's a spa treatment you can make in the comfort of your own kitchen.

3 tablespoons paraffin

1/2 cup mineral oil

1 tablespoon coconut oil

1 tablespoon glycerin

1. In the top of a double boiler over simmering water, combine the paraffin with the oils. Stir until paraffin is melted and the mixture is blended. Stir in the glycerin and remove the pan from the heat. Let mixture cool.

2. Apply cooled cream to cuticle area. Rub in and allow to rest for ten minutes or so.

3. Trim cuticles with a cuticle tool. Massage away cream by applying a gentle body or hand lotion and rubbing lightly, then rinsing with warm water.

Warm Oil Hand Treatment
Manicurists charge $15 to $35 for hot oil hand treatments. Here is a delightfully simple recipe you can create for about 50 cents or less.

1 tablespoon olive or other cooking oil

1 teaspoon almond extract *or* 1 drop lavender essential oil *(optional)*

2 small plastic bags that will fit over your hands

1. Place the oil in a microwave-safe dish and heat it on medium-high for a few seconds until it is warmed, not hot. Add almond extract or lavender, if desired. Stir.

2. Rub the oil on your hands, massaging your fingers and palms. Cover your hands with the plastic bags and wrap a clean hand towel over the bags. Sit comfortably for about 5 minutes.

3. Remove the bags and rinse your hands with warm water, massaging away the oil. Gently pat dry with the towel and apply a light hand lotion.

Cornmeal Hand Scrub
This gentle massage scrub costs about a nickel to make and leaves your hands smooth and soft.

1/4 cup cornmeal

3 tablespoons milk

1 drop almond oil (or almond extract)

1. In a small saucepan, mix the cornmeal with the milk. Heat the mixture over a low flame on the stovetop until it forms a paste. Remove from heat and stir in the almond oil. Allow to cool.

2. Spread mixture on hands and allow to sit for 10 minutes. Gently scrub your hands with the mixture and then rinse off with warm water.

Love Your Feet Cream

Our feet take a lot of abuse. Here's a special treatment to apply to dry, cracked feet that will leave them soft and pretty and costs about one-tenth the price of a visit to the salon for a pedicure.

1 ounce grated or shaved beeswax

3/4 cup almond oil

1. Place the beeswax and almond oil in the top of a double boiler over simmering water. Stir together until they are blended and the wax has melted. Remove from heat and pour into two 4-ounce sterilized containers with tight tops.

2. Allow mixture to cool before applying to feet. Spread on feet at night before bedtime. Wear a pair of clean cotton socks over the cream. In the morning, your feet will be much softer.

Soothing Footbath

This relaxing foot soak will work wonders on your entire body. Use a large dishpan or kiddie tub if you don't have a special foot tub.

1 tablespoon sea salt

2 drops lavender essential oil

1 drop rosemary essential oil

1 drop bay essential oil

1 drop geranium essential oil

Rose petals *(optional)*

1. Fill the soaking pan or tub with enough warm water to cover the feet.

2. Stir in the sea salt until it dissolves. Use your toes to stir, if you wish. Add the essential oils, mixing them well. Float rose petals on the surface.

3. Soak your feet in the basin for 10 minutes, or until the water has cooled off. Pat your feet dry with a towel.

Eucalyptus Foot Lotion

Use this rich and refreshing foot lotion to follow the Soothing Footbath (above) or simply to salve sore feet.

1 tablespoon almond oil

1 teaspoon avocado oil

1 teaspoon wheat germ oil

10 drops eucalyptus essential oil

1. Put all the ingredients in a small, sterilized glass bottle with a tight-fitting stopper. Shake the liquid vigorously until it is completely combined.

2. Store the bottle in a cool, dark place. Shake well before using.

Refreshing Foot Spray

This clean, fresh blend is great for hot summer days. Carry a little spray bottle with you and spritz it on tired feet.

3 tablespoons witch hazel

1 tablespoon rose flower water, orange blossom water, or distilled water

1/8 teaspoon glycerin

10-15 drops of essential oil of your choice

Pour all ingredients into a clean spray bottle and shake. Will keep for two months in plastic container.

Strawberry Foot Scrub

Can't get to the spa for a luxury treatment for those tired feet? Work this simple and sweetly scented natural scrub into your feet and feel like a queen.

2 teaspoons coarse salt

2 tablespoons olive oil

8 fresh strawberries

1. Pour salt into a mixing bowl. Add the oil and stir to combine. Remove caps from strawberries and slice or chop them. Add strawberries to the salt and oil mixture and mash with a potato masher or fork. The resulting mixture should be chunky but well blended.

2. Rub this mixture onto your feet, massaging the balls of the feet and the heels. If desired, use a body puff or foot brush. Rinse off and coat feet with a gentle lotion.

Makes enough for one treatment.

Leg Massage Cream

Treat yourself to a massage from your knees to your toes with this easy-to-make cream especially for the legs.

3 tablespoons anhydrous (water-free) lanolin

3 tablespoons olive oil

2 tablespoons apricot oil

1. Put all the ingredients together in the nonreactive top of a double boiler over simmering water. Heat and stir with a wooden spoon until the lanolin has liquefied.

2. Pour the mixture into a sterilized 4-ounce jar with a tight-fitting lid and allow to cool. Keep in a cool, dark place.

just for men

Rosemary Shaving Soap for Men

Rinse your face with fresh water, then lather up your beard with this fragrant soap before shaving. Be sure to thoroughly rinse off the lather.

2/3 cup rose water

4 ounces pure soap flakes

4 drops rosemary essential oil

3 drops lemon essential oil

2 drops bay essential oil

1 drop sage essential oil

1. Warm the rose water in a nonreactive saucepan over low heat. Place the soap flakes in the top of a double boiler over simmering water. Stir the warmed rose water into the flakes to moisten. Keep stirring the mixture until the soap has melted to a smooth gel (if necessary use a potato masher to dissolve the soap). Remove from the heat and cool to lukewarm.

2. Stir in the essential oils and spoon the soap into a sterilized shallow 7-ounce glass jar with a tight-fitting lid. Set aside to harden for 3 to 5 days. Keep handy in a cool, dark place.

Lightly Scented Aftershave

Aftershave splashes serve two purposes: to soothe the just-shaved beard area and to offer a pleasant scent. Instead of purchasing costly scented aftershaves, make this at home for less than $2 per cup.

1/2 cup witch hazel

1/2 cup rose water

Combine the two liquids in a sterilized jar. Splash on face directly after shaving. Keep tightly covered. Should keep indefinitely on bathroom shelf.

Shaving-Cut Lotion

Apply a drop of this simple, inexpensive, and effective lotion to stop bleeding and prevent infection in the event of a razor nick.

4 teaspoons witch hazel lotion

13 drops lavender essential oil

7 drops geranium essential oil

Put all ingredients in a sterilized 1-ounce glass bottle with a tight-fitting lid. Shake well to combine. Keep in a cool, dark place. Shake before using.

Aloe Aftershave Gel

This alcohol-free gel is suitable for men or women because it refreshes and is safe for sensitive skin. See if you don't love it as much as anything you can buy. Aloe vera gel is available in health food stores—or you can scoop it out of the leaves of a plant.

1/2 cup aloe vera gel

1 1/2 tablespoons distilled water

1 tablespoon witch hazel

10 drops essential or fragrance oils of your choice

1. Combine all the ingredients in the container you'll store the gel in. Stir until well mixed. Cover container with a tight-fitting lid.

2. Keep in a cool, dark location. Should keep indefinitely.

Muscle Rub

This salve really does wonders for hard-working muscles. Massage into stressed, stiff, and aching shoulders, neck, back, or feet. (This is not recommended for pregnant women.)

1 teaspoon lanolin

1 1/2 ounces extra-virgin olive oil

1/4 ounce beeswax, shaved or grated

2-3 drops arnica essential oil

6 drops ginger essential oil

3-4 drops lemon essential oil

1. In an ovenproof glass measuring cup with a pour spout, combine the lanolin, olive oil, and beeswax. Place the cup in a hot-water bath until the wax is nearly melted. At this point, remove the cup from the water bath and stir the mixture with a clean utensil to evenly mix the ingredients.

2. Let the mixture cool. When the mixture begins to harden around the edges of the cup, add the essential oils and stir to incorporate them.

3. Pour into a sterile widemouthed jar and allow to cool before capping. Store in a cool, dark place for several months.

for digestive distress

Soothing Tea for Heartburn
Stomach-Calming Tea
Lemon Settler for Motion Sickness
Hiccup Reliever
Anti-Diarrhea Tea
Electrolyte Drink for Diarrhea
Laxative
Herbal Tea for Flatulence
Hemorrhoid Pads

for colds, congestion, and fever

Chest Rub for Bronchitis
Another Chest Rub
Chest Compress
Mustard Seed Plaster
Mustard Powder Plaster
Cough Suppressant Tea
Cough Suppressant Medicine
Steam Cough Relief
Cough Drops
Gargle Solution
Slippery Elm and Marshmallow Tea
Steam Treatment for Congestion
Herbal Inhalant
Sore-Throat Lozenges
Decongestant Salve
Humidifier Booster
Saline Spray for Clogged Sinuses
Drops for Earache
Fever Tea
Spray for Fever

for bug bites, hives, and itching

Insect Repellent
Soothing Gel for Insect Bites
Essential Oil Itch Soother
Poison Ivy Lotion
Poison Ivy Drying Paste
Healing Oil Bath
Healing Calendula Lotion
Skin Salve for Eczema or Dermatitis
Honey Ointment

Anti-Itching Solution for Hives
Oatmeal Bath for Hives
Anti-Itch Wrap

treatments for skin outbreaks

Acne Facial Scrub
Cleansing Liquid for Acne
Acne Cleansing Pads
Overnight Acne Cream
Hot Compress for Boils
Antibacterial Drawing Paste
Antibacterial Oil
Ringworm Paste
Dandelion/Fig Wart Remover
Herbal Wart Remover

for cuts, bruises, and burns

First-Aid Antiseptic
Calendula Ointment
Healing Ointment
Cleansing Soap
Compress for Bruises
Anti-Bruising Oil
Oil Rub for Burned Skin
Soothing Oil for Burns
Burn Spray
Antiseptic Lotion for Burns
Sunburn Cooler

foot care products

Athlete's Foot Powder
Antifungal Foot Ointment
Antifungal Solution
Corn Plaster
Essential Oil Corn Remover
Salicylic Acid Corn Remover

for mouth and lip irritations

Healing Balm for Chapped Lips
Cold Sore Ointment
Mouthwash for Cold Sores
Cold Sore Paste

dental care products

Mouthwash
Mints
Toothpaste
Antibacterial Mouthwash
Gum Tonic
Super Dental Floss
Toothache-Relieving Rinse
Toothache-Relieving Dental Paste

for joint and muscle aches

Hot Pepper Rub
Massage Cream
Quick-and-Dirty Muscle Rub
Muscle Soak
Liniment
Cold Pack for Strains and Sprains
Castor Oil Rub for Back Pain

for women's problems

Muscle Relaxant for Cramps
Hot Compress for Cramps
Anti-Cramp Tea
Ginger Tea for Morning Sickness
PMS Tea
Yeast Infection Cream

headache treatments

Headache Compresses
Chamomile Tea
Lemon Balm Tea
Migraine Tea
Headache Massage
Headache Oil with Vitamin E

for anxiety and fatigue

Catnip Anti-Anxiety Tea
Hops Anti-Anxiety Tea
Calming Tea for Insomnia
Sleep Pillow
Herbal Milk Bath for
Sleeplessness
Relaxing Aromatic Bath
Invigorating Oil for Fatigue
Energy Tea for Fatigue

chapter 8

Healthy Home Remedies

In a time of soaring health care costs—when a single trip to the doctor's office can cost hundreds of dollars and a visit to the hospital emergency room can balloon into the thousands—it is comforting to know that there are many everyday health problems that you can safely and successfully treat with homemade remedies. As you use the recipes on the following pages, you will be happy to discover that they can make a real difference in how you or a family member feels and in when you start to mend without a budget-busting consultation at a medical facility—or spending a small fortune at the drugstore.

From heartburn and motion sickness to constipation, colds and sore throats to earaches and fever, hives and rashes to acne and warts, cuts and bruises to minor burns, cold sores to gum disease and toothaches, sprains to muscle aches, yeast infections and PMS to headaches, insomnia, fatigue, and many, many more conditions, there are effective home remedies in this chapter that you can make and apply yourself. And all have been checked and approved by an experienced professional.

Many of these homemade recipes use herbs and other natural ingredients that were known to our ancestors and have an honorable place in the history of healing. Many modern medicines were discovered, after all, when scientists took plants that were recognized by herbalists as having special healing properties to the lab for testing. The healing ingredients were then extracted and tested and later manufactured. And with many of these recipes, you are simply going back to the original natural source.

for digestive distress

Soothing Tea for Heartburn

Licorice, ginger, and chamomile are traditional, easy-to-make, and inexpensive digestive tract soothers that still work wonders for occasional flare-ups of heartburn.

1 cup water

1 teaspoon grated licorice root

1 teaspoon chopped fresh ginger

1 teaspoon dried chamomile flowers

1. In a small pan, bring the water to a boil. Add the licorice and ginger. Simmer for 15 minutes. Remove from heat and add chamomile. Cover and steep for 10 minutes.

2. Strain into a teacup and drink.

Stomach-Calming Tea

If you have indigestion, this therapeutic infusion will likely tame your outraged stomach as well as any patent medicine you can buy.

1 cup boiling water

1 teaspoon dried peppermint

1 teaspoon dried chamomile

1. In a small pot, pour boiling water over the dried peppermint and chamomile. Cover and steep for 10 minutes, then strain into a teacup.

2. Drink up to three cups a day to help ease intestinal cramps.

One-Minute Substitute

Quick Antacid from Your Spice Shelf

Some common kitchen spice seeds contain oils that soothe spasms in your stomach and relieve nausea—without costing too pretty a penny. Just chew 1 teaspoon of aniseed, dill, or caraway seeds for a minute, then spit them out without swallowing any. Repeat three times a day.

Lemon Settler for Motion Sickness

While over-the-counter motion-sickness remedies can make you sleepy, ours just take away the sick feeling. This is a tummy-soothing drink.

Juice of 1 lemon

1 cup boiling water

1 teaspoon honey

1 crushed sprig spearmint or peppermint

1. In a large cup, combine lemon juice, boiling water, and honey. Stir to mix and add spearmint or peppermint.

2. Sip as needed. Keep warm in a thermos when traveling.

One-Minute Substitute

Chew Ginger to Settle Your Stomach

Ginger is a traditional tummy settler for nausea and motion sickness, and crystallized ginger—the candy version of it—may save a trip. Just chew on a lump of crystallized ginger as needed. Keep a packet in the car or your purse so you always have it handy.

Hiccup Reliever

You can't even find a remedy for hiccups in the drugstore, but you can make one yourself.

> 2 teaspoons to 1 tablespoon sugar or dry drink mix (cocoa or Ovaltine)

Swallow the dry sugar or drink mix, which isn't easy. Trying to get it down will short-circuit the hiccups.

Anti-Diarrhea Tea

This tea will settle an irate digestive system and help you back to health. It costs nothing if you have raspberries or blackberries in your garden. If your diarrhea persists for more than 24 hours, however, see a doctor.

> 2 teaspoons dried raspberry and/or blackberry leaves
> Boiling water

1. In a teacup, steep the berry leaves in freshly boiled water for at least 10 minutes. Strain.
2. Drink a small cup 3 times a day along with other fluids to prevent dehydration.

making an infusion

Making an herbal infusion is similar to making a cup of tea. Place 3 rounded teaspoons (1/2 ounce) fresh herb leaves or 1 rounded teaspoon dried herb leaves in a teacup. Pour 1/2 cup boiling water over the leaves, cover with a saucer, and let steep for 5 or 10 minutes. Strain the drink while hot—or let it cool if you're going to use it as part of a lotion or gargle with it. Infusions may be stored in the refrigerator for up to 24 hours.

Electrolyte Drink for Diarrhea

Diarrhea can drain your body of liquids and electrolytes quite quickly and quite dangerously. This easily made, inexpensive juice drink helps maintain your body's equilibrium. If your diarrhea persists for more than 24 hours, however, see a doctor.

> 1 cup apple juice
> 2 cups water
> 1/2-1 teaspoon salt
> Juice from a lemon or a lime

1. In a pitcher, combine apple juice, water, salt, and the lemon or lime juice. Store in the refrigerator.
2. Drink throughout the day to maintain hydration and proper balance of electrolytes.

Healthy Home Remedies

Laxative
You don't have to buy expensive psyllium fiber supplements to treat temporary constipation.

1-3 teaspoons psyllium husks

Warm water

1. Stir psyllium husks into an 8-ounce glass of warm water and drink once a day. Follow with a glass of plain water.

2. Drink 6 to 8 additional glasses of water throughout the day.

One-Minute Substitute

Grandma's Always Ready Laxative
This old-fashioned penny-pincher's remedy for constipation sounds simple because it is. Just take 1 to 2 teaspoons castor oil on an empty stomach. It should get things moving within 8 to 10 hours.

Herbal Tea for Flatulence
It's embarrassing to have flatulence and embarrassing to have to buy something to treat it. Instead, make the following tea in the privacy of your home.

1 teaspoon dried chamomile

1/2 teaspoon dried peppermint

1 teaspoon dried catnip

1 teaspoon dried basil

2 crushed fennel seeds

1/2 teaspoon dried marjoram

1. In a large cup, mix the herbs. Pour in 6 to 8 ounces of boiling water and steep, covered, for 10 minutes. Strain and drink tea.

2. Drink 3 or more cups a day.

Hemorrhoid Pads
These work just as well as the commercial brands.

1 ounce witch hazel

5 drops cypress essential oil

3 drops geranium essential oil

5 drops lavender essential oil

2 tablespoons aloe vera gel

Cotton cosmetic pads

1. In an open-mouthed jar with a tight-fitting lid, combine the witch hazel, essential oils, and aloe vera gel. Saturate several cotton cosmetic pads in the liquid and refrigerate for at least an hour.

2. Use a pad on the affected area when it burns and after each bowel movement. Store in the refrigerator for several days.

for colds, congestion, and fever

Chest Rub for Bronchitis

The essential oils in this easy-to-make and easy-to-pay-for rub are therapeutic. You cover them with flannel and a hot pad to warm your chest and help you absorb the essential oil.

30 drops massage or carrier oil such as almond, jojoba, or avocado oil

5-10 drops eucalyptus or wintergreen essential oil

1. In a small bowl mix the carrier oil with the essential oil. Rub the mixture onto your chest.
2. Cover your chest with a cotton towel or piece of flannel, then put a heating pad or hot-water bottle on top of the flannel and snuggle under the blankets.

Another Chest Rub

A warm, homemade chest rub can relax you and calm your cough without bothering your pocketbook.

12 drops eucalyptus essential oil

8 drops hyssop essential oil

4 drops peppermint essential oil

2 tablespoons almond or olive oil

1. In a small dish, mix essential oils with the almond or olive oil.
2. Rub the mixture onto your chest and cover with a damp, warm flannel (try warming the damp flannel in the microwave). Leave on until the warmth fades.

Chest Compress

This warm, soothing compress will make you relax while it helps you to breathe.

A handful of dried, chopped mullein or dried, chopped lobelia

1-2 cups boiling water

1. In a bowl, steep the mullein or lobelia in boiling water for 10 minutes.
2. Saturate a hand towel in the warm liquid, wring it out, and place on your chest. Cover with a warm towel and place a heating pad on top of that.

Healthy Home Remedies   273

Mustard Seed Plaster

It's old-fashioned, but sometimes it's these kinds of remedies that are the best. And you are not risking the family fortune to try it.

2 or more tablespoons olive oil

1/3 cup mustard seed

2 tablespoons grated beeswax

Cloth to cover chest

1. Put 2 tablespoons olive oil and the mustard seed into a blender and blend. Continue adding olive oil until you have a nice, thick liquid.

2. Pour the mixture into the top of a double boiler over low heat; add the beeswax and heat, stirring, until the wax melts. Spread the cloth on a flat surface. Once the mustard-wax mixture is warm and can be spread, apply it to the cloth and let it cool to room temperature.

3. Place the cloth salve-side-down on your chest and cover with a T-shirt or old flannel, then apply external heat on top with a heating pad or hot-water bottle. You should start to feel warmth seeping into your chest in about 10 to 15 minutes. Leave on another 15 minutes. You can store the plaster in the fridge for several days; when needed, remove and let warm to room temperature before using.

Mustard Powder Plaster

You can also make an inexpensive, effective mustard plaster using a strong mustard powder such as Coleman's.

1 tablespoon mustard powder

2 tablespoons flour

1. In a small bowl, mix the mustard powder with the flour. Add enough water to make a paste.

2. Spread the paste over half of a dishtowel. Then fold the towel in half, covering the paste, and apply to chest. Don't apply the mustard paste directly onto the skin. Check chest skin often and remove the mustard plaster if there are signs of irritation.

Cough Suppressant Tea

Now that we know that those commercial cough syrups are pretty useless when it comes to most coughs, why waste your money? Here's a nicer, cheaper alternative.

4 fresh sage leaves or 1 teaspoon dried

Boiling water

In a standard teacup, steep the sage leaves in freshly boiled water for at least 20 minutes. Strain and drink hot or cold.

Cough Suppressant Medicine

You will appreciate onions, garlic, ginger, and honey all the more after they conspire to stop your coughing. And you don't have to worry about ingredients that your body doesn't need or that counteract the suppressing effect as you do with many commercial cough medicines.

1 large onion, finely diced

2 cloves garlic, finely diced

2 tablespoons finely diced fresh ginger

Honey

1. In a small saucepan, combine onion, garlic, and ginger. Add honey to cover and cook over very low heat for 30 minutes. Then mash together and let cool. Strain and store in a clean jar with a tight-fitting lid in the refrigerator.

2. Take one teaspoon every 15 to 30 minutes.

Steam Cough Relief

Sometimes an herbal steam treatment will do more to relieve a cough than any mentholated ointment you can buy.

4 cups water

2 drops thyme essential oil

4 drops eucalyptus essential oil

2 drops hyssop essential oil

1. In a saucepan over medium heat, heat the water until nearly boiling (but don't boil). Pour into a heat-safe bowl and add the essential oils.

2. Hold your head about 8 inches above the water, drape a towel over your head and the bowl to make a tent, and breathe in deeply until the water cools. Keep your eyes closed throughout.

Cough Drops

Do a little steeping and straining, boiling and stirring, rolling and cooling. Voilà! Your very own cough drops at half the price and just as effective as commercial ones. You need a candy thermometer to make these.

2 ounces dried or 6 ounces fresh horehound leaves

3 1/2 cups dark brown sugar

20 drops eucalyptus essential oil

20 drops tea tree essential oil

1. In a saucepan, pour 3 cups boiling water over the horehound leaves and steep for 30 minutes over low heat. Strain into another saucepan and add the brown sugar; stir until the sugar dissolves.

2. Bring the mixture to a boil and boil until it reaches 295°F on a candy thermometer. Stir in the eucalyptus and tea tree oils. Let cool slightly, then, using buttered hands, roll into small balls and let the balls harden on wax paper. Wrap them individually in plastic wrap and use as needed.

One-Minute Substitute

Pepper Spray for a Raw Throat

This quick and easy spray is an antiseptic and a painkiller that costs almost nothing to make. In a clean 8-ounce spray bottle, combine 1 tablespoon of cayenne pepper with just enough water to almost fill the bottle. Shake well and use as a spray to numb the back of your throat. You can also use it for gargling. Just don't get it near your eyes.

Healthy Home Remedies   275

Gargle Solution
This old-fashioned gargle will make your throat feel much better, and it costs very little.

2 heaping tablespoons brown sugar

1/2 teaspoon salt

1/4 teaspoon baking soda

1 quart warm water

1. In a jar with a tight-fitting lid, combine the brown sugar, salt, baking soda, and warm water. Shake well before each use.
2. Gargle with up to 1/2 cup of this mixture as often as needed.

Slippery Elm and Marshmallow Tea
The tea is slippery and the herbs soothing, so they ease throat pain as well as any commercial products for a great deal less.

2 teaspoons powdered slippery elm bark

2 teaspoons powdered marshmallow root

6 ounces boiling water

In a cup, place the slippery elm and marshmallow root. Pour in the boiling water and steep until cool. Strain into a teacup and drink. Store in refrigerator and gently reheat as needed.

Steam Treatment for Congestion
Aromatic herbs and humidity can do wonders for a stuffed-up head. This treatment takes only minutes to put together, and the results are priceless.

3 tablespoons finely chopped fresh thyme, sage, peppermint, eucalyptus, or pine needles

Boiling water

1. Put the herbs in a medium bowl and add boiling water.
2. Lean over the bowl with a towel draped over your head and the bowl and inhale for 10 minutes. Repeat 2 or 3 times a day as needed.

Herbal Inhalant
You can make your own inhalant quickly and safely for pennies.

1/4-1/2 teaspoon rock salt

2-4 drops peppermint essential oil

2-4 drops eucalyptus essential oil

2-4 drops wintergreen essential oil

1. Put the rock salt in the bottom of a small glass bottle or jar with a tight-fitting lid. Add the oils.
2. Carry with you and sniff as needed to open clogged nasal passages.

Sore-Throat Lozenges

These lozenges are called pastilles, and are made with dried plant ingredients. They are cheap, easy to make, and very effective.

1/4 cup violet petals

1/4 cup rose petals

Honey or maple syrup

1 teaspoon dried marshmallow root

Confectioners' sugar *(optional)*

1. With a mortar and pestle, crush the violet and rose petals until you get a fine powder. Mix with just enough honey or maple syrup to form a ball and add marshmallow root. If the mixture is too liquid, add more herbs or powdered sugar until it can hold its shape.

2. Form into small balls about the size of a large pea and place on a greased cookie sheet. Leave 24 to 48 hours or until they harden, then wrap each individually in plastic wrap and store in a cool, dry place.

Decongestant Salve

This rub can give that stuff in the dark blue bottle a run for its money.

4 ounces olive oil

1/2 ounce peppermint oil

1/2 ounce eucalyptus oil

1/2 ounce wintergreen oil

1/2 ounce grated beeswax

4 drops tincture of benzoin

1. In the top of a double boiler over low heat, heat the oils. Add the beeswax and tincture of benzoin and stir until the beeswax is melted and the oils are well mixed.

2. Pour mixture into a clean, widemouthed jar with a tight top and allow to cool. Put under your nose or rub on your chest as a decongestant. You can keep this mixture in a cool, dark place for up to two weeks.

One-Minute Substitute

A Quick Decongestant to Carry with You

The good news about this decongestant is that it doesn't come with a list of warnings! Just put 1 drop of tea tree, peppermint, or rosemary essential oil on a clean handkerchief and carry the handkerchief with you. Inhale as needed.

Humidifier Booster

Getting a good night's sleep is probably the best thing you can do for a cold. This recipe allows you to breathe and sleep through the night.

2-4 drops peppermint essential oil

2-4 drops eucalyptus essential oil

2-4 drops wintergreen essential oil

Cotton ball

1. In a small bowl, mix the oils. Dip a cotton ball into the mixture and put it near the vent of a steam humidifier.

2. Place the humidifier and the cotton ball near your bed when you have a cold.

Saline Spray for Clogged Sinuses
Why pay good money for something that is essentially salt and water? Make your own saline spray.

1/4 teaspoon table salt

1 cup distilled water, warmed to a comfortable temperature

1. Add the salt to the distilled water and stir until it dissolves.
2. To get the solution into your nose, use an ear bulb syringe (like the kind used to clean out a baby's nose), a neti pot (an Indian sinus cleaning tool available in health food stores), or a waterpick on the lowest setting (you'll need a special adapter for this). Flush your nasal passages two to three times a day.

Drops for Earache
In winter weather when earaches are more prevalent, it is smart to keep these bargain ear drops on hand in the refrigerator for emergencies.

1 clove garlic, crushed

2 tablespoons fresh or dried mullein flower

1/2 cup olive or almond oil

1. In a clean jar with a tight-fitting lid, combine the garlic and mullein flower. Cover with the oil, seal the top, and shake to blend. Store in a cool, dark place and shake daily.
2. Make sure the herbs remain under the oil for two weeks, then strain and store the oil in a clean jar with a tight-fitting lid in the refrigerator.
3. To treat an earache, let the oil come to room temperature or run it under warm water. Dispense two or three drops at a time with a sterile eye dropper. Gently massage the ear to help the oil make its way through the ear canal.

Fever Tea
You can certainly take Tylenol or Motrin, but this tea will make you feel better without putting any additional strain on your liver.

Yarrow

Linden flowers

Chamomile

Spearmint

Elder flowers

1 cup boiling water

1. In a small bowl, mix equal amounts of dried, crushed yarrow, linden flowers, chamomile, spearmint, and elder flowers.
2. Combine 3 teaspoons of this mix in a large cup, and add boiling water.
3. Cover and steep for 10 to 15 minutes. Strain and drink hot. After drinking, get under the covers to induce sweating.

Spray for Fever

Spraying pulse points with a cool, soothing solution is said by many to bring down a fever quicker than any pill you can buy. Whether it does work that well or not, it feels great when you are hot and feverish. The pulse points are the places on the body where you can easily feel your heart rate when you touch them with your fingers—typically inside your wrists, just under each side of the jaw, and the back of the knees.

1/4 cup rubbing alcohol

1/4 cup witch hazel

3 drops peppermint essential oil

2 drops lavender essential oil

1. In a clean spray bottle, combine the rubbing alcohol, witch hazel, and essential oils. Shake to mix and then chill in the refrigerator.
2. Spray onto pulse points to reduce fever, avoiding eyes and mouth.

for bug bites, hives, and itching

Insect Repellent

The best way to treat bites is to avoid getting bitten in the first place. But forget spraying poisons on yourself. The essential ingredients of this homemade insect repellent have been shown in numerous studies to keep stinging insects—notably, mosquitoes—far, far away. Keep in mind, however, that if you're in an area with a high rate of mosquito-transmitted diseases, such as West Nile disease, you may need stronger protection.

15-20 drops eucalyptus essential oil

15-20 drops lemon essential oil

15-20 drops lemongrass essential oil

15-20 drops citronella essential oil

1 ounce carrier oil (olive oil or any massage oil)

1. In a small pitcher, mix the essential oils with the carrier oil.
2. Put into a spray bottle and use as needed. Do not use on small children or infants.

Soothing Gel for Insect Bites

Once you've been bitten, you need something to soothe the itch. This easy, inexpensive mixture will do it.

10-20 drops of a combination of lavender, tea tree, chamomile, cedarwood, and/or eucalyptus essential oils

1 ounce aloe vera gel or chamomile or calendula cream

1. In a small bowl, mix essential oils into the gel or cream.
2. Smooth over itchy/painful area. If you make more than you need, you can store the mixture in a clean jar in a cool, dark place for a week.

One-Minute
Substitute

Baking Soda Paste for Itches

Here is an incredibly easy itch reliever that costs just pennies. In a small bowl, mix 1/4 teaspoon baking soda (or meat tenderizer) with a little ice water to make a paste. Then spread the paste over the bite area. Repeat as necessary.

Essential Oil Itch Soother

Instead of messy, expensive anti-itch salves, try this homemade soother, which can be made for under $1.

1 drop lavender, rose, chamomile, or tea tree essential oil

Cold water

1. Fill a bowl with enough cold water to moisten a small washcloth or cotton pad. Swirl the essential oil through the water; then soak the cloth or pad.

2. Squeeze gently to remove any excess water and apply the cloth to the skin. Hold in place with your hand for as long as possible, or cover with plastic wrap and leave in place for about an hour.

Poison Ivy Lotion

The key to healing poison ivy is to dry it up. To make it less annoying, a coating of a heavy lotion keeps it from itching. This may be just as messy as calamine lotion, but it is a lot cheaper.

1/2 teaspoon salt

1/2 cup water

Bentonite clay

12 drops lavender essential oil

12 drops peppermint essential oil

1. In a small bowl, dissolve the salt in the water and add enough bentonite clay to make a creamy mixture. Stir in the lavender and peppermint essential oils.

2. Spread over the affected area.

Poison Ivy Drying Paste

This easily made, inexpensive paste may coat and stick to the skin better than a lotion.

1 tablespoon bentonite clay or finely ground oatmeal

10 drops lavender, chamomile, cypress, and/or geranium essential oil

Water

1. In a small bowl, put enough bentonite clay or finely ground oatmeal to cover the affected area. For each tablespoon of powder, stir in 10 drops of one or more of the essential oils. Moisten the mixture with water to allow for easy application and spread over the affected area.

2. Cover loosely and allow to dry. Rinse off and reapply as needed.

Healing Oil Bath

Dry, irritated skin is the greatest culprit with either eczema or dermatitis. Store shelves are stocked with dozens of creams and lotions, but the natural way is less expensive.

6-8 drops pine, geranium, or lavender essential oils

1. Add essential oil to a hot bath. Swirl to disperse the oil, then get in and soak for about 10 minutes.

2. Carefully get out of the bath (it will be slippery) and massage in any oil still left on the skin. Don't take this bath more than once every 24 hours.

Healing Calendula Lotion

Be sure you have Calendula officinalis *flowers from your garden or a health store for this lotion for treating eczema or dermatitis; they are the ones with the therapeutic effect.*

Calendula flower petals

1. Crush several calendula flower petals between your fingers (or with a mortar or pestle) until the petals are juicy.

2. Rub both petals and juice onto the skin.

Skin Salve for Eczema or Dermatitis

Here is another treatment for rough, dry, irritated skin that outperforms the store-bought versions.

1 ounce grated beeswax

1 cup untoasted sesame oil

1/2 teaspoon tincture of goldenseal

1/2 teaspoon tincture of barberry root

8 drops tea tree essential oil

8 drops chamomile essential oil

1. In the top of a double boiler over low heat, melt the beeswax, stirring occasionally. Stir in the sesame oil.

2. In a small dish, mix tincture of goldenseal and barberry root. Add the tea tree and chamomile essential oils.

3. Stir this mixture into the beeswax-oil mixture. Apply as needed.

Honey Ointment

The honey in this ointment serves as a humectant to draw in moisture, which eases the skin irritation produced by eczema and dermatitis.

1 ounce grated beeswax

1 cup untoasted sesame oil

1/3 cup honey

1 capsule vitamin E, 400 IU

60 drops rose, geranium, chamomile, lavender, or bergamot essential oils in any combination

1. In the top of a double boiler over low heat, melt the beeswax, stirring occasionally. Stir in the sesame oil. Remove from the heat and let cool slightly, then add honey. Pierce the vitamin E capsule and squeeze in the contents. Add up to 60 drops of essential oils.

2. Pour mixture into a clean jars or jars with tight-fitting lids and use as needed to keep skin smooth and hydrated.

Anti-Itching Solution for Hives

You can buy pricey salves at the drugstore to tame the itching of hives, but this easy, pennies-a-pop solution is just as effective.

20-30 drops lavender essential oil

Bowl cold water

1. Stir the lavender essential oil into the bowl of cold water.
2. Dip a cloth into the liquid and apply directly to the hives to reduce inflammation.

Oatmeal Bath for Hives

You know the brand that's famous for its oat-based products. Now you can make your own.

1 handful of rolled oats

1/2 handful dry powdered milk

1/2 handful chamomile

1/4 handful calendula and/or lavender

Double-ply square of cheesecloth

1. Place the oats, milk, chamomile, and calendula or lavender on the cheesecloth square. Tie the ends together to make a bag.
2. Run a warm (not hot) bath. Put the bag under the spout while the water is running. Leave it in the bath and allow the water to cool. (If the water is too hot, it will make the hives worse.)
3. Get into the tub and soak, squeezing the bag over your skin to reduce itching.

Anti-Itch Wrap

Cheaper than cortisone salves, but quite effective, this herbal wrap solution will make life worth living again for people with irritating rashes.

1/4 cup apple cider vinegar

1/4 cup witch hazel

2 cups cold water

4 drops lavender essential oil

2 drops chamomile essential oil

2 drops bergamot essential oil

2 teaspoons baking soda

Clean cloths

1. In a large bowl, mix the vinegar, witch hazel, and 2 cups cold water. In a separate small bowl, mix the essential oils with the baking soda. Stir the baking soda mixture into the water mixture.
2. Soak a cloth in the cool solution and wrap it over the itchy area for 20 minutes at a time or until the cloth begins to dry. Keep the solution chilled in the refrigerator for up to two weeks.
3. May be repeated three times a day.

One-Minute Substitute

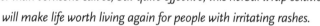

Using Essential Oil to Soothe Rashes

Lavender and tea tree essential oils have soothing properties that can alleviate as well as heal rashes. Try this simple solution before buying expensive ointments. Put 1 drop of lavender or tea tree essential oil directly on the rash, gently smoothing it over the surface. To treat a large area, apply a blend made by mixing 3 drops of either essential oil in 2 teaspoons light olive oil.

treatments for skin outbreaks

Acne Facial Scrub
For a homemade version of an acne-relieving exfoliant that won't break the bank, try this. For more information on green clay powder, see Green Clay Purifying Face Mask, page 242.

2 cups rolled oats

1/2 cup almonds

2 tablespoons dried lavender

1 tablespoon dried peppermint

1 tablespoon calendula leaf

1/2 cup green clay powder

1. In a coffee grinder or blender, grind the oats, almonds, lavender, peppermint, and calendula leaf

2. Add the clay and mix thoroughly, then put in a clean covered container and keep in a cool place. You can keep this scrub for up to three months.

3. To use, in a small open dish, make a paste by mixing a teaspoon of the mixture with water. Massage the paste onto your skin. Let dry, then rinse well.

Cleansing Liquid for Acne
Toners are primarily just water with a few other ingredients, yet they can cost more than $5 a bottle. Instead, make your own (see Making an Infusion, page 271). Dab an affected area three times a day, or use over your whole face after washing.

1 cup distilled water

1 teaspoon dried thyme

1 teaspoon dried calendula flowers

1 teaspoon dried lavender

1 teaspoon dried yarrow

1/4 cup witch hazel

5-10 drops tea tree essential oil

1. In a small pan, bring the distilled water to a boil. Add the thyme, calendula, lavender, and yarrow. Remove from heat and steep covered until cool.

2. Strain and mix strained liquid with the witch hazel. Add the tea tree essential oil, shake, and apply to affected areas with a cotton pad.

3. Store the leftover liquid in the refrigerator and use within two weeks.

Acne Cleansing Pads
Forget those high-priced acne pads that come impregnated with the medicine. Just make your own!

2 cups distilled water

1 tablespoon dried yarrow

1 tablespoon dried chamomile

15 drops tincture of benzoin

6 drops peppermint or wintergreen essential oil

Cosmetic pads

1. In a small pan, bring the distilled water to a boil. Add the yarrow and chamomile. Remove from heat after two to three minutes and steep, covered, for half an hour. Strain and add the tincture of benzoin and peppermint or wintergreen essential oil. Mix well and pour into a sterilized jar with a tight-fitting lid.

2. Put several cosmetic pads in with the liquid. Refrigerate and use as needed.

Overnight Acne Cream

Those little tubes of overnight acne medicine can set you back a pretty penny. Instead, try this homemade paste.

4 drops tea tree oil

1 teaspoon cosmetic clay

1. In a small dish, mix the tea tree oil and the cosmetic clay, and just enough water to make a thick paste.

2. Dab onto blemishes and leave on overnight.

Hot Compress for Boils

This gentle treatment will help relieve the boil in a lovely, aromatic way.

4 teaspoons hot water

2 drops lavender, lemon, tea tree, sage, or clove essential oil

1 cotton ball or gauze pad

1. Put the hot water in a bowl. Swirl your chosen essential oil through the water, then soak the cotton ball or gauze pad in the solution.

2. Gently squeeze out excess fluid and apply the cotton ball or pad directly to the area of the boil. Cover with plastic wrap and secure with a bandage or tape. Leave in place for at least an hour. Repeat twice a day.

Antibacterial Drawing Paste

This therapeutic paste works best if it is applied after putting a hot compress (above) on the boil for 15 minutes.

5 drops total tea tree, lavender, and/or spikenard essential oils

Slippery elm powder or green clay powder

1. Mix essential oils with enough slippery elm powder or green clay powder to generously cover the affected area.

2. Apply the moist powder to the boil and cover with a bandage for 24 hours.

Antibacterial Oil

You don't want a boil to get infected; this antibacterial oil protects you from that. You should, however, test it on a small area of normal skin first to make sure it's not irritating to your skin.

1 tablespoon carrier oil

20 drops tea tree essential oil

20 drops lavender essential oil

10 drops thyme essential oil

1. In a small bowl, combine the carrier oil with the essential oils. Mix well.

2. Hold a hot compress (above) on the boil for 10 minutes, then apply a small amount of the antibacterial oil and cover with a dressing. Repeat every few hours.

Ringworm Paste
Save yourself a trip to the doctor for a prescription with this antifungal paste. If it's not better in a week, see a doctor.

1 tablespoon mustard seeds
Water
1-2 drops sage and/or thyme essential oil

1. Crush the mustard seeds with a mortar and pestle. Stir in enough water to make a paste, then add the essential oil or oils.
2. Apply to the affected area and cover with a light bandage. Reapply once a day until the infection clears.

Dandelion/Fig Wart Remover
Here's an easy wart remover straight from the backyard that won't cost you a thing.

Freshly cut dandelion stalks or fig leaves

1. Use the milky sap that exudes from the dandelion stalks or fig leaves and apply directly to the wart once or twice a day for several days or until the wart pulls away from the skin. Keep the sap away from the skin around the wart, and from sensitive areas such as the eyes.
2. If you are using this treatment on a child, cover the wart area with a bandage to prevent spreading the sap to sensitive skin.

Herbal Wart Remover
Warts are mysterious—they come and go seemingly without reason. You usually don't need a dermatologist or an expensive patent medicine to make them disappear.

1 drop tea tree, lemon, clove, thuja, or thyme essential oil
1 drop almond or olive oil
1 strip bandage

1. Soak the wart in warm water for 15 minutes. Towel off excess water.
2. In a small dish, combine the essential oil with the almond or olive carrier oil. Test this oil mixture on a patch of skin to make sure it isn't irritating.
3. Apply the oil mixture to the wart and cover with the strip bandage. Reapply every 24 hours.

for cuts, bruises, and burns

First-Aid Antiseptic

Here is an all-natural solution with germ-killing properties that will help soothe a minor cut or abrasion. Be sure to wash the affected area well before applying it.

2 ounces Calendula Ointment (below)

40 drops lavender essential oil

20 drops tea tree essential oil

10 drops chamomile essential oil

10 drops lemon essential oil

1. In a small sterile jar with a tight-fitting lid, combine the calendula ointment with the essential oils, mixing thoroughly.

2. Apply a small amount to the cleaned injury. Keep the remainder in a cool, dark place for up to two weeks.

Calendula Ointment

Use the old-fashioned calendula flower (Calendula officinalis) for this therapeutic salve that has many uses.

3 tablespoons fresh calendula petals

1/3 cup light olive oil

2 tablespoons chopped beeswax

1 capsule vitamin E, 400 IU

1. Put the calendula petals in a double boiler and crush slightly with the back of a spoon. Add the olive oil and simmer for two hours over low heat.

2. Strain the liquid into a bowl, pressing against the strainer with the back of a spoon to extract all the oils.

3. Return the liquid to the double boiler. Over medium heat, add the chopped beeswax and stir until it melts. Remove from the double boiler and beat the mixture until it cools and becomes creamy and thick. Pierce the vitamin E capsule with a needle, squeeze in the contents, and mix.

4. Spoon into a sterilized 4 1/2-ounce jar with a tight top, seal, and keep in a cool, dark place for up to two weeks.

Healing Ointment

You can have this ointment on hand to treat everyday cuts and scrapes as they arise, just as you would a tube of pricey commercial antiseptic.

1-1 1/2 ounces grated beeswax

1 cup olive or almond oil

2 capsules vitamin E, 400 IU

30 drops tea tree essential oil

20 drops spike lavender or French lavender essential oil

10 drops chamomile essential oil

10 drops fir essential oil

1. In the top of a double boiler over low heat, melt the beeswax. Stir in the olive or almond oil. Remove from the heat. Pierce each vitamin E capsule with a needle and squeeze the contents into the mixture. Then stir in the essential oils.

2. Pour into a small sterilized jar with a tight-fitting lid and store in a cool, dark place. Use as needed on wounds. Should last a year.

Cleansing Soap

Here is an antiseptic soap you can trust to clean out wounds properly and stave off infections. It smells good and costs very little.

Liquid castile soap

Lavender essential oil

Rosemary essential oil

Tea tree essential oil

1. To the castile soap, add lavender, rosemary, and tea tree essential oils (10 drops total per 2 ounces of soap). Dilute with more soap if skin is especially sensitive to any of the essential oils.
2. Use to clean off cuts and abrasions.

Compress for Bruises

A wet compress can relieve some of the pain of a bruise and help the healing process. This simple formula will have you feeling better in no time and for very little money.

1/4 cup water

1/4 cup witch hazel or cider vinegar

2 drops lavender essential oil

2 drops rosemary essential oil

2 drops peppermint or juniper essential oil

1. In a bowl, mix the water, witch hazel or vinegar, and the essential oils. Soak a flannel cloth in the liquid, wring it out until nearly dry, and then place over injured area.
2. Cover with plastic wrap so the skin absorbs the essential oils and cover the whole thing with a towel. Apply the compress for 30 minutes up to three times daily.

Anti-Bruising Oil

Use this rub very, very gently to help in the healing process.

10 drops rosemary essential oil

10 drops peppermint essential oil

10 drops juniper essential oils

30 drops carrier oil (olive or almond).

1. In a small bowl, mix the essential oils with the carrier oil.
2. Massage the mixture gently into bruised areas every two hours.

One-Minute Substitute

Two Quick Treatments for Burns

Aloe vera gel is a traditional and effective salve for burns. And it costs you nothing if you have aloe vera as a houseplant. Pull a leaf off the plant and with a small spoon, scoop out the clear gel. Apply directly to the burn.

Lavender essential oil provides relief from minor burns, including sunburn. Just apply several drops of the oil directly to the burn.

Oil Rub for Burned Skin

This mixture gives relief. And you can safely use it several times a day.

1 drop tea tree essential oil
1/4 cup organic olive oil

1. In a small dish, dilute the essential oil with the olive oil.
2. Gently massage the mixture over the burned area.

Soothing Oil for Burns

If the burn area is large, you may need to double the ingredients for this soothing oil.

2 capsules vitamin E, 400 IU
5 drops lavender essential oil

1. Pierce each vitamin E capsule with a needle and squeeze the contents into a small dish. Stir in the lavender essential oil.
2. Gently massage into the skin.

Burn Spray

Applying a spray doesn't hurt the burn the way massaging in an oil might. This cool mixture offers relief and healing at very little cost.

1 ounce ice water
1 ounce aloe vera gel
25 drops total lavender, chamomile, spearmint, and yarrow essential oils
1 capsule vitamin E, 400 IU

1. In a small spray bottle, mix the ice water, aloe vera, and essential oils. Pierce the vitamin E capsule with a needle, squeeze its contents into the mixture, and chill.
2. Shake before use and spray over burned area. Keeps in the refrigerator for several days.

---

growing your own aloe vera

You can buy an aloe vera plant at any garden shop or nursery. Aloes like warmth, so in most areas, it is safer to keep the plant potted and place it near a sunny window than to plant it outdoors. (You can move the pot outdoors during the summer months.) Repot an aloe vera in a wide rather than a deep pot; it has shallow, spreading roots. Use one with a drainage hole and fill it with a good potting mix (page 377) with extra perlite. Don't overwater this succulent plant. Let its soil dry completely between soakings. Fertilize it yearly, in the spring, with a half-strength 10-40-10 fertilizer mixture. When you need some aloe vera gel, just cut a lower leaf off the plant and squeeze it.

Antiseptic Lotion for Burns
Nobody wants a burn to become infected. Here's a quick remedy that costs only pennies.

1 handful dried plantain
leaves

1/2 cup hot water

10 drops tea tree essential oil

1. In a blender, add a handful of dried plantain leaves to about 1/2 cup hot water. Begin blending, slowly adding water or plantain leaves as necessary until the mixture becomes thick, like oatmeal. Mix in the tea tree oil.

2. Spread mixture over affected area. You can refrigerate the remainder for several days.

Sunburn Cooler
Brew a pot of regular tea (Lipton, Salada, or a store brand will do fine). The tannins in the tea help soothe the burning feeling.

3 tea bags or 3 tablespoons
loose tea

Boiling water

1. In a teapot, place the tea. Pour in boiling water, cover, and steep 5 minutes. Cool.

2. Use a cloth or cotton ball to dab the sunburn with cooling tea.

foot care products

Athlete's Foot Powder
Dr. Scholl doesn't have a lock on the foot care market. Not when you can make your own antifungal foot powder. It can also be used for jock itch.

1/2 cup arrowroot or
cornstarch

2 tablespoons white cosmetic
clay

10 drops cypress essential oil

10 drops lavender
essential oil

3 drops clove essential oil

5 drops tea tree essential oil

5 drops thyme essential oil

1. In a small container with a tight-fitting cover, mix the arrowroot or cornstarch with 2 tablespoons cosmetic clay. Add the cypress, lavender, and clove essential oils and mix. To make the powder antiseptic, add the tea tree and thyme essential oils.

2. Let the powder sit for a couple of days to absorb the oils, then dust on your feet once or twice a day. Keeps in a dry, covered container for several weeks.

Antifungal Foot Ointment

Treating a fungus with your own aromatic homemade ointment is much pleasanter than paying big bucks for a commercial antifungal ointment. Organic light olive oil is available in health food stores and many supermarkets.

3 tablespoons organic light olive oil

1/3 ounce finely chopped beeswax

50 drops of tea tree, geranium, lavender, pine, myrrh, or peppermint essential oil (or any combination)

1. In the top of a double boiler, warm the oil over simmering water. Add the beeswax to the warmed oil and stir until it melts. Remove from the heat and stir until it cools. Then beat in essential oil.

2. Spoon the ointment into a small, sterilized, widemouthed jar with a tight-fitting lid. Keep in a cool, dark place. Massage a small amount into the affected area twice a day. The ointment should keep for several weeks.

Helpful Hint

Getting Ointment to the Right Consistency
When making ointments, if the salve is too watery, reheat and add more beeswax. If it's too thick, reheat and add more oil.

Antifungal Solution

Use this solution to wipe down areas affected with fungal outbreaks twice a day. It's effective and inexpensive. Before applying this solution, wash the affected area with tea tree soap (available in health food stores).

1-2 tablespoons dried thyme

1-2 tablespoons dried eucalyptus

1-2 tablespoons dried lavender

1. In a large cup, combine the herbs. Cover with 8 ounces of boiling water and steep, covered, for 10 to 15 minutes. Strain and cool.

2. Soak a clean cotton cloth in the solution and apply twice daily to the skin (after your shower in the morning and before bed). You can also use this solution to soak your feet.

One-Minute Substitute

A Quick and Cheap Antifungal Footbath
Here's an easy, pennies-a-pop, footbath to make up in a hurry. Fill a basin with warm water and add 2 or 3 drops of mustard oil or 1 teaspoon of powdered mustard, such as Coleman's. Soak your feet for at least half an hour. The mustard helps kill the fungus. Rinse your feet and dry thoroughly.

Corn Plaster *This homemade corn plaster is very effective and costs only pennies.*

1 banana skin or fig skin or
pulp of a squeezed lemon

1 small dandelion leaf or
garlic clove, crushed

1. Scrape the inside of the banana or fig skin until you have about a teaspoonful of the pulp. Alternatively, you can use the flesh of a squeezed lemon.

2. In a small dish, mix the pulp with the dandelion or garlic to make a paste. Apply paste directly to the corn, binding in place with a small adhesive bandage.

3. When the skin is soft, gently rub the top layer of the corn away with an emery board.

4. Repeat the entire process daily until the corn disappears. For several days after the corn is gone, massage the area with a small amount of Calendula Ointment (page 286).

calendula treatments for blisters

Here are two ways to make use of the healing properties of calendula when treating blisters. Which you use depends on whether the blister is open or still intact.

• For open blisters, make an infusion of dried calendula flowers (see Making an Infusion, page 271). Dab on and let dry.

• For other foot blisters, apply a small amount of Calendula Ointment (page 286) to a clean piece of gauze, and cover the blister. Remove when you're not wearing shoes.

Essential Oil Corn Remover *Here's an easy, inexpensive way to take care of a corn.*

1 drop clove or tea tree
essential oil

2 drops olive oil

1. In a small dish, dilute the essential oil with the olive oil. Spread over corn.

2. Cover the corn with a sterile strip bandage. Repeat application and change bandage daily until corn disappears.

One-Minute
Substitute

Treating a Blister with Essential Oil
Here's a quick fix for a blister that costs pennies. Just place 1 drop tea tree or lavender essential oil on the blister and gently massage it in. Make sure you don't break the skin and don't use tea tree oil on open blisters.

Healthy Home Remedies   **291**

Salicylic Acid Corn Remover

Most commercial corn removers have salicylic acid as their main ingredient—the same ingredient in aspirin. Here's how you can make your own salicylic acid remover.

5 aspirin tablets, 325 mg (adult)

1/2 teaspoon lemon juice

1/2 teaspoon water

1. In a small bowl, with the back of a spoon, crush the aspirin into a powder. Add the lemon juice and water and stir until the mixture forms a paste.

2. Dab the paste onto the corn and cover with plastic wrap, then place a heated towel over the wrap to help the paste penetrate more deeply. It will take several applications over several days before the corn falls off.

for mouth and lip irritations

Healing Balm for Chapped Lips

During winter this homemade lip balm will keep your lips from cracking and peeling, if you use it faithfully. With its lovely smell, it is a true bargain.

4 tablespoons almond oil

1 tablespoon grated beeswax

1 teaspoon honey

1 capsule vitamin E, 400 IU

10 drops chamomile essential oil

10 drops orange essential oil

10 drops wintergreen essential oil

5 drops lavender essential oil

1. In the top of a double boiler, warm the oil, the beeswax, and the honey over low heat until the wax melts. Remove from heat. Pierce the vitamin E capsule with a needle and squeeze its contents into the mixture.

2. Stir in the essential oils. Store in a cool, dark place and use by dipping a finger into the balm and smoothing it on your lips.

One-Minute Substitute

Quickly Soothe a Canker Sore with Aloe Vera

Instead of buying balm in the drugstore to coat that painful mouth sore, make your own instantly. All you need are a cotton swab and an aloe vera leaf. Dry the sore area with a cotton swab, then squeeze a bit of gel from the aloe vera leaf over the area. Repeat as often as necessary.

Cold Sore Ointment

This is really more of a liquid than an ointment, but it works the same way. The jojoba oil serves as a carrier oil.

5 drops lemon balm essential oil

1 drop lavender essential oil

1 drop chamomile essential oil

1 drop bergamot or rose essential oil

10 drops jojoba oil

1. In a small, clean jar with a tight-fitting lid, dilute the lemon balm and the lavender, chamomile, bergamot or rose oil essential oils in the jojoba oil (which serves as a carrier oil).

2. Smooth over the affected area several times a day.

Mouthwash for Cold Sores

This is a simple, certainly inexpensive, mouthwash that helps to heal annoying cold sores as fast as possible.

6 ounces water

3-4 drops clove or tea tree essential oil

1. In a clean jar with a tight-fitting lid, mix the water with the essential oil.

2. Swish the mixture in your mouth for 30 seconds, then spit it out. Cap bottle and keep mixture on the counter. Repeat mouthwash several times a day.

One-Minute Substitute

A Fast Cold Sore Preventive

You probably can't even find a cold sore preventive at your local CVS or Walgreens. If you feel one coming on, here's what to do. Apply 1 drop of lavender or lemon balm essential oil to the area where you feel the cold sore forming. Then hold an ice cube on top of the area for 10 minutes. This should either prevent the outbreak altogether or at least reduce its severity. Repeat the whole procedure several times a day.

Cold Sore Paste

This soothing, not-so-costly paste smothers the irritation of a cold sore and helps to heal it.

1 teaspoon finely chopped licorice root or rhizome

3 ounces distilled water

Slippery elm powder, as needed

Goldenseal powder, as needed

1. In a small saucepan, combine licorice root and distilled water. Bring the water to a boil, then simmer for 10 minutes. Strain into a clean bowl. This makes a strong licorice decoction.

2. In a small, clean container with a tight-fitting lid, mix equal amounts of slippery elm and goldenseal powder and moisten with the licorice decoction.

3. Apply the paste to the sore area to control pain and increase healing. Store extra paste in the refrigerator or dilute with water and use as mouthwash.

dental care products

Mouthwash
You don't need to spend upward of $4 a bottle for artificially flavored mouthwash that is primarily alcohol.

1 teaspoon vegetable glycerin

1 teaspoon aloe vera gel

10 drops peppermint, wintergreen, or spearmint essential oil

1 1/2 cups water

1. In a clean jar with a tight-fitting cap, mix vegetable glycerin and aloe vera gel with the essential oil you have chosen. Add water and shake well. Use as a gargle.

2. Store in a covered jar and shake well before using.

Mints
Instead of sugary candy, chew on breath-freshening herbs and spices.

1-2 fresh leaves spearmint, peppermint, fennel, or parsley

1/4 teaspoon fresh or dried caraway, cardamom, or fennel seeds

Chew on the herb leaves or seeds for two or three minutes. Spit out and discard.

Toothpaste
Although we can't say 4 out of 5 dentists recommend it, we do know this home-made version will cost you far less than any of the commercial brands that fill drugstore shelves. The tea tree oil provides an additional antiseptic boost to help prevent gum disease.

3 tablespoons baking soda

Water

10 drops tea tree essential oil

10 drops peppermint essential oil

1. In a small bowl, mix the baking soda with just enough water to make a paste. Add the tea tree and peppermint essential oils.

2. Use paste to brush your teeth and tongue. Cover the remaining paste and use for the next couple of days.

One-Minute Substitute

Fast Toothache Relief with Clove Oil

Until you can get to the dentist, try this quick numbing trick. Put 1 drop of oil of cloves on a cotton swab, dip the swab in water, and then rub on the aching tooth and gum area.

Antibacterial Mouthwash

Used regularly, this mouthwash can help kill the germs that cause gum disease for a lot less than commercial mouthwashes.

2 cups distilled water

2 tablespoons green tea

2 tablespoon dried, crumbled peppermint, spearmint, or rosemary

10 drops tincture of benzoin or 1 teaspoon tincture of myrrh

1. In a saucepan, bring the water to a boil. In a pint jar with a tight-fitting lid, mix the green tea and peppermint, spearmint, or rosemary. Pour in the boiling water, let cool, cover, and steep overnight in the refrigerator.

2. Strain into a clean bottle with a tight-fitting lid. Add the tincture of benzoin or the tincture of myrrh and shake to mix.

3. Use 2 tablespoons at a time as a mouthwash for sore and/or bleeding gums. Swish and spit without swallowing.

Gum Tonic

This will treat bad gums with respect without running up your grocery bill.

1 dropperful of goldenseal tincture (about 20 drops)

2 drops myrrh essential oil

1 ounce hot water

1. In a glass, combine the goldenseal tincture and myrrh essential oil. Dilute with the hot water.

2. Swish around your mouth and spit.

Super Dental Floss

There may be antiseptic dental floss on the market, but it will cost more than this and may not even work as well.

10 drops goldenseal tincture

3 drops myrrh essential oil

2 drops tea tree essential oil

Dental floss

1. In a small container, combine the goldenseal tincture, myrrh essential oil, and tea tree essential oil. Cut off enough dental floss to clean between your teeth and dip it into the mixture.

2. Use the dipped floss to clean between your teeth. Make a fresh batch every time you want to floss your teeth.

Toothache-Relieving Rinse

To quell the pain until you can get to a dentist, try this inexpensive rinse.

1 1/2 teaspoons whole cloves

1 cup boiling water

1. In a small pot, place the cloves. Pour in boiling water and steep for 10 minutes. Strain into a glass.

2. Rinse your mouth with the warm infusion.

Toothache-Relieving Dental Paste

Some people don't like cloves and need another way to relieve dental pain without using expensive pain pills with lots of side effects. Try this.

2 tablespoons powdered ginger

2 tablespoons red cayenne pepper

Water

1. In a small dish, mix powdered ginger and red cayenne pepper with enough water to make a paste.

2. Saturate a cotton ball with the paste and put on the painful tooth. Keep the paste off your gums, because it may be irritating to gums.

for joint and muscle aches

Hot Pepper Rub

The capsaicin in hot peppers has begun to be appreciated as a pain reliever even by commercial drug companies. Make your own for lots less.

2 tablespoons ground cayenne pepper

1/2 cup Glorious Green Aloe Moisturizing Lotion (page 253) or any commercial moisturizing lotion

1. In a small bowl, combine the cayenne pepper with the moisturizing lotion.

2. Massage the mixture into the painful area, being careful to wash your hands afterward before touching your face or eyes.

Massage Cream

This soothing, painkilling massage cream will take care of sore muscles and your bank balance.

2 teaspoons grated beeswax

1 tablespoon coconut oil

4 tablespoons cayenne-infused oil

10-15 drops wintergreen essential oil

2 tablespoons ginger tincture

2 tablespoons water

2 tablespoons aloe vera gel

1/2 teaspoon borax

1/4 teaspoon powdered vitamin C (from drugstore or health food store)

1. In the top of a double boiler over low heat, mix the beeswax and coconut oil and stir until the beeswax has melted. Stir in the cayenne-infused oil and the wintergreen essential oil.

2. In a separate pan, heat the ginger tincture to evaporate as much alcohol as possible, then add the water, aloe vera gel, borax, and vitamin C and bring to 160°F to 175°F on a candy thermometer. Place the ginger tincture mixture in a blender and whirl at high speed as you add the beeswax-oil mixture. Pour the resulting cream into a clean jar with a tight-fitting lid.

3. Massage cream into sore joints as needed. Keep refrigerated for 4 to 6 weeks.

Quick-and-Dirty Muscle Rub

Again, capsaicin comes to the rescue of tense and tired muscles that need a good massage in a hurry without costing an arm and a leg.

5 drops cayenne-based hot sauce

3-5 drops peppermint essential oil

15 drops massage oil or olive oil

1. In a clean small jar, combine hot sauce, peppermint essential oil, and massage or olive oil and mix thoroughly.

2. Rub the mixture into the affected area by hand or with a cotton ball. This may initially irritate the skin, but the irritation will disappear as the painkilling becomes more effective.

3. Clean your hands with soap and water after each application and avoid touching your eyes.

Muscle Soak

A luxurious hot soak with beneficial herbs is priceless for relieving tight muscles and joints. You can make your own bag of just the right herbs.

1/2 cup baking soda

10-20 drops essential oil of eucalyptus, peppermint, juniper, or pine

1/2 cup Epsom salts

1 tablespoon juniper berries

1 tablespoon dried rosemary leaves

1 tablespoon dried chamomile flowers

1 tablespoon dried eucalyptus leaves

2 teaspoons dried lemon balm leaves

2 teaspoons dried peppermint leaves

1 two-ply square cheesecloth

1. In a small dish, place the baking soda and add the essential oils; mix until the baking soda has absorbed the oils. In a bowl, combine the Epsom salts, herbs, and baking soda mixture. Place in middle of cheesecloth and tie up the ends to make a bag.

2. Hold beneath the running water until tub fills, then massage your body with the bag and let it float in the tub. Soak until water cools.

Liniment

This is a traditional remedy for man and beast, and nothing on the market loosens tight joints and offers relief any better.

4 teaspoons castor oil

2 tablespoon glycerin

2 tablespoon aloe vera gel

2 tablespoons cayenne tincture

20 drops wintergreen essential oil

1. In a clean glass bottle with a tight-fitting stopper, combine the castor oil, glycerin, aloe vera gel, cayenne tincture, and wintergreen essential oil. Shake well.

2. Massage over sore joints as needed. Refrigerate for up to 6 weeks.

Cold Pack for Strains and Sprains

There are all kinds of clever products on the market to use as cold packs. This one is flexible, reusable, and very, very inexpensive.

3 parts water

1 part rubbing alcohol

1 plastic zip-close freezer bag

1. Combine the water and rubbing alcohol in the freezer bag and freeze.
2. Wrap the frozen pack in a towel and apply to the hurting joint. The alcohol keeps the pack flexible.

Castor Oil Rub for Back Pain

You don't have to pay for a special tube of rubbing cream for back pain. Instead, try this easily made rub.

5 drops ginger essential oil

5 drops peppermint or wintergreen essential oil

2 drops camphor essential oil

2 drops rosemary essential oil

1 ounce castor oil

1. In a small bowl, mix together the essential oils and the castor oil.
2. Rub into the painful area and cover with a piece of flannel or an old T-shirt, then put a heating pad over the cloth for 15 to 20 minutes to help the rub soak in. You can double the recipe for larger areas.

for women's problems

Muscle Relaxant for Cramps

Forget the pills marketed just for cramps. Try this less expensive, easy-to-make remedy instead. These tinctures are available in natural food stores.

1/2 teaspoon valerian tincture

1/2 teaspoon cramp bark tincture

Take a dose of valerian tincture and a dose of cramp bark tincture every one to two hours. These are both natural muscle relaxants.

Hot Compress for Cramps

You can enhance the help of a heating pad by using a touch of ginger and oil.

2 tablespoons castor oil

10 drops ginger essential oil

In a small dish, mix castor oil and ginger essential oil. Spread the oil mixture over your abdomen, cover with a cotton or wool flannel cloth, then apply a heating pad for 20 to 30 minutes.

Anti-Cramp Tea
This combination of herbs can safely relax cramps and reduce your discomfort.

1 cup boiling water

1/4 teaspoon dried raspberry leaves

1/4 teaspoon dried chamomile flowers

1/4 teaspoon crushed fennel seeds

1/4 teaspoon dried spearmint leaves

1. In a large cup, pour 1 cup of boiling water over the raspberry leaves, chamomile, crushed fennel seeds, and spearmint. Steep 10 minutes and strain into a teacup.

2. Drink for relief when the cramps hit.

Ginger Tea for Morning Sickness
Here is a simple preparation that will calm your stomach in the morning and reduce nausea without making you sleepy.

1 cup boiling water

1/2 teaspoon minced fresh ginger

1. In a large cup, pour the cup of boiling water over the ginger. Steep 10 minutes, strain into a container, and refrigerate.

2. Sip in the morning when you wake.

PMS Tea
This tea is designed to help regulate hormone levels for all types of premenstrual syndrome without harming your stomach or liver.

1 tablespoon chopped dried dandelion roots and/or leaves

1 tablespoon chopped dried burdock root

4 cups water

1 teaspoon chopped dried black cohosh rhizome or root

1 teaspoon dried cramp bark

1 teaspoon grated orange peel

1 teaspoon chopped dried licorice root

1. In a pot, combine the dandelion roots and/or leaves and burdock root with the water. Add the black cohosh, cramp bark, orange peel, and licorice root. Bring to a boil, reduce the heat, and simmer, uncovered, 40 minutes. Cover and steep for 15 minutes. Strain into a clean container with a tight-fitting lid.

2. Drink 1/2 to 1 cup hot or cold as needed throughout the day. Refrigerate remainder.

Yeast Infection Cream

You don't need those expensive over-the-counter yeast infection remedies. You can make this in no time and for very little money. You can buy capsules of acidophilus bacteria—the bacteria used to make yogurt—in health food stores.

1 capsule acidophilus bacteria

3 tablespoons plain organic yogurt with active cultures

1. In a small dish, open the capsule and mix the bacteria and the yogurt.
2. Apply inside the vagina with a medicine syringe at night and wear a pad to prevent leakage.

headache treatments

Headache Compresses

There's a whole host of treatments beyond pills. But you won't find them in your local drugstore. To ease tension after a hard day, try this cool compress.

Enough chilled lavender toilet water to soak 2 washcloths

2 washcloths

1. In a small bowl, pour in the toilet water. Soak both washcloths in the toilet water and squeeze out the excess.
2. Lie down with a towel behind your neck. Place one wet washcloth on your forehead and the other cloth at the base of your skull. Relax for at least 15 minutes, preferably in a darkened quiet room.

Chamomile Tea

Taking a break in a busy schedule can relieve some of the tension that causes many headaches. Chamomile tea—inexpensive and easy to make—is particularly soothing to frazzled nerves.

3 teaspoons dried chamomile

1 cup boiling water

1 teaspoon honey *(optional)*

1. In a small pot, place chamomile. Pour in boiling water and steep for 5 minutes. Strain into a teacup.
2. Take a few minutes to sip the hot tea slowly while sitting in a quiet spot. Sweeten with a teaspoon of honey if desired.

Lemon Balm Tea

Lemon balm is another soothing tea herb that can relax away headaches for pennies with little fuss.

3 teaspoons dried lemon balm

1 cup boiling water

1 teaspoon honey *(optional)*

1. In a small pot, place lemon balm. Pour in boiling water and steep for 5 minutes. Strain into a teacup.
2. Take a few minutes to sip the hot tea slowly while sitting in a quiet spot. Sweeten with a teaspoon of honey if desired.

Migraine Tea
These vicious headaches are difficult to treat with pills. This inexpensive tea, served in a quiet, darkened room, can be very calming.

2 1/2 cups water

9 teaspoons dried lady's mantle leaves

3 teaspoons dried mint leaves

1. In a saucepan, bring the water to a boil. Add the herbs and boil for 20 minutes. Remove from heat and steep for 10 minutes. Strain into a teacup.

2. Drink 1 cup slowly in a quiet, darkened room.

Headache Massage
The combination of fragrant aroma and gentle massage can bring a throbbing head back to health without jeopardizing your stomach or liver as many headache pills do.

10 drops massage oil

3 drops peppermint essential oil

2 drops lavender essential oil

1 drop lemon, orange, or lime essential oil

1. In a small bowl, mix the massage oil and the essential oils.

2. Dip your fingers into the oil and then massage the oil into the temples, along the hairline, and along the base of the skull, being careful not to get any oil in the eyes.

3. Wash your hands thoroughly after each application.

Headache Oil with Vitamin E
Here is another aromatic solution for safely massaging away a headache.

15 drops lavender essential oil

7 drops wintergreen essential oil

1 1/2 tablespoons almond or olive oil

1 capsule vitamin E, 400 IU

Bowl hot water

1. In a small dish, combine the essential oils with the almond or olive oil. Pierce the vitamin E capsule with a needle and squeeze the contents into the dish.

2. Warm the oil mixture by putting the dish in a bowl of hot water before using. Dab your fingers into the fragrant oil and gently massage your temples and the back of your neck. Wash your hands thoroughly after each application.

for anxiety and fatigue

Catnip Anti-Anxiety Tea
You can ask your doctor for a prescription for an anti-anxiety medication, or you can make a cup of catnip tea (yes, they make it for humans too) and sip it several times a day.

2 teaspoons dried catnip

1 cup boiling water

1. In a teapot, steep catnip in boiling water for five to seven minutes. Strain and drink.

2. Serve yourself catnip tea three times a day.

Healthy Home Remedies **301**

Hops Anti-Anxiety Tea
Your cat is casting jealous glances at your catnip tea. So try hops, the critical ingredient in beer, instead.

2 teaspoons dried hops

1 cup boiling water

1. In a teapot, steep hops in boiling water for five to seven minutes. Strain and drink.
2. Serve yourself hops tea three times a day.

Calming Tea for Insomnia
All those over-the-counter sleep aids are just repackaged antihistamines. Instead, try this natural (and less expensive) alternative.

Boiling water

3 teaspoons dried chamomile or lemon balm

1. In a small pot, pour boiling water over chamomile or lemon balm. Steep 10 minutes, strain, and drink an hour before bed.
2. Once you start falling asleep more easily, cut the amount of herb in half.

One-Minute Substitute

Lavender Rub for Insomnia
Massage a single drop of lavender essential oil into each temple before going to bed.

Sleep Pillow
This aromatic small pillow will work its wonders—with no side effects—on your sleep habits.

4 tablespoons sweet woodruff

2 tablespoons lemon balm

2 tablespoons lavender

1 tablespoon chamomile

1 tablespoon hops

1 tablespoon rosebuds

10-15 drops chamomile essential oil

10-15 drops lavender essential oil

10-15 drops clary sage essential oil

10-15 drops marjoram essential oil

1 tablespoon powdered or freshly grated orrisroot

1 small zippered pillowcase

1. In a large bowl, mix the woodruff, lemon balm, lavender, chamomile, hops, and rosebuds. In a separate small bowl, mix the essential oils with the orrisroot. Stir this mixture into the large bowl.
2. Fill the pillowcase, zip it, and add it to your bed pillows for sweet dreams.

Herbal Milk Bath for Sleeplessness

What is more relaxing than a nice soak in a soothing herbal bath? And there are no bad aftereffects in the morning.

1/2 handful lavender
1/2 handful chamomile
1/2 handful rose petals
1/2 handful dry powdered milk
Double-ply square of cheesecloth

1. Place the lavender, chamomile, rose petals, and powdered milk on the cheesecloth and tie the ends to make a bag.
2. Place under the spigot of the tub while the water is running. Start with warm water but allow it to cool before getting in. The cool water helps lower your body temperature, important for sleep.
3. Soak for 15 minutes while listening to relaxing music or a relaxation tape.

Relaxing Aromatic Bath

Here's another way to get sleepy or anxiety-free without any pills. Keep the water relatively cool to maintain a low body temperature, important for sleep.

10 drops lavender, rose, geranium, and/or bergamot essential oil.

1. Add the essential oils to a cool bath.
2. Soak for 15 minutes while listening to relaxing music or a relaxation tape.

Invigorating Oil for Fatigue

These essential oils have fragrances that help to stimulate you and keep your mind alert.

Eucalyptus essential oil
Juniper essential oil
Grapefruit essential oil
Clary sage essential oil
Ginger or peppermint essential oil
Rosemary essential oil

1. In a clean small spray bottle, mix 2 parts eucalyptus, 2 parts juniper, 2 parts grapefruit, 1 part clary sage, 1 part ginger or peppermint, and 2 parts rosemary essential oils. Shake to mix.
2. You can use this spray in a variety of ways: Spritz an entire room when you feel tired and need to keep reading. Spray a cloth, hold it up to your nose, and breathe deeply. Rub into your hands. Use in a diffuser or humidifier.

Energy Tea for Fatigue

This tea is a real homemade pick-me-up that beats the pricey specialty teas you find at the grocery.

1 teacup boiling water
1/2 teaspoon dried rosemary leaves
1/2 teaspoon dried ginseng root
Honey *(optional)*

In a teacup, make an infusion of boiling water, dried rosemary leaves, and dried ginseng root. Sweeten with a bit of honey, if you like, and drink as often as necessary.

chapter 9

Wholesome Natural Pet Care Products

Our animal companions provide us not only with comfort and amusement but also with an uncritical devotion and loyalty that is difficult to obtain

elsewhere. And a loving pet provides therapy that instantly lifts its caretaker's spirits. So all of us who love pets tend to be suckers for buying them expensive treats and toys. As this chapter will show you, however, you don't have to spend a fortune to keep your pet—dog, cat, bird, hamster, guinea pig, gerbil, rat, turtle, or fish—well fed, healthily groomed, and happily occupied.

You can indulge your pets with nutritious meals that they will gobble up eagerly and healthy treats that they can enjoy without jeopardizing their health and well-being. None of these foods will strain your budget and most are actually fun to make. And it is always reassuring to know exactly what goes into your pet's food. In the recipes that follow, you will find not only healthy everyday foods and treats but also special-occasion treats such as a dog's birthday cake, feline catnip crackers, and parrot pops.

You will also find great recipes for natural wet and dry shampoos, flea dips, breath-saving dog biscuits, even a formula for dealing with skunk spray. For backyard bird lovers, there are recipes for inexpensive seed combinations you can mix to feed wild birds outside your window. And for young families, there are salads and treats for gerbils, hamsters, turtles, and other childhood favorites.

dog food

Calcium-Rich Dog Food

This easy-to-make recipe appeals to dogs and strengthens their bones. Although it is not inexpensive, it costs less than canned dog foods and you can vouch for the quality of its ingredients.

1 pound ground chicken or hamburger

4 cups cooked oatmeal or brown rice

1/2 cup bread crumbs

1/4 cup vegetable oil

1 tablespoon bonemeal (available at garden centers)

1 pet vitamin, crushed

1/2 cup shredded cheddar cheese

1. In a skillet over moderate heat, brown meat, stirring frequently. Remove from heat.

2. Stir in other ingredients and enough water to keep the mixture from being crumbly.

3. Cool and store in the refrigerator for one week or in the freezer for up to three months.

Feed according to weight of dog. Feed a 5-pound dog 1/2 cup daily; double the serving for every 5 pounds. Monitor your dog's weight and adjust portions to avoid obesity.

Makes 6 cups

Low-Fat Chicken and Rice Dog Dinner

If you want a nutritious beef- and-wheat-free diet for your pet, this combination will satisfy its appetite and may even keep its weight under control. This is also an economical dog food with fresh ingredients.

3 pounds chicken, with skin and bone

1 1/2 cups cooked oatmeal or brown rice

1 pint fat-free cottage cheese

1 dog vitamin

1. Poach, bake, or microwave chicken until well done. Cool and cut into 1/2-inch cubes. Drain and reserve pan juices to use as soup stock. Discard bones. Cook oatmeal or rice according to package directions and let cool.

2. In a large bowl, mix together cubed chicken and grains. Crumble vitamin and stir it in. Drain cottage cheese and fold it into the mixture.

3. Store in a covered container in the refrigerator for up to one week.

Feed according to weight of dog. Feed a 5-pound dog 1/2 cup daily; double the serving for every five pounds. Monitor your dog's weight and adjust portions to avoid obesity.

Makes 12 servings, 1/2 cup each

Delectable Dog Biscuits

The combination of dog food and oatmeal makes these biscuits a healthy and much-desired treat for your dog. You are assured of good ingredients and a better price than commercial dog biscuits. For a nutritional boost, add a crumbled dog vitamin.

2 pounds Calcium-Rich Dog Food (opposite) or canned dog food

1/4 cup whole wheat flour

3/4 cup oat bran

1 cup rolled oats

1 dog vitamin, crushed (*optional*)

1/4 cup Parmesan or cheddar cheese, shredded (*optional*)

1/2 cup vegetable oil

1. Preheat oven to 250°F.
2. Mix dog food, flour, bran, rolled oats, vitamin (if desired), and cheese (if desired for a flavor boost).
3. Add oil slowly, mixing dough to a consistency that can be rolled and cut with a cookie cutter.
4. Roll and cut or mold biscuits; place on an ungreased baking sheet. Bake for 3 1/2 hours, or until hard.
5. Cool and store in a covered canister in refrigerator for one week, or in a freezer for up to one month.

Makes 16 medium biscuits

homemade comforts for a new puppy

Puppies suffer from separation anxiety when they first leave their mother.

• To ease the transition, ask the breeder to put an old T-shirt or other piece of clothing into the puppy's box for a few days. When you bring the puppy home, bring along the clothing with the smells it recognizes and put it into the puppy's new bed.

• Along with this security blanket, add something that smells of you, so that the pup will soon get used to its new home.

• Another helpful transition aid is an old-fashioned ticking alarm clock, which emulates the mother's heartbeat.

• Also try filling an old sock with dried beans and microwaving it for a few seconds to create a soft, warm "body" for the puppy to snuggle up to.

Dog Slaw

Here's a dietary supplement for your dog, such as you will only find at very expensive pet emporiums. Making your own costs less than a dollar per serving. Dogs like carrots, which aid in digestion, freshen breath, and provide vitamins. The yogurt is digestion-friendly.

1 cup shredded carrots, raw

1/3 cup cooked brown rice

1/2 cup fat-free plain, live-culture yogurt

1/4 cup salad oil

1. Mix carrots and raisins in a bowl and set aside. In a second bowl, stir together the yogurt and salad oil. Pour this mixture over the slaw and toss.
2. Store in a covered container in the refrigerator for up to three days. Serve 1/4 cup every day along with meals or as a treat.

Makes 4 servings

Lucky Liver Snaps

The secret of many successful show and obedience trainers is nothing more than a little chewy liver nibble that dogs can't resist. Try it—your pet will jump through hoops for this homemade treat that has much more liver flavor than the store-bought kind.

1 pound beef or chicken livers
1 egg
1 cup flour
1/4 cup bran meal
3/4 cup cornmeal
1 tablespoon garlic powder

1. Preheat oven to 400°F. Chop raw livers, and then liquefy them in a blender. Add egg, pulse to blend, and then pour mixture into a mixing bowl. Stir in flour, bran, cornmeal, and garlic powder.

2. Spread mixture evenly into 9 x 13-inch greased sheet-cake pan and bake for 15 minutes.

3. While still warm, cut sheet into 1-inch squares. Turn squares out onto baking rack to cool and harden.

4. Store cooled treats in a plastic zip bag in the freezer to preserve freshness for up to three months. Serve either frozen or at room temperature.

Makes 117 liver snaps

Sweet Breath Dog Treats

Puppies often have "puppy breath" that they naturally outgrow by the age of 6 months. If an adult dog has occasional bad breath, this tasty recipe will combat the problem. If bad breath persists, however, it may be a sign of dental or digestive problems that a vet should treat. Here is a specialty dog biscuit that you don't have to shell out a fortune for at a pet store.

1 tablespoon activated charcoal (available in fish section of pet shops)
1/2 cup whole wheat flour
1 cup white flour
1/4 cup bran cereal
1/2 cup cornmeal
4 tablespoons vegetable oil
1 egg
1/2 cup chopped fresh basil, wintergreen, or mint
1/2 cup chopped fresh rosemary or thyme
1 cup of acidophilus milk

1. Preheat oven to 400°F. Process charcoal in coffee grinder until finely ground. Mix flour, bran, cornmeal, and charcoal together in a bowl. Stir in other ingredients.

2. Form into bite-size patties and place on a greased cookie sheet. Bake 20 minutes, or until dry and hard.

3. Store in a covered container in the refrigerator for one week, or in the freezer for up to three months.

Makes 24 medium biscuits

One-Minute Substitute

A Quick Water Bowl for Dog Walkers
Pick up an inexpensive plastic shower cap (or save a free one from a hotel) to use as a portable pet water dish. Stick it in your pocket when walking your dog, and when needed, pull it out and fill it from a water bottle or the nearest faucet or water fountain.

Doggie Birthday Cake

People do like to make a fuss over their dogs. For a birthday or adoption anniversary, you can go to a very fancy pet store and spend a lot of money or you can make up this nutritious treat (to be meted out during the week) for a few dollars. Here's a cake that you can feel good about offering him.

1 small package cornbread mix or 1/3 cup flour

1/3 cup cornmeal, bran, or rolled oats

1 1/2 teaspoons baking powder

1/2 teaspoon garlic powder

1 pound ground chicken

2 tablespoons honey

1 large egg

1/4 cup live-culture plain yogurt

4 teaspoons vegetable oil

1 container (4 ounces) whipped cream cheese

Delectable Dog Biscuits, as needed to decorate cake (page 307)

1. Preheat oven to 350°F. In a medium bowl, stir together dry ingredients. Make a well in the center and add chicken and wet ingredients. Stir just until mixed (or substitute cornbread mix made according to directions and combined with chicken).

2. Pour into greased cake pan and bake for 25 minutes or until chicken is done and a toothpick inserted in the center of cake comes out clean.

3. Turn out onto a cake rack to cool.

4. Frost with cream cheese (thin, if needed, with a little milk) and decorate with dog biscuits. Refrigerate in a covered container for up to one week.

Makes one cake with 4 to 6 servings

canine care products

Brush-and-Go Dry Dog Shampoo

You can save $5 a pop by substituting this single ingredient for a commercial dry pet shampoo. Although your pet will still need the occasional soap-and-water shampoo to remove ground-in dirt, dry shampoo will keep your dog clean and fresh smelling during cold weather or when you're traveling.

1 box (1 pound) baking soda

1. Test for sensitivity by rubbing a little baking soda into your dog's coat between the ears (where it can't be licked off). Wait 5 minutes and check for reddening or other signs of irritation. If there are none, proceed.

2. Rub baking soda into the dog's coat, working it in all the way to the skin. Be careful to avoid eyes, nose, mouth, and ears. Allow soda to remain in coat for a full minute to absorb oil and odor.

3. Brush fur with a pet brush until all the baking soda and debris are removed.

Makes one or more shampoos, depending on the size of dog

Minty Skunk Cure

When a skunk sprays your dog, confine it outdoors and run to the bathroom supply cabinet for help. Speed is important: Dried skunk essence is harder to remove and lingers longer.

1 or more large tubes traditional-formula white toothpaste (colored or gel pastes can discolor fur)

1 bottle dog shampoo

1/4 cup cider vinegar

1. Work toothpaste into the dog's fur from head to tail, nose to toe. Allow toothpaste to air-dry for 20 minutes.

2. Wet the dog and apply dog shampoo, working up a full lather.

3. In a large bucket, combine vinegar with 1 gallon of warm water. Rinse the dog with this solution (double it for a big dog) and dry as usual.

4. Repeat treatment as needed.

Makes one treatment

Cocktail Flea Dip

To check for fleas, comb your pet over a sheet of white paper. If black specks (flea frass) drop onto the paper, treat the animal at once with this dip (double it for large pets). There are many expensive flea dips on the market but this one—pennies a pop—works without harsh chemicals. To get rid of flea eggs—and future infestations—wash the animal's bedding and vacuum your house thoroughly.

2 tablespoons vodka or dry vermouth

1 3/4 pints water

1. In a 2-quart saucepan, stir alcohol into water and bring to a boil.

2. Remove from heat, cover pan, and allow solution to steep for two hours.

3. Rub cooled solution into pet's fur, rinse, and comb out.

Makes one treatment

Flea-Begone Bandanna

Here's a safe, renewable, flea-repelling bandanna to make for your dog that is much healthier for the dog and anyone who plays with it than expensive toxic flea collars. It's prettier too. The active ingredients are essential herb oils, which smell good to us, but fleas and mosquitoes can't stand them. Herbal oils are readily available at health food stores.

1 cotton bandanna (color and pattern of your choice)

1 small vial rose geranium essential oil

1 small vial lavender essential oil

1. Sprinkle several drops of each oil on the bandanna.

2. Roll the bandanna and tie it loosely around your dog's neck.

3. Launder the bandanna; retreat with oil when the scent fades.

Note: If your dog won't wear a bandanna, dab oil between its shoulder blades where it can't be licked off. Don't get oil near a dog's eyes, nose, or mouth.

natural ways to make fleas flee

Consider aromatic leaves, wood shavings, and soap the first defense in your arsenal of flea repellents.

• Fill small drawstring bags (available at cooking supply and natural foods stores) with fresh or dried chamomile leaves, walnut leaves, or cedar shavings, and tuck them into your dog's bedding (where they can't be chewed) to repel fleas.

• Sprinkle garlic powder or mix a crushed garlic clove into your dog's food to ward off fleabites. Both garlic and chamomile are attractive flowering perennials, so for a free supply, try growing these herbs in your flower or vegetable beds.

• Sprinkling brewer's yeast on your pets' food daily is also generally thought to help them repel fleas.

Brewer's yeast is available at health food stores.

• Soap kills fleas on contact. When bathing your dog, begin by lathering the neck area first and then work your way toward the tail, because fleas tend to congregate around the neck.

• After rinsing, rub apple cider vinegar through the fur to repel fleas, and add a teaspoonful of cider vinegar to the dog's drinking water.

Flea Powder
This inexpensive powder will leave your dog fresh smelling and free of pesky fleas. It is safe to apply as often as needed. Mix and match the oils according to your own scent preference. Commercial flea powders cost much more and contain toxic chemicals.

1 box (1 pound) baking soda

10 drops peppermint, lavender, rosemary, cedar, eucalyptus, or rose geranium essential oil

1. Empty baking soda into a mixing bowl, sprinkle with your personal blend of oils, and stir to blend.

2. Work treated baking soda into your pet's fur, beginning at the neck (where fleas congregate) and working toward the tail. Keep the powder away from nose, mouth, eyes, and ears.

3. Allow the powder to remain on the dog for 10 minutes, then comb or brush it out, along with dirt and fleas.

Makes one treatment

Note: If you have a large dog, you may need to make two or more recipes.

Helpful Hint

Easy Way to Remove Burrs and Gum from Fur
Burrs and chewing gum can be nearly impossible to comb or shampoo out of a pet's tangled fur. To make burrs easier to comb out, coat them with vegetable or mineral oil. Allow the oil to soften the burr for a few minutes, and then comb it out. To remove chewing gum, work creamy-style peanut butter into the gum until it dissolves, then comb out.

Wholesome Natural Pet Care Products   **311**

Ear Mite Oil

Ear mites can lead to serious infections and problems, including hearing loss in dogs. You can head off problems—and expensive vet bills—with this simple treatment. If you are too late and the problem persists, consult a veterinarian. It could be a yeast infection and not mites at all.

1 vitamin E capsule, 400 IU
1/4 cup mineral oil

1. Pierce a vitamin E capsule with a needle and squeeze the contents into a small dropper bottle. Add oil and shake. Store at room temperature.
2. To apply, hold the bottle in your hand for a few minutes to warm the oil. Put two or three drops of warm oil into the dog's ear canal and massage gently for a count of ten. Allow the dog to shake its head, then carefully swab oil and dirt from the ear. Repeat in the other ear.
3. Apply every other day for a full week.

Makes 1/4 cup

---

free pooper scoopers

• Save used zip-shut plastic sandwich and food storage bags to recycle as puppy poop bags. To use a bag, turn it inside out and reach inside the clean side of the bag to grab the poop. Then pull it right-side-out, zip it closed, and toss it.
• If you don't like the hands-on approach, relegate a cheap or decommissioned pair of scissors-style salad tongs to the status of pooper scooper—they work better than the real thing, and you can still make deposits into used zipper bags.

Firm Stool Fix

If your pup or dog suffers occasionally from loose or runny stools, try this cheap and easy high-fiber remedy. If the problem persists, it could indicate internal parasites and you should consult a vet.

2 teaspoons canned pumpkin
1 tablespoon cream cheese
1/4 cup corn flakes

1. In a bowl, mix pumpkin and cheese; roll into a ball and coat with corn flakes.
2. Serve as a treat.

Makes 1 treatment

cat food

Wholesome Kitty Dinner

This nutritious meat and vegetable meal will be a welcome change of pace for your cat. You know exactly what is in it, and it's budget-friendly too.

2/3 cup ground chicken or hamburger

1 jar mixed vegetable baby food

1 cat vitamin, crumbled *(optional)*

1/3 cup plain dry bread crumbs

1. In a small saucepan over medium heat, poach the ground meat in a small amount of water until medium rare. Remove from heat and allow to cool.

2. Stir together the meat, meat juices, vegetables, and vitamin, if desired. Form into bite-size balls and roll in bread crumbs.

3. Serve as much as your cat will eat in one sitting. Store the rest in a covered container in the refrigerator for up to three days.

Makes 2 or 3 servings

Helpful Hint

Trick Your Cat into Taking Medicine

Cats are choosy about what they eat, and often turn their noses up at the taste of medicine. If you have trouble getting yours to take its medicine, try smearing the medication on the back of a front paw—the cat will lick it off. If it is in pill form, crush the pill and mix it with a little cream cheese to make it adhere to the paw.

Tuna Treats

Cats are famous for loving tuna, and yours will jump for joy when you whip up these healthful treats that use a can of "people" tuna and a few pantry staples. As a bonus, the oil-packed tuna will help prevent hairballs. You won't find fresh treats like this at any pet store.

1 can oil-packed tuna

1/4 cup cornmeal

1/4 cup bran cereal

1 1/2 cups whole wheat flour

1. Preheat oven to 350°F. In a large bowl, mix all the ingredients together.

2. Press dough out on a floured board and cut into small cookies with a cookie cutter or pizza roller.

3. Place cookies on a greased cookie sheet and bake for 20 minutes or until light brown. Turn out onto a cake rack to cool. Store in a covered container in the refrigerator for up to a week or in the freezer for up to a month.

Makes 24 or more depending on size of cookie

Catnip Crackers

Cats will go bonkers for these catnip crackers, so save them for rainy-day treats and special occasions. You can pay a lot more for commercial cat treats, but they won't measure up to these fresh, homemade ones.

3/4 cup flour

1/2 cup whole wheat flour

2 tablespoons dried catnip (available at pet shops and in pet aisle at most supermarkets)

1/2 cup yogurt

1 egg

1 tablespoon honey

3 tablespoons vegetable oil

1. Preheat oven to 350°F. In a medium bowl, mix flours and catnip together. Stir in yogurt, egg, honey, and vegetable oil.

2. Press out dough on a floured surface and cut into tiny treats using a cookie cutter or pizza wheel. Place on greased cookie sheet and bake for 15 minutes or until golden brown.

3. Store in a covered container in the refrigerator for a week or in the freezer for up to three months.

Makes 24 or more depending on the size of crackers

Quick Fish Stick Treats

Cats and their human companions alike will love these instant treats made from inexpensive frozen fish sticks. Adding a sprinkle of garlic powder will help your cat to repel fleas, and you won't find any treats as fresh or wholesome as these in a pet store.

1 package frozen, breaded fish sticks

1/2 teaspoon garlic powder

1. Empty a box of frozen fish sticks onto a cutting board. Sprinkle with garlic powder and cut the frozen sticks into 1-inch squares.

2. Store the squares in a zipper plastic bag (along with cooking instructions from the package) in the freezer for up to three months.

3. To serve, remove a square and microwave according to package directions, cool, and serve at room temperature.

Makes approximately 36 treats

Sardine Balls

Cats will meow for the fishy flavor of these wholesome little fish balls. They're easy to make, easy on the budget, and the oily fish will help keep hairballs from forming. You won't find the likes of these in any store.

1 can (6 1/2 ounces) sardines, packed in oil

3/4 cup plain bread crumbs

1. Empty the can of sardines into a mixing bowl. Mix in 1/2 cup bread crumbs. Roll the mixture into bite-size balls. When all balls are made, roll them in the remaining bread crumbs to coat.

2. Store in a sealed container or zipper plastic bag in the freezer.

3. To serve, thaw a ball to room temperature and place in your cat's bowl.

Makes 6 or 8 treats

make your own cat toys

Cats love a variety of toys, and are especially fond of small, lightweight, flexible, and sparkly toys. Avoid a costly trip to the pet store by offering these found toys to your pet.

• Save foil wrappers from chewing gum and other snacks, and roll them into little balls for your cat to bat around.

• Twist a foil wrapper into a little "bow tie" and fasten it on the end of a piece of string, then dangle it for your cat to play with. You can even tie these string toys to doorknobs throughout the house. Your cat will love hiding behind the door and reaching around to bat at them.

• Create little rolling noisemakers by filling film canisters with nontoxic items such as pieces of breakfast cereal and chopped nuts. Your cat will spend many happy hours rolling and chasing these toys.

Melon Squares *Some cats love the flavor of melon. If yours is among them, keep some of these mixed melon treats on hand.*

1/2 orange-fleshed melon
1/2 green-fleshed melon

1. Peel and cube the melon flesh as you would for a salad.

2. Store in a sealed container in the refrigerator for up to one week.

3. Serve one or two cubes as a treat daily.

Makes 1 cup

Cat Grass Buffet *House cats like green "grass" to nibble on, and this recipe offers your cat long-lasting variety for pennies. You can buy untreated sprouting grains inexpensively at health food stores or even cheaper at feed mills. Keep grains in sealed plastic containers in the refrigerator. Save an empty Parmesan cheese shaker to fill with seed mix: It makes sowing easier.*

1 cup whole oat berries
1/2 cup wheat berries
1/2 cup barley seeds
1/4 cup alfalfa seeds
1/4 cup rye grass

1. Put grains into a sealed plastic container and shake to mix. Fill shallow, tip-resistant pots with potting soil and moisten with tepid water.

2. Sprinkle the grains thickly over the top of the soil and cover grains with a sprinkling of soil. Set the pots in a sunny window and water as needed to keep the soil as moist as a wrung-out sponge. When the grass is an inch tall, set a pot beside your cat's dinner dish and watch the fun.

3. For an ongoing supply, start a fresh pot of cat grass every other week.

Makes four 4-inch flowerpots of grass

Wholesome Natural Pet Care Products   **315**

feline care products

Baby-Fresh Litter

Cat litter to cover bottom of
litter box
1/3 cup baby powder

*The most effective way to prevent cat litter odor is also a money
saver: Instead of throwing money away by filling the litter box to
the top, pour in a shallow layer. Use only 2 or 3 inches so that
the litter can air-dry rapidly. Between litter changes, you can keep
even the cheapest brand of litter smelling fresh with this simple,
baby-safe recipe.*

1. Pour litter into cat pan to a depth of 3 inches.
2. Sprinkle baby powder over the top of litter and stir to blend.
   For best results, change litter at least once a week.

Makes filler for one litter box

Helpful Hint

Clever Cat Litter Storage

If you keep your litter box in the laundry room, bathroom, or a
closet, try storing new kitty litter in an open bag at the bottom
of your clothes hamper, corner of a closet, or near the washer.
Not only will the litter absorb odors and help keep these rooms
smelling fresh, but you'll also be reminded to change the litter
every time you change clothes.

Dry Cat Shampoo

1/3 cup bran
1/3 cup cornmeal
1/3 cup rolled oats

*Take the stress out of bath time for your cat by bathing it with this
soothing, dry shampoo. As an added bonus, you'll save some
pocket change because it's made from common pantry staples.*

1. Pour grains into a microwave-safe plastic container, seal, and
   shake to combine. Warm in microwave set on low for 10 seconds.
2. Rub warm grains into fur. When finished, brush the meal out
   along with oil, dirt, and dander.

Makes 1 shampoo

Fragrant Flea Treatment

Cats can be sensitive to any flea treatment, particularly toxic commercial flea powders. So try this mixture on a small patch of skin on the cat's stomach and wait for a day to see if there is a reaction. You must also wash the cat's bedding and vacuum the house thoroughly to get rid of flea eggs.

6 drops lavender essential oil
1 tablespoon mineral oil

1. Drop the lavender essential oil and the mineral oil into a small bottle and shake to combine.
2. Warm the oil by holding the bottle in your hands for a few minutes.
3. Massage the warm oil into the neck area and the base of the tail where fleas congregate, then all parts of the cat, being careful to avoid contact with the cat's ears, eyes, nose, and mouth. Repeat treatment when the scent is no longer detectable.

Makes 1 treatment

Help Hint

Free Disposable Cat Litter Boxes
Why clean a smelly plastic litter box when you can get bio-friendly ones for free and toss them, dirty litter and all? Make a habit of stopping by your local convenience or beverage store and asking for empty plastic-wrapped, shallow soda boxes—the kind that hold a dozen cans of soda pop. Keep the plastic on the box while in use, pull it off and toss in the recycle bin before dumping the litter-filled box into the trash. They also make convenient toss-and-go litter boxes for traveling with your cat.

Tick Removal from Cats

Cats are sensitive to many kinds of medications and herbal treatments, including tick repellents that are safe to use on dogs. Your best bet is to watch for ticks, especially around the face, ears, and neck, and remove them according to the following recipe. It will save you a trip to the vet.

Petroleum jelly
Hydrogen peroxide

1. Coat the tick and surrounding skin with petroleum jelly applied with a cotton swab.
2. After the tick smothers, gently pull it, with the head intact, from the cat's skin.
3. Swab the area with hydrogen peroxide to disinfect it.
4. If you remove a tiny deer tick (a potential transmitter of Lyme disease), seal it in a plastic container, such as a film canister, and take it and the cat to a veterinarian for testing.

Makes one treatment

Wholesome Natural Pet Care Products   **317**

treats for birds

Pet Bird Honey Treats

Parakeets and songbirds like sweets. This calcium-rich sweet treat is an inexpensive, wholesome snack. Most of the ingredients are already in your kitchen. You can find cuttlebone and bird grit at any pet supply store or in the pet aisle of your grocery.

1/3 cup cornmeal

1/2 cuttlebone, finely ground (in coffee grinder or mortar and pestle)

1/4 teaspoon fine bird grit

1/4 cup mixed parakeet, finch, or canary seeds

1 piece spray millet, crumbled

2 tablespoons honey

1/4 cup wheat germ

1 egg

1. Preheat oven to 350°F. Place all ingredients into a bowl and mix well. If mixture is too thick to mold, add a little water. Press with hands into small logs onto a greased and floured cookie sheet.

2. Bake for 30 minutes or until lightly browned.

3. Remove from oven, and turn logs out onto a cake rack to cool. Store in covered container in the freezer for up to three months.

4. To serve, thaw a log and fasten to cage bars with a treat clip. Renew when well nibbled.

Makes approximately 12 treats

making your home safe for birds

Birds are very sensitive to environmental pollutants and poor air quality. In the 1800s canaries were routinely carried into coal mines—if a canary died, the miners knew they, too, were in danger and should evacuate.

• **Beware of household fumes.** The kitchen may seem like a friendly place for a bird, but it is actually filled with potential poisons. Nonstick pans placed over high heat can give off fumes that are toxic to birds, and it's best not to expose birds to aerosol cleaner and detergent fumes.

• **Watch the temperature.** Study references for the care needed by the type of bird you have. Most thrive in a very specific and narrow range of temperatures. Put your bird in a room where you can regulate the temperature year-round, and where there are no drafts. Place the cage well away from windows, and if possible, cover it at night with a breathable cloth cover.

• **Use a safe, secure cage.** Antique and decorative cages are often beautiful, but may have sharp edges, bars far enough apart to either trap or let birds escape, or wood bars that birds can chew through. Even worse, they may have been painted with lead-based paint. Use such cages as decorative objects, and house your birds in cages with stainless steel or nontoxic enameled bars.

• **Avoid dangerous treats.** Chocolate can be lethal to birds. Wash vegetable and fruit skins to remove pesticide residue. While it's safe to offer apples, cherries, peaches, and pears to birds, the seeds are toxic, as are all parts of avocado, onions, mushrooms, tomatoes, salt, dried beans, and rice.

Pet Bird Snacking Salad

For optimum health, offer your bird fresh or thawed frozen fruits and vegetables daily. Forget expensive dried treats from a pet shop—they can't compare in freshness, flavor, or vitamins. This salad appeals to all bird species, and is easy to put together by saving a little here and there from your meal preparations. Modify it as needed: You will learn quickly which ingredients your bird devours and which ingredients it leaves uneaten.

3 leaves leaf lettuce or 1/2 cup fresh spinach, chopped

1/2 cup fresh or frozen, thawed, broccoli florets

1/2 cup frozen and thawed whole kernel corn

1/2 apple, diced

1/2 segmented orange, diced

1/4 cup dried currants

1/2 cup unsalted peanuts (for large birds only)

1. Toss all ingredients in a covered bowl and store in the refrigerator for up to 5 days.

2. To serve, put 1/3 cup salad in a shallow bowl or clay flowerpot saucer in the cage. Offer daily and make new salad as needed.

Makes 6 servings

Helpful Hint

The Easy Way to Trap Bird Ticks

If your bird has ticks, hang a disposable white cloth (or a paper towel) on one side of its cage. The ticks are attracted to the bright object. After the ticks congregate on the cloth, remove and dispose of it in a sealed plastic bag.

Sweet and Crunchy Bird Muffins

Small-quantity corn, bran, and oatmeal muffin mixes are sold in envelopes for less than 50 cents apiece—using them as a basis for these yummy bird treats lets you whip up treats faster than you could make them from scratch—but you can substitute your favorite muffin recipe (omit salt, which can harm birds). Plus, this all-in-one treat takes the place of several pricey commercial single-ingredient treats. For variety's sake, make all three flavors at the same time and alternate the flavors you offer your bird each day.

1 small package of commercial corn, bran, or oatmeal muffin mix

1/3 cup milk

1 egg

1/4 cup applesauce

1/2 cup mixed dried fruits (not sugared)

1/2 cup birdseed mix (appropriate to the species of bird)

1 bird vitamin (crumbled)

1. Preheat oven to 375°F. Prepare muffin mix according to directions, substituting applesauce for oil. Stir in the dried fruit and seed.

2. Pour batter into greased muffin tins and bake according to package directions, baking for 20 minutes or until golden brown.

3. Store muffins in sealed container in the freezer for up to three months.

4. To serve, thaw a muffin and place part or all of it in the bird's cage. You can refrigerate unused portions for up to a week.

Makes 6 muffins

Finch and Canary Treat

Here's a bite-size nutritious treat that's easy to make for small songbirds like finches and canaries. It is fresher and far less expensive than store-bought treats.

1/4 cup crunchy homemade Peanut Butter (page 33) or crunchy, unsweetened, low-salt commercial peanut butter

1/2 cup high-quality finch seed mix

1/4 cup wheat germ

1. In a medium bowl, mix peanut butter and seeds together, adding more seeds if needed to make a stiff batter.
2. Pour wheat germ into a shallow saucer. Form the peanut butter mix into small balls and roll the balls in wheat germ to coat.
3. Serve one ball as a treat, in a bird-proof bowl. Store leftovers in a covered container in the refrigerator for up to one month or freeze for up to three months.

Makes 8 treats

homemade toys for parakeets and parrots

Birds in the parrot family, including parakeets, love toys, but they can be pricey, and the bigger birds can destroy them quickly. Try these time-tested, and inexpensive, homemade toys.

• Parakeets love to preen in a mirror. So, instead of paying for a fancy and often fragile bird mirror, just remove the hinge from a sturdy old compact and fasten the mirror securely to the cage bars near a perch.

• Parrots love to climb. Satisfy this urge by tying knots along a sturdy cotton rope and hanging it from the top of the cage.

• Parrots also love to bite and chew, and a dog-chew toy is often less expensive and just as long lasting as a parrot chew toy. Try a rawhide "bone," or one made from nylon.

• Both parakeets and parrots like colorful toys, so string big wooden beads onto cotton rope and hang it for them to bat around and chew.

Parrot Pops

These chewy sweet treats will keep your parrot happily occupied for hours. Whip them up inexpensively, then sit back and watch the fun.

1 cup high-quality mixed commercial parrot treats

1/2 cup round oat cereal pieces

1 cup dried mixed fruit, unsweetened

1 cup unsalted peanuts

1/2 banana, mashed

1 egg white

6 craft sticks or sucker handles (available at craft or kitchen supply stores)

1/2 cup honey

1. Preheat oven to 100°F. In a medium bowl, mix together parrot treats, oat cereal, dried fruit, and peanuts. Add banana and egg white and stir to coat.
2. Spray muffin or corn-stick tin with nonstick spray, fill compartments with mixture, insert a stick or handle in each and press to compress. Bake for two hours, or until very hard. Remove pops from pan, coat each pop with honey, place on a greased cookie sheet, return to oven and bake for another 10 minutes or until honey is dry.
3. Serve one treat at a time. Remove and discard uneaten parts after 4 hours. Store pops in a sealed container in the refrigerator for up to one month or in the freezer for up to three months.

Makes 6 treats

Wild Bird Food

Watching backyard birds brings hours of enjoyment to adults and teaches children valuable nature lessons. This easy and inexpensive recipe—better than a store-bought packet of birdseed—will attract a wide variety of colorful and interesting birds, including doves, woodpeckers, blue jays, nuthatches, chickadees, tufted titmice, cardinals, goldfinches, and many others, depending on where you live.

1/2 cup sunflower seeds

1/2 cup cracked corn

1/2 cup raisins

1/2 cup crunchy homemade Peanut Butter (page 33)

1. Mix all ingredients together in a bowl. Press the mixture into an empty suet feeder or small string bag.

2. Hang the feeder in a tree.

Makes 2 cups

One-Minute Substitute

Quick Treat for Wild Birds

Don't discard day-old doughnuts. They are great for feathered visitors to your backyard! These oily, carb-rich treats make a high-energy food that will help keep wild birds warm in winter. Just drive one or more nails into a fence post or tree trunk at eye level. Then hang a glazed cake or yeast doughnut on each nail. After you mount them, sit back and enjoy watching a congregation of hungry birds devour them.

Premium Wild Bird Mix

Avoid high-priced, and often inferior, wild birdseed blends. Buy premium individual types of seeds in bulk and mix your own feeder food for less money and greater quality. These individual seeds are available at feed, hardware, and wild-bird stores. The addition of live mealworms may entice elusive bluebirds to your feeders in the northeastern and western areas of the United States. Mealworms can be purchased at pet shops and through the Internet.

1 pound striped sunflower seeds, hulls on

1 pound black-oil sunflower seeds, hulls on

1 pound raw peanuts

1 pound dark raisins, dried blueberries, apples, or other dried fruits, chopped

1 pound cracked corn

1 small carton live mealworms

1. In a rodent-proof metal container with a tight lid, mix together the striped sunflower seeds, black-oil sunflower seeds, peanuts, fruit, and cracked corn and store in a cool area, such as the basement or garage. Store mealworms in the refrigerator according to package directions.

2. Spread one or two scoops of the seed mixture onto a tray-type feeder and sprinkle with mealworms.

Makes 5 pounds

Healthy Hummingbird Nectar

Why buy expensive hummingbird nectar when you can make your own for pennies? This nectar will attract both hummingbirds and orioles. Choose a feeder with a red base to attract the birds, so there's no need to use potentially harmful red food coloring. To prevent fermentation in hot weather, empty your feeder every three days and sterilize it by rinsing it out with boiling water.

2 cups water
1/2 cup granulated sugar

1. In a small saucepan over medium heat, bring water to a boil and then stir in sugar until it dissolves. Return solution to a boil. Remove from heat and cool, uncovered.
2. Store the nectar in a clean tightly capped jar in the refrigerator for up to one month.
3. Sterilize feeder by rinsing it with boiling water. Fill with fresh nectar and hang in the shade, at eye level.

Makes 2 1/2 cups

food for exotic pets

Guinea Pig Salad

Fresh vegetables and fruits should be essential parts of a guinea pig's diet. The dried treats sold in pet shops are good in a pinch, but they're expensive and a poor substitute for fresh treats. This is a vitamin-rich fresh salad that's easy to make and good enough to share with your guinea pig.

1/2 cup fresh spinach
1/4 cup shredded carrot
1/2 cup chopped strawberries
1/4 cup orange juice

1. Toss spinach, carrots, and strawberries in a bowl with juice.
2. Serve in a feeding bowl. Remove and discard uneaten salad after 4 hours. Store leftovers in a sealed container in the refrigerator for one day.

Makes 2 servings

One-Minute Substitute

Quick Free Playthings for Pet Rodents
Rodents have a never-ending need to chew, and they can rapidly demolish expensive store-bought toys. Save your pocketbook by collecting household "chew toys" for mice, rats, guinea pigs, and bunnies, such as empty cardboard egg cartons, rolls from paper towels, food wrap, and toilet paper, as well as small blocks of wood left from woodworking projects.

Hamster Fruit Cup

Experts agree that dried hamster pellets and treats do not provide a complete diet, and pet shops don't include a salad bar, but your hamster can scurry to its bowl for this budget-friendly sweet treat that you can whip up in no time, using fresh fruits and vegetables.

1/2 banana
1/4 cup carrot, grated
Lemon juice
1 tablespoon dark raisins
1 teaspoon honey

1. Slice banana and toss with grated carrot in a bowl, adding a sprinkling of lemon juice to keep them from discoloring. Drain juice from bowl; add raisins and honey and mash with a fork.

2. Serve half in a treat bowl, and store the remainder in a covered container in the refrigerator for one day. Remove and discard uneaten treats after 4 hours.

Makes 2 servings

Gerbil and Rabbit Salad

It's important to offer pet rodents vitamin-rich fresh fruits and vegetables, and your gerbils and bunnies will welcome this healthy salad. For budget-boosting ingredients, ask for discarded outer leaves (which are more vitamin rich than inner leaves) at your produce counter, farmers' market, or a restaurant salad bar. For variety, alternate seed and nut toppings.

1/4 cup spinach or leaf
   lettuce, chopped fine
1/4 cup carrot, grated
1 teaspoon sunflower or
   pumpkin seeds, unsalted

1. Toss vegetables together in a bowl, top with seeds or nuts, and serve in a small treat bowl. Store leftovers in a sealed container in the refrigerator for one day.

2. Remove and dispose of uneaten fresh foods after four hours.

Makes 1/2 cup

Pet Rodent Tabbouleh

You just can't substitute dried pellets or grains from the pet store for fresh foods when it comes to feeding a balanced diet to rodents. This is a nutritious treat recipe for pet mice and rats. You can make it easy by saving plain, leftover grains from the family table.

1 cup bulgur wheat,
   uncooked
1 ounce boiling water
   (1 jiggerful)
1/4 cup brown rice, cooked
1/4 cup rolled oats, cooked
1/4 cup parrot seed mix
1/4 cup dark molasses
1 rodent vitamin, crushed
   (optional)
1/4 cup wheat germ

1. Put bulgur in a bowl, add boiling water, and allow to stand five minutes. Stir in remaining ingredients to make a thick, crumbly mixture.

2. Form into small balls and roll in a saucer of wheat germ to coat.

3. Serve 1 ball daily as a treat. Discard uneaten treats after four hours. Store extra treats in a sealed container in the refrigerator for up to one week, or in the freezer for up to one month.

Makes 1 3/4 cups

Turtle and Reptile Treat

To give your pet turtle a calcium boost, try this fortified daily vegetable medley. With a few additions, this treat will also benefit iguanas and other cold-blooded vegetarian pets. Reptiles have very specific dietary needs and must be housed at the proper temperature to induce an appetite.

1/2 cup carrot, shredded

1/2 cup lettuce or spinach, chopped

1 stalk celery, chopped

1 calcium tablet, crushed

1 teaspoon alfalfa sprouts (available at pet or health food stores)

1/4 cup melon or strawberries, chopped

1. Place vegetables into a bowl, sprinkle with calcium, and toss for turtle snack. For iguanas and other reptiles, add alfalfa and fruit.

2. Serve half in a chew-proof bowl. Store the remainder in a covered container in the refrigerator for one day.

Makes 1 1/2 cups

---

pet emergency kit

Set a pet carrier—or a cage for birds or reptiles—where it's easy to find. Place a lightweight nylon backpack inside the carrier and fill it with the following items:
• Photocopies of your pet's license and shot records
• Address and telephone number of your veterinarian, kennel, and breeder
• Your cell phone number and another emergency contact phone number
• Identifying photos of your pet
• Food and water bowls
• Packaged food (for dog or cat), seed mixes and supplements (for birds and cold-blooded pets), and instructions for feeding
• Bottled water
• Leash (for dog or cat)
• A couple of old toys
• Pet sweater (for dog or cat)
• Litter bags (for a dog), a small bag of litter and disposable litter box (for a cat)
• Newspapers to use as carrier or cage liners

Aquarium Fish Treats

The best food for your aquarium fish is a high-quality commercial fish food formulated for the species of fish, but, for variety, they especially enjoy fresh or fresh-frozen live food and fresh vegetables. Experiment with treats listed here. Crickets, mealworms, and bloodworms are sold at pet shops.

1/4 cup spinach, pureed

1 earthworm, finely chopped

6 crickets

6 mealworms

6 bloodworms

1/4 cup raw beef liver (blended)

1 raw shrimp (blended)

1. Mix spinach plus any two other ingredients. Store a week's worth of the mix in a sealed container in the refrigerator. Freeze the rest for up to one month.

2. To serve, drop a piece of the mix the size of a pencil eraser into the aquarium. Continue until fish stop feeding. After five minutes, remove uneaten food from the bottom of the aquarium, using a siphon or cooking bulb baster.

Makes 2/3 cup

Part 3

around the
house

*

chapter 10

Spit-and-Polish
Cleaning Products

Advertisements for "new and better" cleaning supplies fill home-oriented magazines, and they virtually subsidize daytime broadcasting (that's why they are called soap operas). Many of these highly touted products do have seemingly miraculous ingredients that can make dirt vanish, but you should think twice before using these chemicals in your home, and they are often no better than traditional cleaning compounds that you can made yourself. As the recipes here show, there are many safer ways to clean everything in your house, using simple mixtures of inexpensive, everyday staples that you probably already have in your pantry.

Homemade cleaning solutions not only get the job done easily and inexpensively, but more important, they do it without harming you or your possessions. Most of these cleaning solutions have a long and honorable history—your grandmother probably used many of them. As you might expect, you'll see recipes that use many time-tested ingredients such as baking soda, vinegar, and lemon juice. But you might be surprised to know that you can still buy borax and washing soda among the laundry detergents in your local supermarket. And you might be even more surprised to find that tomato ketchup is a fine copper polish.

These homemade cleaning products are all very economical. White vinegar and baking soda, for example, are much cheaper than commercial fabric softener for keeping lint off your clothes and stopping static electricity. Old newspapers are cheaper than paper towels for cleaning windows. And dried herbs refresh your house far more inexpensively than any commercial room deodorizer.

general housecleaning

Basic Window and Glass Cleaner

Forget about all of those store-bought window cleaners. Your windows can get a professional shine for just pennies. This recipe will clean a houseful of windows. You can make a smaller batch in a quart spray bottle by mixing 1/4 cup vinegar with enough water to fill the container.

1/2 cup white vinegar
2/3 gallon water
1 clean gallon container
1 clean 32-ounce
   spray bottle

1. Mix the ingredients in the gallon container.
2. Fill the spray bottle and spray on windows and glass items as needed. (Save the remaining cleaner for another day.)
3. Dry glass with crumpled newspaper for added brightness—and savings!

Super Window and Glass Cleaner

The alcohol in this formula helps prevent streaking.

1/3 cup white vinegar
1/4 cup rubbing alcohol
3 1/2 cups water
1 clean 32-ounce
   spray bottle

1. Mix all the ingredients in the spray bottle. Shake well before using.
2. Spray on dirty windowpane or other glass surface.
3. Dry with crumpled newspaper.

Citrus Disinfectant

If you like pricey commercial orange cleaners, you'll love this fresh citrus-scented vinegar spray that is easy to make and costs less than a dollar. You can also deodorize a room by setting out a small bowl of citrus vinegar.

Peel from 1 orange, grapefruit, lemon, or lime
3 cups white vinegar
1 clean quart jar with lid
1 clean 32-ounce
   spray bottle

1. Combine the citrus peel and vinegar in the quart jar. Fasten the lid on the jar and store the mixture in a cupboard for two weeks, giving it an occasional shake.
2. Remove the peel from the jar, strain the vinegar, and return it to the jar.
3. To use as a spray cleaner, pour 1 cup of citrus vinegar in the spray bottle and fill with water.
4. To clean linoleum floors, add 1 cup citrus vinegar to 2 gallons water.

Tough Multipurpose Cleaner

When it comes to cleaning non-wood surfaces around your home, this cleaner is tough to beat—you might even say it's "fantastic." And it costs only pennies.

- 1 1/2 pints water
- 1/3 cup rubbing alcohol
- 1 teaspoon clear household ammonia
- 1 teaspoon mild dishwashing liquid
- 1/2 teaspoon lemon juice
- 1 clean 32-ounce spray bottle

1. Combine the ingredients in the spray bottle and shake well before each use.

2. Spray on countertops, kitchen appliances and fixtures, and tile or painted surfaces.

3. Wipe down with a clean cloth or damp sponge.

Fresh-Smelling Multipurpose Cleaner

This formula has a clean smell and works hard, despite its inexpensive ingredients. You can buy liquid castile soap at health food stores.

- 3 1/2 cups hot water
- 1/2 cup white or apple cider vinegar
- 1 teaspoon borax
- 1 teaspoon washing soda
- 1 teaspoon liquid castile soap
- 1 clean 32-ounce spray bottle

1. Fill spray bottle first with hot water; then add vinegar, borax, washing soda, and liquid castile soap. Shake well before using.

2. Spray on countertops, kitchen appliances and fixtures, and tile or painted surfaces.

3. Wipe down with a clean cloth or damp sponge.

Wall and Cabinet Cleaner

If you have dingy cupboards, this cleaning solution will deodorize them as well as wiping up the dust and dirt.

- 1 cup clear household ammonia
- 1 cup white vinegar
- 1/4 cup baking soda
- 1 gallon warm water

1. Combine the ammonia, vinegar, and baking soda in a large bucket, add water, and give it a few stirs.

2. Use a sponge or cloth rag to wash walls, ceilings, floors, or cabinets.

3. Wipe up the excess liquid with a clean cloth and allow to dry thoroughly before replacing contents.

One-Minute Substitute

Use Bread to Spot-Clean Wallpaper

Cut the crusts off a slice of white bread and roll it up into a ball. Once the bread starts to feel slightly doughy, roll it over the bad spots on the wallpaper to lift off the dirt or fingerprints. Test the bread ball first on an inconspicuous corner.

Interior Wall Cleaner

Those scuff marks and stains on your painted walls seem to appear out of nowhere. This potent cleaner will remove them without harming your paint job.

1/2 cup borax

1 tablespoon clear household ammonia

1/4 cup vinegar

1 gallon warm water

1. In a large bucket, mix all the ingredients.

2. Apply the solution to the wall with a clean sponge. Use a second clean sponge to rinse the wall with plain water.

3. To minimize streaking, start at the bottom of the wall and work up.

Herbal Carpet Freshener

Many commercial air and carpet deodorizers work to mask odors by deadening the nerves associated with your sense of smell. To truly freshen carpets around your home, try this inexpensive natural formula instead. (If you don't like the smell of lavender, you can also freshen up carpets with plain baking soda.)

1/2 cup lavender flowers

1 cup baking soda

1. In a large bowl, crush the lavender flowers to release their scent.

2. Add the baking soda and mix well. Pour the mixture into a cheese shaker or a can with holes punched in the lid.

3. Sprinkle liberally on the carpet. Wait 30 minutes; then vacuum.

Pine Floor Cleaner

You shouldn't have to spend a small fortune to give your no-wax floors a pine-fresh smell. This excellent cleaner will do the job for only a few cents a floor. Since soap flakes are not widely available, as they once were, it's usually necessary to make your own by grating a soap bar; it takes only a minute or so.

1/2 cup soap flakes

1/4 cup washing soda

1 cup salt

2 cups water

2 teaspoons pine oil

1 clean 16-ounce plastic bottle with a tight-fitting lid

1 cup white vinegar

1. To make the soap flakes, lightly grate a bar of pure soap, such as Ivory, on a coarse kitchen grater.

2. In a saucepan over low heat, combine the soap, washing soda, salt, and water and stir until the soap, soda, and salt have dissolved.

3. Remove from the heat and allow the mixture to cool until it is lukewarm. Add the pine oil. Stir well, pour into the plastic bottle, and secure the top.

4. To use, pour 2 or 3 tablespoons of the cleaner into a half-bucket of hot water, stirring well. For large areas, you may need to double the amount.

5. After cleaning, add the vinegar to a half-bucket of clean water and rinse the floor.

Spicy Carpet Freshener
Add a nice smell to your rooms while you freshen the carpets with this simple mixture.

1 cup baking soda or cornstarch

7-10 drops essential oil in your favorite scent (eucalyptus or rosewood, for example)

1. In a large bowl, combine the baking soda or cornstarch with the essential oil. Break up any clumps with a fork and stir well. Pour the mixture into a cheese shaker or a can with holes punched in the lid.
2. Sprinkle liberally on the carpet. Wait 30 minutes, then vacuum.

air fresheners

Spicy Room Freshener Spray
Why waste your money on commercial air fresheners when it's so easy to make your own favorite scents? Use this spray judiciously, however. A room should have a hint of the spicy scent, not an overpowering perfume. You can combine up to three different essential oils to create a fragrance that suits you. Other popular choices include eucalyptus, lavender, geranium, grapefruit, orange, peppermint, pine, juniper, rose, and spearmint.

1 clean 12-ounce spray bottle

1/4 cup rubbing alcohol

25 drops bergamot essential oil

8 drops clove essential oil

5 drops lemon essential oil

1 cup distilled water

1. In the spray bottle, combine the alcohol and the essential oils and shake well to disperse the oil. Add the water and shake for a minute or two more to thoroughly blend all the ingredients.
2. Let the mixture sit for a few days before using to allow the fragrance to blend and mature. A quick spritz is all that's needed to freshen a room.

Pie Spice Room Freshener
This homey and aromatic mixture can be made for pennies and makes you think an apple pie is in the oven; real estate agents sometimes suggest that homeowners put this mixture on the stove before prospective buyers come to see the house. No commercial room freshener at any price smells as good.

3 cups water

6 cloves

1 cinnamon stick

6 pieces dried orange peel

In a small saucepan, combine all the ingredients and bring to a boil over medium heat. Reduce the heat and simmer, uncovered, until your home is filled with a fresh, spicy scent. (Don't let the water boil away.)

furniture polishes

Lemon Oil Furniture Polish

Shine up your wood furniture, paneling, and knickknacks with this all-natural polish that will take you only a minute to prepare, and costs less than a bagel. Discard any leftovers and make up a fresh batch each time you want to polish your wood treasures.

1 cup olive oil
1/3 cup lemon juice
1 clean 16-ounce spray bottle

1. Combine the oil and lemon juice in the spray bottle. Shake well before using
2. Apply a small amount to a soft flannel cloth or chamois, and apply it evenly over the wood surface.
3. Use a clean, dry flannel cloth to buff and polish.

No-Fuss Furniture Polish

How would you like a furniture polish that you can just wipe on and forget? Well, your prayers have been answered—and for a lot less money than you might expect!

1/4 cup boiled linseed oil
1/8 cup vinegar
1/8 cup whisky
1 clean 16-ounce spray bottle

1. Combine all the ingredients in the bottle. Shake well.
2. Apply a small amount of polish to a clean, soft cloth and wipe on. No need to buff; the dullness evaporates along with the alcohol.

Cabinet Polish

Why burn through your household budget on furniture polish for those large wood kitchen cabinets, bookshelves, or wardrobes around your home? Here's the perfect polish to use on big jobs—and it costs a couple of pennies to make. Be sure to mix up a fresh batch for each use.

1 teaspoon lemon juice
1 teaspoon olive oil
2 cups warm water

1. Combine the ingredients in a bowl or container.
2. Dip a soft flannel cloth into the solution and wring it out. Wipe over the wood.
3. Buff and polish with a soft, dry cloth.

mold and mildew removers

Spot Mold and Mildew Remover
Mix up a batch of this powerful but benign-smelling disinfectant to get rid of small patches of mold and mildew that breed in bathroom medicine cabinets, windowsills, and other surfaces around your home.

1 cup white vinegar
2 tablespoons borax
4 cups hot water
1 clean 32-ounce spray bottle

1. Combine the ingredients in the spray bottle. Shake well.

2. Spray on surfaces where mold or mildew is forming. Wipe off mildew, but leave cleaning solution residue to keep mildew from returning.

Paint and Tile Mold and Mildew Remover
This formula will take mold and mildew off painted and tile surfaces for only pennies a pop. Be sure the room is well ventilated as you work.

1/4 cup chlorine bleach
1 tablespoon borax
1 1/2 cups water
1 clean 16-ounce spray bottle

1. Combine all the ingredients in the spray bottle and shake to mix.

2. Spray painted or tile surface and wipe off mildew and mold with a clean cloth. Rinse with clean water and dry with clean cloths.

Mold Remover for Leather and Luggage
If you discover mold on your expensive luggage or leather jacket, don't race to the dry cleaners. Instead, remove the offending growth with this simple, inexpensive mold-removal recipe.

1/2 cup rubbing alcohol
1/4 cup water
1 clean 8-ounce spray bottle

1. Combine the ingredients in the spray bottle and shake well to mix.

2. Spray affected area. Let solution set 10 to 20 minutes, then wipe off mold with a clean rag and allow the item to thoroughly air-dry.

metal polishes

Brass and Copper Paste Polish
Use this simple, nontoxic—and very inexpensive—polish to brighten up all your tarnished unlacquered brass and copperware. (Lacquered items only need dusting.)

1/4 cup flour
1/4 cup salt
1/4 cup vinegar
1/4 cup hot water
1 teaspoon lemon juice

1. In a small bowl, combine all the ingredients to form a paste.
2. Using a soft cloth, rub the mixture onto the metal surfaces to remove tarnish.
3. Rinse the object thoroughly in warm water (remember, salt is corrosive).
4. Dry with soft, clean cloths and then buff to a shine with a soft flannel cloth or chamois.

Cut-Lemon Brass and Copper Polish
Here's an even easier way to shine up unlacquered brass or copper objects—and a useful way to use up leftover half lemons.

1/2 cup white vinegar
2 tablespoons salt
1/2 lemon

1. In a saucepan over medium heat, heat the vinegar 5 minutes, then pour it into a small bowl and stir in the salt.
2. Dip the lemon into the mixture and rub it over the object, concentrating on the most heavily tarnished areas.
3. Thoroughly rinse the object in warm water and dry with soft, clean cloths. Buff to a shine with a soft cloth.

Ketchup Copper Polish
This simple polish can be a bit messy, but it works like a charm on unlacquered copper—and it's completely nontoxic. Can your old copper polish say that?

1/2-1 cup tomato ketchup
1/4-1 lemon, juiced

1. In a small bowl, combine the ketchup and lemon juice and stir to mix. How much you need of each ingredient depends on the size of the object you want to polish, but keep the ratio of ketchup to lemon juice about 8:1.
2. Spread out some old newspapers on your work surface. Rub the mixture over the copper piece's surface. Let it sit 5 to 10 minutes.
3. Thoroughly rinse the copper piece in warm water and dry with soft, clean cloths. Buff to a shine with a soft cloth.

One-Minute Substitute	**Potato Rust Remover for Tin Pans**

Tin pie plates and other kitchen utensils are subject to rust if they are not dried carefully after each washing. Here, for little more than the price of a potato, is a way to restore your tinware without harsh chemicals. Peel a potato and cut it into easy-to-handle pieces. Put some baking soda or salt in a saucer. Then dip a cut piece of potato in the soda or salt, and rub it over the rust spots. Rinse the tin utensil and dry thoroughly.

Chrome and Stainless Steel Polish

Baby the chrome and stainless steel finishes around your home with this simple one-two set of cleaners. They remove stains as well as dirt and fingerprints in no time for less than a quarter.

1/4 teaspoon baby oil
1/2 cup club soda

1. Apply a few drops of baby oil to a soft cloth or piece of flannel and wipe down the chrome or stainless steel surface. Use a second soft cloth, moistened with club soda, to rinse off the oil.
2. Dry and buff with a soft, dry cloth.

Quick and Easy Silver Shine

Want a really easy, inexpensive, and amazingly effective way to polish your silver without any smelly chemicals or commercial products? This is easier than using a silver dipping cleaner.

1 quart hot water
1 tablespoon baking soda or washing soda
1 tablespoon salt
1 sheet aluminum foil

1. Fill the kitchen sink with about 1 quart hot water.
2. Dissolve the baking (or washing) soda and salt in the water, then place the sheet of aluminum foil at the bottom of the sink.
3. Rest the tarnished silver on the foil for 10 seconds. Remove and dry with a soft flannel cloth.

in the kitchen

Automatic Dishwasher Detergent
Even if you live in a hard-water area, this simple, inexpensive detergent recipe will give you shiny, spotless dishes.

2 cups borax

2 cups washing soda

1 clean 32-ounce plastic container with cover

1. Combine the borax and washing soda in the container and seal it tightly for storage.

2. For each load of dishes, put 2 tablespoons of the mixture in the dishwasher soap dispenser.

One-Minute Substitute

Fast, Cheap Rinsing Agent for Your Dishwasher
Here's an easy way to get those dishes sparkling in your automatic dishwasher without using any chemical rinsing agents. Just stop the dishwasher during its rinse cycle and add 1 to 1 1/2 cups of white vinegar. Or pour the vinegar into the rinse compartment beforehand (being careful not to overfill). Wash dishes as usual.

Dishwashing Liquid
This dishwashing soap for washing dishes by hand costs less than a dollar for a 16-ounce bottle and really gets your dishes clean. And unlike some of its commercial counterparts, it's mild on your hands too.

1/4 cup soap flakes

1 1/2 cups hot water

1/4 cup glycerin

1/2 teaspoon lemon oil

1 clean 16-ounce squirt bottle

1. To make the soap flakes, lightly grate a bar of pure soap, such as Ivory, on a coarse kitchen grater.

2. In a medium pitcher, pour the soap flakes into the hot water and stir with a fork until most of the soap has dissolved. Let the solution cool for 5 minutes.

3. Stir in the glycerin and lemon oil. A loose gel will form as it cools. Use the fork to break up any congealed parts and pour the liquid into the squirt bottle. Use 2 to 3 teaspoons per sink or dishpan of hot water to clean dishes.

Microwave Oven Cleaner

You don't need harsh cleansers and lots of elbow grease to clean your microwave. For the price of a lemon, some baking soda, or some white vinegar, you can just wipe away the splatters and stains inside the oven.

1 1/2 cups water

3 tablespoons lemon juice or 1 cup water

3 tablespoons baking soda or 2 cups white vinegar

1. In a microwave-safe bowl, combine the water and lemon juice, water and baking soda, or just the vinegar. Place the uncovered bowl inside the oven, and run the oven on high for 3 to 5 minutes, allowing the liquid to condense on its inside walls and ceiling.

2. Carefully remove the bowl with a towel or pot holder (it will be very hot!), and wipe the interior with a dishrag or paper towel.

Basic Oven Cleaner

Use this odorless recipe the next time you need to clean your oven, and leave those caustic chemical-based oven cleaners where they belong—on the store shelf.

2 tablespoons liquid soap

2 teaspoons borax

2 cups warm water

1 clean 16-ounce spray bottle

1/2 cup baking soda in an open bowl

1. Pour the soap and borax into the spray bottle, and add the warm water. Shake well to dissolve the borax.

2. Spray the solution on the oven's surfaces, giving special attention to dried, cooked-on spills.

3. Let the mixture set for 30 minutes to an hour, then scrub the oven surfaces with a damp scrub pad dipped in the baking soda. Rinse with clean water.

Lazy Person's Oven Cleaner

Here is the recipe for a cheap, almost effortless oven cleaner that rivals any commercial counterparts.

3/4 cup clear household ammonia

1 cup baking soda in a widemouthed dish

1. Pour the ammonia into a small bowl and leave it overnight in a closed, cool oven.

2. The next day, remove and discard the ammonia and wipe down the oven's interior surfaces with moistened paper towels or damp sponges dipped in baking soda.

Oven Floor Cleaner

This recipe is for cleaning up the oven floor after a sticky sweet pie or a too-full casserole has spilled over and caused a real mess. You don't need expensive, caustic commercial oven cleaners to deal with it. You probably already have everything you need on hand.

1/2 cup water
1-2 cups baking soda
1 teaspoon liquid detergent

1. Sprinkle water along the bottom of the oven.
2. Spread enough baking soda over the surface to coat it entirely, and sprinkle more water on top of it.
3. Let the paste set overnight. The next morning, the grease and grime will be loosened enough for you to wipe it up with damp paper towels or dishrags.
4. Once you've wiped up the core of the mess, use the liquid detergent on a damp sponge to remove any remaining residue. Rinse with water and let dry.
5. Repeat if necessary.

Garbage Disposer Cleaner

Those in-the-sink garbage disposer units are great for cutting down on bagged waste, but they can produce some unpleasant odors from time to time. Here is an easy and efficient way to get rid of any unwanted smells.

1 quart white vinegar
Ice-cube tray

1. Fill an ice-cube tray with white vinegar and freeze it. Remove cubes, place in a sealed plastic bag, and return to the freezer.
2. Once a week run 2 to 3 vinegar ice cubes through your garbage disposer.

One-Minute Substitute

Quick Garbage Disposer Sweetener

Instead of buying a commercial product to keep your garbage disposer smelling good, try this easy solution. Save leftover orange, lemon, and grapefruit peels in a sealed plastic bag in your refrigerator. Then, once or twice a week, run a few peels through the disposer.

Scouring Powder

You don't need chlorine bleach to clean stains off the nonporous surfaces in your kitchen and bathroom. This scouring powder is just as effective, a lot safer to use, and far more economical.

1 cup baking soda
1 cup borax
1 cup salt
1 clean 32-ounce plastic container with cover

1. Combine the ingredients in the container and mix well. Close the container tightly to store.
2. To clean a stained surface, sprinkle some of the powder onto a damp sponge or directly on to the surface to be cleaned. Scour, rinse, and dry.

Homemade Scrub Powder

Use this mixture to scrub off grease and grime from your stainless steel and enameled cookware. (If you use baking soda on aluminum cookware, it may cause darkening.) You don't need pricey commercial products.

2 1/2 cups baking soda

1 1/2 cups salt

2 tablespoons cream of tartar

1 clean 32-ounce plastic container with lid

1. Mix the ingredients well, and store in a tightly sealed plastic container.

2. To use, pour 2 to 3 tablespoons of powder onto cookware and scrub with a brush or nylon scrubber that's been slightly moistened with water. Rinse well and dry with a soft cloth.

Steel Wool Soap Pads

Those popular prepackaged steel wool soap pads are great for getting tough stains and cooked-on foods off your pots and pans, but they can be rough on your hands. These homemade steel wool pads work just as well, and are easier on both your wallet and your skin.

1 bag steel wool pads (available at hardware stores)

3 tablespoons Homemade Scrub Powder (above)

1. If you've purchased large pads, use a sharp scissors or shears and carefully cut them into rectangles approximately 3 inches long by 2 inches high.

2. Spread a layer of scouring powder over the cooking surface, moisten the steel wool pad with warm water, and scrub away stains. Rinse well with water. Dry with a soft, absorbent towel.

3. To make your pads last longer, squeeze out remaining water and keep them in a bowl lined with aluminum foil.

in the laundry

Fabric Softener

Here's a simple recipe for keeping your fabrics soft and fluffy. It's a lot gentler on your clothes than commercial fabric softeners, and much easier on your wallet as well.

1/4 cup baking soda

1/2 cup white vinegar

1. Fill the washing machine with water.

2. Add the baking soda and then the clothing.

3. During the final rinse cycle, add the vinegar (pour it into the softener dispenser if your washing machine has one).

Laundry Soap

This basic laundry soap gets clothes as clean as those fancy single-name commercial cleaners; it just costs a lot less.

1/2 cup soap flakes

1/2 cup baking soda

1/4 cup washing soda

1/4 cup borax.

1 clean 16-ounce plastic container with lid

1. To make the soap flakes, lightly grate a bar of pure soap, such as Ivory, on a coarse kitchen grater.

2. In a large bowl mix all the ingredients together. Store in a tightly sealed plastic container.

3. Use about 1/2 cup of the mixture instead of detergent in each load of laundry.

Stain Remover

Stains are always easier to get out if you treat them before they set (club soda is effective for lifting many types of stains before they dry). You can also use other ingredients found around your home to remove many common types of stains (see Removing Common Stains, below).

1/3 cup clear household ammonia

1/2 cup white vinegar

1/4 cup baking soda

2 tablespoons liquid castile soap

1 1/2 quarts water

1 clean half-gallon (64-ounce) recycled plastic container

1 clean 16-ounce spray bottle

1. Mix all the ingredients in a 1/2-gallon container. Pour some of the solution into the spray bottle. Shake well before each use.

2. Spray liquid onto the stain and let set 3 to 5 minutes. Launder as usual.

removing common stains

Automotive Oil and Grease Stain Remover

1 liter cola

For severe stains, soak the garment in cola overnight. Rinse and launder the next morning.

Grass and Bloodstain Remover

1 teaspoon 3% hydrogen peroxide

1/4 teaspoon clear household ammonia

Mix the ingredients in a small bowl. Rub the mixture on the stain. As soon as the stain fades, rinse and launder.

Perspiration Stain Remover

1 cup white vinegar

1/4 cup salt

2 quarts warm water

Mix the ingredients in a bucket and soak garment for one hour before washing.

Red Wine Remover

1 tablespoon borax

2 cups warm water

Dip garment in solution, let it soak for one minute, then launder.

Tomato Sauce Remover

1/2 cup 3% hydrogen peroxide

3 cups water

Mix ingredients in a dishpan or bucket. Soak garment in the solution for 30 minutes before laundering.

Whitening Yellowed Whites

1/2 cup white vinegar

6 cups warm water

Mix ingredients in a dishpan or bucket. Soak clothes overnight and launder the next morning.

Vinegar: Fabric Softener Plus

Who would have guessed that a single cup of an everyday staple—white vinegar—which costs about a quarter, could do everything that many people use a fabric softener, a color setter, a disinfectant, and a bleach to do? Just add 1 cup distilled white vinegar to your washer's rinse cycle, and it will kill any bacteria in the wash, set the color of newly dyed fabrics, keep clothes lint- and static-free, brighten small loads of white clothes, and eliminate the need for fabric softeners.

Washer Disinfectant

Just because your washer sees a lot of soap and water doesn't mean it doesn't get dirty. Use this simple recipe to disinfect it twice a year. This rinse also removes some of the built-up soap scum from your washer's hoses, so it may even spare you a visit from your local repairman.

2 cups white vinegar
2 cups bleach

1. Let the tub fill with water, then add the vinegar. Let it soak for 1 hour, then restart and let it run through a complete cycle.
2. Repeat process using the bleach.

in the bathroom

Multipurpose Disinfectant Cleaner

Here's a good all-purpose disinfectant that is as easy to use and effective as any commercial bathroom cleaner but much less expensive.

2 teaspoons borax
1/2 teaspoon washing soda
2 tablespoons lemon juice
4 tablespoons white vinegar
3 cups very hot water
1 clean 24-ounce spray bottle

1. Combine the borax, washing soda, lemon juice, and vinegar in the spray bottle.
2. Slowly add the hot water, then vigorously shake the bottle until the powdered ingredients have dissolved. Shake the bottle before each use.
3. Spray on tile and ceramic surfaces and wipe with a damp, clean cloth.

Soft Scrub

You don't need to buy special cleaners for your vulnerable kitchen and bathroom surfaces. This homemade soft scrub gets out tough stains on surfaces that are easily scratched, including ceramic sinks and countertops, and costs just pennies per cleaning job.

1/4 cup borax

1/2 teaspoon vegetable-oil-based liquid soap (such as Murphy's Oil Soap)

1/2 teaspoon lemon juice

1. In a small bowl, combine the borax and liquid soap to make a smooth paste.

2. Stir in the lemon juice and mix well.

3. Place a small amount of the paste onto a clean, damp sponge, apply to the surface, then rinse off and dry surface with a clean rag.

Eucalyptus Tile Cleaner

This fresh, tangy powder will leave your kitchen and bathroom tiles as shiny and clean as any commercial cleaner and for less than half the price.

1/2 cup soap flakes

1 cup chalk or diatomaceous earth

1 cup baking soda

1 teaspoon essential oil of eucalyptus

1 clean recycled 16-ounce jar with metal top

1. To make the soap flakes, lightly grate a bar of pure soap, such as Ivory, on a coarse kitchen grater. Then, in a small bowl, crush the soap flakes with the back of a spoon until powdered (or whirl them in a blender).

2. Mix in the chalk or diatomaceous earth and the baking soda, breaking up any lumps.

3. Sprinkle the essential oil over the surface of the powdered mixture and stir it with the spoon. Continue stirring for several minutes to disperse the oil throughout the mixture, then spoon the mixture into a screw-top jar or can with several holes punched in the lid.

4. Cover the holes with masking tape to keep the powder dry between uses. Let the mixture sit a week before using to be sure the essential oil has been thoroughly absorbed. Sprinkle surface with powder, scrub with a damp sponge, and rinse with clear water. Dry with soft towel.

Nontoxic Bathroom Cleaner

This is a terrific deep-cleaning cleanser for any bathroom surface. It cuts through soap scum and mildew as well as any commercial bathroom product and costs just pennies.

1 2/3 cups baking soda

1/2 cup liquid soap

1/2 cup water

2 tablespoons white vinegar

1 clean 16-ounce squirt bottle with closing cap

1. Mix baking soda and liquid soap in a bowl. Dilute with water and add the vinegar. Stir the mixture with a fork until any lumps have been dissolved. Pour the liquid into the bottle. Shake well before using.

2. Squirt on area to be cleaned. Scrub with a nylon-backed sponge. Rinse off with water. Keep cap on between uses.

Showerhead Cleaner

Use this "explosive" mix to blast away mineral deposits blocking up your showerhead. You don't need the plumber at $75 an hour to clean out your showerhead. Use this recipe to do it yourself.

1/4 cup baking soda

1 cup vinegar

1 plastic sandwich bag

Adhesive tape or a large bag tie

1. Pour the baking soda and vinegar into the bag over a sink. Wait a minute or two for the foaming to stop and then place the opened end of the bag over the showerhead, which should be submerged in the solution.

2. Secure the bag to the showerhead stem with the tape or bag tie. Let the showerhead soak in the solution 1 to 1 1/2 hours. Wipe off showerhead with a soft cloth.

Nontoxic Rust Remover

Commercial rust removers are among the most toxic compounds found around the home. But here's a completely safe and surprisingly effective way to give rust stains on bathtubs and sinks the brush-off.

1 lime (a second one may be needed for some jobs)

1/4 cup salt

1. Squeeze the lime over the rust spots, then cover the moistened area with salt.

2. Let the mixture set 3 to 4 hours.

3. Use a nylon scrubber to scrub the mixture off. The rust will be gone.

Nontoxic Toilet Bowl Cleaner

Clean and sanitize your toilet bowl without harmful chlorine! For no-scrub convenience, simply pour in this mixture and leave overnight. No commercial product at any price matches that.

1 cup borax

1/2 cup white vinegar

1. Flush the toilet to wet the sides of the bowl.

2. Sprinkle the borax around the toilet bowl; then liberally drizzle some vinegar on top. Let the toilet sit undisturbed for 3 to 4 hours before scrubbing with a toilet brush.

Tougher Toilet Bowl Cleaner

For tougher jobs, try this potent paste that still has no chlorine and costs much less than commercial toilet bowl cleaners.

2/3 cup borax

1/3 cup lemon juice

1. In a small bowl, combine the ingredients to form a paste.

2. Apply the paste to the toilet bowl using a sponge or rag. Let the paste set for 2 hours, then scrub off. Flush the toilet.

Spit-and-Polish Cleaning Products   **343**

Drain Opener

Commercial drain cleaners are not only extremely toxic; they can actually harm the pipes in your home with repeated use. Don't bother with those caustic cleaners; use this simple, inexpensive, and safe way to unclog drains instead.

1/2 cup baking soda
1 cup vinegar
1 teapot boiling water

1. Pack the drain with the baking soda, then pour in the vinegar.
2. Keep the drain covered for 10 minutes, then flush it out with boiling water.

One-Minute Substitute

Fast and Easy Drain Freshener

Here's an easy way to eliminate drain odors while maintaining the proper pH and health of your septic system. Run warm tap water for several seconds, then pour 1 cup baking soda into the drain. Wait an hour and flush with a teapot of boiling water. For best results, repeat once every two weeks.

Septic Tank Activator

If you detect a persistent unpleasant odor from your septic tank, it's probably due to a "die-off" of sewage-digesting bacteria. Before you call in your local septic tank specialist, try using this simple recipe to give the little beasties a boost.

2 cups sugar
1 quart simmering water
2 cups cornmeal
2 packages dry yeast powder

1. Dissolve the sugar in a saucepan of simmering water and cool to lukewarm. Mix in the cornmeal and the yeast.
2. Once the solution has been mixed, flush it down the toilet (flush twice, if necessary). For best results, do this before turning in for the night, or when there will be no activity in the bathroom for several hours.

cleaning the car

Basic Car Wash

Taking your car to a commercial car wash can be a costly habit to maintain—and the results are never as satisfying as when you do it yourself. This soap is tough on grime but gentle on your car's finish and your wallet.

1/2 cup mild liquid dish soap
1/2 cup baking soda
1 gallon warm water

1. Mix ingredients in a clean gallon container. Shake until all the baking soda is dissolved.
2. To use, mix 1 cup solution in a pail of warm water.

Upholstery Shampoo

Use this shampoo on a regular basis to freshen up fabric interiors that get a lot of use. It's much cheaper than commercial upholstery cleaners, and does the job just as well.

6 tablespoons soap flakes
2 tablespoons borax
1 pint boiling water

1. To make the soap flakes, lightly grate a bar of pure soap, such as Ivory, on a coarse kitchen grater.

2. In a large bowl, mix the soap flakes and borax together. Slowly add the boiling water, stirring well to thoroughly dissolve the dry ingredients.

3. Let cool, then whip into a foamy consistency with an eggbeater.

4. Brush dry suds onto the furniture, concentrating on soiled areas. Quickly wipe off with a damp sponge.

Vinyl and Leather Interior Cleaner

Put the life back into your car's vinyl or leather interior with this fresh-scented polish without paying auto-parts-store prices.

2 tablespoons vegetable-oil-based soap (such as Murphy's Oil Soap)
1/4 cup olive oil
1 teaspoon lemon essential oil (available at aromatherapy or health food stores)

1. Mix the ingredients well in a small bowl, and apply with a sponge.

2. Wipe off with a soft cloth.

Windshield Cleaner

You shouldn't drive with a dirty windshield, and you shouldn't have to buy a commercial windshield cleaner either. Fill up a spray bottle with this solution and keep it in your trunk (along with some old newspaper to wipe off the grime). It will also keep steam and frost from forming on your car's windshield. Be sure to wipe off any solution that gets on rubber or plastic gaskets or wipers with a damp cloth, because prolonged contact with alcohol may damage them.

3 cups glycerin
1 cup rubbing alcohol
2 cups water
1 clean 32-ounce spray bottle

Combine the liquid ingredients in the spray bottle and shake well before using.

Spit-and-Polish Cleaning Products   **345**

chapter 11

Useful House and Garden Products

Running a household is a challenge. These days, just keeping a house operating smoothly takes a fat billfold and ingenuity. But you can lessen the drain and

strain with some of the easy-to-make products in this chapter. Here you will find time-honored recipes for wallpaper pastes and strippers, furniture stains, and other useful household compounds. You will also find safe natural ways to keep your home pest-free, along with ideas and recipes for providing fun for children—and adults—with busy hands. And you can make them all with a minimum of money and a maximum of good results.

Keeping your yard and garden beautiful and productive without spending a fortune or using a lot of questionable chemical compounds is also a major concern of most householders. There are recipes and formulas here for keeping your garden weed-free without using expensive manufactured herbicides and for making your own organic compost and natural soil conditioners and fertilizers. The many recipes for homemade garden pest controls will provide you with a choice of effective solutions to classic garden problems that neither cost very much nor taint the atmosphere. Just using ingredients that you already have in your kitchen, you can foil everything from black spot on your roses to slugs in the marigolds—and keep rabbits and deer out of your vegetable patch or shrubs. You will also discover some useful seed and potting mixes and other natural products that you can make to give your indoor plants a boost.

household compounds

Fabric Paste

Covering a less than perfect wall with an attractive fabric is an old decorating trick that you probably already know. Using liquid starch as your glue may surprise you. It's now cheap and easy to add some color to a wall, under the wainscoting, or inside an alcove.

Fabric to cover the area
Bottled liquid starch

1. Select a fabric that is medium to light weight. Cut the fabric to the lengths needed and soak the cut pieces, one at a time, in a tub filled with liquid fabric starch.

2. Press the fabric to the wall as you would if wallpapering, smoothing out wrinkles, and allow it to dry.

3. When you want to remove the fabric, simply pull it away from the wall and rinse away any starch that remains on the wall with a sponge or wet towel.

Wallpaper Stripper

Removing old wallpaper is never fun, but you can make it easier by heating up your own homemade stripper. For a large room, make up batches of the stripper so that it always goes on hot.

Wallpaper scoring wheel or wire-bristle brush
1 1/3 cups very hot water
2/3 cup liquid fabric softener
Sponge
Paint roller
Wallpaper scraper or putty knife

1. Score wallpaper lightly with scoring tool or wire-bristle brush so that stripper solution will be absorbed beneath the paper's water-resistant surface.

2. In a bucket, mix hot water and fabric softener. Apply this stripper to small areas with a sponge. You can cover larger areas with a paint roller soaked in the hot solution.

3. Allow stripper to soak into wallpaper for 20 minutes, then scrape paper off the wall with a wallpaper scraper or putty knife, being careful not to gouge the wallboard or plaster underneath.

4. Reapply stripper solution to stubborn spots, or if stripping multiple layers of paper. When paper is removed, rinse the wall with a sponge and clean water, and allow it to dry before priming to paint, or applying new paper.

Oil-Paint Stain

This stain is perfect for coloring wooden picture frames because you can use the exact colors of a painting to make the artwork coordinate with the frame, thinning the pigment to allow the natural wood grain to show. If you want traditional wood colors, choose raw umber (equivalent to walnut), burnt umber (mahogany), and yellow ocher (golden oak).

Artist's oil paints in tubes (one or more colors, as needed)

Turpentine

1. Mix equal parts oil paint and turpentine in a clean, wide-mouthed jar. Test the hue and opacity of the stain on a scrap of wood. This flexible stain can be easily modified. If it is too opaque, add turpentine; if it is too transparent, add more oil paint. If you want a unique shade, mix paints as needed. Be sure to mix enough stain for the entire project, as it is hard to duplicate a custom stain if you run short.

2. Brush the stain on the wood and allow it to dry to the touch before varnishing. If you want more grain to show, wipe the freshly stained wood with a clean, lint-free cotton cloth (such as an old T-shirt) moistened with turpentine.

One-Minute Substitute

Fast Fix for Furniture Scratches

You don't have to refinish a piece of wooden furniture, trim, or floor just because it has a few scratches. (In the case of an antique, refinishing can actually reduce its value.) Here is an easy, inexpensive way to disguise a scratch. Get a children's crayon in a color that closely matches the wood's finish. Burnt sienna, sienna, and yellow ocher are among the most useful colors. Then just rub the sharpened crayon over the scratch and buff to blend it in. If you want permanent coverage, and the piece is less valuable, use a felt-tip marker instead; then apply paste wax as directed to add sheen.

Varnish-Based Stain

Some wood species, such as maple, are so hard that they don't absorb stain satisfactorily. If you find that this is the case, you can still "stain" a piece of furniture by tinting the sealer and varnish with the wood stain of your choice. This custom-tinted varnish recipe solves the problem as no commercial product can, and is a little less expensive to boot.

Varnish

Paint thinner

Stain

1 varnish-quality natural- or nylon-bristle brush

Extra-fine sandpaper

Tack cloth

1. Stir together 1 part varnish, 1 part paint thinner, and 1/2 part stain in a widemouthed jar to create a tinted sealer coat. Stir slowly to avoid bubbling. Brush onto a smoothly sanded piece of wood and allow to dry overnight before varnishing.

2. Sand the sealed piece of furniture lightly and wipe down with a tack cloth. To deepen the stain color, add stain, as desired, to tint the varnish in the can. When mixing the color, remember that the color will deepen with each coat of varnish. Test the color on a scrap of wood or inconspicuous part of the project before proceeding. When the color is right (it should be transparent enough to allow wood grain to show through), brush varnish onto the entire piece, taking care to avoid drips or streaks. Allow varnish to dry overnight.

3. If a second coat of varnish is needed, repeat Step 2. Allow the varnished piece to dry for 2 days before using.

four unexpected uses for vinegar

Shock Cure

If you struggle with static electricity around the house in winter, try this simple, cheap vinegar cure.

1. Mix 1 cup white vinegar with 1 cup water in a 16-ounce or larger spray bottle.

2. Spritz a dust cloth with the solution and wipe plastic tabletops, venetian blinds, and upholstery to remove dust and discourage it from coming back on static currents.

Glue Begone

You don't need to buy small bottles of expensive glue removers—you can wipe stubborn adhesive tags from store-bought products with a little household staple.

1. Dip a clean cloth into white vinegar and rub it over glue spot until it loosens. Remove the glue with a dry corner of the cloth. Use a plastic spatula to lift any stubborn spots.

2. Rinse spot with a clean, damp cloth, and polish with a dry cloth.

Hand Deodorizer

There is nothing more irritating than a strong fish, onion, or garlic smell that sticks to your hands. Here's the cheap and easy answer.

1. Wash your hands with soap and water as usual, pour vinegar over your clean hands, and rub it in for a few seconds.

2. Rinse and dry hands as usual.

Mineral Deposit Remover

If you live in an area with hard water, sooner or later you'll notice that your coffee maker takes longer to brew and the coffee doesn't taste as good, your rug steamer doesn't work as well as it did, and your steam iron may stop steaming. Here's how to make them all like new again.

1. To clean coffee makers, steam-cleaning machines, and steam irons, pour 1/2 cup (or more as needed to fill reservoir) white vinegar into the water reservoir, turn the machine on, and allow it to run until all of the vinegar passes through.

2. Follow up by filling the reservoir with clean water and running the entire reservoir of clean water through the machine to rinse out the vinegar residue. Repeat with a coffee maker, if needed.

Nontoxic Stain for Children's Wood Projects

If you have a child who is old enough for simple woodworking projects, or for painting precut blocks and plaques, you'll want to try this recipe. It gives you brightly colored, safe stains that cost pennies compared to a few dollars for a name-brand counterpart.

1/3 cup powdered tempera paint

1 cup water

Widemouthed quart jar

Paintbrush

Nontoxic spray or brush-on, water-based varnish

1. Pour powdered paint into jar. Add water, screw on cap, and shake to mix.

2. Apply to wood with a paintbrush and allow the project to dry overnight.

3. Paint details and allow to dry overnight. Varnish with a water-based, nontoxic varnish, according to package directions, to preserve the color and add an attractive glossy surface. Dry as directed before using.

Test for Finish Remover

With this simple process, you'll be able to determine the kind of finish used on a piece of furniture, and the type of stripper you'll need to buy, saving both time and money. When working with chemical finish removers, use eye protection, rubber gloves that are designed for this use, and work in a well-ventilated place, such as a garage with opened doors.

Nail-polish remover
Cotton balls

1. Saturate a cotton ball in nail-polish remover and hold it briefly against an inconspicuous part of the furniture, such as the bottom of a chair runner, side of a drawer, or back of a table leg.

2. If the furniture finish becomes sticky or begins to dissolve, it is a lacquer-based finish like shellac or oil-based varnish, and you should buy a liquid furniture refinisher or denatured alcohol to remove the finish.

3. If the covering is unaffected by nail-polish remover, it is a plastic-based varnish, such as polyurethane, and you should strip it with paint remover.

Leaking Toilet Test

Toilets can leak undetected, leading to an expensive waste of water, and sometimes ruined floors. You don't need a plumber to find out. Here's how to test a toilet for leaks yourself.

10 drops food coloring

1. Add food coloring to the tank on the back of the toilet and leave it for 1 hour.

2. When the hour is up, examine the water in the toilet bowl. If colored water has leaked into it, you need to replace the toilet-tank ball. Buy a replacement at a hardware store and, following directions on the package, put in the new ball.

3. If colored water has leaked onto the floor, you likely need a new wax ring under the toilet. Replacing this takes some strength—a porcelain toilet bowl is heavy to lift—so you may want a plumber to do this job. It's not hard to do: Shut off the water supply to the toilet (the shutoff valve is usually on the wall at the base of the toilet). Flush the toilet, and when it is empty, unscrew and lift the toilet from the floor. Buy a replacement wax ring to match the worn one under the toilet. Install the new wax ring and set the toilet back in place, screw it down, and turn the water back on. Repeat the food coloring test to make sure the leak is stopped.

craft-making supplies

Craft Paste
Flour paste is a time-honored favorite for paper crafts like decoration making and papier-mâché. It is easy and cheap to make at home.

1 quart water
1/4 cup salt
1 1/2 cups white flour (more or less as needed)

1. In a saucepan, bring the water to a boil, and then remove from heat.
2. Stir in salt and add flour a little at a time, stirring constantly to prevent lumping, until the mixture reaches the consistency of very thick gravy. Cool and use.
3. Store leftover paste in a sealed container in the refrigerator for up to 5 days. Discard paste if mold forms or it smells spoiled.

Pottery Glue
Use this traditional homemade recipe to make durable glue for repairing broken pieces of crockery or china.

1 1/2 teaspoons glycerin
4 1/2 teaspoons gum arabic
1/4 teaspoon water
Rubber bands *(optional)*
Duct tape *(optional)*

1. In a small bowl, mix glycerin, gum arabic, and water thoroughly and store in a small, sealed bottle.
2. Coat both sides of the surfaces to be glued with the mixture and clamp them together with strong rubber bands or duct tape until glue dries (about 1 hour).
3. Wash mended objects carefully by hand; do not place mended pieces in a dishwasher or stove.

Paper Glue
This inexpensive homemade glue is more transparent than flour paste and is good for gluing pieces of paper together where looks count, such as scrapbooking or making greeting cards.

1 cup cornstarch
3 cups water
4 tablespoons light corn syrup
2 teaspoons white vinegar

1. Mix and cook 1/2 cup cornstarch, 1 1/2 cups water, and other ingredients over medium heat until thickened. Remove from heat.
2. In a separate bowl, stir together the remaining 1/2 cup cornstarch and 1/2 cup water. Blend into heated mixture. Store in a sealed container in the refrigerator for up to 2 months.

Homemade Art Chalk

Whether you need an ongoing supply of chalk for the family note board or simply want to supply budding artists with an endless supply of sidewalk chalk, here is an easy and inexpensive way to make your own chalk.

Cardboard toilet-tissue tubes or plastic taper candle molds (available at craft stores)

Masking tape

Wax paper

1 1/2 cups plaster of paris

3/4 cup water

Disposable milk or ice-cream carton

Paint stir stick

3 tablespoons powdered tempera paint color (or mix 4 teaspoons colored paint and 4 teaspoons white paint for pastel colors)

1. Cover one end of each mold (toilet-tissue tubes for fat sidewalk chalk and taper candle molds for chalkboard-size chalk) with masking tape to prevent leaks. Line the molds with wax paper so that the finished chalk will release easily.

2. In a disposable container, stir the plaster of paris and water together slowly with a paint stirring stick. Divide the solution into two or three containers if you are making more than one color of chalk. Add paint powder to each container and stir to color evenly.

3. Set wax-paper-lined molds upright on a flat surface, fill with chalk mix, and tap the sides of the mold to release air bubbles. Allow chalk to air-dry for 3 days before unmolding. The chalk should slide out of the cardboard tubes and candle mold.

4. Make up a new batch as needed until all desired colors are made.

Homemade Play Clay

This simple, money-saving recipe is great for making children happy on a rainy afternoon, but it is also the basis of Christmas tree ornaments, beads, and other sophisticated crafts. The recipe makes doughlike "clay" that bakes hard in the oven, and can be painted and coated with a craft varnish for a permanent and professional finish.

4 cups flour

1 cup salt

1 1/2 cups water

1. Preheat oven to 350°F. Mix ingredients together and knead for 5 minutes. You can divide the dough into portions and add drops of food coloring at this point, or model the white "clay" and paint the finished piece. Put unused clay into sealed plastic bags and use within 4 hours of mixing.

2. Place finished pieces on a cookie sheet and bake for 1 hour (until hard).

Finger Paints

You can feel good about giving little artists finger paints that you make yourself from kitchen pantry staples that you know are safe—and washable.

1/2 cup cornstarch

2 cups cold water

6 small plastic containers with snap-on lids

Food coloring kit

1. In a small saucepan, combine the cornstarch and water. Bring to a boil over high heat, stirring constantly until thickened. Remove from heat and let cool to room temperature.

2. Divide cornstarch mixture evenly among the containers. Put several drops of food coloring into each container and stir to distribute colors evenly.

Play Bubbles

Bubbles are a great party starter for kids of all ages, and this easy recipe makes lots of bubbles. Use your imagination—you can create bubble blowers out of open-ended cookie cutters and empty juice cans with both ends cut out. Instead of blowing bubbles, hold these blowers and whisk them through the air to release streams of bubbles.

1/2 cup dishwashing detergent

1 1/2 cups water

2 teaspoons sugar

1 teaspoon glycerin

1. In a medium bowl, slowly mix the ingredients, using a spoon or whisk to avoid foaming.

2. Pour the mixture into shallow bowls, dip blowers into the bowls, and wave them through the air to make big bubbles.

Vegetable Easter Egg Dyes

You can make your own colorful Easter egg dyes from vegetable juices for pennies. To make patterns on the already hard-cooked eggs, draw the design with a nontoxic wax pencil or crayon and then dip the eggs into hot dye long enough to color the egg without melting the wax. For a lacy pattern, soak a piece of fabric lace in melted paraffin and wrap around an egg while the wax is still soft. Put the wrapped egg in a spoon and dip into hot dye just long enough to color it. Remove the egg, and peel the fabric off to reveal a lacy colored pattern.

Peels of two or more onions

1/2 cup frozen spinach, thawed

1 fresh beet

1. For yellow eggshells: In a saucepan of water, boil onion peels for 20 minutes or until the water turns yellow. Remove peels, add eggs, and boil for 5 minutes. Remove eggs and set aside to cool.

2. For green eggshells: In a saucepan of water, boil spinach for 20 minutes, or until the water turns green. Strain out spinach and return green water to saucepan, add eggs, and boil for 5 minutes. Remove eggs and set aside to cool.

3. For red eggshells: Cut the beet into small pieces and put in a saucepan of water, boil for 20 minutes, or until the water turns red. Remove beet pieces, add eggs, and boil for 5 minutes. Remove eggs and set aside to cool.

basic flower drying

Dried flowers can make a very natural-looking floral arrangement that will last you a long time. And if you do the drying yourself, the cost is minimal. Some candidates can come from your own garden and others you can find elsewhere. If you like roses, for example, you can often get wilted ones from a florist at no cost. (They won't look wilted when they are dried.) Try to get a dozen or more flowers with stems. Besides roses, other flowers that can be successfully dried this easy way are hydrangeas, strawflowers, Queen Anne's lace, and baby's breath. Here's how to proceed:

1. Remove the leaves from the stems. Then bundle the stems together in groups of six with a rubber band. Hang the bundle upside down by string from a rod or a clothesline in a dry, warm place, such as a closet or the attic. The stems are hung upside down so that the flowers don't flop over during drying.

2. Leave bundles for a week or two or until the flowers are dry to the touch.

Drying Medium for Preserving Flowers

Many flowers dry better in a drying medium, which you can make yourself much more economically than if you buy it. Most flowers dry best and last longest when they are picked fresh and are just beginning to open. This drying medium will dry many kinds and colors of flowers and buds, although you must re-create their stems with floral wire and floral tape. To preserve their color, display dried flowers out of direct sunlight.

1 pound borax
1 pound cornmeal
1 1/2 teaspoons salt
Flowers and flower buds
Artist's brush with pointed tip

1. Preheat oven to 200°F. In an open casserole, mix borax, cornmeal, and salt. Bake uncovered for 30 minutes, stirring occasionally, to completely dry the contents.

2. Pour half of the drying mixture into a shoebox or plastic storage container. Set aside the remainder of the drying mixture.

3. Make a shallow well in the center of the mix. Trim the stem of a bud or flower to 1 inch long. Hold the flower and trickle cornmeal mix between its petals to fill the blossom. Place the flower into the well in the container of mix, stem-end-down. Repeat with as many flowers as will fit in the container.

4. Pour the remainder of the mix over all flowers until they are buried. Set the container in a warm, dry, dark place, such as a closet, for two weeks.

5. After drying, remove flowers carefully from the mix and brush cornmeal mix from petals with an artist's brush. Fasten flowers and buds for arrangements onto floral wire stems with floral tape. You can hot-glue short stems to wreaths and gift packages.

Potpourri Mixes
A bowl of fragrant, flowery potpourri can fill a room with the essence of summer—even in the dead of winter. Make potpourri to perfume your own home—or as homemade gifts. If you don't have a garden, ask your florist for past-their-peak flowers, such as lavender, statice, and roses, and lemon leaves that you can dry (see Drying Medium for Freezing Flowers, page 357).

3 cups dried flower petals, herb leaves, and small pine cones *(optional)*

3 tablespoons dried orrisroot (available at craft or herb stores)

10 drops essential oil (one type or a blend of your choosing)

1. In a large bowl, mix flower petals, herb leaves, small pine cones, if using, and orrisroot together.
2. Sprinkle essential oils over the dry ingredients and stir to distribute the fragrance.
3. Display in an open bowl out of direct sunlight, and add a couple drops of oil, as needed, to refresh the fragrance.
4. Store, or give as a gift, in a sealed glass or plastic container.

Bayberry Wax for Candles and Soap
For many, the spicy fragrance of bayberry candles brings warm holiday memories. It is easy to make traditional bayberry wax for candle or soap making if you have access to a bayberry, or wax myrtle, shrub (Myrica cerifera).

Bayberries

Water

Strainer

1. Pick bayberries in November. Put berries into a pan of water large enough to accommodate the quantity you've picked. Bring water to a boil, reduce heat, and simmer until the solution is thick and syrupy.
2. Strain the berries and seeds from the solution. Allow the solution to cool in a heatproof bowl. When the bayberry wax floats to the top of the liquid and solidifies, lift it off and store it in a sealed container in the refrigerator until you have collected enough to dip or mold candles.

Molded Candles

If you love making candles, you may want to invest in metal molds for tapered candles. You can, however, make many molded candles in containers that you already have around the house. A soup can, for example, will mold a fine pillar candle. Look around and see what other shapes you have. Buy wicking, paraffin, and mold seal at a craft shop or on the Internet.

1 packet wicking

1 10-pound block paraffin

Crayons (colors of your choice)

Scented oil (scent of your choice)

Molds

Nonstick cooking spray

1 packet mold seal

1. Cut wicking 4 inches longer than the height of the mold. Melt some of the wax in a double boiler over very low heat and soak the wicks in melted wax until saturated. Lay the wicks out straight on a piece of wax paper to cool and dry.

2. Lightly spray the inside of each mold with nonstick cooking spray, and if it doesn't have its own seal, use a mold seal product.

3. Stick the wick to the bottom of the mold with a bit of mold seal. Tie the other end to a small stick or skewer, pull the wick taut and lay the stick across the mouth of the mold.

4. Melt the rest of the wax in a double boiler. Never let the wax exceed 200°F (use a candy thermometer to check the temperature). Use pot holders or mitts to handle hot wax to prevent burns. Lower the heat, add crayon bits and a few drops of scented oils, and stir to distribute evenly.

5. Pour wax into molds, stopping 1/2 inch from the top. Place the molds in a pan of cold water (use pot holders), taking care not to splash water into the mold. Let cool 1 hour.

6. When the mold is cool, remove the candle. Trim the wick and smooth the bottom of the candle by standing it in a pot of warm water. If you used a 2-part mold, trim any ragged seams with a paring knife.

Rolled Beeswax Candles

Candles rolled from sheets of beeswax are simple to make and long-burning. They make elegant gifts.

Sheets of beeswax (as many as the number of candles desired)

Wicking

1. Cut wicking 3 inches longer than the sheets of beeswax.
2. Melt a small amount of beeswax in a double boiler over low heat. Soak wicks to saturate in wax, remove, and stretch out straight on a sheet of wax paper to cool.
3. Warm beeswax sheets until malleable with an electric hair dryer set to its lowest setting. Lay a prepared wick on the edge of a sheet of beeswax, placed on a flat surface. Roll the beeswax sheet tightly and evenly around the wick until it is as thick as desired.
4. Trim excess beeswax off with a utility knife, and seal the candle seam with a heated butter knife. Repeat steps for remaining candles.

household pest repellents

Cockroach Repellent

Cockroaches are attracted to damp areas, but they'll stay away if you use this inexpensive solution. Remember to store pest treatments, such as this, in capped and labeled bottles in a childproof cabinet.

1 metal coffee can with plastic lid

1 old-style beer-can opener (that cuts a V notch)

2 tablespoons borax

1 tablespoon flour

1 tablespoon sugar

1. Punch holes around the base of an empty coffee can, using a beer-can opener. Label the can with a sign that reads "Cockroach Killer."
2. In a small bowl, mix the ingredients together. Put in the coffee can, snap on the lid, and place it under the sink or wherever you've seen roaches. Lock the undersink cabinet if you have children or pets.
3. Refill the can, or create additional cans as necessary.

Moth Repellent Cedar Sachets

You can have the benefits of a moth-repellent cedar closet or cedar-lined drawers at a fraction of the cost of the real thing with these fragrant cedar sachets.

2 pairs colorful adult or baby socks

1 bag cedar shavings (sold at pet shops as hamster bedding)

Satin or grosgrain ribbon

Clothes hanger

1. Fill socks with cedar shavings—adult-size for closets and baby-size for drawers.
2. Tie the tops of the socks closed with coordinating ribbon.
3. Tie large sachets to clothes hangers and hang in closets to freshen air and repel moths. Tuck the little ones into lingerie and sweater drawers.

Homemade Flypaper

Why buy flypaper when you can make your own? All you need is a brown paper bag, a little sugar, and some corn syrup.

3 1/2 ounces corn syrup
1 tablespoon brown sugar
1 tablespoon white sugar
6 strips brown paper
  (cut from a paper bag)

1. Combine the syrup and sugars in a shallow bowl.

2. Poke a hole at the top of each strip of brown paper. Soak paper in the syrup mixture overnight.

3. Scrape paper strips across the edge of the saucer to remove excess syrup and hang the finished flypaper strips near windows and doors.

4. Replace when strips are covered with insects.

Pungent Moth-Repelling Bundles

Moths dislike the strong fragrance of certain herbs. They also avoid cupboards that are regularly aired out, so every once in a while leave your closet or dresser drawers cracked open for a day, and make an herbal repellent.

1 small bundle southern-
  wood, camphor, tansy, or
  sweet woodruff
1 rubber band
String
1 coat hanger

1. Bind together a small bundle of fresh herbs (one kind or a blend) by fastening a rubber band around the stems.

2. Tie a bundle to an empty coat hanger and hang it in the closet among woolen clothes, or tuck it under drawer-liner paper in a drawer containing woolens.

Aromatic Moth-Repelling Sachets

This sachet containing lavender and elder flowers makes a nice gift, and will also keep your drawers fragrant and moth-free.

10 inches fine material, such
  as silk or nylon netting
Dried lavender flowers
Dried elder flowers

1. Fold the fabric with right sides together and cut to create an 8 x 8-inch square plus a 1/2-inch seam allowance on all four sides. Sew three seams.

2. Turn the pouch right side out, and fill with flowers. Tuck the remaining seams inside and stitch the bag closed by hand.

3. Place in drawers or chests with woolens to repel moths

Ant Traps

Here's an easy, inexpensive way to round up the ants that begin to invade your house each summer.

3 cups water

1 cup sugar

4 teaspoons boric acid

Cotton balls

3 clean 8-ounce screw-top jars

Old-style beer-can opener (that cuts V notches)

1. In a pitcher, mix the water, sugar, and boric acid together. Loosely pack the jars half-full of cotton balls, and saturate with the solution.

2. Pierce jar lids with the can opener, making two or three holes just large enough to admit ants.

3. Place the baited jars where ants are active, but make sure jars are out of the reach of pets and children. Attracted by the lethal sugar and boric acid mixture, ants will crawl into the traps.

Helpful Hint

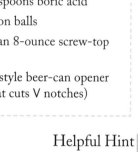

How to Keep Pet Food Ant-Free

Placed on the floor, pet food bowls are like a natural magnet for ants. Here's a simple, totally nontoxic way to keep ants away. Set an empty pie pan where you usually feed your pet. Fill the pet's dish with food and set it into the pie pan. Pour water into the pie pan, filling it to the rim. Ants and other crawling insects cannot cross this "moat" to reach the pet food.

Carpet Flea Remover

If fleas hitchhiked indoors on your pet, try this simple, effective, and cheap fix for freshening and debugging your carpets, using your vacuum.

3 mothballs

Duct tape

1. Cut a small slit into the disposable vacuum bag liner and drop in mothballs. Seal the slit with a piece of duct tape. If you have a bagless vacuum, simply drop the balls on the floor and vacuum them up, or open the canister and drop them in.

2. Vacuum as usual. Fleas that are vacuumed up will be killed by the mothballs in the bag or canister. Drop in new mothballs when you change the disposable bag or empty the canister.

garden helpers

Spot Weed Killer
Weeds that pop up between flagstones and in cracks of the sidewalk are hard to dig out of the small crevices. Kill weeds in your terrace or walkway by dousing them with this simple laundry-room solution.

Household bleach
Boiling water

1. Prepare a solution of 5 percent bleach and 95 percent boiling water.
2. Douse weeds with the solution, wait a day and check for withering. If the weeds resist, increase the percentage of bleach and repeat.

Helpful Hint | **How to Protect Plants When Spot-Treating Weeds**

It's difficult to spot-treat weeds that sidle up to your favorite garden plants without killing the good plants. Here's how to keep the weed killer on the weed and off your prized peonies: Cut the bottom out of a large, 2-liter clear plastic soda bottle or 1-gallon milk jug and remove the cap. To isolate a weed for treatment, set the bottomless jug over it, stick the weed-killer spray applicator into the cap opening and spray. Be sure to label the bottomless bottle with the pesticide being used and to store it in a locked cabinet with other pesticide equipment.

Red Clay Stain Remover
If you garden in an area with clay soil, you know all too well how its red color stains your clothes. Set aside an old pair of jeans just to garden in. When they're caked with mud, use this simple recipe to keep stains off the clothes you wash them with.

1 part table salt
Vinegar

1. Drape muddy jeans over the back of a lawn chair or lay them out on a picnic table and rinse vigorously with a garden hose.
2. In a small jar, add vinegar to the salt, a little at a time, to make a paste. Rub the paste into the mud stains, allow to sit for 20 minutes, then launder as usual.

In the old days gardeners had to outsmart weeds because there were no chemical weed killers. Take a few tips from the old-timers, save an expensive trip to the garden center, and keep your garden weed-and chemical-free.

1. Weed early and often to keep weeds from taking hold. Hold the hoe blade horizontal to the ground and scrape weed seedlings from the vegetable garden and around ornamentals. Avoid tilling deeply—it can bring buried weed seeds to the soil's surface, where they will sprout. To save your back, use an ergonomic hoe with a gooseneck that allows you to stand up straight.

2. Burn weeds that pop up between pavers and in the driveway with a small propane torch or kill them with boiling water.

3. Spread a 3-inch-deep layer of organic mulch, such as straw, wood chips, or compost, at the base of plants to smother weeds and retain soil moisture.

4. Pull weeds from potted nursery plants before setting them into your garden.

5. Apply granulated lime according to package directions to lawns in the fall, using a fertilizer spreader. Most lawn weeds can't thrive in alkaline soil.

Rust Remover

Vinegar makes an inexpensive rust remover for old hinges, screws, and metal lawn furniture that have started to rust from outdoor exposure.

White vinegar
Steel wool
Paper towels

1. Fill a widemouthed jar half-full of vinegar, drop in small rusty parts, screw the lid on, and soak for a few days until rust loosens. Remove the objects, rinse, and carefully dry.

2. Soak a paper towel in vinegar and lay it over furniture surfaces to loosen rust. If the rust is stubborn, cover the saturated towel with plastic wrap to keep the towel damp. Set the piece out of direct sunlight for a few days. Remove the wrapping, steel-wool the spot smooth, rinse, dry, and paint if desired.

Fire Starters

If you use this simple recipe to make your own fire starters, you'll never have to dash to the hardware store at the last minute when you'd rather be enjoying your patio fire pit or charcoal grill.

Scraps of particleboard or kindling
1 pound paraffin wax
Cake cooling rack

1. Melt paraffin in the top of a double boiler over low heat or in a slow cooker set on low heat.

2. Dip wood scraps into the melted wax to cover completely, remove, and set on the cooling rack to harden.

3. When the wax cools, store the waxed scraps in an old coffee can in a cool place. To use, place one or two scraps at the bottom of your fire pit or charcoal grill and stack logs or charcoal over them. Use a long-handled match to light the waxed starters, which will act as long-burning igniters for your fire.

Whitewash

Whitewash is a wood coating that has been used for hundreds of years. In the days when paint was an expensive luxury, whitewash was popular for painting farm buildings and fences. Whitewash has no binders and will slowly wear away in rain, which is why it was routinely painted on greenhouse roofs to shade plants in summer. To finish a traditional project, or to shade your greenhouse, try this simple recipe. While whitewash must still be mixed by hand, the ingredients, including color tints, are sold at concrete supply stores.

1 cup table salt
2 cups hydrated lime
1 gallon water or milk

1. Stir ingredients together slowly in a metal bucket, taking care not to splash. Add more lime or water as needed to achieve the color and consistency of milk. For a more permanent paint, substitute fresh milk for water.

2. Allow mixture to cool before painting on wood and allow it to air-dry.

Caution: Mix whitewash outdoors; wear protective eye goggles and old clothes. Be careful not to splash the mixture on your skin when mixing, and rinse it off right away if it does get on your skin. Mix whitewash in a metal bucket, because it heats up as the ingredients combine and may affect a plastic container.

Water Repellent for Exposed Wood

Try this recipe for a long-lasting, waterproof coating for decks, shutters, and other wooden items that are exposed to the elements. If you plan to stain the wood, do so before applying the water repellent. If you want to paint or varnish, apply the water repellent first and allow it to dry before painting or varnishing.

1 quart exterior varnish
   (spar or polyurethane)
1 clean 1-gallon paint can
1 cup grated paraffin wax
1 stirring stick
Mineral spirits
Paintbrush or roller

1. Pour varnish into can. Add wax and stir slowly until wax dissolves.

2. Add mineral spirits until the can is full, and stir slowly to mix all ingredients, without creating air bubbles.

3. Brush or roll the treatment onto raw or stained wood and allow to dry for 4 hours before using, painting, or varnishing.

4. If you want to paint the wood, prime with oil primer after the water repellent dries, allow primer to dry as directed on package label, then paint.

garden soil care

Compost
Compost is the best all-natural soil amendment you can use. It contains valuable plant nutrients and plant disease-fighting organisms, and it also makes soil moisture-retentive and easier to till. Best of all, compost is free when you make your own. You can make compost in a bin (3 feet square is ideal) or simply pile the ingredients on the ground. If you turn the pile periodically, it will break down faster, but even if you pile it and leave it for a year, it will break down.

6 parts dried (brown) plant material (dry leaves, straw, sawdust, paper)

1 part fresh (green) plant material (grass clippings, vegetable scraps, coffee grounds, horse, cow, or chicken manure)

1. Put a layer of brown material directly on the ground, then add a layer of green material. Continue to layer brown and green material to a height of 3 feet. Water with a hose as needed to keep the pile as moist as a wrung-out sponge.

2. To speed up decomposition, use a hay fork to puncture and turn the pile to allow air into its center. In rainy weather cover the pile with a tarp to prevent saturating it.

3. If the pile becomes smelly, it is too wet—mix in more brown ingredients. When the pile looks like rich, crumbly black soil and has a sweet, earthy fragrance, it is ready to use in the garden or as mulch.

Helpful Hint

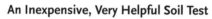

An Inexpensive, Very Helpful Soil Test

A complete soil test—available from your local Cooperative Extension office or your state agricultural university—costs less than $20 and is the best investment you can make in your garden. The results will provide an exact prescription for fertilization, liming, and adding trace elements. Knowing what your soil needs allows you to furnish your plants with ideal conditions with no wasted effort. For testing locations and to order a kit by mail, check the government pages of your phone book or do an Internet search.

Green Manure Soil Conditioner *Often called green manures, these annual crops thrive in cool weather, protecting garden soil from erosion and weeds.*

Hairy vetch or
winter rye seeds

1. After clearing vegetables or annual flowers from a bed in fall, sow hairy vetch or winter rye seeds in cleared beds according to package directions.
2. In early spring, three to four weeks before planting time, dig the green manure right into the soil. As it decomposes, it adds humus to the soil and acts as fertilizer for the coming season's crop.

Seaweed Soil Conditioner *Seaweed is actually higher in nitrogen and potassium than most animal manures, and is also a rich source of trace elements. Many municipalities with beaches are glad to have you haul it away.*

Seaweed

1. To cleanse seaweed of salt, pile it where runoff will be directed to a storm drain, such as on your driveway. Allow several rains to rinse away the sea salt, then add the seaweed to your compost pile or dig it into garden beds in the fall.
2. To make seaweed tea, steep an old pillowcase filled with seaweed in a bucket of water for a week. Remove and discard the bag, dilute the liquid to the color of weak tea, and water plants with it.

water-wise gardening techniques

You can save water and still have a beautiful garden. All it takes is noting moist and dry areas of your property and choosing the right plant for the right place.

Think of your yard as radiating outward from your house like a bull's-eye target. The wettest areas are closest to the house—particularly around outdoor faucets where water drips, and the next wettest area is within reach of a 50- or 100-foot garden hose. Beyond the reach of your hose are the driest areas.

For efficient water use and healthy plants, grow water lovers like ferns and woodland perennials near the house, and select drought-tolerant perennials with deep roots that can reach groundwater, such as coneflower, rudbeckia, and ornamental grasses, outside the reach of your garden hose.

If you live in a mild-winter climate, consider water-conserving garden plants that are native to South Africa, Australia, and the Mediterranean. Or select plants that are native to your region, which are naturally adapted to your local soil and rainfall.

Wood-Ash Potassium Boost

Wood ashes from a fireplace or woodstove (not coal or charcoal ashes) are a free source of the plant nutrients potassium, calcium, and phosphorus. They can also be used, like lime, to decrease soil acidity. Benefits of treating soil with ashes include improved hardiness and flavor of fruits. Be sure to apply in small amounts or compost well before applying to keep the caustic ashes from burning plants. Water-soluble nutrients can leach from ashes, so be sure to use fresh ones that have not been exposed to rain.

Wood ashes

1. Apply 5 to 10 pounds of ashes per 100 square feet of garden in the fall.
2. To reduce soil acidity, use as a substitute for ground limestone: Apply up to twice as much wood ashes as limestone package recommends, and allow ashes to weather over the winter before planting.

Helpful Hint

Fertilizer, Free for the Asking

Healthy plants are naturally resistant to insects and diseases, and natural fertilizers are the best way to ensure healthy plants and a balanced garden ecosystem. No matter where you live, good sources of fertilizer, free for the hauling, are available at farms and from neighbors who have pet rabbits or chickens. All you have to do is ask for animal manure to enrich your compost.

Coffee Grounds Fertilizer

Acidic coffee grounds make an excellent soil conditioner or mulch for acid-loving plants like conifers, azaleas, and rhododendrons. You can often have as much of the used grounds as you need, free for the taking, from chain coffeehouses.

Coffee grounds

1. Apply a 3-inch-thick mulch of coffee grounds around the base of acid-loving plants, leaving a 6-inch ring of bare soil around the trunk of the plant to discourage trunk-eating insects and voles that like to nest in mulch.
2. For a complete fertilizer, 2-4-2 analysis, mix 4 parts coffee grounds with 1 part composted wood ashes, and work into soil in autumn.

garden pest fighters

Blood Meal Rabbit Repellent

They may be cute, but when bunnies munch on your prized garden produce or gnaw the bark of young trees, they wear out their welcome. Blood meal is an organic fertilizer that is high in nitrogen, the nutrient most needed by green plants. But more important, rabbits associate the smell of blood meal with predators, and will avoid gardens treated with it.

Blood meal

1. Sprinkle over the soil around garden perimeters and in garden beds according to package directions.
2. Reapply after heavy rains.

Helpful Hint | **Use Fencing to Keep Rabbits Out**
Use fence wire or hardware cloth with holes small enough to discourage chewing and exclude the tiniest rabbit. Wrap young tree trunks with hardware cloth to keep rabbits from gnawing the bark. To protect a vegetable garden, staple chicken wire that has small holes along the inside of your garden fence. For most effective control, bury the fencing a foot deep to keep rabbits from digging under it.

White Flag Deer Repellent

Deer flash the white undersides of their tails as a warning signal when predators or other dangers are near. Frighten deer away from your garden by duplicating this reaction with flags you can make from recycled materials.

Stakes (2 or 3 feet tall)

Several white plastic grocery bags or rags (such as strips torn from old white T-shirts)

1. Hammer stakes that are nose-high to a deer into the ground around your garden at 6-foot intervals.
2. Tie grocery bags to the stakes so that wind will billow them out, or tie strips of white fabric long enough to flutter in the wind.

Soap Deer Repellent

Deer dislike the smell of deodorant soap. Scraps collected and tied into an old sock make a long-lasting, environmentally safe protection for prized shrubs, flowers, and vegetables. Fresh bars of soap make an even stronger deterrent. One bar can protect a 9-square-foot area, so space bars as needed to protect vulnerable plants.

Several bars or scraps of deodorant bath soap (not floral scented)

Long nail (12 penny), or drill with 1/8-inch bit, or old socks

String

1. Remove soap from wrapper, make a hole in one end of a bar with the nail or the drill, and run a piece of string through the hole. If using soap scraps, drop them into the toe of an old sock and tie the open end shut with string.

2. Tie soap (or soap-filled sock) to the branch of a shrub or tree with string or attach to a stake in the garden bed. Replace when soap is diminished by rain.

Stink 'Um Deer Spray

Deer have sensitive noses, and are repelled by animal odors, especially that of spoiled eggs. Whip up this stinky brew and deer will soon be feeding elsewhere.

1 egg

1 cup water

1/4 cup garlic juice

1 tablespoon liquid dish detergent

Scrap of panty hose

Rubber band

1. In a blender, mix egg, water, and garlic juice. Stir in detergent to avoid foaming. Pour solution into an open container and set in an out-of-nose-range spot outdoors to age for 3 days.

2. Cover the siphon of a spray bottle with a scrap of panty hose held on with a rubber band to prevent clogging. Fill spray bottle with Stink 'Um and spray vulnerable plants. Repeat applications after rains.

Repellent for Four-Footed Pests

Whether it's raccoons treating your trash like an all-you-can-eat buffet or mice looking for a barbecue-grill condo, you can get four-footed pests to scram with a couple of inexpensive household products.

Ammonia

Water

Mothballs

1. In a spray bottle, mix a solution of half water and half ammonia. Liberally spray trash cans or other areas visited by animal pests. If trash cans sit outside, swab them out with full-strength ammonia after every emptying.

2. Place a handful of mothballs in a shallow dish or pan and set into an unused barbecue grill to repel mice, opossums, and raccoons. Remove the mothballs when the grill is in use. Tuck a few mothballs into patio furniture cushions before storing them over the winter to repel nesting mice. Be sure to keep mothballs, which are toxic, out of the reach of children and pets.

One-Minute Substitute

A Quick Slug and Snail Barrier

When you don't have time to set elaborate traps for these garden pests, make an unbroken ring of wood ashes around your favorite flowers. Snails and slugs will turn away from caustic ashes. Make sure to reapply the ashes after a rain.

Slug and Snail Trap

Slugs and snails devastate prized garden plants by chewing round holes in the leaves, leaving telltale shiny slime trails. They climb up into plants like hostas and marigolds to feed after sundown, and in the morning, crawl down to hide in mulch or garden debris. Here's a nontoxic recipe for catching them.

1 or more clear plastic drinking-water bottles and caps

1 teaspoon dry yeast

1 teaspoon sugar

1 cup tepid water

Stale beer *(optional)*

1. Mix yeast, sugar, and water together and allow it to rest for 5 minutes. Pour just enough yeast solution (or stale beer) into an empty drinking-water bottle, so that when you lay it on its side the liquid does not run out.

2. Lay the bottle on its side under a plant that shows slug damage or place under a vulnerable plant as a preventive measure. Slugs and snails will be attracted by the yeasty odor, crawl in, and drown.

3. Check the bottle daily, and when full, replace the cap, throw it away, and make a new trap. Make as many as you need—these traps may not be beautiful, but they look better than the skeletal remains of a slug-eaten plant in the garden.

Easy Earwig Trap

These fearsome-looking insects can be identified by the pincers at the ends of their tails. Although they don't hurt people, these nocturnal feeders can nibble plants overnight. Try this nontoxic control made with recycled newspaper.

Several sheets of used newspaper

String

1. Roll several thicknesses of newspaper into a tight cylinder and secure with string. Dampen the rolled paper and place on the soil near eaten plants.

2. Check the roll each morning to see if earwigs are hiding inside. If so, dispose of them in a securely tied trash bag and set out a new roll. Continue this routine until earwigs are under control.

Homemade Insecticide

When aphids, whiteflies, and other insect pests become a problem in the garden or on your houseplants, don't rush to the market for an expensive spray. Make your own from these kitchen-tested ingredients. Store all garden treatments, such as this, in a capped and labeled bottle in a childproof cabinet.

10 garlic cloves

1 tablespoon vegetable or mineral oil

3 cups hot water

1 teaspoon dishwashing soap (not laundry or dishwasher detergent)

1. In a blender, puree the garlic, skin and all, and oil.

2. Strain mixture through a sieve into a quart jar. Add water and dishwashing soap. Cap the jar and shake gently to mix.

3. Decant the mixture into a spray bottle (you can clean and reuse a cleaning product spray bottle). Spray infested plants, making sure to cover both sides of the leaves. Apply every 3 days for a week to control hatching insect eggs. Repeat as needed after rains or when problems arise.

Alcohol Insect Treatment

Rubbing alcohol is a time-tested treatment for soft-bodied garden pest insects like aphids and mealybugs. Traditionally, it was advised that you dab it onto individual insects with a cotton swab, but this is a time-consuming task. Try this speedy spritz instead.

1 cup rubbing alcohol

1 cup water

1. Combine the alcohol and water in a spray bottle and shake to combine.

2. Before treating, spray one leaf of the infested plant as a test to make sure there are no reactions, such as browning. If not, spray the entire plant, including undersides of leaves and flower buds. Avoid spraying open flowers, which may turn brown if treated with alcohol.

3. Repeat every other day for 3 days to kill hatchlings. Monitor plants and spray again as needed. Label the bottle and store it out of the reach of children and pets.

You can avoid attracting stinging insects, such as bees, yellow jackets, and mosquitoes, by being careful about what you wear or how you smell while gardening or sitting on the patio. Here are some suggestions.

• Stinging insects that strike during daylight hours are attracted to flower colors—red, pink, yellow, orange, and purple—so wear clothes in cool shades of blue, green, black, gray, or white for yard and garden work.

• Many stinging insects are also attracted to floral and fruity scents, so forgo perfume, scented shampoo, scented hair conditioners, and scented lotions.

• These insects are often repelled by herbal scents. Wear a broad-brimmed hat and tuck sprigs of rosemary or chrysanthemum or marigold flowers into the brim to repel insects. Or, if you don't want to wear a hat, put the sprigs into the pocket of a T-shirt.

Aspirin Systemic Insecticide

Plant experts have experimented successfully with watering plants with aspirin-water as a systemic insecticide and promoter of plant growth. Plants naturally produce some salicylic acid, which aspirin contains, as a natural protection. When watered with the aspirin solution, treated plants absorb extra salicylic acid, which helps them repel sucking insects, and they produce strong, healthy growth.

3 regular-strength aspirin (325 mg)

5 gallons water

1. In a large watering can, stir aspirin into water until dissolved. Water plants as usual with treated water or put it in a spray bottle and use as a foliar spray.

2. Treat plants twice monthly with aspirin water.

Antifungal Compost Tea

Compost is not just a great soil conditioner and fertilizer. It also contains beneficial organisms that resist soil-borne fungal diseases. To discourage formation of fungus on plants, such as brown patch, sooty mildew, and powdery mildew, make a "tea" treatment using common garden compost.

1 gallon container compost

1 burlap bag or old pillowcase

String

3 gallons water

1. Place compost in the bag, tie the bag shut with string, and drop it into a bucket of water.

2. Set the bucket in a sunny spot, and steep the bag in the water for 2 or 3 days—until the water turns dark brown.

3. Remove the bag of compost (use the contents as mulch). Dilute the remaining solution with water to the color of weak tea. Spray it on roses, rudbeckia, phlox, and other plants that are susceptible to fungal infections. Repeat twice monthly during the growing season to prevent outbreaks.

Baking Soda Fungal Fix

When a baking soda solution is applied to fungus-prone plants, such as roses and bee balm, before signs of mildew appear, it can prevent diseases including powdery and sooty mildew and black spot. And because this spray is cheap and easy to make, you can keep it on hand and apply as needed. To further discourage fungal diseases, keep plant leaves as dry as possible by watering the soil without splashing the leaves, and mulch plants with disease-fighting compost.

1 teaspoon baking soda

1 teaspoon liquid dish-washing soap (do not use laundry or dishwasher detergent)

1 quart warm water

Pour ingredients into a large spray bottle and shake to mix. Spray both sides of leaves and stems.

Bug Blaster Soap Spray

Dishwashing soap is harmless to the environment and is safe to use in the house. Outdoors it also makes an effective control for soft-bodied insects, such as caterpillars, thrips, aphids, and mealybugs, because soap breaks down their protective coverings, causing the pests to dehydrate.

1 tablespoon liquid dish-washing soap (do not use laundry or dishwasher detergent)

1 gallon water

1. Pour soap into water and stir to dissolve. Fill a spray bottle and test-spray one or two leaves of an infested plant. Wait a day, and if the leaves are not damaged, spray the entire plant. Be sure to coat the stems as well as both sides of the leaves.

2. Repeat the treatment twice a week until the pests are no longer visible. Then repeat as often as needed.

Catnip Bird Repellent

There are times when you may want to attract birds to your garden. In the spring, when they are feeding nestlings, birds can rid your garden of harmful insects. But later on, if they decide to eat your freshly planted corn and vegetable seeds, you will want to discourage them. Here's how.

Catnip plants or seeds

1. Plant catnip plants or seeds near, but not right next to, vulnerable garden seeds and seedlings.

2. The catnip will draw neighborhood cats, which in turn will scare the birds from your garden.

Rhubarb Insect Solution

Rhubarb is an attractive perennial plant that not only makes good pies but also makes an insecticide that is toxic to sucking insects. This recipe is for ornamental plants only. Do not spray on herbs, fruits, or vegetables, because rhubarb leaves are toxic to humans.

3 stalks rhubarb with leaves

1 gallon water

1. Chop rhubarb leaves and stems. In a stockpot, combine rhubarb and the water. Bring to a boil, reduce the heat, and simmer, uncovered, for 1 hour.
2. Cool to room temperature, and strain liquid into a spray bottle through a funnel. Spray on infested plants at 3-day intervals for 10 days. Repeat as necessary.

Ammonia Plant Conditioning Spray

Ammonia is a concentrated form of nitrogen, which is the nutrient most needed by green plants. You can make an inexpensive all-purpose fertilizer and insecticidal spray using ammonia and soap. The soap helps the ammonia stick to the leaves and also kills soft-bodied insects. Mix as much as you need for garden plants and lawns. Store all garden treatments, such as this, in a capped and labeled bottle in a childproof cabinet.

1 part household clear ammonia

1 part liquid dishwashing soap (do not use laundry or dishwasher detergent)

7 parts water

1. In a large container combine the ingredients.
2. Fill a spray bottle and apply mixture to stems and both sides of leaves for garden plants. Use a hose-end applicator to spray the lawn.

Helpful Hint

Use Scented Mulch to Keep Insects Away
Trimming herbs frequently, especially removing flower stalks, helps them maintain lots of tender, flavorful new growth. Sprinkle the sprigs and flowers that you don't use in the kitchen along garden paths as aromatic and insect-repelling mulch.

Oil Spray Insecticide Concentrate

Some plant pests and fungal infections are hard to eradicate because they have shells or waxy coatings that protect them from traditional treatments. You can, however, smother tough-shelled scale, the eggs of many insects, and even mildew infections by coating them with oil. Store all garden treatments, such as this, in a capped and labeled bottle in a childproof cabinet.

1 tablespoon liquid dishwashing soap (do not use laundry or dishwasher detergent)

1 cup vegetable oil

1. In a pint container, combine soap and oil to form a concentrate. Store it in a sealed, labeled container.

2. To apply, mix 1 or 2 teaspoons concentrate with 1 cup water in a spray bottle and apply to stems and both sides of plant leaves. Reapply after it rains.

Insect Repellent

Insects won't bug your next patio cookout if you try this fragrant, non-toxic herbal fix.

Sprigs fresh rosemary

Sprigs fresh basil

Sprigs fresh thyme

1. When you remove food from the grill, spread out a handful of pungent culinary herbs on the top rack of the grill where they will smoke, but not burn.

2. Allow the herbs to cook and release their insect-repelling fragrances.

houseplants

Sterile Seed-Starting Mix

Mature plants develop defenses against many kinds of insects and diseases, but fragile seedlings can be wiped out by soil-borne diseases or insects. Use this money-saving recipe to make a sterile potting medium for sprouting garden seeds, and also for making potting soil to protect valued houseplants.

1 part sifted garden soil

2 parts sphagnum peat moss

2 parts coarse sand

1. In a large container, mix all ingredients together.

2. To sterilize, moisten and place ingredients in a shallow baking pan with a baking potato and bake at 200°F until the potato is done. This is a smelly process, ideal for doing on an outdoor grill.

Helpful Hint

How to Overwinter Herbs Indoors

To preserve culinary herbs for use in winter, dig the plants from the garden in August and transfer them to pots. Place the pots on a sunny windowsill indoors. For best results, select vigorous but compact plants and use 6-inch clay pots.

Lightweight Seed Mix
This mix is made of sterile materials bought at a garden center and does not need to be baked.

1 part vermiculite
1 part milled sphagnum moss
1 part perlite

1. In a large container, mix all the ingredients together.
2. Moisten with warm water before using

Flowerpot Sterilizer
Just because a flowerpot is used and dirty, you don't need to toss it. Whether clay, plastic, or ceramic, the pot can be superficially cleaned with a strong blast from a garden hose. If the pot has white, crusty mineral deposits, scrape them off with an old knife (scraping clay pots will sharpen the knife). When the pot is free of dirt and minerals, sterilize it to kill insect eggs and plant diseases.

1 part household bleach
10 parts water

1. Mix the bleach and water, making enough to fill a tub that is deeper than the largest pot you want to sterilize.
2. Place the cleaned pots in the tub and allow them to soak for 20 minutes.
3. Remove sterilized pots, rinse again with clear water, and set them in the sun to dry. They are now ready for new plants.

General Purpose Potting Mix
The compost in this mix contributes disease-fighting microorganisms and nutrients to help mature indoor and patio potted plants thrive.

1 part perlite
1 part finished compost
1 part topsoil

1. Mix all ingredients together and store in a waterproof, sealed container.
2. To modify this mix to suit succulents, cacti, and other plants that need sharply drained soil, increase the perlite to 2 parts, or add 1 part builder's sand to the original recipe.
3. Before filling a large pot, invert several small plastic pots on the bottom of the larger pot, then fill with soil. The air space beneath the small pots will aid drainage and lighten the overall weight of the pot.

reblooming holiday houseplants

When you receive a special flowering plant as a gift, it can be heartbreaking to have to toss it after the holidays, but it doesn't have to end this way. With a little effort, you can keep these plants from year to year, and get them to rebloom.

Amaryllis. After blooming, set the plant in a sunny spot and water as usual, letting it die back naturally, as you would for any bulb. This will occur sometime between late spring and early summer. Remove the withered foliage. Put the plant in a cool (about 55°F), dark place (such as a closet or garage), and do not water it. In August, bring the plant out into the light and warmth. Water and fertilize it, and flowers should appear in time for the holidays.

Poinsettia. As the length of the day increases in spring, poinsettias will stop blooming, but their foliage will remain fairly attractive. They can be placed outside in the warm months, but be sure to do a hard pruning in midsummer (cut stems back to 2 inches above the soil). During September and October, put the plants on a strict light schedule: 14 hours of total darkness at night, 10 hours of bright light during the day. Any light at all during the dark period can disturb the cycle, which is why some people place the plants under garbage cans or in a closet at night. Once the flower heads have formed, you can bring the plants back into normal conditions.

Booster for Early Spring Flowers

Get a jump on spring by forcing branches of flowering shrubs and trees to bloom early indoors. In late winter, watch for flower buds to swell on forsythia and on quince, ornamental cherry, and dogwood trees. Prune enough branches to fill a tall vase.

1 1/2 gallons warm water
   (110°F-115°F)

1 three-gallon bucket

1 cotton ball

Sudsy ammonia

1 plastic garbage bag

1. Cut stems, crush the cut ends with a hammer, and place them in the bucket of warm water.

2. Saturate a cotton ball in sudsy ammonia and drop it into the bucket.

3. Set the bucket of stems in a clean garbage bag, tie it closed, and set it in a warm place indoors until the buds begin to open. Then arrange the stems in a vase of clean water and set out in a room for a long-lasting bouquet.

Helpful Hint

How to Create a Lush Indoor Garden

If you display your houseplants all in one area, you will get a lush effect, and the plants will benefit from the heightened humidity gained by grouping the pots of moist soil.

In a sunny corner of a room, place a large trash bag on the floor and cover it with attractive, weatherproof decking, tiles, or an outdoor rug that coordinates with the room's décor. Arrange the potted plants on the covering, with the shorter ones at the front and rows of successively taller ones behind. For extra protection, set water-collecting saucers under each pot. To increase humidity, include a few vases or decorative bowls filled with pebbles and water. To add to the garden effect, you can include a small figure, such as a bird, child, or frog statue, if you want.

Repellent for Houseplant Pests

If you have a houseplant that is bothered by aphids, mealybugs, or other insect pests, you can banish them with this simple, no-mess recipe.

6 mothballs

1 large clear plastic dry-cleaning bag

1 twist tie

1. Set the infested plant, pot, saucer and all, into the dry-cleaning bag. Moisten the soil, drop mothballs into the bag, and tie the bag closed with a twist tie.

2. Set the bagged plant in a bright place that is out of direct sunlight for a week. At the end of the week, remove the plant and put it in its usual home, and dispose of the bag and mothballs. Repeat the treatment as needed until pests are gone.

Houseplant Food

For an easy organic food for houseplants, try this recipe for "manure tea."

2 bucketfuls fresh horse or cow manure or 1 bucketful poultry manure

1 burlap bag

Rope

1 barrel or garbage can

Water

1. Dump manure into the burlap bag. Tie the bag shut with one end of a long rope and place it in an empty barrel or garbage can.

2. Fill the barrel or garbage can with water and leave the bag to steep for a week, using the rope occasionally to jerk it up and down and mix the liquid.

3. Thin the "tea" to the color of weak tea and apply monthly to the soil around houseplant roots. Keep reserved tea in labeled jars with tight lids out of the way of children and pets.

index